Excerpts from *Unspeakable Truths*:

"Leaving the Rich Suckers who bought those unregulated Derivatives to wake up one morning to find themselves holding soggy Toilet Paper whose value had collapsed. Learning for the first time what <u>Risk is really all about</u>. (But 'if they were so <u>Rich</u>, why weren't they <u>Smart</u>?')"

"Like Siberian Tigers, markets are '**Serial Killers**' in too many respects. And their best future from the social perspective is to exist in Regulated Environments akin to the Bronx Zoo's *Tiger Mountain*. Where their many benefits can be harnessed to serve the public good. While the anti-social downsides inherent in their nature are properly restrained."

"We may be forgiven for seeing certain parallels here with the relationship between a Hooker and her John. Not the street corner kind of Hooker, of course. More like an elegant Call Girl from a prestige escort service. With everything very couth and kosher-looking. Which begs the question of who's really the Hooker and who's the John."

"'Efficient Markets' theorists in the ivory tower world and among Wall Street's crews of Rocket Scientists had been telling us for years that such horrendous one-day losses '*couldn't possibly happen in the lifetime of the Universe.*' Because their much-abused **Gaussian Bell-Shaped Curve** showed that the 'Probabilities' of such events were too small to worry about. But these losses did happen. Just ask any Baby Boomer on the verge of retirement."

"As the Financial Meltdown of 2008 reminded us, under-regulated markets have a long history of going on periodic murderous rampages. Just like hungry tigers roaming free in the wilderness. With their Serial Killer behavior overflowing as they rip away jobs and homes from Millions of people who depend on them. Gulp down Trillions of dollars in hard-earned life savings. Ravage the flesh of thousands of small businesses whose bones are flung on the ash heaps of Bankruptcy. Lay waste to the civilized landscape, Big Time."

Also by Joseph M. Giglio

Fast Lane to the Future: The Privatization Route
(Hudson Institute, 1996)

Mobility: America's Transportation Mess and How to Fix It
(Hudson Institute, 2005)

Driving Questions: Developing a National Transportation Vision
(Hudson Institute, 2007)

Judges of the Secret Court (Hudson Institute, 2008)

UNSPEAKABLE TRUTHS

IS TRANSFORMING TRANSPORTATION A KEY TO SOLVING AMERICA'S ECONOMIC CRISIS?

JOSEPH M. GIGLIO

HUDSON INSTITUTE
Washington, D.C.

"Behind every great fortune, there is a crime."
—Honoré de Balzac

"When money speaks, the truth is silent."
—Russian proverb

JOSEPH M. GIGLIO

Mr. Giglio's unique background in business, public policy, and finance is rooted in his experience on Wall Street, in management consulting, in government service, and in academia.

Mr. Giglio served as the Special Advisor to the Office of the Secretary of Transportation. He is also a Trustee Emeritus at Hudson Institute, a leading public policy think tank. In addition, Mr. Giglio teaches strategic management at the Graduate School of Business at Northeastern University in Boston. He has served as full-time faculty since September 1997. During the three years between 1998 and 2000 he was selected as the outstanding professor at the Graduate School of Business.

Mr. Giglio has served as Executive Vice President at Smith Barney, President of Chase Municipal Securities, and as Senior Managing Director at Bear, Stearns & Co. Inc. The American Banker recognized Mr. Giglio as the "Outstanding Investment Banker" for several years. Also, he served as Chairman of Apogee Research Inc. Prior to going to Wall Street, Mr. Giglio held a series of senior management positions with the Federal Government as well as the City and State of New York.

Mr. Giglio served as Chairman of President Reagan's National Council on Public Works Improvement, which released its report "Fragile Foundations" in 1988. He also chaired the U.S. Senate Budget Commission on Innovative Financing of Infrastructure from 1983-1986. Mr. Giglio served as Chairman of the Board of Directors for the Intelligent Transportation Society of America (ITSA), a federally charted advisory committee addressing public and private sector technology applications. He served as Vice Chairman of ITSA from 1998-1999, and is a former board member of the Massachusetts Higher Education Financing Authority. Also, he is the former Chairman of the Public-Private Division of the American Road and Transportation Builders Association.

Mr. Giglio was appointed to the board of the Special Commission on Transportation Finance and the Health and Education Facilities Authority by Gov. Mitt Romney. Additionally, Mr. Giglio is an adjunct faculty member at Polytechnic University in New York City.

Mr. Giglio sits on the board of a number of private corporations and has been a prolific author on finance and transportation public policy. He holds a B.A. degree from Rutgers University, an M.P.A. degree from New York University, an M.B.A. degree from Columbia Business School, and a Ph.D. degree from Northeastern University.

The views in this book are solely those of the author. No opinions, statements of fact or conclusions contained in this document can be properly attributed to the Hudson Institute, its staff, its members, its contracted agencies, or the other institutions with which the author is affiliated.

For more information about obtaining additional copies of this or other Hudson Institute publications, please visit Hudson's website at **www.hudson.org/bookstore** or call toll free: 1-888-554-1325.

For media and speaking engagement purposes, email Hudson Institute at info@hudson.org or call 202-974-2400.

ABOUT HUDSON INSTITUTE:

Hudson Institute is a nonpartisan, independent policy research organization dedicated to innovative research and analysis that promotes global security, prosperity, and freedom.

Founded in 1961 by strategist Herman Kahn, Hudson Institute challenges conventional thinking and helps manage strategic transitions to the future through interdisciplinary studies in defense, international relations, economics, health care, technology, culture, and law.

With offices in Washington and New York, Hudson seeks to guide public policymakers and global leaders in government and business through a vigorous program of publications, conferences, policy briefings, and recommendations.

Hudson Institute is a 501(c)(3) organization financed by tax-deductible contributions from private individuals, corporations, foundations, and by government grants.

Visit **www.hudson.org** for more information.

To Daniel J. McCarthy and James Molloy Jr.
Two Exceptional Teachers

Credit Where It's Due

As with my previous books, this book owes much to a number of folks.

My first thanks are due to Dean Thomas Moore of the College of Business, Northeastern University, and the Group Coordinator of the International Business and Strategy Department, Professor Nicholas A. Athanassiou, for giving me the freedom to pursue my writing. Closely related, I am grateful to the Center for Strategic Studies for supporting this project.

For advice and feedback, I thank Mike Abrams, Joe Aiello, Bill Ankner, Martin Capper, Charles Chieppio, Dan Dornan, Linda Marie and Michael Doyle, Butch Eley, David Fink, John Friar, Kevin Kiley, Jack Lettiere, Mario Marsano, Dick Mudge, Bob Muh, Carl Nelson, Kathy Ruffalo-Farnsworth, Michael Shinn, and Pamela and Michael Woodnick. I have been lucky to have had the opportunity to debate and argue with them about many of the issues discussed in this book, especially Professor John Friar, who always provides unique insights.

Special thanks to Jack Basso for bringing to bear his good judgment on several key sections of the book.

I offer a special thanks to Mary Lynn and Kevin Kiley for their friendship and support over the years.

At the Hudson Institute, I want to especially thank several people who made this book possible. I thank Grace Terzian, who always manages to keep everything on an even keel. I also thank Miriam Himmelfarb for her editorial work and Mitzi H. Pepall for her usual good taste. I want to thank Burke Malek, who served as my research assistant during the last months of this project. He is a part-time MBA student who is intellectually strong with high energy levels, a super achiever.

It is fitting to acknowledge that Joshua Martiesian suggested Chapter 12 and Johanna M. Storella made a timely and serendipitous visit to my office and helped triage the various book titles.

Enough said.

CONTENTS

Chapter 1
TRANSFORMING WHAT?

Of the making many books there is no end.
—Ecclesiastes

Transportation in America.
But why?

Because the major <u>Capital Investment Programs</u> needed to do this can help us **Grow Our Way** out of the <u>Economic Mess</u> we're in.

What's the connection?
Simple.

Capital Investment Programs of this magnitude can do **Three Important Things**:

1. <u>Pump Up the All-Important Growth Rate</u> of the nation's **Gross Domestic Product.**
2. <u>Generate the Millions of New Jobs</u> needed to **Put Americans Back To Work.**
3. <u>Goose the Tax Revenues</u> of our Federal, State, and Local Governments to levels that **Get Them Off the Bread Lines.** So they can start doing the things needed to **Make America Strong.** All <u>without</u> any increase in Tax Rates.

See?

■ ■ ■

1

How The Economic Crisis Changed Everything

The **Financial Meltdown of 2008** didn't merely plunge us into a **Major Recession**. It <u>Drove Us Off a Cliff</u> into the worst **Economic Crisis** since the 1930s.

- During October 2009, for example, the nation's **"Official" Unemployment Rate** finally shot up past the Terrifying Milestone of <u>10 Percent</u>. Closing out the month at a sickeningly high <u>10.2 Percent</u>. And you already know how much "improvement" there's been since then.

- Even worse was the **"Real" Unemployment Rate**. The one that <u>adds in</u> Americans whose jobs can only give them <u>Part-Time Work</u>. Plus those who've become <u>so discouraged</u> by futile job searches they've simply <u>dropped out</u> of the work force, so they <u>don't get counted</u> in the "Official Figures." Giving the nation a <u>Real</u> Unemployment Rate of **17.5 Percent**. Just like during the **Great Depression of the 1930s**. When many people wondered whether our version of Capitalism could <u>ever again</u> produce enough decent jobs for **All Americans** who wanted to work.

- Yet during the <u>same October</u> that generated these dismal job numbers, the Federal Government's **Department of Commerce** was reporting that the "<u>Recession seemed to be over.</u>" Because the nation's **Gross Domestic Product** had <u>grown</u> at an annual rate of 3.5 Percent during the 3 months ending

September 30, 2009. Breaking a string of <u>4 straight three-month periods</u> when GDP <u>shrank</u>.

- Sure. Great. Three cheers for GDP. But <u>where</u> were the New Jobs we needed to **Put Americans Back To Work?** The nation's business firms were <u>still</u> announcing <u>More Layoffs</u>. And again, I don't have to tell what's been happening on this score since the Department of Commerce made its "cheery announcement."

Clearly, we've got some **Serious Huffing and Puffing** to do if we're going to pull ourselves out of this Economic Crisis. But it must be the <u>Right Kind</u> of Huffing and Puffing. The kind that <u>grows our economy</u> fast enough to produce the many Millions of steady New Jobs needed to Put Americans Back To Work full-time.

This means our Huffing and Puffing must emphasize **Major New Capital Investment Programs.** The kind of Big-Ticket programs that are <u>Proven Growth Generators</u> for a national economy stuck in low gear. Programs that can produce New Jobs by the Millions as they <u>Transform the Basic Tools of our Economy</u> into what America needs to be a <u>Twenty-First Century Leader.</u> Instead of a limping Also-Ran.

In short, **Infrastructure Programs.** To transform and modernize the Essential Sinews of America's over-age, obsolete, horse-and-buggy capability to <u>Produce Goods and Services</u> efficiently and <u>Get Them to Market</u> with dispatch.

And Capital Investment Programs to **Transform Transportation** can lead the way.

■ ■ ■

Why Transportation?

The current **Economic Crisis** has given fresh <u>Urgency</u> and <u>Importance</u> to the Ideas for **Transforming Transportation in America** we've shared in my previous books.

But our Thinking about these Ideas has to reflect <u>What's Happened</u> since 2007.

So we need a New Book to bring us up to date.
And <u>this</u> is that New Book.

My previous books (***Mobility*** in 2005, ***Driving Questions*** in 2007, and ***Judges of the Secret Court*** in 2008) explained <u>How</u> the nation's transportation problems are crippling the nation's Growth Potential. And <u>Laid Out</u> our options for dealing with these problems.
  In simple terms, we have only <u>Four Options</u>.
  Here they are in a nutshell:

  • <u>OPTION 1</u>: *Do Nothing.*

  Forget about spending huge sums of money to build the new Transportation Capacity our economy needs. <u>Learn to live with what we've got</u>. Stop bellyaching about transportation bottlenecks that diminish our Mobility. Leave earlier in the morning to accommodate a more time-consuming trip to work. Have dinner an hour or 2 later in the evening after the kids are in bed. Make fewer discretionary trips. Spend more time at home watching TV. Muddle through. This way, at least we'll be able to keep more of our income in our own pockets, instead of paying it out in higher prices and taxes to support transportation.

Of course, this assumes our incomes won't shrink as Transportation Bottlenecks choke off economic activity. Leaving a smaller income pie to be divided among more people as the nation's population increases.

Not to mention forcing us to pay higher prices for consumer goods and services because of the added costs Transportation Bottlenecks impose on their producers. Higher prices we'll try to offset by Buying Less. Reducing our Living Standards.

Needless to say, some Sharp Entrepreneurs will make out like bandits as they learn how to exploit the Decline of American Society. Remember what Rhett Butler told Scarlet O'Hara in *Gone with the Wind*?

"There are as many fortunes to be made from the decline of a society as from building one."

So let's keep our fingers crossed that we can be among the lucky few.

- **OPTION 2**: *Have the Federal Government move aggressively to deliberately Shrink the nation's economy to a level where its mobility needs can be comfortably met by existing transportation capacity.*

The assumption here is that a formal National Policy of **Planned Shrinkage** can spread the inevitable pain more equitably among the American people.

The Main Focus of this policy would have to be the nation's 100 top Metropolitan Regions. Because that's where most of the economic action is. They generate <u>three-quarters</u> of the nation's Gross Domestic Product and are home to <u>two-thirds</u> of its people. Their dominance as Economic Engines means that the effect of shrinking their economies will spill over to the rest of the nation. Placing all Americans on a low-cal diet of reduced living standards. (Except, of course, the Very Rich.)

We can expect such a Federal Policy to include **Strict Regulations** that bring Immigration to a screeching halt.

<u>Plus</u> **Limit the Number of Children** women are allowed to have. So the size of the nation's population is effectively frozen.

<u>Plus</u> **Impose Residency Rules** directing where people can live. To achieve "Rational Allocations" of population density. According to the dictates of Federal Planners.

<u>Not to mention</u> **Rationing Health Care** services to favor the nation's most productive (i.e., "Highest Paid") workers and their families. While limiting services to the elderly and other dependent Americans.

You get the idea.

All this may sound like one of those "Graphic Novels" (what intellectuals like to call Comic Books these days to justify their sky-high prices) depicting the End of America in properly shocking terms.

On the other hand, <u>think of the money we'll save</u> by not having to pay for elaborate new programs to improve transportation. Even if most of these savings quickly run through our fingers to pay the extra costs imposed by a Declining Society.

• <u>OPTION 3</u>: *Convert our top 100 Metropolitan Regions into true twenty-four-hour societies so we can make use of <u>existing</u> transportation capacity now lying idle during the nighttime hours when most people are asleep.*

By spreading Economic Activity more evenly across all hours of the day, we can effectively acquire <u>New Transportation Capacity</u> that would otherwise cost many Billions of dollars to build from scratch. So we can make <u>more efficient</u> use of the transportation capacity we already have. Just like factories that operate 3 Shifts per day. So the money invested in their plant and equipment can generate profits around the clock.

Of course, the **Social Engineering** needed to accomplish such a transformation is scarcely trivial.

Roughly <u>Half the People</u> living in each of these 100 metropolitan regions will have to switch from living during the day to living at night. Working at night. Commuting at night. Going to School at night. Shopping at night. Patronizing doctors and dentists at night. Attending religious services at night. Doing at night all the other human activities they now do while the sun's up.

No doubt some fairly heroic **Government Regulations and**

Policing would be necessary to assure the "Right Balance" (as defined by Government Planners) between our daytime and nighttime populations.

But think how cheaply we could obtain additional transportation capacity this way.

• OPTION 4: *Do the "Unthinkable" and Move Aggressively to acquire the additional transportation capacity we need.*

Marshall the best talents of Government and Private Enterprise to get it all done in sensible ways. Shame them into it, if necessary. Face up to the costs and figure out clever new ways to cover them. Act like Big Kids for a change.

Political commentators who like to think they're as witty as Groucho Marx may smile droll smiles and tell us this is the Worst Option—except for all the others. Well, let them have their fun. It's a small price to pay as long as they get on board.

For years, the Federal Government has told us: *"We can't build our way out of Congestion."*

Of course we can. And we must, if we expect our children to live better than we do.

Otherwise we're looking into an **Abyss of Lost Dreams.**

When *Driving Questions* was first published back in 2007 (which may seem like an eternity ago), nearly everyone assumed that the shape of America's near-term future would look pretty much the same as its recent past. So the book could discuss various proposals for transforming America's transportation systems in the context of a Leisurely Evolutionary Process occurring over the next 10 years or so.

In other words, we could view the Challenges of Transportation (and so much else on the American scene) as a group of **Temporary Problems**. Like Broken Legs. And when we break a leg skiing or riding a motorcycle, we go to the doctor to have it set and a cast put on. Fully confident that the doctor's use of conventional treatment methods and technology will enable our leg to heal completely in due time.

But since 2007, America's been hit by events that produced the current **Economic Crisis**. And it's begun to dawn on us that its Impact is likely to influence the nation's life for years to come.

So the challenges we face in transforming transportation aren't just temporary problems.

Instead, they represent something more like a **Permanent Condition**. Like **TYPE 2 DIABETES**. Which will never go away of its own accord and could even be Life Threatening if not promptly treated. And the necessary treatment inevitably involves some significant Lifestyle Changes and new Technology. As well as short-term "Emergency Room" measures.

Obviously, **Emergency Room measures** had to come first.

We had to get our semi-conscious patient stabilized. Shoot him full of insulin to get his blood sugar under control so his body would function more or less normally again. Wake up his brain so he could be made aware of the facts about his medical condition and appreciate how he's going to have to change the way he lives.

Then the first round of **Lifestyle Changes**.

Like teaching our patient to test his blood sugar at home each day. Giving himself insulin shots each morning. Paying serious attention to the lists of No-No foods and Okay foods we give him. All designed to avoid a repeat of the collapse that brought him to the Emergency Room in the first place.

Finally, we get to the **Long-Term Measures** that can (hopefully) remove Type 2 Diabetes as a health concern in our lives.

Such measures can involve exploiting new drugs and other forms of advanced treatment technology that have the potential for enabling our bodies to naturally produce the insulin we need. This can require making Large Investments that may take years to bear fruit.

But we have to start this process Now. The time for idle speculating between cold beers on warm summer afternoons is over.

We need a **New Moses** to lead us out of the Wilderness.

And that New Moses will be wearing <u>Engineer Boots</u> and a <u>Hard Hat</u>. With plans for <u>New Construction</u> rolled up under his arm.

But <u>First</u> we have to take a look at <u>How</u> the Economic Crisis came about and <u>What</u> it means. So we'll know what we're up against.

This gets us into some really <u>Tough Subjects</u>. Like the many faces of **Derivative Securities**. The **Housing and Mortgage Mess**. **How Free Markets Really Work**. And (toughest of all) **Monetary Theory**.

Or at least, the so-called "Experts" who write about these subjects like to claim they're Really Tough. <u>Much too tough</u> for Normal People to understand.

But I'll let you in on a Secret.

This claim is nothing but a **Con Job** by the Experts to intimidate us into standing in awe of them. Because there's <u>Nothing</u> about these subjects Normal People can't understand when they're explained in clear, down-to-earth language. Like you find on the Sports Pages of reader-friendly tabloid newspapers.

And that's what this book's going to do.

<u>Explain Everything</u>.

In the kind of gutsy English we use every day when we're talking to each other face-to-face. With appropriate Body Language.

So sit back and read. You'll find it a lot more interesting than the Sports Pages.

■ ■ ■

How This Book Is Organized

The issues laid out above in the 4 Options are more relevant than ever. But the Economic Crisis has changed their focus in some important ways. Like forcing us to appreciate the critical differences between:

- **Emergency Room Measures** (like resurfacing our crumbling roads and fixing our bridges).

- **Lifestyle Changes** (replacing obsolete <u>Taxes</u> with sensible <u>User Charges</u>, just like in Movie Theaters).

- **Long-Term Programs** (exploiting new technology and management methods that transform how we develop and operate transportation facilities).

To help us understand <u>Why</u> our focus must change, this book begins by explaining <u>How</u> the current Economic Crisis developed and <u>What Impact</u> it's likely to have on critical aspects of Life in America.

All this is covered in **Chapters 2 through 5.** They include detailed explanations of the **Great Financial Meltdown of 2008.** The Whys and Wherefores of **Oil Prices.** The **Crazy World of Financial Derivatives.** And the **Housing and Mortgage Mess.**

My previous books emphasized the importance of incorporating beneficial aspects of **Free Market Capitalism** in how we Plan, Finance, Build, and Operate transportation facilities.

But it's become apparent (and not just because of the Economic Crisis) that standard views about **How Markets Work** are seriously flawed and have led to much confusion.

Therefore, **Chapter 6** discusses the down-and-dirty realities of **Markets in the Twenty-First Century**. So we can get rid of our Myths and Hang-Ups about their True Benefits.

Needless to say, Markets need **Money** if they're to function effectively on any but the most simpleminded Barter level. This brings us face-to-face with the supposedly formidable branch of economics known as (shudder) "**Monetary Theory**."

Professional economists like to make a <u>Big Deal</u> about Monetary Theory. Presumably so the rest of us will admire them for having mastered a subject that's way over the heads of Normal People.

But as we'll see in **Chapter 7**'s discussion of the "**Secrets of Money**," its critical importance to a modern society doesn't automatically make it too complicated to understand. Because, like Markets themselves, the <u>Invention and Evolution of **Money**</u> is a natural product of Instinctive Human Pragmatism in our ongoing efforts to make our societies Work Better.

Also, Money is intensely "**Mystical**." Because the adult males who dominate our societies have gotten it hopelessly intertwined with Sex in their minds. This confusion can lead to Major Problems. (But it also makes for some Great Stories.)

The book's <u>**First 7 Chapters**</u> give us the <u>Background</u> we need to come to grips with the issues raised by the Economic Crisis. This paves the way for the **<u>Next 4 Chapters</u>**, which explore some of the things we'll have to do to <u>Make It Big</u> in the much-changed world of the Twenty-First Century.

Like transforming our Transportation Systems into serious **Economic Growth Generators**. As discussed in **Chapter 11**.

■ ■ ■

Why Did the Economic Crisis Happen?

Experts are still squabbling over answers to this question. Here's a short list of the Usual Suspects (in no particular order of importance):

- **Greed.**
- **Easy Money.**
- **Crazy Leverage.**
- **Unregulated Derivatives.**
- **Credit Collapse.**
- **Bernie Madoff.**

Let's take a look at each one.

GREED

Always a Popular Scapegoat whenever anything goes wrong. Because we assume it's <u>inherent</u> in Human Nature.

But however inherent Greed may be, it takes the right kind of <u>Incentives</u> to make it burst forth in Full Glory. For example:

Suppose you hire me to sell your line of Christmas Cards door-to-door. And you offer me a lucrative commission on the <u>retail price</u> of all the cards I sell each day. So what's my <u>Incentive</u>?

Is it to push the cards that generate the <u>highest profits</u> for you (maybe because their production costs are very low)?

Or, is it to push the cards that can generate the <u>highest retail sales volume</u> for me (even if they're Loss Leaders that don't earn you a dime)?

You already know the answer to that one.

Now let's switch places.

Suppose we work on Wall Street and I hire you to sell the glitzy **Derivative Securities** my brilliant Rocket Scientists have packaged up from pools of solid and not-so-solid home mortgages. And your year-end bonus is based on the <u>dollar volume</u> of these securities you've sold during the year. So what's your <u>Incentive</u>?

Is it to act responsibly and sell high-priced Derivatives backed by not-so-solid mortgages <u>only</u> to really savvy investors who understand the <u>Higher Risk</u> accompanying their high yields? While selling less-savvy investors lower-price Derivatives with modest yields backed by solid mortgages?

Or is it to <u>maximize your dollar sales volume</u> pushing the high-priced Derivatives to <u>all</u> investors? By touting their "fabulous yields" and not mentioning their greater risk?

You know the answer to that one too.

So who's at fault when Judgment Day comes and the Market Value of all those high-priced Risky Derivatives collapses? Leaving stunned investors holding the bag?

<u>You</u>? Because you gave in to your Inherent Greed?

<u>Me</u>? Because I gave you an impossible-to-resist <u>Incentive</u> to push my high-priced toxic Derivatives to all and sundry? And never mind the consequences?

We all remember Gordon Gekko's "*Greed is Good*" speech in Oliver Stone's 1987 movie **Wall Street**.

But there's a much more articulate and compelling Defense of Greed in Ayn Rand's classic Libertarian novel **Atlas Shrugged**. With entrepreneur John Galt insisting that Greed is the <u>only</u> thing we can really depend on to move human society ahead.

Or is all this just the old story of Satan conning Faust to <u>Sell His Soul</u>?

EASY MONEY

One reason why there were so many Fausts selling their souls during the years leading up to 2008 was the increasing number of <u>Satans</u> holding out baskets full of cash. Begging these Fausts to take it. Why?

Because the world was <u>Overflowing with Cash</u> from skyrocketing profits during the Boom Years. All seeking low-risk investments offering decent returns.

The end of the Cold War led to an explosion in Global Trade. With the American public gulping down ever-greater volumes of Consumer Goods from traditional exporters like Japan.

While low-wage nations like China rushed to set up their own cheap factories to get in on the party.

Fueled by capital from American corporations seeking to exploit bargain-priced labor pools overseas. Eventually becoming "Full Partners" with foreign companies by moving ever-larger portions of their domestic manufacturing capacity and technology Offshore. And in the process, transforming themselves from traditional <u>Manufacturer/Distributors</u> into new, more streamlined, higher-profit <u>Importer/Distributors</u> serving hungry American consumer markets.

All of which led to a rapid escalation in the global supply of New Investable Cash from trading profits seeking Profitable Deals. Further stoked by a growing American <u>Trade Deficit</u> (as the dollar value of U.S. <u>Imports</u> far outpaced the value of U.S. <u>Exports</u>).

And what do economists tell us happens when the <u>Supply</u> of anything increases?

The <u>Price</u> it can command in the marketplace <u>decreases</u>. (Exactly as happened in the World War II German POW camps for Allied bomber crews. With cans of Spam and other Red Cross Package goods <u>falling in price</u> the day after these packages arrived. We'll look at this in **Chapter 6**, on How Free Markets Really Work.)

And in the case of Investable Cash, this "price" takes the form of the <u>Investment Return</u> it can obtain from new Deals.

The Owners of this investable cash found their <u>Pricing Power</u> further undercut by the actions of Federal Reserve Chairman **Alan Greenspan.** He insisted on keeping the **Federal Funds Rate** as low as possible for as long as possible in order to restart the Stock Market boom that had collapsed during the Dot.Com Meltdown of 1999.

(**Chapter 7** explains how the Federal Reserve sets the all-important Federal Funds Rate. This is the basic Interest Rate that provides the <u>floor</u> against which all other American interest rates are determined. Influencing the level of interest rates in the rest of the world. Plus the <u>Investment Return</u> owners of investable cash can expect from new Deals.)

So the Owners of new Investable Cash had to start looking for "Riskier Deals" if they wanted the kind of Investment Returns they'd gotten used to. Deals they wouldn't previously consider but now had to "Take Seriously" (which too often meant "Ignoring Risk").

Inevitably, so much **Easy Money** sloshing around the world brought all kinds of "have I got a deal for you" Lascivines swarming out of the woodwork. In the <u>Mortgage Broker</u> industry, for example. (For the definition of "Lascivine," see the end of this Chapter.)

A Mortgage Broker is a <u>Financial Middleman</u>. He lives off the fees he earns by matching up <u>Home Buyers</u> seeking mortgages with <u>Lenders of Cash</u> for new mortgages. With no concern for minor nuisances like Credit Risk. So his <u>only</u> interest is to generate new mortgages for as many home buyers as he can.

Bad credit history? Unstable family income? No cash for a down payment?

"No problem. I've got lenders banging down my door to bring them home buyers they can give mortgages to."

"Yeah, but what about the monthly payments?"

"Don't worry. I can get you an Adjustable-Rate Mortgage. Costing you only pennies a day for the first year."

"And after that?"

"Come see me. We'll do a Refinancing for you. The way home prices are skyrocketing these days, I ought to be able to get you cash to pocket plus low monthly payments a year from now."

"Really?"

"Here. Breathe on this shaving mirror. That's it. See? Your breath fogged the mirror. That means you qualify."

(**Chapter 5** details how these mortgage scams worked.)

And this sort of thing wasn't limited just to home mortgages. The same kind of scam reasoning was behind all kinds of wild **Derivative Securities** packaged up by investment banks and other financial firms to take advantage of the tsunamis of Investable Cash seeking Deals.

We'll look at this in a minute. But first . . .

CRAZY LEVERAGE

I once knew a hard-working Chinese accountant, originally from Hong Kong, whose American name was **Jack**. His only hobby was placing a few Two-Dollar bets on the horses each Saturday in the OTB parlor around the corner from his house.

So each Saturday after lunch, Jack would leave his house with a Ten-Dollar wad of Betting Capital in his blazer pocket. Carrying his worn-out blue Land's End shoulder bag containing his Dell laptop, pad of graph paper, and handful of different-colored roller ball pens.

He'd pick up a copy of the *Daily Racing Form* at the corner candy store. Settle into a comfortable chair in the OTB parlor. And start typing numbers from the *Racing Form* into the custom-tailored Excel spreadsheets on his laptop. Looking for favorable bets.

Jack never bet more than $2 on any horse. And always "To Show" (finish Third or better). Never "To Win." Or even "To Place" (finish Second or better). Because Show Betting gave him 3 times the chances to make a few dollars on each race than Win Betting. And twice the chances of

17

Place Betting. His goal was to come out ahead for the afternoon rather than occasionally Scoring a Big Payoff.

Very Conservative.

But early one Saturday afternoon, Jack noticed that the man sitting next to him in the OTB parlor was watching intently as he crunched numbers on his laptop. The man was wearing a cashmere sport jacket and a prominent diamond pinkie ring. Probably a Loanshark, Jack figured. But that was no big deal in any OTB parlor on a Saturday afternoon.

"Excuse me for talking," the Loanshark said finally in a quiet voice. "But you look like a Serious Bettor. I mean, with that laptop."

"Just a hobby," Jack said.

"You got a System?"

"Not really. I just crunch the numbers and see what comes up."

"Yeah, that makes sense. Systems are a dime a dozen. And they never work."

"As I said, it's just a hobby."

"Sure. Anyway, tell me. You know about the Arrangement on the Third Race at Bowie?"

"What arrangement."

"You know. Who's going to win. It's all Arranged, if you know what I mean."

"The race is Fixed?"

"These things happen all the time. But you're probably onto that. Being a Serious Bettor."

"How do you know about this?"

"Phone call last night from a guy who works at the track. He's never been wrong yet."

"You going to bet the race?"

"Sure. Fifty to Win. It's too good to pass up. The odds were 12 to 1 when I checked a few minutes ago."

"Well, I only bet at the Two-Dollar window. I haven't got that kind of money on me."

"That's okay. I can lend you the cash."

"Lend it to me?"

"That's my business. I'll lend you $48 so you can bet $50 to Win. You can pay me back after the race. Out of your winnings."

"What terms?"

"The usual. 6 for 5."

"Let's see. You lend me $48. And I pay you back . . . um, $57.60."

"Right."

"So the interest rate is . . . ah, 20 Percent. For a loan of maybe half an hour."

"Jesus, you did all that in your head?"

"I'm an accountant."

"I should have figured. But look at it from the standpoint of your winnings. A fifty-dollar bet pays off $600 at 12-to-1 odds. Plus you get your original $50 back."

"And out of those $600 winnings, I pay you back $57.60. Leaving me with a net of . . . um, $542.40. That's a return on my $2 of . . . um, wait a second . . . My God. About 27,000 Percent."

"Isn't that what you financial guys call Leverage?"

"Well, the Leverage part is when I match my $2 with the $48 I borrow from you. That's a Leverage Ratio of 24 to 1. Pretty hefty."

"But look at your profit of over $540 on your $2."

"What's the name of the horse?"

"You'll go for it?"

"Tell me the horse first. I want to check his numbers."

"How can I do that unless I know you'll go for it? After all, this is Business."

"Then how can I go for it without checking out the horse first?"

"Jesus . . . All right, look. You seem like an okay guy, so I'll trust you. But promise you won't say anything to anybody."

"I promise."

"Fine. The horse is . . . *Angel's Mercy*."

"Third race at Bowie?"

"Yes, yes. But keep your voice down."

Jack turned to his laptop. Found he'd already typed in the numbers for the third race at Bowie. And marked *Angel's Mercy* as a possible candidate for one of his regular Two-Dollar Show Bets. But that was before the Loanshark had told him about the "Arrangement."

In his professional world, Jack was always hearing inside tips on supposedly Hot Stocks. And always ignored them because he was too conservative to expect easy money from the Stock Market.

But this was different somehow. The Loanshark's words had stirred an unfamiliar sense of Excitement inside him that was becoming hard to suppress.

Besides, what was the most he could lose? Only $57.60 to pay back the loan from the Loanshark. Plus his $2. Pocket change. After all, one of his accountant partners was an amateur photographer who always seemed to be spending upwards of a thousand dollars to buy the latest digital camera. That's what hobbies were all about.

Sure. Why not take a chance? For once in his life.

"Okay. I'm in," Jack said to the Loanshark.

"Great. Believe me, you won't regret this. Here. Let me give you the cash so we can get our bets down."

The Loanshark removed an alligator wallet from the left inside breast pocket of his cashmere jacket. It was thick with large-denomination bills, and he handed a Fifty to Jack. Who took out his modest Betting Wad of Singles and handed back two of them.

Then they walked to the Fifty-Dollar window and placed their bets on *Angel's Mercy*. To Win. And sat down to watch the race on the TV monitors.

Angel's Mercy ran in the middle of the pack until the final turn for home. Then, as the leading horses seemed to run out of gas, he surged to the front and won by two lengths going away.

As soon as Jack collected his $600 payoff, he paid the Loanshark

$57.60 to retire his $48 loan. And as the two of them were walking back to their seats, the Loanshark abruptly noodged him.

"Listen," the Loanshark said in a low voice. "I know of another Arrangement. In case you're interested."

"I'm listening."

"This one's on the next race at Aqueduct. So we'll have to hurry if we're going to get our bets down."

"You're betting this one?"

"Sure. A Hundred to Win. The horse is paying, like, 17 to 1. But there'll be a lot of Smart Money on this one. So I don't know if those odds will hold until post time. Still, it's too good to pass up."

"A <u>Hundred Dollars</u>? That's more than I bet in 2 months."

"If you really want to Score Big, you have to invest a few dollars."

"I'm not interested in Scoring Big. I just want to come out a few dollars ahead by the end of the afternoon."

"All right, look. You're a Conservative Guy. I can see that. So put your winnings in your wallet where they'll be safe."

"But . . . "

"Just use the $2 you'd bet anyway. And I'll <u>lend</u> you the rest."

"Lend me $98?"

"Sure. Why not? We did fine together last time."

"Same terms?"

"Same terms."

"So I'll owe you . . . um, $117.60."

"Right."

"Well, what the Hell."

"You'll go for it?"

"May as well."

"Great."

By the time they got their bets down at the Hundred-Dollar window, the odds on the horse had dropped to 10 to 1. But that still meant a pay-off for Jack of <u>$1,000</u> when the horse came in First. More money than he'd ever won in a <u>year</u> of betting. And even after he paid $117.60 to the Loanshark for his loan, that <u>still</u> left him with a net win of $882.40. Which meant he'd pocketed $1,424.80 so far that afternoon.

It turned out that the Loanshark had inside information about "Arrangements" for three other races in different parts of the country. So they bet those races in the course of the afternoon. With the betting amounts rising steadily until they reached $1000 on race Number 5.

And the pattern was always the same. Jack would put up $2 from his Betting Wad and the Loanshark would lend him the rest. With Jack's Leverage Ratio soaring to <u>499 to 1</u> by the fifth race. Which brought his cumulative net winnings for the afternoon to an astonishing $5,992. And his original Ten-Dollar Betting Wad was still intact. This was betting success like he'd never dreamed possible.

"You got anything else?" Jack asked the Loanshark eagerly at the end of the afternoon as they were pocketing their winnings from the fifth race. "The West Coast tracks are still open."

"A guy from LA was supposed to phone me about something at Santa Anita. But I haven't heard from him."

"The cell phone reception's bad in here. Maybe he called but you didn't hear the ring."

"That's possible. I'll go outside and call him from the sidewalk. Just in case."

The Loanshark was gone for nearly 5 minutes. But came back all smiles.

"There's this hot two-year-old Filly owned by some movie people," the Loanshark said in a confidential voice. "She's running at Santa Anita this afternoon. LA time. Everything's been Arranged."

"Sounds good."

"But listen. I gotta show my LA guy I'm serious or there won't be any Next Time, if you know what I mean. So we have to Bet Big."

"How big?"

"I told him we'd go 10K."

"Are you saying $10,000?"

"My LA guy'll be watching the wires. He's got to see 10K cross the screen. Otherwise . . . "

"My God, $10,000 on a single bet . . . "

"Naturally, we'll have to spread it around among the various windows so nobody gets suspicious. But my LA guy knows how to count. And he'll be watching."

"Wow . . . "

"Listen. I'll tell you what we can do if 10K bothers you."

"What?"

"We'll go Partners. Fifty-fifty. I'll bet 5K and you'll bet 5K. That way . . . "

"Yeah, but . . . "

"Don't worry. You'll still put up your usual $2 and I'll lend you the rest of the 5K. Same terms as before. Just so long as our bets total 10K."

"Yeah, I guess that'll be okay."

"Good. Then let's go. We've got a lot of work to do and not much time to do it."

Between the two of them, they got 20 individual bets placed at seven different windows by two minutes before post time. Jack borrowed $4,998 from the Loanshark for his share. Giving himself an astounding Leverage Ratio of <u>2,499 to 1</u>. He'd owe the Loanshark $5,997.60 when the race was over. But his payoff would be at least $30,000, so that didn't bother him.

The race went pretty much the way Jack expected it to as he watched the TV monitor closely. The Filly ran most of the race back in the pack, which was the usual pattern. And right on schedule, she started closing on the lead horses as they rounded the Turn for Home.

But then something Really Bad happened.

Jack saw the Filly stumble as she was just about to catch the first horse. Stumble again. Then crash down heavily onto the track, flinging her jockey over her head. And all the other horses barreled past her in a matter of seconds as she lay writhing in agony on the track. The race was over. And they had lost. Big Time.

"Jesus Christ, did you see that?" the Loanshark said in a shocked voice.

"Yeah. We lost big."

"Shit, I've never seen anything like that in my life. Did you see how the bone was sticking out of the Filly's front leg? The whole fucking bone, for Christ's sake."

"Yeah. While all the other horses ran past her."

"I mean, I've heard about things like that happening. But, you know, just once in a while. I never actually saw anything like this. Jesus, the whole fucking bone sticking right out of her leg . . . "

"Too bad for us."

"Too bad for the Filly. They'll have to put her down."

"Put her down?"

"You know. Give her a death needle."

"Kill her?"

"No horse can survive with a broken leg like that. With the whole fucking bone sticking right out through her skin. Jesus, what a disaster."

"Yeah."

"Well, I guess we better settle up. I don't want to stay here any longer than I have to. The whole thing is making me sick. Jesus, that fucking bone . . . "

"Right."

Jack pulled out his wallet, fat with his afternoon's winnings. Started pulling out hundred-dollar bills and handing them to the Loanshark.

His winnings covered nearly all of his $5,997.60 loan payment. All except the last $5.60. Which he covered with Singles from his Betting Wad. Leaving him walking home with his Betting Wad thinned down to a mere $2.40. His worst loss in all the years of placing nice safe Two-Dollar bets.

As soon as he got home, Jack closed himself into the small bedroom

24

he used as a study. Set up his laptop on the desk. Cobbled together an Excel spreadsheet to give himself a picture of what had happened. Plugging in the numbers he could remember and typing in formulas to generate the rest. And twenty minutes later, the whole picture was clear on the laptop's monitor.

He'd walked into the OTB parlor with his usual Betting Wad of <u>10 Singles</u>.

After the Fifth Race, his cumulative winnings had reached <u>$5,992</u> after paying off the Loanshark.

For the Sixth Race, he borrowed <u>$4,998</u> from the Loanshark to make his Five-Thousand-dollar bet. Giving himself an incredible Leverage Ratio of <u>2,499 to 1</u> when matched against the $2 from his Betting Wad. Which could have given him net winnings from the Sixth Race of <u>$24,002.40</u> after paying back the Loanshark.

But after the Sixth Race turned into a disaster, he <u>still</u> had to pay back the Loanshark <u>$5,997.60</u> (including the usual 20 Percent interest). This wiped out his total winnings for the afternoon. <u>Plus</u> took an additional <u>$5.60</u> from his original Betting Wad.

So he left the OTB parlor having lost <u>76 Percent</u> of his original Ten-Dollar Betting Wad (since he <u>also</u> lost the $2 of his own cash he'd put up for his Sixth Race bet).

Meanwhile, the Loanshark left with <u>$1,367.60</u> in total interest on the cash he'd loaned out.

Not to mention his <u>$8,200</u> cumulative winnings on the first 5 races (assuming the bets he placed were made entirely with his own cash). Offset by his loss of the entire <u>Five-Thousand-Dollar</u> cash bet he had placed on the Sixth Race. Letting him walk away with a <u>$4,567.60</u> net profit for the afternoon.

Jack sat there with a growing sense of astonishment over <u>how easily</u> the Loanshark had conned him.

Previously, he'd <u>always</u> crunched the numbers carefully on his laptop for each horse who looked like a possible bet. Estimated the Potential Cost of losing his Two-Dollar bet. Versus the Potential Gain from winning. Adjusting each by the Relative Probabilities. Looking for <u>Risk-Reward Ratios</u> that made sense. Always so Prudent and Conservative.

But all that went by the boards after the first race. When he'd won over <u>270 times as much cash</u> for each dollar he'd put up from his Betting Wad, even <u>after</u> paying back his loan from the Loanshark. Because of his <u>24-to-1</u> Leverage Ratio from that loan. And the Loanshark's confident words about why the bet was a <u>sure thing</u>.

So he never touched his laptop for the rest of the afternoon. Just listened to each new deal the Loanshark brought him. Involving ever-larger bets. Ever-higher Leverage Ratios. And ever-more spectacular winnings. All of which he found impossible to resist.

Until everything came crashing down in the Sixth Race. Which wiped out all his winnings. And sent him home having lost <u>76 Percent</u> of his original Betting Wad.

Too bad about the Filly.

Leverage is obviously a Great Thing when you're Winning. Because it can <u>Multiply Like Mad</u> the value of your Winnings versus the few dollars of your own capital you have to put up.

But it can be an <u>Absolute Disaster</u> when you're Losing. Because then it <u>Multiplies Like Mad</u> the cost of your <u>Losses</u>. And can wipe out most of your Original Capital.

<u>That's</u> what happened (a few Million times over) to all those "Risk-Ignorant" managers in the financial industry during the **2008 Meltdown.** Running hedge funds. Asset portfolios in banks, insurance companies, pension funds, major charities. And so on.

Not to mention deep-pocket private investors buying "something-for-nothing" derivatives in their Mad Passion for higher returns.

Or homeowners who bought houses they couldn't afford by Leveraging their few down-payment dollars with bait-and-switch mortgages. Because losing a horse race was supposedly a "thing of the past" . . .

Yeah, sure.

Reader Note: Loansharking is one of the most lucrative sources of income for New York City's Five Families, who do business all over the country through a Cartel popularly known as the **Mafia** (but is far from being exclusively Italian). So this Cartel is one of America's largest and most politically powerful industries and is wired into all kinds of so-called "Kosher Industries." Including the financial community. But most economists pay no attention to the Cartel because it isn't "Respectable." This skews their understanding of the whole American economy by leaving out a Cartel that accounts for a very roughly estimated 10 Percent of reported Gross Domestic Product. Maybe more.

UNREGULATED DERIVATIVES

Let's suppose you bought the home of your dreams back in 2005. With the aid of an easily affordable fixed-rate thirty-year mortgage to cover 75 Percent of the purchase price.

What do you think happened to your mortgage after that? Did your lender stick it away in the safe mattress of its loan portfolio to live off the Interest until it was paid off?

Not very likely.

Your lender probably sold it right away for Fast Cash to a Wall Street investment bank. Along with all the other home mortgages it had closed on that month (some of which may well have been less creditworthy than yours).

And what did that Wall Street investment bank do with all those mortgages it had bought?

Packaged them up in a "Mortgage Pool." Divided into groups based on their assumed "Credit Quality."

Then it created a New Issue of dividend-paying debt securities backed by the monthly income generated by all the home mortgages in that pool. Securities known as "**Collateralized Mortgage Obligations**" (CMOs). A form of **Derivative Securities**. So-called because their value is derived from the value of all those home mortgages in the pool. (See **Chapters 4 and 5** for a full explanation of what Collateralized Mortgage Obligations and other Derivatives are all about.)

The Wall Street investment bank knew these new Collateralized Mortgage Obligations would be a lot easier to sell to investors at nice high prices if they carried a high credit rating from a major rating firm. The best known of which are **Moody's, Standard & Poor's,** and **Fitch.**

Such privately owned rating firms are in the highly profitable and unregulated business of selling credit ratings to issuers of securities like that Wall Street investment bank. Just like **Dell** is in the unregulated business of selling PCs to consumers. (But not like pharmaceutical companies selling prescription drugs that have to be approved as "Safe" by the Federal Government.) So naturally these rating firms tend to lean over backwards to provide their customers with the "products" they need.

What determines how high a credit rating a particular issue of securities receives?

In Theory, lots of conscientious number crunching and data analysis by the rating firm's professional staff to evaluate the True Credit Strength of the mortgage pool backing those Collateralized Mortgage Obligations.

In Practice? Well, you know how it is when Wall Street's Big Swinging Dicks who do a lot of business with each other get together to buy and sell unregulated "products." Their Sales Instincts rule the day. The rating firm guys want to sell their profitable rating products to the investment banker guys. And the investment banker guys want to sell their profitable new securities on the strength of Triple A ratings. So what do you think happens?

The investment bank gets the Triple A rating it wants from the rating firm for its new issue of Collateralized Mortgage Obligations. Then turns its salesmen loose to sell these products to the usual suckers. Like hedge funds. Other banks. Pension Funds. Mutual funds. Insurance companies.

So-called "sophisticated" private investors. All the other deep-pocket buyers of securities craving attractive returns that carry so-called "Minimal Risk."

And what <u>Incentives</u> does the investment bank use to goose its salesmen into maximizing their sales of these products?

Why, what better than seven-figure annual bonuses based on the <u>retail sales value</u> of what they sell each year?

All of which seemed okay until 2008. When some of the dicier mortgages packaged up with your solid mortgage in the pool backing those Collateralized Mortgage Obligations started defaulting on their monthly payments. And the same thing happened in hundreds of other similar mortgage pools backing similar Derivatives.

Leaving the Rich Suckers who bought those unregulated Derivatives to wake up one morning to find themselves holding soggy Toilet Paper whose value had collapsed. Learning for the first time (apparently) what <u>Risk is really all about</u>. (But "if they were so <u>Rich</u>, why weren't they <u>Smart</u>?")

So panic spread throughout the whole financial community. With nobody knowing what the securities in the <u>other</u> guy's portfolio were really worth. Therefore, how could anybody do normal business with anybody else?

Any if nobody can do business with anybody else, the nation's whole economy screeches to a halt.

CREDIT COLLAPSE

"Neither a Borrower nor a Lender be," prattled Polonius to Laertes in Shakespeare's **Hamlet**.

Well, maybe.

But in the <u>Real World</u>, few business firms of any size can operate without regular access to short-term credit to smooth out the mismatches in their normal cash flows.

Suppose you run your family's Widget factory. And you have to pay your employees their wages every Friday. That means a <u>cash outflow</u> each week.

But most of your prime customers are Wholesale Distributors who pay their bills for Widget purchases from firm's like yours on the last day of the <u>month</u> <u>following</u> each month you make Widget deliveries to them. So your <u>cash inflows</u> from sales are about <u>4 times</u> more widely spaced than your cash outflows for weekly payroll. How do you cope?

Like the overwhelming majority of business firms, you cover these cash flow mismatches by drawing down a long-established <u>credit line</u> from your local bank each week to cover payroll. And you repay these credit Drawdowns (plus the usual interest) as soon as each monthly payment comes in from your Wholesale Distributor customers. That's the way the commercial world normally works. Until 2008, that is.

But one Friday morning in October 2008, you had a Very Disturbing Experience.

You've been writing checks for this week's payroll. And you get on your desktop PC to access your firm's bank accounts so you can transfer to your main checking account enough cash from your credit line to cover these payroll checks. Just as you do every Friday.

But this morning, you see a chilling message from the bank on your PC's monitor screen.

"All credit lines are frozen until further notice."

Well, you scrounge around among your firm's various bank accounts and manage to come up with enough Cash to cover this week's payroll. Leaving you pretty well tapped out for operating cash until a big group of customer payments is due to arrive in 3 weeks. Too tapped-out to meet your next 3 payrolls.

So what do you do?

> <u>One Option</u> is to simply close the factory and lay off your employees until that big group of customer payments arrives. But a closed factory doesn't produce any Widgets. So you can't

deliver any to your customers, who may turn to other suppliers in the meantime. In any case, your future cash inflows from Widget sales will be lower. Meaning <u>smaller profits</u> this year.

<u>Another Option</u> is to close the factory and lay off your employees just for next week. And see if you can find enough Emergency Cash somewhere to cover payroll for the 2 weeks following. If you can, this will <u>reduce</u> your profit loss for the year because only a week of production will be lost. But if you can't? Well, you can always go back to the first option and keep the factory closed.

So it goes . . .

The Widget company's experience got repeated a few Million times throughout the nation during the Fall of 2008. Among all kinds of companies that suddenly found themselves without access to normal credit. The result was massive waves of worker layoffs. Lost wages (which meant less consumer spending). And lost company profits. All of which made a disastrous Recession even worse.

<u>Why did this happen</u>?

Because too many banks woke up one morning to find that some of the dicey unregulated Derivative securities they held in their portfolios had become <u>toxic waste</u> and lost most of their value. So in a panic, they tried to conserve as much Available Cash as they could. By <u>freezing</u> their lending activities. To business firms and individuals alike. Causing vast portions of the nation's business activity to grind to a halt.

(Incidentally, what <u>exactly is</u> a Widget? Well, it's no different from one of Alfred Hitchcock's **MacGuffins**. Like the microfilm full of mysterious "state secrets" hidden inside a Chinese figurine in his movie *North By Northwest*. Of no importance by itself, in other words. Simply the "Thing" the plot revolves around.)

31

BERNIE MADOFF

Oh come on, you're thinking. I've got to be kidding.

Wasn't Madoff just another two-bit Con Artist operating on the smarmy fringes of Wall Street? Who happened to hit it Very Big suckering rich acquaintances from his mistress on down to invest their money with him by promising high returns. Which he paid them from cash invested by his <u>next</u> round of suckers. Whom he paid from cash invested by the round of suckers <u>after that</u>. And so on. In what became history's biggest **Ponzi Scheme.**

Nothing to do with causing the Economic Crisis. Right?

Well sure. Technically.

But there's more to it than that.

What turned Madoff into one of the year's Biggest Ongoing News Stories was <u>when</u> his Ponzi scam blew up. During the **Financial Meltdown of 2008.** Because <u>that</u> turned him into a **Symbol** of a <u>World Gone Terribly Wrong</u>. Leaving his bones to be picked over with glee by carrion voices of the news media.

Any other time, Madoff would simply have been one more page-one **Financial Crime Story** the media would drool over for a day or so. Before moving on to the next **Celebrity Sex Scandal.** Or **Big Sports Upset.** Or **20-People-Killed-Auto-Pileup** in Wyoming.

But coming when it did, Madoff's story reminded too many people of the undercurrent of <u>Pervasive Sociopathic Behavior</u> that seemed to lie beneath the Great Meltdown. Making him an **American Legend** in his own time.

After all, didn't the Meltdown happen because too many people were driven by a <u>Make-Money-at-Any-Cost</u> craving that blinded their common sense? Just like Madoff. Not to mention his so-called "Victims."

And that <u>same</u> craving drove other people to buy houses they couldn't really afford in the belief that housing prices had nowhere to go but up.

Confident that rising prices could let them refinance their mortgages before their low teaser rates expired and pocket extra cash. (See **Chapter 5** for the details.)

Plus drove overpaid <u>managers at investment banks</u> to embrace the crazy Derivatives engineered by their Rocket Scientists. Which they didn't really understand. But So What, as long as they could be sold for big fast profits to schnook investors who thought "Risk" was something limited to OTB parlors. While chanting the **IBG** mantra ("I'll Be Gone") that became Wall Street's swan song. (**Chapter 4** explains Derivatives.)

Not to mention so-called <u>Professional Investors</u> driven to multiply the dollars in their pockets 30 or 40 or 100 times with <u>borrowed cash</u>. So they could place ever-more Gigantic Bets on whether a security's price would go up or down in the next few days. Or minutes. Ignoring the possibility that a Gigantic Bet could be a <u>Gigantic Loser</u>. And hang them out to dry, owing 30 or 40 or 100 times <u>more</u> than the cash in their pockets. Getting their knees broken (even if only figuratively) when their lenders sent their "Uncle Brunos" around to collect.

Interestingly, the flip side of what Bernie Madoff really meant can be found in that all-time favorite 1942 movie *Casablanca*. The great story of how lead character **Rick** (Humphrey Bogart in one of his most iconic roles) was transformed from "Innocent Idealist" to "Me-First Cynic" to "Worldly Moralist" by his experiences during World War II (the <u>Good</u> war).

During the 1930s, Rick "ran guns to Ethiopia" and "fought for Loyalist Spain" (two powerful symbols of Liberal Idealism back when the movie was made). But during the Fall of Paris in 1940, he suffered a "traumatic romantic betrayal" by **Ilse** (the Ingrid Bergman character).

So he retreated, emotionally shattered and bleeding self-pity, to City-of-Intrigue Casablanca in North Africa. Where he opened a popular nightclub. Complete with the obligatory fixed roulette wheel in its illegal backroom gambling casino. And went out of his way to try and convince everyone (including himself) that he was simply a Cold-Hearted, "I stick my neck out for no man," New York City Tough Guy with a shady past. (Which, of course, didn't extend to his loyal club pianist friend **Sam**. Or to **Annina**, the young Romanian refugee who sought his help while her husband was unsuccessfully trying to win enough money at the club's roulette wheel to buy their way to neutral Lisbon. Or to any of the refugees from Nazi-occupied Europe who worked for him.)

But everything changed when Ilse unexpectedly showed up in Rick's night club. Accompanied by her impossibly pure-hearted anti-Nazi underground leader husband **Victor**. And in a private late-night visit, told Rick she believed Victor to have died in a concentration camp when they became lovers in Paris. But when she found out that Victor was actually alive and had escaped, she had no choice but to return to him. Begged Rick to understand. And help Victor get to Lisbon so he could carry on his anti-Nazi Cause. Even offering to stay behind with Rick and resume their romance.

So Rick saw a Golden Opportunity. He could arrange passage to Lisbon for Ilse and himself. With Victor conned into staying behind in Casablanca and martyring himself to save Ilse's life. What could be a more perfect conventional romantic ending (so long as Victor gets heroically killed in time)?

But when push came to shove in the movie's climax, Rick's long-dormant Liberal Social Conscience woke up at last. So he put Ilse and Victor on the plane to Lisbon ("the problems of two people don't amount to a hill of beans in this crazy world," he told her). Then went off to join a Free French garrison and Fight the Nazis. Accompanied by his glibly corrupt police chief friend **Louis**, who's also seen the light.

Bernie and Rick. Archetype bookends of America's moral spectrum.

With **Bernie** and his "victims" insisting that Feathering Our Own Nests is the Only Thing that <u>Really Counts</u>.

While **Rick**, the savvy but emotionally battered New York City boy, rose to Heroic, Self-Sacrificing proportions when the chips were really down during World War II. Becoming the kind of American we all wanted to be (and Millions of us <u>actually were</u>) during those **Noblest Years** in the nation's history.

So we don't all have to be <u>Schmucks</u>. As Rick shows us, it's simply a matter of **Moral Choice.**

■ ■ ■

Some Locker-Room Terminology

Meanwhile, here are some <u>Definitions</u> of popular Locker-Room Terms we'll be seeing often in the pages that follow.

(Stained-glass academic books like to call such definitions a **Glossary**. But this word makes my eyes glaze over and quickly skip past it. Or even skip the whole book. So let's not poison the well right here at the start.)

- **Economic Crisis:** What we seem to be stuck in right now. Marked by a <u>Constipated National Economy</u> that can't seem to grow its way out of a paper bag. Having to <u>Kiss Goodbye</u> to Millions of American jobs that may be gone forever. Plus low housing prices that might have seemed like "bargains" a few years ago if we were looking to buy, but now represent hard-earned savings dollars down the drain if we're stuck owning those houses. Plus the flip side of "Early Retirement" (having to keep working until we drop because Half the Value of our 401(k)s vanished into thin air). Ditto college for our children.

- **The Financial Meltdown of 2008** (known for short as **"The Great Meltdown"** or simply **"The Meltdown"**): A

Bible-style plague that <u>Tanked the Stock Market</u> by nearly 60 Percent in the Fall of 2008. <u>Killed Off</u> other financial and credit markets in the process. <u>Bled Dry</u> banks and other business firms that either vanished into Bankruptcy or had to be rescued by Taxpayer Bailouts. And <u>Saddled Us</u> with the **Economic Crisis.**

- **Lascivines:** The modern equivalent of those <u>Smarmy Saloonkeepers</u> in classic Western Movies. Paying the usual "Gaudy Ladies" to hover at the bar and croon us into drinking overpriced, watered-down whiskey while their painted eyes seem to promise that we can "take them upstairs" later. As these Saloonkeepers take Big Cuts of the crooked card games they let Fast-Shuffle professional gamblers run in their back rooms. And have cattle rustlers on retainer to "maintain order" among the drunks and other losers. Plus pay off the local sheriff to look the other way. (You get the idea.)

- **Rocket Scientists:** Bright young nerds with Ph.D.'s in Math or Physics from major universities. Who found that earning a decent living in the academic world was <u>tougher</u> than earning a decent living as Broadway actors. So they ended up earning fabulous livings on Wall Street. Where their technical backgrounds let them quickly master the intricacies of "<u>Quantitative Finance Theory.</u>" And engineer all kinds of wild new **Derivative Securities** too complicated for most people to understand. But very profitable for the financial firms that employed them.

- **Big Swinging Dick:** An infantile macho term of "Respect" for anyone in the financial industry who's aggressive enough to generate <u>Really Big Dollars</u> for his firm (by hook or crook), and gets paid accordingly. Reflects the typical confusion about "Money and Sex" that befuddles the minds of the "chronic little boy" adult males who dominate American business and industry. Which is often expanded to include <u>Murder</u> itself (as in "I made a <u>Killing</u> in the Market").

- **Yiddish Words:** Sprinkled throughout the book. But never in *italics* to make them seem like a Big Deal. Because they aren't. Just part of Wall Street's local color. As in the popular saying: "*Dress <u>British</u> but talk <u>Yiddish</u>.*"

■ ■ ■

Crossroads

The **Financial Meltdown of 2008** was one of the most Critical Events in American history.

- It **WIPED OUT** some **$11 Trillion of the nation's wealth.** Which is going to take years to get back.

- **DESTROYED** more than **8 Million American jobs through September 2009** (and you know how many more since then). Too many of which are Gone Forever.

- **FROZE UP** the nation's vast **Financial Credit System.** Leaving Millions of business firms too short of cash to operate.

- **FORCED** the Federal Government to spend **$2.8 Trillion** (**and commit another $8.2 Trillion) in Taxpayer funds** bailing out crippled major corporations. Like General Motors, Chrysler, Citigroup, Bank of America, AIG, and a host of other "too-big-to-fail" private sector institutions.

- **COST Millions of Americans** their **JOBS. HOMES. LIFE SAVINGS.** Hopes for **DECENT RETIREMENTS.**

This was a Cataclysm far worse than any Natural Disaster in the nation's experience.

And it's important that we understand What Happened and Why. So we'll know how to choose the <u>Right Kind</u> of Huffing and Puffing to claw our way back from the **Abyss.**

Well, so much for the Big Picture. Now let's look at some of the <u>Appalling Details</u>.

■ ■ ■

Chapter 2
THE "GUNS OF AUGUST" ALL OVER AGAIN

No man is an island, entire of itself. Every man is a piece of the continent, a part of the main. If a clod be washed away by the sea, Europe is the less. As well as if a promontory were. As well as if a manor of thy friend's or of thine own were . . .

And therefore never send to know for whom the bell tolls. It tolls for thee.
—*John Donne*

Believe it or not, the Summer of 2008 wasn't the first time successful, know-it-all, big-power Western industrial nations looked into the **Abyss**. Responded in all the wrong ways. And ended up in **Deep Doo-Doo**.

In 1914, **Archduke Franz Ferdinand** was heir to the throne of the multi-ethnic **Austro-Hungarian Empire**. And on the bright Sunday morning of June 28, he and his wife **Duchess Sophie** made an official state visit to the **Bosnian city of Sarajevo**. Which was then an occupied province of the Austro-Hungarian Empire.

In late morning, the cars in their imperial procession made a wrong turn on the unfamiliar streets of Sarajevo and halted to get their bearings.

At that moment, **Gavrilo Princip**, a young Bosnian Freedom Fighter (or Terrorist, take your pick), stepped out of the crowd holding a revolver. And fired 2 shots into the back seat of the open car carrying the Archduke and Duchess.

One bullet shattered the Archduke's left jugular vein. The second buried itself deep in the abdomen of the Duchess. Both died within minutes.

And Europe proceeded to come apart at the seams.

Less than 6 weeks later on August 3, the armies of Kaiser Wilhelm's **Germany** invaded **Belgium**. As the first step in their long-standing **Schlieffen Plan** to score a quick knock-out military victory over Republican **France**. Why?

- Because France had a <u>military alliance</u> with **Tsarist Russia**. Which had already begun <u>mobilizing</u> its huge army in support of its client Balkan state of **Serbia**.

- Because Serbia, as the "spiritual leader" of occupied Balkan states like Bosnia, was being <u>threatened with invasion</u> by the **Austro-Hungarian Empire** (with the support of its **German** ally) for "refusing to cooperate fully" in the investigation of the assassination of Archduke Franz Ferdinand.

- But **Germany** regarded Russian mobilization as an <u>invasion threat</u> against its eastern provinces. And assumed this would prompt Russia's ally **France** to attack it from the west. Hence its decision to mount a preemptive invasion of France through neutral **Belgium** <u>before</u> Russia could complete its mobilization.

- However, the constitutional monarchy of **Great Britain** had <u>guaranteed</u> the territorial integrity of **Belgium**. So it declared war against rampaging **Germany** on August 4. And began landing contingents of its small but highly trained professional army in France on August 7 to support the French and Belgian armies.

- By the middle of August, therefore, the major league lineup was basically complete. The alliance of **Britain, France,** and

Russia was formally at war with the alliance of **Germany** and **Austro-Hungary**.

Clear?

I thought not.

And the parties of the two alliances seemed equally confused.

But they still plunged ahead with great enthusiasm in the 5 local wars that broke out during August within days of each other in different parts of Europe:

1. **Austro-Hungary vs. Serbia** in the Balkans
2. **Austro-Hungary vs. Russia** in southern Poland and Galicia
3. **Russia vs. Germany** in East Prussia
4. **France vs. Germany** in Alsace-Lorraine
5. **Germany vs. Belgium/France/Britain** in Belgium and northern France

All of which they confidently expected would be over by Christmas.

Well, they got the Christmas part right.

But not the Year.

Because what became the unimaginable catastrophe of **World War I** dragged on with **Maximum Mismanagement** by all parties until **November 1918**. Which destroyed the remains of Nineteenth-Century European society and wasn't really settled until 1945. When the Western Allies and the Soviet Union finally smashed the resurgent monster Germany had become in the wake of the 1918 Armistice and established a New Europe (for better or worse) amid the ruins.

But however inconclusive World War I may have been, its **staggering costs** horrified the world. All told, the 16 nations that ended up fighting each other spent the equivalent of some **$3,000 Trillion** (in inflation-adjusted 2009 U.S. dollars) on the War. Mobilized **65 Million troops**. With

12 Percent of these troops being killed and another **33 Percent** wounded. For an overall casualty rate of **45 Percent**.

Among the 3 original major Allies, for example:

- **Russia** spent **$275 Trillion** (again, in inflation-adjusted 2009 U.S. dollars) to fight the War. Mobilized **12 Million** troops. Of whom **15 Percent** (or 1.8 Million) were killed in battle. While another **42 Percent** (or 5 Million) were wounded. For a total casualty rate of **57 Percent**. Which doesn't include some **2 Million Russian civilians** killed as a result of the fighting.

- **France** spent **$537 Trillion** on the War. Mobilized **8.7 Million** troops. With **16 Percent** (or 1.4 Million) killed and **49 Percent** (4.3 Million) wounded. For a total casualty rate of **65 Percent**.

- The **British Empire** spent **$560 Trillion** fighting the War. Mobilized **8.8 Million** troops. Of these, **10 Percent** (about 900,000) were killed and **24 Percent** (2.1 Million) were wounded. For a total casualty rate of **34 Percent**.

Among the so-called "Original Bad Guys," the costs were equally severe:

- **Germany** spent **$625 Trillion** fighting the War. Mobilized **13.4 Million** troops. Among whom **15 Percent** (2 Million) were killed and **43 Percent** (5.7 Million) were wounded. For a total casualty rate of **58 Percent**.

- The **Austro-Hungarian Empire** spent **$255 Trillion** on the War. Mobilized **7.8 Million** troops. Of whom **26 Percent** (2

Million) were killed, and another **24 Percent** (1.9 Million) were wounded. For an overall casualty rate of **50 Percent**.

In terms of "collateral damage":

- <u>Three</u> of Europe's four leading monarchs lost their crowns (only Britain's royal family survived, since it was already constitutionally based). To be replaced by "republican governments" of varying stability.

- The Austro-Hungarian Empire collapsed and was replaced by some half-a-dozen ethnically based nations. Most of which were overrun by Germany in World War II and became puppet states of the Soviet Union thereafter.

- The people of Europe, having borne the brunt of the suffering, lost all confidence in the so-called "Ideals of Western Civilization" they'd taken for granted before 1914. Especially the credibility of their governments. Whom they were convinced had persistently lied to them. Protected their own elites at the cost of everyone else. And squandered Millions of lives by mismanaging the War.

- And virtually <u>everyone</u>, Victors and Vanquished alike, was left bankrupt afterwards. Owing more money to the United States (which sat out most of the War and became the world's leading creditor nation) than they could ever possibly repay.

Quite a scorecard for a major war that settled virtually nothing.

Perhaps the only real winners were the generations of writers who produced hoards of books (fictional and otherwise) that tried to explain what happened and why and what the impact was.

But did <u>Our Generation</u> experience its own version of the "**Guns of August**" during the **Summer of 2008** when the World of International Finance melted down so catastrophically?

■ ■ ■

The World of Banks

Some people may find obvious parallels to 1914 in the "assassination" of the famed investment banking house of **Lehman Brothers** on **September 15, 2008**. When the Federal Government "allowed it to collapse into Bankruptcy."

But a more telling parallel (equivalent to Gavrilo Princip drawing his revolver in the first place) may have occurred more than a year earlier, on **July 31, 2007**. When investment banking firm **Bear Stearns & Company** placed two of its hedge funds in **Bankruptcy** because they had <u>run out of cash</u>. Then "<u>temporarily suspended</u>" withdrawals from a third hedge fund because it had been swamped by requests from clients to get their money back.

We'll look at some of the key things that led up to these unnerving actions by Bear Stearns in a minute.

But first a little background about <u>what banks actually do</u>.

Throughout history, banks of one kind or another have been the primary **Financial Intermediaries** in most civilized societies.

In other words, they provide the essential (and highly profitable) services involved in <u>bringing together</u>:

- **Those who <u>Have Excess Cash</u>** that they wish to invest for profit, and

- **Those who <u>Need Cash</u>** to build or buy hard assets (like income-producing factories and equipment, entire profit-making companies, homes to live in, etc.).

In the course of operating successful businesses as Financial Intermediaries, banks have had to be aware of a basic **Fact of Life:**

The <u>More Time</u> that Cash must be committed to an investment, the <u>Higher</u> its annual profit payment is expected to be. This is most clearly illustrated in the world of **Lending and Borrowing.**

For example, a corporate bond that matures in <u>10</u> years is normally going to pay a <u>higher interest rate</u> than a bond that matures in only <u>5</u> years. But this interest rate will be <u>lower</u> than for a bond that matures in <u>20</u> years. With the actual level of all these interest rates being determined by constantly changing perceptions of those who buy and sell these securities in the marketplace.

This relationship between **Interest Rate** and **Time** can be plotted on a chart called a **Yield Curve.** With the resulting curve usually sloping upwards (towards higher interest rates) to the right (as maturity time becomes longer). Financial newspapers like *Investors' Business Daily* and *The Wall Street Journal* publish such Yield Curve Charts for U.S. Treasury debt securities on a daily basis.

For a bank, this relationship defines a **Profit Opportunity.** If it lends out Cash for (let's say) <u>10 years</u> and funds this loan by borrowing the necessary Cash for only <u>1 year at a time</u> at annual intervals, it can earn an **Automatic Profit** (if all goes well) from the **Spread** between <u>higher</u> ten-year interest rates on the Cash it **lends out** and <u>lower</u> one-year rates on the Cash it **borrows.**

This has given rise to the classic banking mantra: *"Lend Long and Borrow Short."*

But sometimes the standard relationship between interest rates and time becomes <u>reversed</u>. With short-term interest rates rising <u>higher</u> in the marketplace than long-term rates. This phenomenon is known in financial circles as an **"Inverted Yield Curve"** and is usually a harbinger of Bad Times.

For a bank, an Inverted Yield Curve means that it's <u>losing money</u> on its long-term loans. Because its receipts of loan interest are <u>lower</u> than the interest payments it must make on its short-term borrowings to fund these loans. And the bank's ability to survive these temporary periods of financial stress depends on how much **Equity Capital** it has to cover its losses.

But a bank's <u>ultimate protection</u> against getting into this kind of trouble is having **Prudent Management**. Savvy enough not to overreach itself by bowing to the temptation to chase maximum profits by making too many questionable loans when Good Times are rolling.

By long tradition, banks can choose to engage in the following activities to pursue their business of serving as Financial Intermediaries:

- Take <u>Deposits</u> **of Funds** from business firms and individuals. That banks can hold either in "immediately available, no-questions-asked" **Checking Accounts** for these depositors. Or in interest-paying **Time Deposit Accounts** available only on fixed maturity dates or by "advance notification" by depositors.

  (Taking Deposits is the whole basis for the seemingly magical process by which such banks can literally <u>Create New Money</u> out of thin air. This process is fully described in **Chapter 7**, which covers "**The Secrets of Money**.")

- **Make short-term, medium-term, and long-term** <u>Loans</u> to business firms and individuals. Using Depositor funds, their own Equity Capital, or funds borrowed from other sources.

- Trade <u>Financial Securities</u> for their own account. Supporting these trading activities with their own Equity Capital or with funds borrowed from other financial institutions.

- Buy entire <u>New Issues of Stocks or Bonds</u> from their business clients for an agreed price. Then resell these stocks or bonds through their retail networks at slightly higher prices to private individuals and institutions. This practice is known as **Underwriting** and is usually very profitable. However, the bank must place its <u>own funds at risk</u> temporarily to buy these new issues and hope it can quickly recoup its funds (and earn a profit) by turning around and selling the new securities to private investors.

(Just like the age-old process where a **Fish Wholesaler** <u>buys</u> the entire catch of a fishing boat for a negotiated cash price when it ties up at the dock. Then turns around and <u>resells</u> the fish in numerous small parcels at higher prices per pound to local restaurants and retail food stores. Hopefully, before they go bad.)

- Provide <u>Financial Advisory Services</u> to business clients. For fees that can be quite lucrative and don't require committing any of the bank's capital.

Until <u>1933,</u> banks in the United States were allowed to engage in any or all of these activities.

But the perception developed that this wide-open approach to banking led to various "abuses" that had brought about the Financial Meltdown in 1929–30, which helped to create the **Great Depression**. (The Meltdown of 2008 was scarcely the only example of a financial "Guns of August" event in American economic history.)

So in 1933, the Roosevelt Administration persuaded Congress to pass the **Glass-Steagall Act** as part of its efforts to overhaul the crippled financial industry.

Among other things, this landmark legislation defined <u>2 entirely</u>

separate kinds of banks and erected a formidable "Chinese Wall" between them:

1. "Commercial Banks" were those that chose to continue in the business of **Taking Deposits** from business firms and individuals. Usually as publicly traded "bank holding companies" theoretically owned by large numbers of stockholders. To encourage this, depositors would have their accounts Fully Insured by a new government agency known as the **Federal Deposit Insurance Corporation** (FDIC). And in financial emergencies, Commercial Banks could temporarily Borrow Cash from the **Federal Reserve** (the nation's "Central Bank") to tide them over.

   But these protections came with a price. For example, Commercial Banks were prohibited from underwriting securities. Or providing brokerage services to the public. Or offering fee-based financial advisory services. And they were required by Federal regulators to maintain "prudent" capital structures. Which meant having more Equity Capital relative to their Debt Capital than had previously been the case.

   (As a result, the legendary banking firm of **J. P. Morgan** split into two entirely independent companies. With its "Commercial Bank" portion becoming a publicly traded bank holding company known as **Morgan-Guarantee Trust Company**).

2. "Investment Banks" were those that preferred to continue in the business of **Underwriting** new issues of stocks and bonds for business clients and providing fee-based **Financial Advisory Services** to these clients. They were usually owned by "private partnerships of their principals" and re-

mained largely unregulated by the Federal Government. Which meant no meaningful limits on the amount of <u>Debt Capital</u> they could have in their capital structures relative to <u>Equity Capital</u>.

But they were <u>prohibited</u> from **Taking Deposits** from business firms and individuals. And they had <u>no statutory right</u> to **Borrow Cash** from the Federal Reserve in the event of Emergencies.

(The remaining portion of **J. P. Morgan** became a private Investment Bank known as **Morgan-Stanley.**)

As the years passed, <u>Commercial Banks</u> developed a reputation for being dull, predictable, conservative institutions hamstrung by all sorts of government rules and regulations. Run by dull, predictable, conservative white males. Who made ultra-prudent loans to dull, predictable, conservative business firms and upscale individuals with unquestioned credit pedigrees.

But the reputation of <u>Investment Banks</u> was just the opposite. They became known as exciting, risk-taking, aggressive Swingers largely free of rules and regulations. Staffed by exciting, risk-taking, aggressive men and women whose sharp eyes were always on the lookout for new opportunities to help build exciting, risk-taking, aggressive new business concepts into the kind of enterprises that could be the Future of America. (**Bear Stearns** was one of these investment banks.)

By the 1980s, in fact, Investment Banking had entirely replaced **Advertising** as Manhattan's **Number One Glamour Industry**. Where the Best and Brightest graduates of the nation's leading business schools were eager to establish their careers. While Commercial Banking stumbled along as a safe-haven bureaucracy for unimaginative time-servers who "just wanted to make a decent living."

But during the 1990s, as the "deregulation mania" began sweeping across the country, all this started to change.

An ambitious Brooklyn boy named Sandy Weill who was overflowing with entrepreneurial chutzpah and Wall Street smarts began acquiring control of various banks, insurance companies, retail brokerage firms, and similar financial institutions. Some of these he cobbled together into an increasingly large financial conglomerate under the umbrella of his publicly traded insurance company, known as **Travelers Group**. Others became part of his publicly traded commercial bank holding company, called **Citicorp**.

In 1997, Weill's Citicorp acquired the investment banking firm of **Salomon Brothers**. And in 1998, he proposed a $70 Billion merger between Citicorp and Travelers. Which would be the biggest corporate merger in American history and would create the world's largest one-stop financial services institution, to be known as **Citigroup**.

Sandy Weill's Citigroup proposal presented the Federal Government with a major challenge. Its **"Do Everything"** approach to financial services would make a mockery of the Chinese Wall and other New Deal restrictions on banks embodied in the Glass-Steagall Act.

But this approach was being strongly advocated throughout the financial industry as the best way for the nation to compete with foreign banks like **UBS**, **Deutsche Bank**, and **Credit Suisse First Boston** for larger shares of the world's burgeoning financial business.

So the Federal Government bowed (not all that unwillingly) to the inevitable and granted Weill a "temporary waiver" to complete his Citicorp/Travelers merger. And in 1999, the Republican-controlled Congress passed the **Gramm-Leach-Bliley Financial Services Modernization Act** (with President Clinton's support), which effectively repealed Glass-Steagall.

Now the road was wide open for other entrepreneurs to try and emulate Sandy Weill. To create their own versions of **Full Service Financial Institutions** to make huge profits doing business throughout the world.

Assuming they could come up with enough capable management talent to make it all work successfully.

■ ■ ■

The Stillborn Management Revolution

Ah, Management . . .

Presumably the <u>most essential requirement</u> for business success.

During the first half of the Twentieth Century, it became increasingly apparent that the <u>Challenges</u> of managing large organizations had grown to such a level of complexity that only individuals with the right mix of skills could meet them effectively.

Because business success depended on smoothly integrating such disparate functions as:

- **Producing Products Efficiently.**
- **Marketing Them at a Profit to Customers.**
- **Financing the Firm Intelligently.**
- **Keeping Accurate Records of What Was Happening.**

Thus was born the distinct career of "**Professional Manager.**" Someone able to "<u>run the whole enterprise</u>" effectively. To make sure it was "**Doing Things Right.**" And, at the Top Management level, to make sure it was "**Doing the Right Things.**"

One of the first and most famous of these Professional Managers was **Alfred P. Sloan.** Who became head of General Motors (yes, <u>that</u> General Motors) in 1920. And proceeded to build it from a ragtag mishmash of independent automobile brands into one of the world's largest and most successful industrial corporations.

A number of the nation's leading universities became aware of the success of Sloan and others as Professional Managers. And realized that this was a profession that demanded a unique sets of skills. Just as a **Physician** needed a unique set of professional skills. Or an **Attorney**. Or a **Dentist**. Or an **Accountant**.

Skills that could be <u>taught</u> to properly motivated individuals in appropriately structured university graduate programs. Whose acquired competence could be recognized on completion of these programs by awarding them **Professional Degrees as <u>Managers</u>**. Equivalent in status to the professional degrees awarded to Medical Doctors, Attorneys, Dentists, and Accountants.

So a number of universities picked up on this marketing opportunity and established graduate programs in **Business Administration** to produce **Professional Managers**. With their students being required to achieve a certain level of **working literacy** in the basic technical specialties of business, like Accounting, Marketing, Finance, etc., so they would know how to make them serve the larger goals of the **Business Enterprise** as properly integrated "skill teams."

And at the end of their periods of study (usually two years), students in these programs would be awarded the degree of **Master of Business Administration** (MBA). Testifying to their ability to <u>run a business</u>. Just as the degree of **Doctor of Medicine** awarded to medical school graduates testified to their ability to <u>treat the sick</u>.

The result was a flow of truly professional managers into the business world. Gifted people who had learned in business school how to connect all the dots in a complex enterprise so its **Portfolio of Assets** could generate maximum value for its shareholders. People like **Jack Welch**, who turned sclerotic giant **General Electric** into a heads-up growth company. And **Lou Gerstner**, who became CEO of **IBM** when everybody was writing it off as a day-is-done leftover from the old era of mainframe leasing and made it a cutting-edge leader in information technology. And **Jaime Dimon** of **JPMorgan Chase,** who showed how a financial conglomerate could really get its act together.

But as the years passed, something happened to derail this sensible concept.

An increasing number of students in MBA programs found that what they <u>really</u> wanted was to have careers as recognized **Technical Specialists** in the business world. As **Accountants,** for example. Or **Marketing Professionals.** Or **Finance Mavens.** As opposed to simply being **Professional Managers.**

- Some of these students got the idea that they could obtain more highly paid entry-level jobs after graduation if they possessed technical skills that could immediately be put to work by potential employers. Rather than having to serve as "Executive Trainee" gofer-types for mid-level managers.

- Others believed that promotions and raises would come faster if their employers perceived that they had superior skills as Technical Specialists.

- Still others felt that their "personalities" better suited them to work in technical areas, especially during their younger years.

- And if, in the course of events, they should reach the point of being offered a true **Management Job?** Well, they'd deal with that when the time came. If it ever did.

Needless to say, students didn't reach these conclusions on their own. They were the result of dormitory scuttlebutt ("feedback") reaching them from recent graduates, as well as job interviews with prospective employers. And it became apparent that what these prospective employers <u>really</u> wanted were **Technical Specialists.**

The universities bowed to these realities by allowing those students who so desired to focus increasing portions of their two years in graduate business school on becoming Technical Specialists. Even to the point of awarding them degrees like "**MBA in Marketing,**" or "**MBA in Finance.**" Thereby tending to bury the original concept of business school as a training ground for **Professional Managers.**

Nowhere was this increasing focus on training Technical Specialists more welcome than in the financial world. Whose firms fell all over themselves to hire boatloads of business school graduates with MBAs in Finance. In an effort to help themselves cope with the increasingly math-oriented and arcane "Science of Finance." (For a full discussion of how complicated and esoteric this so-called "Science" became, see the explanation of **Derivatives** in **Chapter 4.**)

But this left financial firms starved for qualified <u>Professional Managers,</u> even as they overflowed with technical specialists. So they had no choice but to staff their top management ranks with hurriedly converted technical specialists (who tended to find themselves completely at sea when it came to their new and unfamiliar responsibilities). Or with smooth-talking "Power Players" who had mastered the art of manipulating the internal politics of their organizations to serve their own private agendas.

This problem became especially serious in investment banks as they converted themselves from <u>private partnerships</u> into <u>publicly traded corporations</u> in order to increase the amount of Equity Capital they had available to expand their underwriting and trading operations.

As "<u>Partners</u>" their top managers had virtually all their personal wealth tied up in illiquid investments in their firms. So when they erred, it was usually on the side of being "too cautious" (which isn't a bad mind-set for managers who don't really know what they're doing).

But as "<u>Stockholders</u>" in publicly traded corporations, their personal wealth was highly liquid. Enabling them to cash out whenever the moment seemed right. And move on to more gracious lives of upscale philanthropic activities and support of fashionable cultural institutions.

So is it any wonder that many investment bank managers became bitten by the eager-beaver bug? Stumbling all over themselves to rush into risky situations that seemed to promise "greater profits" (and therefore skyrocketing year-end bonuses to compound the size of their stock holdings in their firms) without really understanding the risks they were exposing their firms to?

Needless to say, there were exceptions here and there. Like famously colorful **Alan Greenberg,** who became CEO of Bear Stearns in 1978 and led it into its glory years with a sure hand.

Greenberg had come up through Bear's highly profitable trading ranks and had never been to business school. In fact, he was skeptical of standard MBA types with their elaborate spreadsheets. Preferring what he called "PSDs" (*"Poor, Smart, Deep Desire to be Rich"*), who tended to be classic New York City ethnic types from the "Bridge and Tunnel Crowd" with sharp minds and lots of ambition. He had a trader's gut instinct for insisting on knowing at the end of each day how many Dollars the firm had committed to each outstanding trade. Plus, how Risky each trade was. Not to mention what the firm's Leverage Ratio was on each trade. Which isn't a bad recipe for **Staying Out of Trouble.**

But great instinctive managers like Greenberg are all too rare. And when he stepped down as Bear's CEO in 1993, there was no one of his talent to replace him. So the flaws in Bear's top management became little different from the amateur-hour klutziness that afflicted the rest of the financial industry. All of which were nakedly exposed with terrible consequences in 2008. When the world's financial institutions repeatedly "shot themselves in the foot" because their clueless, untrained, wildly overpaid, generally incompetent top managers hadn't the foggiest idea of how to cope with the Noah's Flood of problems that were inundating them.

■ ■ ■

The Bear
Stearns Story

(*Disclosure: Between 1977 and 1988, I worked for Bear Stearns and got to know a number of people who were on the scene during its subsequent decline. But none of them contributed any "tales told out of school" to the discussion that follows.*)

The unsettling actions that Bear Stearns took on July 21, 2007 affected 2 hedge funds that Bear had set up as **"Structured Investment Vehicles"** (SIVs).

Despite being managed by the firm's **Bear Stearns Asset Management** subsidiary, being SIVs meant (at least in theory) that these hedge funds were "legally independent" companies whose balance sheets and income statements would have no impact on Bear's reported financial performance as a publicly traded corporation.

Their purpose was to make profits trading with their own capital in the largely free and unregulated markets for **Collateralized Mortgage Obligations**, using "appropriate" amounts of <u>Leverage</u>.

- For a full description of what Collateralized Mortgage Obligations are and how they developed, see **Chapter 5**, which covers **Housing and Mortgages**. Right now, all we have to remember is that Collateralized Mortgage Obligations are simply one form of **Collateralized Debt Obligations**, or CDOs (also known as **"Collateralized Loan Obligations"**), whose underlying security happens to be home mortgages. As **Chapter 4** (about **Derivatives**) notes, other Collateralized Debt Obligations may be based on automobile loans. Or consumer credit card debt. Or virtually any kind of loan made to a Borrower by a Lender.

- To understand how trading in free markets actually works in the real world (as opposed to the fairyland world of many economics textbooks) and how Leverage can boost trading profits, see **Chapter 6**, titled "**Is Market Capitalism Still Alive?**"

(If these words should tempt you to <u>immediately jump ahead</u> to either or both of these chapters, feel free to do so. The rest of this chapter will still be here when you get back. After all, this book <u>isn't</u> like one of those childhood meals where your mother absolutely forbade you from tasting so much as a tongue-lick of the chocolate ice cream for dessert until you had finished your dreary plate of overcooked carrots or spinach or whatever. You can read this book's chapters in any order that makes sense to you. That's why its Table of Contents is so detailed.)

Meanwhile, a few words about **Leverage**.

Suppose you buy a financial security for $100 entirely with your own cash (i.e., your "Equity Capital"). And after a month or so, you're able to sell that security in the marketplace for $101. That gives you a profit of $1, or a return on your Equity Capital of **1 Percent**.

Which isn't very exciting.

But suppose instead, you <u>borrow</u> $100 and add it to your $100 of Equity Capital. Now you can buy <u>2</u> of those securities for $100 each. And if you sell both for $101 each, you've made a profit of $2. All of which can be allocated to your Equity Capital. Raising its return to **2 Percent**.

That's a little better. In <u>Leveraging</u> your Equity Capital by a 1-to-1 ratio, you've <u>doubled</u> its return.

So why not borrow **$1,000**? That way, you <u>Leverage</u> your $100 in Equity Capital by a 10-to-1 ratio. Enabling you to buy <u>11</u> of those securities at $100 each. And when you sell all 11 for $101 each, your profit is $11. So after you've allocated this profit to your Equity Capital, you've raised its return to **11 Percent**.

Now things are starting to get interesting.

Bear's 2 "independent" hedge funds typically employed Leverage Ratios as high as <u>30 to 1</u> (i.e., borrowing $3,000 for each $100 in Equity Capital). Using the same numbers as in the example above, this meant being able to buy <u>31 securities</u> at $100 each for <u>each</u> $100 of Equity Capital. And if they were sold for $101 each, that meant a profit of $31 for each $100 of Equity Capital. Which translates into a Return on Equity of **31 Percent**.

Equity returns of this magnitude make it possible to attract **Outside Investors** willing to contribute additional Equity Capital to your hedge fund in order to participate in these great-looking returns. If the hedge fund maintains its 30-to-1 Leverage Ratio, then each <u>additional</u> $100 in Equity Capital contributed by Outside Investors increases the fund's **Total Trading Capital** (Equity plus Debt) by $3,100. Making it possible for the fund's sharp traders to buy and sell more and larger blocks of securities. Generating (if all goes well) <u>increasingly large</u> dollar profits.

Is it any wonder that those Big Swinging Dicks on Wall Street's trading floors received such enormous year-end bonuses during the boom years prior to 2008? And were therefore motivated to make ever-more extravagant trades, with no concern for their long-term implications?

But wait a minute. What about all that borrowed cash?

Well, here are four things to keep in mind:

- **<u>FIRST</u>:** A hedge fund obviously has to pay interest on its borrowed cash at regular intervals. But these interest payments are made out of its gross trading profits. So they reduce the fund's **Net Return on Equity** somewhat. But not so much as to lessen its appeal to Outside Investors. Who keep pouring in their dollars while the good times roll.

- **<u>SECOND</u>:** To keep interest costs as low as possible, this cash is borrowed on a <u>very short-term basis</u> (as short as overnight, in some cases). Reflecting the principle we considered earlier that <u>the shorter the loan's term is, the lower its interest rate is</u>. Many of these short-term loans took the form of "**Repos.**" In which the Borrower received cash by selling the Lender a marketable security that he was committed to <u>buying back</u> at a slightly higher price by a fixed date a few weeks or days (or even hours in some cases) later.

- **THIRD:** This borrowed cash is usually <u>secured</u> by the securities the hedge fund purchases with it. Just as a mortgage on a borrower's house is secured by the house itself. This means that the lender can <u>seize</u> these securities and sell them in the open market if the borrower should fail to repay the loan on time.

- **FOURTH:** The banks and other financial institutions lending this cash want to keep their loan capital working as efficiently as possible. So they're more than happy to more or less automatically "**Roll Over**" (i.e., Renew) each short-term secured loan as it comes due. Especially if the hedge fund's success make it seem like a potential customer for <u>more and larger</u> loans in the future.

Bear Stearns was known as one of Wall Street's most aggressive and successful trading firms. And it was always looking to expand its customer base in imaginative ways.

That's why it created the theoretically "independent" SIV known as the "**<u>High Grade</u> Structured Credit Strategies Fund**" in October 2003. Gave it a modest amount of seed capital. Arranged to have it managed on a contract basis (for fee payments) by its **Bear Stearns Asset Management** subsidiary. And opened it to investments of Equity Capital by wealthy individuals, pension funds, and other Outside Investors through the purchase of Limited Partnership units.

The Fund's stated business goal was to earn safe returns for its limited partners by investing in "top-rated debt securities." Using "prudent" amounts of leverage.

Note the following points:

- The **High Grade Fund** limited its investments to <u>Interest-Paying Debt Securities</u> (no "risky" common stocks, in other words). This meant that, in addition to any possible market profits from the future sale of these securities, it <u>also</u> earned secure, predictable income from regular payments of interest by these securities. In fact, these interest payments were the Fund's <u>primary</u> source of profits. And the use of <u>Leverage</u> to buy the securities boosted their <u>actual</u> return on the Fund's Equity Capital (i.e., the limited partners invested cash) to a Percentage level that was significantly <u>higher</u> than the nominal interest rate on the Debt Securities themselves. Pretty neat.

- The Interest-Paying Debt Securities that the Fund purchased were mostly long-term Collateralized Mortgage Obligations that Bear Stearns <u>itself</u> had created from large pools of **Home Mortgages** it had bought from a variety of mortgage lenders (see **Chapter 5** for the details of how this works). These mortgages generated monthly interest payments, which were the <u>cash source</u> of the interest payments the Collateralized Mortgage Obligations made to the Fund. This made them appear to be quite safe and enabled these Collateralized Mortgage Obligations to be rated <u>Triple A</u> by such highly respected Wall Street rating firms as Moody's, Standard & Poor's, or Fitch. Really neat.

- In order to <u>further</u> protect its investors, the Fund also purchased **Credit Default Swaps**. These tradable securities theoretically <u>insured</u> the Fund against any interruption in regular interest payments by its Collateralized Mortgage Obligations, or any decline in their market values. (See **Chapter 4** on **Derivatives** for a description of Credit Default Swaps.)

- Since Bear Stearns itself was the **Underwriter** for these Collateralized Mortgage Obligations and Credit Default Swaps, it could sell them directly to the High Grade Fund for a price that included the normal Underwriter's Markup. Therefore, Bear profited in **three ways**. From (**a**) its Underwriter's Mark-Up. <u>Plus</u> (**b**) the management fees earned by its wholly owned **Bear Stearns Asset Management** subsidiary. <u>Plus</u> (**c**) its return on the modest amount of Equity Capital it had invested in the Fund to get it started. Super Neat.

At first, everything went at least as well as planned (hoped?).

The High Grade Fund's portfolio of long-term Collateralized Mortgage Obligations grew by leaps and bounds as the continued rise in housing prices stimulated more home buying. Not to mention an increasing wave of mortgage refinancings by existing homeowners eager to tap the cash value of the skyrocketing equity in their homes. (See **Chapter 5** for an account of this phenomenon.)

All of which provided Bear Stearns with a constant flood of <u>new</u> mortgages that it could bundle into <u>new</u> pools to support <u>additional</u> issues of long-term Collateralized Mortgage Obligations for sale to customers like the High Grade Fund. Whose Percentage returns on the cash invested by its limited partners danced merrily along at attractive two-digit levels because of the Fund's use of leverage. Which made it especially attractive to investors seeking decent returns during an era of <u>record low</u> interest rates.

But as the housing markets began to cool during 2006, Bear Stearns created a <u>second</u> theoretically "independent" hedge fund in August. Called the "**High Grade Structured Credit Strategies <u>Enhanced</u> Master Fund**," this one targeted investors seeking higher returns who were willing to accept "limited additional risk."

The **Enhanced Fund**'s game plan for delivering these higher returns was to build its portfolio around long-term Collateralized Mortgage Obligations backed by pools of so-called "**sub-prime mortgages**." Whose higher interest rates generated income flows that would enable the Collateralized Mortgage Obligations they backed to produce higher returns for the Fund's limited partners. Especially when goosed by much higher Leverage Ratios. At least, that was the plan.

(The whole story of how low-income home buyers were suckered into signing up for unaffordable sub-prime mortgages by fee-hungry lascivines in the mortgage broker industry sounds like one of those hokey made-for-television movies where Big Bad Capitalists rip off the American public and precipitate a disaster. Unfortunately, it's all too true. See **Chapter 5** for the details.)

By the beginning of 2007, the bloom was clearly off the rose in the housing and mortgage markets. And the **Dragon of Chaos** was starting to breathe serious fire in all directions. In the form of falling home prices, higher mortgage default rates, and general investor panic.

In **March 2007**, Bear's 2 hedge funds suffered their first monthly losses after riding high during the housing boom. This caused some nervous limited partners to demand their invested capital back.

But the only way the hedge funds could accommodate these demands was to <u>raise cash</u> by selling off some of their long-term Collateralized Mortgage Obligations in whatever crude over-the-counter markets existed for them.

However, traders in these markets had never shown much interest in buying Collateralized Mortgage Obligations. During the housing boom, when everyone was on top of the world, this hadn't mattered to the hedge funds. Their whole schtick was based on steady interest payments from Collateralized Mortgage Obligations. Which they could goose into high returns with their robust leverage ratios.

But steady interest payments didn't count for much now. What really mattered was how much Fast Cash the hedge funds could generate by dumping their Collateralized Mortgage Obligations.

And the dismal answer turned out to be, "**Not Much.**" There was no buyer demand except at ridiculous fire-sale prices. The Collateralized Mortgage Obligations had become (as they say in the trade) "illiquid," and worth nothing close to what their sellers claimed.

There are <u>two</u> main ways to determine the fair value of a security. If it's a widely traded common stock like IBM, you can simply check out its most recent transaction price on the New York Stock Exchange. This is known as "**Marking to Market**" and provides a clearly <u>objective</u> value that's hard to argue with.

But what if the security is a Collateralized Mortgage Obligation that isn't listed on any formal exchange and rarely trades? Then you have to use a valuation approach known as "**Marking to Model.**" This is a <u>sub-jective</u> approach intended to show what the security **should** be worth. It generally involves lots of number crunching with financial spreadsheets and is subject to wide differences of opinion. But this was all the hedge funds had. And potential Collateralized Mortgage Obligation buyers had little confidence in it.

In **May 2007**, Bear Stearns came up with a new plan to save the hedge funds.

It attempted to issue an **Initial Public Offering** (IPO) of common stock in an independent company (in which Bear Stearns's hedge funds had a $400 Million investment) called **Everquest Financial**. Which started buying Collateralized Mortgage Obligations from Bear Stearns in September of 2006. The intention was to hold these Collateralized Mortgage Obligations in a "long-term portfolio" until they matured. Living off their regular interest payments in the meantime. In fact, in what couldn't exactly be called a proper "arm's-length negotiation," Everquest initially agreed to buy $550 Million worth of Collateralized Mortgage Obligations from Bear Stearns's hedge funds. And then continued these purchases well into 2007, even as the market plummeted. These purchases were intended to give the hedge funds sufficient cash to see them through their rough period. By May, Everquest's assets were valued at over $700 Million.

And who would receive the shares generated from the IPO? Well, most of them would go to Bear Stearns's hedge funds, seeing how they had invested $400 Million in Everquest. Which Bear's funds could then sell for Cash. Wiping Bear's hands clean of the "toxic waste" it sold to Everquest to begin with. And because Bear was willing to underwrite the deal, they would take the associated fees as well.

"*No thanks,*" said various large private investors and financial institutions that Bear informally sounded out about taking significant chunks of Everquest's IPO. And it quickly became apparent that there was no meaningful market for the IPO. So Bear had to cancel it. The first time in living memory that one of its underwritings had failed.

After that, things went from bad to worse relatively quickly:

- The collapse of Everquest's IPO, plus growing losses by the hedge funds and disturbing rumors about the "reliability" of their monthly performance reports, caused increasing numbers of their nervous limited partners to demand that their equity investments be returned.

- To meet these redemption demands, the funds had no choice but to sell their Collateralized Mortgage Obligations for whatever cash they would bring. Which further reduced the market value of these assets. Leading short-term lenders to demand more collateral as still more limited partners demanded their money back.

- On **June 15, 2007**, Merrill Lynch and JPMorgan Chase seized the Collateralized Mortgage Obligations that the hedge funds had put up as **collateral** for $1.5 Billion in short-term cash they'd borrowed from these lenders but couldn't repay. (In other words, the lenders "foreclosed" on these assets. Just like mustache-twirling Simon Legree in the old stage melodrama.)

- And on **June 25**, Bear Stearns itself loaned **$3.2 Billion** to the High-Grade Fund to try and shore it up. But increasing redemptions by its limited partners quickly soaked up this cash. So eight days later, the Fund suspended all further redemptions.

- So on **July 31, 2007**, Bear bowed to the inevitable and placed both the High-Grade Fund and the Extended Leverage Fund in **Bankruptcy**. Candidly telling the limited partners that their equity investments in the funds were "virtually worthless." The usual round of lawsuits and arbitration claims followed.

Now concerns about financial strength shifted to Bear itself.

In 2007, it had been the nation's fifth largest investment bank, with nearly $400 Billion in assets and more than 14,000 employees worldwide. As recently as **February 2007**, it had been valued in the stock market at $25.1 Billion. And it had a Triple A credit rating.

But all this went out the window in the months following the bankruptcy of the hedge funds. The perception grew that Bear was a firm "In Trouble." So its stock market price plunged. And short-term lenders who had always rolled over their loans to Bear without question now started saying "*Goodbye*." Or demanding more collateral for their loans.

On **November 1, 2007**, the *Wall Street Journal* published a front page story documenting what seemed like "wildly irresponsible" lack of attention to Bear's problems by its top managers. And on December 20, Bear reported the first loss in its history and had to write off $1.9 Billion in losses on its loan portfolio. Thereafter, the Wall Street rating agency **Standard & Poor's** downgraded Bear's senior long-term debt to "Single A."

These events further increased the general sense of "Nervousness" about Bear in the financial community. Leading to more firms shying away from investing in, lending to, or otherwise doing business with Bear. Such a **"Loss of Confidence"** is the worst thing that can happen to any financial firm because it creates negative perceptions (justified or not) that spread like California wildfires.

So Bear's top managers began looking for a proverbial "deep-pocket" investor to come forward with a large equity investment. Or even another bank to buy Bear outright on reasonably favorable terms. But nothing worthwhile was forthcoming.

A significant contributor to Bear's collapse was the deplorable **"Snob Factor"** that still permeated too much of the financial industry in 2008.

The specific circumstances can be traced back to **September 1998** when Bear was one of the banks called upon by the **Federal Reserve Bank of New York** to help bail out the swinging hedge fund **Long-Term Capital Management,** which had overreached itself with its trading activities. (See the last section of **Chapter 7, The "Secrets of Money,"** for the story of how this hedge fund came to grief and why.)

The other banks in the New York Fed's bailout syndicate had always perceived Bear as being dominated by (horrors) "sweaty Jewish and Italian trader types" from down-market Brooklyn and Queens, who'd gotten their degrees from unwashed commuter schools like Pace University and St. John's. Rather than traditionally upscale bankers with Ivy League degrees who lived on Manhattan's Upper East Side.

So Bear wasn't invited to attend the critical Sunday meeting at Long-Term Capital Management's headquarters to examine its books. To which it responded by refusing to participate in the bailout when push came to shove. The other banks regarded this as an infuriating "act of rebellion against their betters." And swore to themselves that one day they'd "make those Kikes and Wops pay."

That day came during the early months of 2008, when Bear ran out of cash to cover its trading losses and was running all over town begging for temporary credit extensions so it could survive. Giving the other banks the opportunity they'd been waiting for since 1998. To turn up their aristocratic noses and hang Bear out to dry.

All of which climaxed during the wee hours of **Monday, March 24, 2008** (just before the Asian markets opened). When Bear was forced by the Federal Government to announce its sale for a few pennies on the dollar to **JPMorgan Chase**. Backstopped by a commitment by the **Federal Reserve** to buy upwards of **$30 Billion** worth of mortgage-based securities in Bear's portfolio that Morgan regarded as "too toxic to touch."

One of the things that made this such a watershed event was the <u>direct involvement</u> by the Federal Government in saving Bear Stearns from having to file for Bankruptcy.

Previously, the Federal Government would <u>only</u> do something like this when a deposit-taking <u>commercial or savings bank</u> got itself into financial trouble. <u>Investment banks</u> like Bear were strictly on their own. Just like corner grocery stores and other unregulated business firms that were free of any government-imposed limits on the amount of borrowed funds they could use to leverage their Equity Capital.

And if they screwed up and failed? **Tough.** That's what's <u>supposed</u> to happen under Capitalism. Let others learn from their mistakes.

So the Federal Government had cruised along, seeming like a beat-everybody-in-sight NFL team on its way to the Super Bowl. Until it got unexpectedly bushwhacked by a "don't get no respect" underdog of a Financial Meltdown on a rainy Sunday afternoon. And found itself down by three touchdowns at the end of the First Quarter.

So it had to throw out its standard Game Plan. Change its Offensive

Lineup. Call some unorthodox plays that nobody had ever seen before (like saving investment bank Bear Stearns from Bankruptcy). Anything it could think of to get itself back in the game.

Even to the extent of having the Federal Reserve actually <u>buy</u> $30 Billion worth of rotting mortgage-based securities from Bear that nobody else would touch with a ten-foot pole.

As the financial tsunami of 2008 began rolling across the world like Noah's flood. Leaving devastation in its wake.

■ ■ ■

Aftermath

Bear Stearns may have ceased to exist as an independent firm on **March 24, 2008**. But it continued to haunt the financial world like Marley's Ghost for months thereafter. As the Global Meltdown continued. Marked by a growing pattern of formerly solid financial institutions turning into basket cases that could no longer survive on their own. After their years of kindergarten management games, shooting up on short-term borrowings, and boozing away on risky trades blew up in their faces.

Just like Bear. When it started the ball rolling, as it were.

At first, some publicly traded investment banks like **Morgan Stanley** and **Goldman Sachs** tried to protect themselves by becoming "Bank Holding Companies." This enabled them to <u>borrow emergency cash</u> from the Federal Reserve if the need arose.

More importantly, it allowed them to <u>Take Deposits</u> from business firms and individuals (just like regular commercial banks). Since these deposits were <u>insured</u> by the Federal Deposit Insurance Corporation, they tended to act like "permanent debt capital." Remaining in place (at no risk to depositors) even if the bank's financial position deteriorated. This made the banks much less dependent on cash borrowed in the volatile short-term debt markets, whose lenders could pull the cash plug at any time.

But these benefits came at a price. As Bank Holding Companies, these investment banking firms were now subject to the <u>same</u> Federal regulations as regular commercial banks. Most notably, they could no longer <u>leverage</u> their Equity Capital with borrowed cash to anything like the same extent as before. Therefore, each $1 Million of profit yielded a <u>much smaller</u> Percentage return on Equity Capital because it could no longer be goosed by high leverage ratios.

Given the circumstances, however, this price seemed worth paying. Especially when the basic issue seemed to involve "survival."

Anyway, the next domino to fall was the ancient and much-respected investment banking firm of **Lehman Brothers**. Whose "aristocratic image" was as different from Bear Stearns as could be imagined but whose terminal decline was remarkably similar.

■ ■ ■

The Lehman Brothers Story

Lehman Brothers was founded in 1850 in Alabama by three Jewish brothers (Henry, Emmanuel, and Mayer) who had emigrated to the USA from the German province of Bavaria. Originally a dry-goods business, the firm began focusing increasingly on cotton trading (the South's Number 1 cash crop). As the center of cotton trading moved to New York during the late 1850s, Lehman opened a branch office there. Which eventually became its headquarters as the firm broadened its activities to include bond trading and financial-advisory services.

By 1900, Lehman had begun moving into the business of underwriting new issues of common stocks for corporate clients. And during the ensuing decades, it underwrote new issues for many name-brand corporations like Sears Roebuck, Woolworth, Gimbels, Macys, Studebaker, and Goodrich.

Interesting sociocultural note: Within the American Jewish Community, Jews descended from Nineteenth-Century German and Austrian immigrants are regarded as "Natural Aristocrats." Traditionally seen as being well educated and super-couth. Highly successful in the "learned professions" and business. Devoted to actively supporting classic charities and cultural institutions (supposedly a reason why New York City—which is, among other things, the world's preeminent Jewish city—is the "International Capital of Culture"). Also, the pejorative term "*Kike*" is said by a number of sources (such as the popular book *Our Crowd*, by Stephen Birmingham) to have originated around 1900 among New York's wealthy and assimilated German Jews to distance themselves from the Millions of poverty-stricken, Yiddish-speaking, generally "unwashed and vulgar" Jewish immigrants from Poland, Russia, and other Eastern European countries, who were then pouring into New York City. Subsequently, the term became popular in American Christian anti-Semitic circles to define "all Jews."

In 1984, Lehman Brothers was acquired by **American Express,** which merged it with its Shearson brokerage subsidiary to create **Shearson Lehman/American Express**. This lasted until 1994, when American Express decided to get out of the banking and brokerage business. So it spun off Lehman in an initial public offering, and Lehman once again became an independent investment banking firm.

The next twenty years marked a period of considerable success for Lehman, as it increased its net revenues more than six-fold, to $19.2 Billion, and its worldwide headcount to some 28,600. By the end of 2007, it was one of the 5 largest investment banks in the United States and seemed poised to continue its stellar growth.

Meanwhile, Lehman had become increasingly reliant on **Fixed Income Trading** and **Securities Underwriting** for profit growth. This went hand-in-hand with a 46 Percent increase in its Leverage Ratio, from 24 to 1 in 2003 to 35 to 1 in 2007. And much of this leverage took the form of short-term debt with maturities as short as a single day. So Lehman had to continuously romance its lenders with sweet talk about the "solid value" of the assets it had pledged as collateral for these "here-today-gone-tomorrow" loans. (Does this sound familiar?)

But much of this sweet talk was undercut by the continued erosion of the housing and mortgage markets during the summer of 2007. While Lehman's common stock price fell 37 Percent from June to August. As the firm closed it sub-prime mortgage arm. Wrote off $3.5 Billion in the value of its mortgage-related assets. And laid off more than 6,000 employees by the end of the year.

And matters only grew worse in 2008. In January, Lehman closed its wholesale mortgage lending unit and laid off another 1,300 employees in a vain attempt to stem further cash hemorrhages from its sub-prime mortgage operations. And as Bear Stearns collapsed in March, Standard & Poor's rating arm downgraded its outlook on Lehman from **"Stable"** to **"Negative"** on the expectation that its revenues would decline by at least another 20 Percent. Which immediately caused Lehman's stock price to plunge by another 48 Percent.

Lehman attempted to counter this by selling $4 Billion in Convertible Preferred Stock (which is an options-like quasi-debt security paying a fixed dividend that gives the holder the right to convert it to common stock for a specified price).

But this fresh cash was quickly soaked up by more write-offs, including Lehman's $1.8 Billion bailout of 5 of its short-term debt funds (just as Bear had done a year earlier when it bailed out its hedge funds). As ravenous short-sellers (the "Vultures of Capitalism") began circling. And rumors flew that other firms were refusing to trade with Lehman in the securities markets. Which threatened its ability to remain in business.

With its common stock price in a virtual free fall, Lehman contemplated "taking itself private." But this had to be abandoned when it became clear that the necessary financing wasn't available.

So Lehman's next move was to try and locate buyers for $30 Billion of its commercial mortgages (i.e., mortgages on office buildings, shopping malls, and the like) whose actual market value couldn't be determined because their trading activity was virtually non-existent. So talks with the Korea Development Bank, China's CITIC Securities, and the Royal Bank of Canada went nowhere.

Obviously, the time had come for the Federal Government to step in if Lehman was to be saved.

But any such moves were complicated by the enormous public outcry that had arisen over the $29 Billion "Federal Bailout" of Bear Stearns. With voices from all sides of the political spectrum screaming at the Feds for *"using taxpayer funds to bail out big Wall Street firms that had caused this mess, while refusing to lift a finger to help American families in danger of losing their homes."*

Since a contentious presidential election loomed in a matter of weeks, Treasury and the Federal Reserve felt that nothing short of an unambiguous Congressional directive to "save Lehman" would allow them to move. But the Bush Administration chose not to approach Congress.

So the Federal Government was reduced to informally jawboning Bank of America, HSBC, Nomura Securities, and Barclay's Bank to "rescue Lehman on their own." Which proved fruitless. And on **September 11, 2008,** Lehman had no choice but to file for Chapter 11 Bankruptcy. Listing assets of $639 Billion and liabilities of $768 Billion (meaning that its Equity Capital—Assets minus Liabilities—had become worthless). Leaving its viable businesses to be snapped up at fire-sale prices by sharp-eyed bottom fishers.

This was the largest Chapter 11 Bankruptcy in American history up to that point. And in retrospect, it's generally regarded as the most disastrous decision by the Federal Government since the early 1930s. When the Federal Reserve chose to <u>shrink the nation's money supply by one-third</u>. Thereby shattering the American economy for the rest of the decade.

■ ■ ■

The Merrill Lynch Story

Merrill was founded in 1914 by Charles Merrill and Edmund Lynch. During the next 30 years, it grew by a series of mergers and acquisitions into the nation's largest and best known retail brokerage firm. By the early 1940s, it had become **Merrill Lynch, Pierce, Fenner & Beane.** Informally known as *"We The People"* (after the popular CBS network radio show of the time) and *"the Thundering Herd."*

Just as Lehman Brothers had epitomized the "aristocratic German-Jewish culture" in the financial industry, Merrill Lynch became a symbol of "working-class Irish Catholic culture" (like New York City's police and fire departments). Not that it mattered much when push came to shove in September 2008.

But interestingly enough, its appointment of Stanley O'Neal as CEO in 2001 marked the first time an <u>African-American</u> became head of a major American financial institution. Even more interesting is the <u>$161 Million Golden Parachute</u> given to O'Neal in November 2007 to "just go away" as Merrill was melting down.

Social commentators may regard this as evidence of how far American society has come in matters of racial equality. When "even an African-American" can rise to such a staggeringly lucrative level of incompetence in a major industry like Finance (shades of the old **Levy's Rye Bread** commercial tag line: *"You don't have to be Jewish . . . "*). Which may actually be more significant than "white shoe" Harvard Law School alumnus Barack Obama winning the Presidency in 2008.

In 1971, Merrill Lynch became a publicly traded corporation. And in 1978, it acquired the small but prestigious investment bank **White Weld & Company** to expand its underwriting activities and take advantage of its huge retail brokerage arm's ability to place new common stock issues with investors directly rather than through syndicates composed of other firms.

But by 2000, Merrill was (like Lehman and Bear Stearns) becoming increasingly dependent on its <u>in-house trading</u> and <u>Collateralized Mortgage Obligations</u> businesses for profit growth. By goosing this growth with a <u>105 Percent increase</u> in its Leverage Ratio (to 39 to 1 in 2007 from a much more modest 19 to 1 in 2003), Merrill was able to provide its common stock holders with a 13 Percent increase in their investment return during this period.

By **2006**, Merrill had leaped to the Number 1 spot in the nation's Collateralized Mortgage Obligations business as it underwrote $35 Billion in these securities (40 Percent of which were backed by sub-prime mortgages).

To help secure this leadership position, Merrill spent $1.3 Billion to acquire **First Franklin,** one of the nation's largest originators of sub-prime residential mortgages. This gave it a major in-house mortgage originator and reduced its dependence on buying mortgages in the open market from numerous banks and home loan firms to back new underwritings of Collateralized Mortgage Obligations. But this acquisition got mixed reviews from various analysts in the financial community, who expressed concern that Merrill might have "overpaid" for First Franklin.

These concerns increased during the **Summer of 2007,** when two of Bear Stearns's hedge funds defaulted (see above). As a short-term lender to these funds, Merrill seized $800 Million of Bear's mortgage assets (which Bear had posted as collateral on these loans) and proceeded to auction them off in the secondary markets.

But the auctions failed to generate reasonable bids for the sub-prime mortgages and highlighted Merrill's exposure to these "toxic waste securities." Leading to its write-down of nearly $8 Billion in the balance sheet value of such assets. Followed later in 2007 by a further $12 Billion write-down on mortgage-backed securities. Plus an outright $2.9 Billion loss on "hedges-gone-wrong" for its Collateralized Mortgage Obligation securities.

Such write-downs can have severe consequences for any firm forced to take them, as happened with all the firms discussed in this chapter. For example:

- **The firm's stock price may fall significantly.** (By February 2008, Merrill's stock had plunged 46 Percent from its May 2007 high.)

- **Credit downgrades by Wall Street rating agencies may increase borrowing and hedging costs.** (Early in 2008, Moody's Investors Service placed Merrill's long-term debt *"on review for a possible downgrade"* based on its forecast of $6 Billion in additional write-downs in the months ahead.)

- **Traders in other firms may lose confidence in the firm's ability to meet its trading obligations and refuse to do business with it.**

- **The firm may have to increase its equity capital by selling off assets and even entire business units, or by issuing new common stock.** (In July 2008, Merrill sold back its 20 Percent stake in Bloomberg to that firm for a much-needed $4.4 Billion. And began negotiations to sell controlling interest in its Wealth Management Services subsidiary and other units.)

- The firm's management may need to implement cost-cutting measures to boost future performance. Such as significant employee layoffs and revisions in its compensation schemes to <u>discourage</u> risk taking. (Between May 2007 and September 2008, Merrill laid off over 7 Percent of its employees. Leading to a wave of "rats-leaving-the-ship" defections to other firms among its most productive remaining employees.)

Merrill's continued write-downs of toxic mortgage assets, increasing operating losses, and difficulties in refinancing its short-term borrowings made it clear that its days as an independent firm were numbered. And on **September 14, 2008** (three days after Lehman filed for bankruptcy), Merrill agreed to sell itself to the **Bank of America** in an exchange-of-stock transaction worth only <u>39 Percent of its stock market value</u> 12 months earlier.

This acquisition more than doubled the size of Bank of America's investment banking operation and gave it Wall Street's largest retail brokerage operation.

But it significantly increased its exposure to mortgage-backed securities of questionable value. To which Standard & Poor's rating arm responded by cutting Bank of America's long-term credit rating by one point (to AA-) and putting the Bank on *"Credit Watch with negative implications"* (the usual precursor to further rating downgrades).

■ ■ ■

The AIG Story

Manhattan's legendary overcrowded parties are rumored to exist primarily to provide young guys on the make with ways to connect with young gals to be made.

And in New York City, people have always tended to define themselves by the kind of work they do. So whenever you saw an interesting-looking woman at one of these parties, you'd approach her with a fairly standard opening line.

"Hi. My name's Joe. I'm in investment banking / neurosurgery / advertising / real estate development / publishing" (or some other supposedly "glamorous' field").

Then watch her eyebrows rise with obvious interest. And you were on your way.

Of course, you had a tougher row to hoe if your field wasn't one of the cliché glamorous ones. For example, suppose you were stuck with this opening line:

"Hi. My name's Joe. I'm in the insurance business."

Then her eyes would immediately glaze over and you'd see her glance past you to scan the room for potentially more exciting prospects.

Because it was <u>inconceivable</u> in those days that a drab-sounding field like insurance could <u>ever</u> become a springboard for the kind of outrageous con artistry that **American International Group** practiced so effectively. Conning the Federal Government out of Billions of taxpayer dollars. From which top managers would pay themselves extravagant seven- and eight-figure bonuses while their firm was incurring record losses. Not to mention covering the costs of "executive retreats" for its top managers at fashionable Scottish hunting estates well stocked with slaughterable birds and small animals.

Will wonders never cease.

AIG began life in 1919 when American expatriate Cornelius Vander

Starr founded a small insurance agency in Shanghai, China. In 1926, he opened a New York brokerage office to sell an increasing variety of insurance policies to individuals and business firms in the North American market.

By the 1960s, AIG began transforming itself into an increasingly large underwriter of all kinds of different life and casualty insurance policies. And in 1969, it "went public" to increase its Equity Capital.

But insurance underwriting is a <u>regulated business</u>. Insurance underwriters are required to set aside significant reserves of Equity Capital to assure that they can meet any claims by policy holders and maintain ultra-safe Triple A credit ratings. This hamstrings their ability to engage in the kind of high-leverage business activities that can boost their Return on Equity to levels capable of attracting large investors seeking better-than-market yields.

So in 1987, AIG got together with 2 former executives from investment bank **Drexel Burnham Lambert** to establish an unregulated <u>hedge fund subsidiary</u> called **AIG Financial Products** (AIGFP). Managed by the former Drexel executives. Who were given a large degree of management autonomy and a significant up-front share of AIGFP's profits. And eventually opened other offices in offshore financial centers like London and Tokyo.

From AIG's perspective, AIGFP offered the following benefits:

- AIGFP could take advantage of <u>new business opportunities</u> outside the regulated insurance industry to profitably exploit AIG's Triple A credit rating, strong capital base, and risk-management skills.

- As an unregulated hedge fund, AIGFP could use <u>high leverage ratios</u> to generate substantial profits by trading exotic derivatives. And could produce even more profits by <u>packaging up its own glitzy derivatives</u> and selling them at high markups to other financial firms, pension funds, and large private investors hungry for attractive (and seemingly low-risk) returns.

• So AIG could use AIGFP's growing profits to <u>offset occasional insurance losses</u> from high-cost "disaster events" like Hurricane Katrina (thereby "diversifying its risk"). Plus <u>attract new buyers for its common stock</u> among the many stock market investors eager to participate in the growing profitability of corporations with obvious "Star Quality."

The first crack in AIG's success story mirror occurred in **2001** when the federal **Securities and Exchange Commission** accused it of selling "nontraditional insurance products" that enabled its publicly traded customer firms to <u>evade established accounting standards</u> for reporting their financial performance. After an investigation that lasted until 2004, AIG settled with the SEC by paying a $126 Million fine.

But almost immediately, AIG got caught up in an <u>insurance industry bid-rigging investigation</u> by the SEC and New York State Attorney General Eliot Spitzer (then flying high as the nation's most visible "financial industry Jeremiah"—before being elected Governor, but subsequently feeling compelled to resign after publicly confessing to having been the favorite John of an upscale Washington Escort Service). This investigation soon expanded to include accusations that <u>AIG had been playing fast and loose with standard accounting regulations</u> about how it reported its financial performance. Which it ultimately settled by paying $1.6 Billion in fines.

As a result of these scandals, AIG fired both its CEO and its board chairman. Publicly reported that it had revised some of its prior years' earnings downward by $3.5 Billion. Hired independent consultants to help make its internal controls "more kosher" (which didn't extend to eliminating all financial pork and shellfish from its diet).

But none of this could prevent <u>all three major rating firms</u> from downgrading AIG's credit rating from Triple A to Double A in March 2005. Or having its stock market value decline by more than $40 Billion.

Meanwhile, AIGFP had become a <u>Really Big Macher</u> in the derivatives business. By the end of 2004, its portfolio of Credit Default Swaps alone had soared to $290 Billion. With most of this exposure <u>totally unhedged</u> against potential losses (to save money) because it claimed that its "conservative portfolio management" made any losses unlikely. And during 2005, in the inevitable pursuit of higher returns, increasing portions of this portfolio became concentrated in Credit Default Swaps AIGFP had written on Collateralized Mortgage Obligations backed by <u>sub-prime residential mortgages</u> (i.e., "insuring Derivatives on high-risk mortgages against default"). Which the continued rise in housing prices throughout the nation appeared to make "as safe as houses."

But the **March 2005** downgrade of AIG's credit rating caused AIGFP's trading partners to insist that it post an additional $1.2 Billion in collateral against the Credit Default Swaps it had written. And AIGFP's managers became sufficiently "nervous" about the $80 Billion in Collateralized Sub-prime Mortgage Obligations it was (in effect) "insuring" with its Credit Default Swaps to start pulling back from this business.

As housing prices turned south during 2007, the credit markets (especially for mortgage-backed securities) became seriously disrupted. And in September, AIG had to report a third-quarter loss of $352 Million on its Credit Default Swap portfolio. Followed by an additional loss of $550 Million in October. Ultimately topped by a reported net loss of $5.3 Billion for 2007's fourth quarter, driven by AIGFP's staggering $11 Billion loss in the value of its Credit Default Swap portfolio.

The continuing decline in housing prices and resulting increase in mortgage defaults shattered market values for all mortgage-backed derivatives. This forced AIG to post increasing amounts of collateral against the Credit Default Swaps it had written against these securities. But in **February 2008**, AIG's independent auditor found that its "Mark to Model" valuation methods seriously <u>overstated</u> the "fair value" of its Credit Default Swap portfolio by some 300 Percent. Causing one of the rating agencies to put AIG on *"rating watch negative."* Which led to an unprecedented <u>12 Percent single-day decline</u> in AIG's stock.

Following JPMorgan Chase's "emergency acquisition" of Bear Stearns in <u>March 2008,</u> worries over the health of other financial firms began spreading like a California wildfire. With AIG at the top of the list. Especially after its announcement in May 2008 of <u>another</u> $8 Billion loss in the value of its Credit Default Swap portfolio. Bringing its <u>total losses</u> so far to nearly $20 Billion. Which rose to $25 Billion by August 2008, when it had to report <u>still another</u> $5.6 Billion loss <u>plus</u> the posting of $7 Billion in additional collateral for its Credit Default Swaps.

By now, other AIG businesses were bleeding cash like Tsarist hemophiliacs. Especially involving "Lending Securities for Cash." With AIG (ever hungry for higher yields) investing this cash in various Asset-Based Securities containing sub-prime mortgages. Whose market values tanked as the credit markets seized up. Forcing AIG to sell them at a loss.

By **September 2008**, it was obvious that AIG was "Running on Empty" as far as operating cash was concerned, and Standard & Poor's cut its credit rating by three whole notches. Which triggered another $15 Billion increase in AIG's collateral for its Credit Default Swap portfolio and threatened it with **Bankruptcy**.

But AIG was so large and interconnected with so many other financial firms in its trading activities that Bankruptcy would clearly result in a calamity akin to the Great Depression. So the Federal Government had to step in.

In retrospect, it's clear that the Federal Government had abandoned its hands-off stance with respect to the investment banking industry on **March 24, 2008**. By brokering and financing the sale of Bear Stearns to JPMorgan Chase.

So the Federal Government knew that it had to "save AIG" when the time came. And since there were no "white knights" left in the financial community with sufficiently deep pockets to buy AIG, it had only one option.

Which was to effectively "**Nationalize**" AIG. Giving it an $80 Billion credit line from the Federal Reserve to draw against. Plus additional loans and other direct investments that eventually totaled <u>more than $170 Billion</u> in all. In exchange for an <u>80 Percent equity stake</u> in its ownership and functional control over its management.

So the die was cast. Henceforth, the federal government would be the business community's **Big Daddy**. Passing out allowance money by the Billions to its new family of unruly children (which eventually included **General Motors, Chrysler,** and other companies). While trying to keep them from squandering too much of it on "tooth-rotting candy" (in the form of huge bonuses and lavish perks for top managers).

In **Chapter 8,** we'll look at the details of what the federal government <u>actually did</u> during this critical period.

■ ■ ■

Consequences

By no stretch of the imagination could Bear Stearns's top guys during the period leading up to its "Emergency Acquisition" by JPMorgan Chase be called <u>Competent Managers</u>.

For the most part, they were simply highly skilled Power Players who rose to their level of "<u>Dangerous Incompetence</u>" by artfully manipulating Bear's internal politics for their own purposes. And when they reached the top, generally failed to exert the kind of Responsible Leadership we could reasonably expect from the top managers of such a large and important firm. It simply wasn't in them.

But what's really shocking is that Bear's top managers were scarcely an exception among the top guys who ran the financial industry. In fact, they typified the whole breed. At Lehman Brothers. Merrill Lynch. AIG. And so many other firms.

Incompetent bunglers all.

Totally clueless to the <u>real dangers</u> of excessive Risk Taking. Of massive use of Leverage built around short-term borrowings. Of lack of protective Equity Capital. Of kindergarten-level Risk Management. Of abuse of Lax Regulation . . .

More outrageously overpaid than any other top managers among the world's major industries.

Puffing away on hundred-dollar cigars in their separately ventilated mahogany-paneled executive suites.

Like so many irresponsible children who had somehow gained access to Cold War missile control rooms.

Playing uncomprehendingly with the shiny buttons that could launch nuclear warheads against an unsuspecting world.

Which they ultimately did.

Wiping out more than $11 Trillion dollars of wealth in the process.

Leaving the rest of us to clean up the mess. While we lick our wounds.

Is it any wonder that increasing numbers of Normal People—outraged by their loss of jobs, homes, and savings—began screaming that there ought to be <u>Laws</u> against allowing <u>Just Anybody</u> to hold top manager jobs in industries that are so important to the public welfare. Shouldn't they be required to possess **<u>Government Licenses</u>** testifying to their superior qualifications for such jobs?

- Just like **Physicians?** Who are <u>prohibited</u> from treating the sick and injured until they're awarded state licenses after passing stiff written exams.

- Or **Lawyers?** Who are <u>prohibited</u> from dispensing legal advice until they've been admitted to the State Bar after passing equally stiff exams.

- Or **Accountants?** Who are <u>prohibited</u> from expressing formal opinions about the "adequacy" of corporate financial statements unless their state governments have granted them "**Certified Public Accountant**" licenses. After they've passed the required exam and demonstrated a certain number of years of successful professional work in their field.

So why not have the <u>same kind</u> of rigorous licensing requirements for **Professional Managers** before they're permitted to hold top management jobs in critical industries?

A perfectly understandable question. But for a variety of reasons, such manager licensing requirements are unlikely ever to happen in the Real World.

However, this is <u>not</u> to say that there shouldn't be **Serious Regulation** of critical industries like Finance. Which can wreak such terrible havoc on the world when they screw up.

Chapter 9 examines the Regulatory issue in detail.

■ ■ ■

Too Big to Fail?

A lot's been said about this syndrome in the wake of all that's happened. And most of it misses the point.

Because the simple fact of sheer <u>size</u> isn't what matters.

It's being "**Too <u>Interconnected</u> to Fail**" that counts most.

<u>That's</u> why the Federal Government decided so many financial institutions had to be bailed out. Sold off to others with government guarantees to sweeten the deal. Loaned enormous sums of taxpayer money. Recapitalized with government equity. Etc.

Because it finally dawned on the Feds that these financial institutions were <u>interconnected</u> in so many horrendously complicated ways that the collapse of <u>any one of them</u> could set off a massive chain reaction of disrupted connections. Causing the whole elaborate process by which money flows through society to **Seize Up.**

Seize Up?

Yeah, you know. Shut down. Stop working. Whatever you want to call it.

Like, you go to Macy's to buy a box of shirts. And when you hand your American Express Card to the payment clerk, she shakes her head and points to a hastily hand-lettered sign on her cash register. Which reads: "**<u>CASH ONLY</u>. No Credit Cards. No Checks.**"

Or your wife fills her shopping cart with the week's groceries at the supermarket. But when she goes to the checkout counters with her MasterCard ready, she sees that same sign hanging over each cash register: "**<u>CASH ONLY</u>. No Credit Cards. No Checks.**"

Or you're the president of a nice little family-owned wholesale hardware distributor that your father built up from nothing. And it's time to do the biweekly payroll for your employees. Your desktop PC has already printed out their paychecks and stubs ready for your signature. So you get online with your bank to transfer the payroll cash from your credit line to the checking account against which the paychecks have been written. Just like you always do.

But something's different this time. Your PC's monitor flashes a message telling you that all credit lines have been "**<u>temporarily frozen.</u>**" You hurriedly phone your banker to ask what gives. But all you get is a recorded message asking you to leave your name and number. Because hundreds of other small businessmen like you are also trying to ask him what gives.

So how are you supposed to pay your employees today? With monkey wrenches? Screwdrivers? Bags of six-penny nails?

Want to know what the **Apocalypse** really looks like?

Well you've just had a preview.

Makes your knees tremble, doesn't it.

The elaborately interconnected nature of the financial industry greatly boosts the speed and efficiency with which Money can move through the arteries of our society. And the industry has exploited this through its vast investments in better and more sophisticated technology.

- Like lighting-fast communications systems that can let traders in Europe and America know in an instant what kind of bet a trader in Hong Kong has just placed on the direction of the Yen/Dollar spread.

- Or automated computer models that can spot interesting price anomalies in the relationship between 2 securities on opposite sides of the world. And a microsecond later, place Multimillion-dollar bets on the likely development of those anomalies.

- Or the complex mathematical models developed by Wall Street's super-brain Ph.D. Rocket Scientists. That can tell you in real time the probability that your trading positions can't lose more than (say) $30 Million during the next 24 hours. So you can decide whether to reduce your exposure just to be on the safe side. Or increase it to pursue more profits.

But all the sophisticated technology in the world ultimately depends on a <u>Sacred Principle</u> that's as old as markets themselves. And as Mystical. ***A Guy Keeps His Word.***

For every **Seller** wanting to complete a transaction, there has to be a willing **Buyer** on the other side (and vice versa). For every **Borrower** wanting a loan, there has to be a willing **Lender** (also vice versa). These crucial **Other Guys** on the other side of transactions are known in the trade as <u>**Counterparties**</u>.

So your particular Counterparty in a transaction may be a trader at the other end of a phone line agreeing to a specified price for a certain transaction. Or an investment banker telling you he'll commit his firm's capital to underwriting your IPO. Or a lender agreeing to a $10 Million loan so your firm can go ahead and build that new factory in Toledo. Or somebody promising to meet you for lunch tomorrow at your favorite restaurant to discuss a deal. Whatever . . .

But it's all so much smoke unless you can believe that:

A Guy Keeps His Word.

Because you can't waste time having crews of lawyers spend days haggling over every word in a formal contract. And no contract means anything anyway unless you can <u>trust that Sacred Principle</u>:

A Guy Keeps His Word.

Otherwise, nobody can do business with anybody else. Because that Sacred Principle is the <u>mortar</u> that holds all the bricks together in a society as complex as ours.

But on **July 27, 2007,** the Top Guys at Bear Stearns **<u>Broke Their Word</u>** to the limited partners in those 2 hedge funds by placing them in Bankruptcy.

Maybe they didn't have any other choice, given the circumstances.

On the other hand, those circumstances hadn't been caused by some Vengeful God who came roaring out of the King James Bible to pull down their House of Cards.

They had been caused <u>directly</u> and <u>exclusively</u> by those Top Guys themselves. Who had royally screwed up their responsibility to manage things wisely. They just didn't know any better. Like all the other backward children running the financial industry.

So suddenly people in the financial industry <u>stopped trusting each other.</u>

Stopped trusting what the Other Guy said about the true value of the securities in his firm's portfolio that he wanted to offer as collateral on the loan he was seeking.

Stopped trusting his promises about "risk-free" portfolio management and "no-questions-asked" redemptions and a whole host of other "I'll-love-you-forever-darling" avowals.

And if you can't trust the Other Guy, how can you do business with him?

So naturally the entire financial world melted down.

And the Feds had to come rushing in with wide-open checkbooks to stave off the **Apocalypse**.

■ ■ ■

The 2008 Stock Market Collapse

In less than 3 months between September 1 and the stock market's autumn <u>low</u> on November 20, **Standard & Poor's 500 Index** lost a staggering **41 Percent of its Value**. That's like each dollar <u>shrinking in value</u> to only 59 cents. With some **$4 Trillion** of stock market value disappearing into Thin Air. As panic-stricken investors dumped their shares for whatever price they could get.

The **American Stock Market** is a vast marketplace made up of more than 5,500 corporations in hundreds of different industries. Their common stocks are publicly traded on the nation's various organized stock exchanges, like the **New York Stock Exchange.** Plus in numerous **Over-The-Counter** markets maintained by large brokerage firms. And the S&P 500 Index is the "market proxy" used by most financial professionals to track the performance of this huge marketplace. Reflecting the daily <u>Buy and Sell</u> decisions by literally Millions of investors in one of the most exciting examples of "free market capitalism" in action.

According to Ivory Tower Theorists, these investors are all coldly rational "**Mister Spock**" types. Who possess complete information about all publicly traded companies. Know everything there is to know about Accounting and Finance. And base their investment decisions on carefully quantified "**Risk/Reward**" ratios.

Well, maybe you can find a few stock market groupies who match this bloodless profile. If you look under enough rocks.

But most investors are more like those described by British economist John Maynard Keynes in his landmark 1936 book *The General Theory of Employment, Interest, and Money.*

> *Professional investment may be likened to those <u>newspaper competitions</u> in which the competitors have to pick out the <u>6 prettiest faces</u> from a hundred photographs, the prize being awarded to the competitor whose choice <u>most nearly corresponds to the average preferences</u> of the competitors as a whole. So that each competitor has to pick, not those faces which he himself finds prettiest, but those which <u>he thinks likely to catch the fancy of the other competitors,</u> all of whom are looking at the problem from the same point of view.*

So this vast majority of stock market investors represents a diverse collection of personality types who spend their time (in Lord Keynes's words) *"anticipating what the 'average opinion' expects the <u>Average Opinion</u> to be."* And their personal agendas range widely across the so-called "Rationality Spectrum."

Therefore, the collective buy and sell decisions of these many millions of stock market investors with a wide variety of views about stock values and their future prospects reflect what Lord Keynes liked to call "**Animal Spirits.**" (Though the animal in question is more likely to be a herd-following Sheep than a go-it-alone Siberian Tiger.)

Their decisions may be irrational and wrongheaded much of the time.

But taken together, they're what determine the value of the S&P 500 Index at any given moment.

This means that the Index closely tracks the <u>changing perceptions</u> (or <u>misperceptions</u>) about what's happening in the American economy among those millions of individuals who (wisely or not) are willing to "Put Their Money Where Their Mouths Are" in one of the best examples of a more or less free marketplace.

<u>This</u> is what makes the S&P 500 Index an excellent indicator of **Public Confidence** (or lack thereof) in the American economy, and of how this level of confidence is changing over time. And this is why it can help us track what happened during the Fall Meltdown.

Another important indicator of how "Crazy Wild" the markets became during the Fall of 2008 is the "**Volatility**" of the S&P's daily Index Values during this period. This is a quantitative measure of how wildly market prices are jumping up and down from day to day. So this variable shows us the relative "**Nervousness**" of the stock market. Which tends to be as high strung and neurotic as that mythical Jewish Princess of New York City folklore.

<u>That's</u> why the stock market often seems like a perplexed gargoyle standing at the corner of Wall and Broad. Trying to decide whether <u>this</u> is the week it should "***Climb a Wall of Worry.***" Or whether it "***Hates Uncertainty***" enough to <u>decline</u>. Unless, of course, it's July and therefore time for the so-called "***Summer Rally.***" In which case, we can all go on vacation while stock prices fall (as they generally do during the summer months).

Wall Street types really do parrot such nonsense phrases. Especially when they're talking to "civilians" at parties or on cable television news shows. But it's not clear whether this is simply a Con Job or whether these self-appointed gurus actually believe such myths and enchantment tales.

In any case, <u>Changes</u> in the daily value of the S&P 500 Index—along with the <u>Volatility</u> of these changes—reflect what literally millions of stock market investors <u>believe</u> is going on in the American economy.

The terrifying Autumn 2008 Meltdown represented an average loss of nearly **One Percent** for each of the 58 trading days between September 1 and the market's Fall low on November 20. And included such un-precedented <u>one-day losses</u> as:

- **7.7 Percent** on October 9.
- **8.8 Percent** on September 29.
- **9 Percent** on October 15.
- **10.8 Percent** on October 28.
- **11.5 Percent** on October 13.
- Not to mention **14 days** (nearly <u>one-quarter</u> of those 58 trading days) when one-day losses were greater than **Five Percent**.
- And **9 days** when they were greater than **Six Percent**.

Needless to say, "**Efficient Markets**" theorists in the ivory tower world and among Wall Street's crews of Rocket Scientists had been telling us for years that such horrendous one-day losses *"couldn't possibly happen in the lifetime of the Universe."* Because their much-abused **Gaussian Bell-Shaped Curve** showed that the "Probabilities" of such events were too small to worry about.

But these losses <u>did</u> happen. Just ask any Baby Boomer on the verge of retirement. Who saw the value of his 401(k) cut nearly in half while the autumn leaves were falling.

- **September** began with a continuation of the summer's grad-ual downtrend. With Wall Street's cliché "**Summer Rally**" failing to materialize (as usual).

But the downtrend worsened as the month progressed. So September's <u>S&P Volatility</u> closed out at a relatively high

91

55 Percent. Not all that surprising in view of the S&P Index's <u>loss</u> of **9.2 Percent** for the month.

- <u>October</u> maintained its storied reputation on Wall Street as *"the month when disasters happen."* Because the Stock Markets went <u>**TOTALLY NON-LINEAR.**</u>

Just like super-volcano **Mount Pinatubo** in the Philippines on June 15, 1991. When it **blew up catastrophically and flung nearly <u>Three Cubic Miles</u> of toxic waste particles into the earth's atmosphere.** Poisoning it for the next two years and lowering the earth's average temperature by several degrees. Turning thousands of square miles on the island of Luzon into a lifeless moonscape of mud flows and volcanic ash. (And Ma Nature didn't even bother filing an <u>Environmental Impact Statement</u> first.)

So the <u>S&P's Volatility</u> skyrocketed to **80 Percent** (nearly 1.5 times as Crazy Wild as September's number). As **17 Percent** of its market value disappeared into the Abyss of free-falling prices.

- <u>November</u> brought some easing in the battered markets.

The S&P's Volatility backed off slightly to **71 Percent**. And its market value fell for the month by "only" **7.5 Percent**. With values reaching their exhausted autumn low on November 20.

- <u>December</u> saw the prostrated markets too weak to do much more than moan. Even Wall Street's so-called "**Santa Claus Rally**" took a vacation that year (as it so often does).

So the S&P's Volatility sank to a comparatively somnolent **50 Percent**. And its Index value for the month was only down a "basically flat" **0.8 Percent.**

In terms of sheer dollar losses, the "Fall of 2008" (along with the fall of so many other illusions) was probably the <u>**Greatest Financial Disaster**</u> in world history. And its cost in shattered wealth and wrecked human lives is still being counted throughout the world.

Even in **Iceland**. Where the <u>entire</u> banking system collapsed when it became apparent that its bank portfolios were stuffed full of American-made toxic derivatives that had little value. Which virtually <u>bankrupted</u> the entire country.

(The following exchange was heard on a late-night TV talk show during the final days of 2008:

Question: *"What is the capital of Iceland?"*

Answer: *"About $25. Give or take.")*

■ ■ ■

And I heard a great voice out of the Temple saying to the 7 Angels: "Go your ways and pour out the vials of the Wrath of God upon the earth."

And the <u>First Angel</u> went, and poured out his vial upon the earth. And there fell a noisome and grievous sore upon the men which had the mark of the beast, and upon them which worshipped his image.

And the <u>Second Angel</u> poured out his vial upon the sea. And it became as the blood of a dead man. And every living soul died in the sea.

And the <u>Third Angel</u> poured out his vial upon the rivers and fountains of waters. And they became blood . . .

And the <u>Fourth Angel</u> poured out his vial upon the sun. And power was given unto him to scorch men with fire . . .

And the <u>Fifth Angel</u> poured out his vial upon the seat of the beast. And his kingdom was full of darkness. And they gnawed their tongues for pain . . .

And the <u>Sixth Angel</u> poured out his vial upon the great river Euphrates. And the water thereof was dried up . . .

And the <u>Seventh Angel</u> poured out his vial into the air. And there came a great voice out of the Temple of Heaven from the throne, saying: "It is Done."

And there were Voices. And Thunders. And Lightnings. And there was a Great Earthquake, such as there was not since men were upon the earth. So mighty an earthquake. And so great.

—The Revelation of Saint John

■ ■ ■

Chapter 3
WHAT HAPPENED: OIL PRICES

So we beat on, boats against the current,
borne back ceaselessly into the past.
—F. Scott Fitzgerald

The 75 Percent collapse in Crude Oil prices that began in mid-2008 makes it easy to forget the outright panic that spread across the nation during earlier months while oil prices were galloping frighteningly towards an <u>inconceivable $150 per barrel</u>. (And you all know what's been happening to gasoline prices in recent months.)

Historical evidence shows that spikes in Oil Prices have preceded most American recessions since the end of World War II. Though their significance as a direct "cause" of each recession remains a matter for experts to cluck over.

But it's difficult to avoid a sense that the panic induced by the latest Oil Price spike <u>traumatized large segments of American society</u> in ways that greatly contributed to the current Economic Crisis. In fact, it may even have permanently changed significant aspects of the nation's culture because of its cost impact on:

- **Americans dependent on private automobiles as their principle means of transportation.** Who watched the critically important "discretionary" portion of their personal spending patterns shrink as escalating fuel prices at the pump sent their non-discretionary spending careening out of control.

- **Detroit's Big Three auto industry.** Which saw the evaporation of its last defense against loss of market share to increasingly dominant Asian-owned auto manufacturers.

- **Transportation-dependent American industries.** Whose traditional cost structures suffered massive and destabilizing inflation as their transportation costs escalated.

- **Housing markets.** Where new issues affecting housing locations helped shatter the established perception that home prices "had nowhere to go but up."

■ ■ ■

Auto-Dependent Americans

Automobile commuters facing costs of $100 or more to fill the tanks of their SUVs and other gas-gulping vehicles had to ask themselves some troubling questions. About such critical lifestyle issues as:

- How to <u>spend less</u> on food, housing, entertainment, and other personal expenditures so they could afford to drive to work.

- <u>Never again being able to buy a car</u> that didn't get at least 30 miles per gallon. Even if that meant joining the mass migration to less-exciting vehicles produced by Asian-owned manufacturers.

- <u>Moving to more densely developed neighborhoods</u> closer to their jobs. Giving up their backyard barbecues, swimming pools, and extra bathrooms if necessary.

- Not to mention (the real stunner) <u>switching in droves</u> to bus lines and other forms of public transportation for their trips to and from work.

These issues cut to the heart of traditional American consumer spending patterns. On which the standard business models for major components of the national economy are based.

■ ■ ■

Detroit's Big Three

During the 1990s and much of the current decade, increasing numbers of Americans became <u>convinced</u> that automobiles produced by Toyota, Honda, and other Asian-based manufacturers offered better quality, reliability, and operating efficiency at more attractive prices than vehicles produced by General Motors, Ford, and Chrysler. The result was a <u>significant decline</u> in the Big Three's share of the all-important North American market.

In an effort to preserve their profitability in the face of this dramatic loss of market dominance, the Big Three's less-than-sure-footed top managers evolved <u>defensive business models</u> that emphasized selling fewer vehicles at higher profit margins.

This meant increasing their dependence on selling SUVs, high-performance cars, light trucks, and similar gas-guzzling vehicles in which the Asian-based companies were regarded as being less competitive. And so long as gasoline prices remained more or less stable, the Big Three's defensive business models seemed viable.

However, the impact of Oil Price inflation on gasoline prices cut the ground out from under these business models. The Big Three saw buyer demand for their high-profit, fuel-gulping vehicles vanish like cigarette smoke in sports bars. Leaving them so financially crippled that they required Multibillion-dollar taxpayer bailouts in order to survive.

But Big Three survival took the form of <u>much-shrunken also-rans</u> in the global auto industry as they were forced to cut production. Close factories. And lay off employees. In a desperate effort to stem their horrendous financial losses. With little in the way of fuel-efficient new vehicles in their development pipelines to offer much hope for future recovery.

So the once-dominant American auto industry (including its suppliers and dealers) now lies <u>moaning in the weeds</u> like a crippled elephant beset by hungry lions. Surrounded by nearly a quarter million cast-off American workers. Who face the prospect of <u>never again</u> enjoying the decent livings that had once been their reward for showing up on time for each shift. And whose consumer buying power had once been an important mainstay of so many other industries.

■ ■ ■

Transportation-Dependent Industries

Making products for consumers and other business firms still remains an important segment of the American economy. This is true despite the increasing popularity of products made in China and other low-labor-cost countries. Not to mention the explosion in the contribution of financial services to the nation's GDP.

But manufacturing has always been <u>highly dependent</u> on transportation. A manufacturing firm must receive regular shipments (mostly by truck) of the raw materials and semi-finished parts it needs to make its products. And these products must be shipped (again, mostly by truck) to customer markets. So transportation costs are an important component of the firm's overall cost structure and therefore its profitability.

Oil Price inflation directly increased the pump prices of truck fuel to providers of transportation services. Since most transportation providers are low-margin operations, they had little choice but to pass these higher fuel prices along to their customers.

This meant that many manufacturing firms confronted increases in their transportation costs large enough to destabilize their overall production cost structures.

So these manufacturers had to make some difficult choices among various disagreeable options:

- *Do we pass on our transportation cost increases to our customers in the form of higher prices for our products? Even if this leads to reductions in unit sales and therefore lower profits?*

- *Do we simply eat these transportation cost increases so we can avoid price increases on our products and keep unit sales at the same level? Even if this shrinks our profit margins and diminishes our overall profitability?*

- *Do we try to offset these transportation cost increases by cutting other production costs? Even if this means laying off some of our employees? Cutting pension and medical benefits for remaining employees? Reducing our total output and therefore our sales revenue? Generally becoming a smaller firm generating fewer profit dollars?*

• *Do we subcontract the entire production of some products to lower-cost firms (perhaps in Mexico, or even China) so we can continue to offer our customers a "full line" of products at existing prices that cost us less to produce? Even if this effectively means shifting some of our production activity offshore and therefore permanently reducing the size of our American work force?*

• *Do we simply abandon the production of some products with especially burdensome transportation costs as "no longer worth making"? Even if this ends our status as a "full-line manufacturer" in the eyes of our customers and causes some of them to shift all their purchases to other sources?*

All of these choices can contribute to further declines in American manufacturing capability and employment. Leaving the nation <u>more dependent on imports</u> to meet its product needs.

Firms that <u>produce</u> transportation services found themselves in even worse shape, because fuel purchases are usually their second largest production cost (after labor). This was especially true of the domestic airline industry, already crippled by fairyland business models and clueless top managers. Who found a <u>new way</u> to add to their industry's astonishing record of having <u>lost more money than it's ever made</u>. By ignoring opportunities to hedge the skyrocketing costs of jet fuel in the futures and options markets.

■ ■ ■

Housing Markets

An important factor in the price of a house is <u>how near it is</u> to concentrations of the jobs homeowners depend on for their personal incomes. In general, the closer a house is to job locations, the higher its price is likely to be (and vice versa). From a national perspective, this is especially significant for auto-dependent metropolitan regions in California, Florida, Arizona, and similar states.

During the 1990s and the first half of the current decade, various other factors caused housing prices to rise faster than personal incomes. Many home builders responded by constructing an increasing proportion of their new houses in previously undeveloped "fringe areas" of metropolitan regions where they could take advantage of significantly lower land costs. But these fringe areas tended to be much farther from regional job centers than existing residential areas.

In effect, home builders were offering potential home buyers a <u>trade-off</u> between the Cost of Housing and the Cost of Commuting (usually by automobile). During a period of stable gasoline prices, many home buyers (especially first-timers) found this trade-off sufficiently attractive to choose less-expensive fringe area houses and absorb somewhat higher commuting costs.

So home builders had little difficulty selling their new fringe area houses for decent profit margins. Especially with the growing proliferation of "tantalizingly cheap" adjustable-rate mortgages featuring low initial interest rates. And shrinking down-payment requirements. And "relaxed" credit standards. And optimistic assumptions about future growth in housing prices. (See **Chapter 5** for more details about this "cheap mortgage" phenomenon.)

But the onset of soaring Oil Prices shattered this comfortable trade-off. As gasoline pump prices skyrocketed, the costs of auto commuting (especially for people living in "long-commute" fringe areas) became an increasing burden. This destabilized housing prices in several ways:

101

- **Home Builders** with large inventories of newly constructed houses in fringe areas found it increasingly difficult to sell these houses for anything close to their normal profit margins (and, in some cases, even had to sell them below cost simply to clear their inventories). Among other things, this diminished the ability of many home builders to repay their construction loans from local banks. So banks stopped offering construction loans and home builders stopped constructing new houses (if they didn't go out of business entirely). Which increased the level of unemployment among construction workers, effectively removing them from the home buyer market. All of which caused housing prices in the affected regions to stop growing and even decline.

- **Home Owners** (especially first-timers) in these regions found that the market value of their homes had begun to decline instead of continuing to rise. Leaving them with shrinking home equity—or growing negative equity if they had bought their homes with modest or zero down payments. This robbed them of the ability to refinance their adjustable-rate mortgages when low initial "teaser interest rates" expired. Confronting them with much higher monthly housing payments. And few options for selling their now-unaffordable homes in stagnant markets, where prices had often fallen to levels below the balances due on outstanding mortgages. Causing the rates of home abandonments and foreclosures to escalate. Dumping more houses on already saturated markets. Which placed further downward pressure on house prices.

■ ■ ■

Why Are Oil Prices So Volatile?

Ask 100 experts and you're likely to get 100 different answers. But they all boil down to classic market issues involving **Supply** and **Demand**. (For more information about how markets actually work in the real world, see **Chapter 6**.)

Throughout much of its history, the Oil Industry's main problem has been "**Too Much Supply**." New oil field discoveries in areas like Spindletop in Texas, the Gulf of Mexico, and the Middle East had an annoying habit of coming online at the worst possible times. Flooding the world with more new oil than the industry knew what to do with. Causing market prices to collapse. Despite the endless warnings of Cassandra types that "the world is destined to run out of oil." (Yeah, but not soon enough to boost next year's profits.)

During the later part of the Nineteenth Century, **John D. Rockefeller** (grandfather of banker **David** and Governors **Nelson** and **Winthrop**, and great-grandfather of current Senator "**Jay**") came up with his own solution to the "Oil Glut" problem. This involved building his giant **Standard Oil Company** into a functional Monopoly. So it could "rationally" control the supply of oil "for the benefit of all concerned."

But after 1900, the Powers That Be in Washington decided they couldn't stomach the idea of a private corporation wielding this kind of power. So they forced Standard Oil to be broken up into a number of "separate and independent" companies. Thereby ending Rockefeller's "experiment." And letting the supply of oil run wild again.

Oil producers struggled to respond to this problem by developing "Gentlemen's Agreements" among themselves to control Supply "in rational ways." The most notorious of these producer cartels is OPEC. But OPEC is only the newest and most highly publicized cartel.

The difficulty with oil-producer cartels is that too many of their members aren't exactly "Gentlemen." So they can't resist opportunities to make hay while the sun shines by sneaking extra quantities of oil onto world markets to take advantage of temporary price spikes. Causing other members to wrinkle their noses in disgust—before joining the party so they don't get left behind.

(One of the few Economic Laws that's truly <u>ironclad</u> is the practical impossibility of enforcing cartel supply and price restrictions. Except with the kind of outright physical violence that only seems acceptable among New York's Five Families.)

Meanwhile, recent decades saw what amounted to a revolution in the **Demand** for oil products.

First World industrial nations began improving both their economic growth rates and the equitable distribution of their enhanced prosperity. And the ranks of major economic achievers were swelled by the emergence of formerly developing Third World nations—especially population giants like India and China.

The combined result was a significant and growing increase in the number of people eager to enjoy the more lavish personal lifestyles previously limited to upper-class types in the West. Lifestyles that inevitably meant higher per capita consumption of oil products.

Despite the innovative policies adopted by many First World nations to dampen the growth of oil-product consumption, the rapid increase in the global population of new middle- and upper-class consumers led to strong growth in the world's overall per capita rate of oil-product consumption. This generated strong upward pressure on the trend of oil prices generally.

An interesting wrinkle affecting both the Supply and Demand for oil products was President Nixon's 1971 decision to end the convertibility link between the U.S. Dollar and Gold.

As the world's functional "**Commodity Money**" reserve currency, the Gold-linked Dollar's stable value relative to all other goods and services had been the underlying basis for their prices in world markets (which was why oil has always been priced in Dollars). But the end of the Dollar's link to Gold and apparent conversion into a purely "**Paper Money**" currency raised disturbing questions in many minds about its continuing "stable value." (See **Chapter 7** for a discussion of the real and perceived issues concerning "Commodity Money" versus "Paper Money.")

On the one hand, oil producers worried about how to preserve the future "buying power" of their Dollar-denominated oil revenues.

- Should they explicitly raise the Dollar price of the oil they supplied in order to protect themselves against an uncertain future?

- Should they restrict the supply of oil in the hope that world markets would raise its Dollar price for them?

- Should they price their oil in a currency other than the Dollar? Or in a basket of other currencies?

- Should they try to convert their oil reserves into other (hopefully more stable) forms of wealth as quickly as possible so they could abandon what appeared to be the increasingly risky business of producing oil?

Individually and collectively, oil producers have never been able to settle on a consistent strategy for preserving the future value of their oil revenues. The result has been a chaotic pattern of fits and starts. Try this strategy. Not working? Try that strategy. Not working either? Then let's try Charlie's strategy.

So it goes.

Leading inevitably to price spikes followed by price declines. Followed by more spikes, and more declines. With oil prices becoming increasingly

<u>volatile</u> because Supply can never quite manage to remain in sync with Demand for very long.

On the other hand, traditional oil-consuming societies feared that greater oil price volatility would lead to an escalating trend of permanently higher prices. High enough to threaten the viability of their oil-dependent economic lifestyles. So they mounted a full-court press to find ways of protecting themselves:

- **Greater energy independence?** By all means. Let's limit our oil consumption only to whatever oil we can pump and refine at bargain prices within our own borders. Start drilling wherever new sources of oil look promising. In our national parks. Off our highly developed tourist beaches. Under the White House and Empire State Building if necessary. Whatever it takes so we can continue to afford our traditional lifestyles.

- **Higher energy efficiency?** Yes, yes. Let's reduce our per capita rate of oil consumption. Mandate fifty-mile-per-gallon automobiles as the only models legal to sell, even if they're too small to accommodate most families. Convert all the land in empty-closet-space states like Iowa to the production of corn-based Vodka (sorry, I mean Ethanol).

- **More alternative energy sources?** Of course. Let's become less dependent on fossil fuels from any source. Cover all our western deserts and other vacant land with solar panels. Install huge windmill forests on every conceivable hill where the wind blows with any consistency. Construct massive pump-storage water reservoirs high up in all our mountain ranges. Even follow France's example and generate three-quarters of our electric power with (horrors) nuclear reactors. (<u>Question</u>: How many people were killed by Pennsylvania's **Three Mile Island** nuclear disaster? <u>Answer</u>: Zero. How many were injured? Also zero.)

Needless to say, even the fledgling efforts in such directions by oil-consuming societies have had some noticeable impact in reducing oil demand. Adding to the worries of oil producers about the future buying power of their petroleum reserves. Leading to further volatility in oil prices.

So the historical pattern has been long periods in the past when oil products like gasoline have been available at what seemed like "bargain prices." With the frequency and length of these periods causing many industrial nations to be suckered into adopting economic lifestyles (like "passionate" auto love) that assumed permanently cheap oil.

Only to be panicked by recent oil price spikes and increased volatility. Which are perceived as harbingers of permanently higher prices in the future. High enough to jeopardize the viability of these oil-dependent lifestyles.

That's the real message of the frightening 2007–08 oil price spike among too many Americans. Whose impact (more psychological than physical) may have helped turn the latest recession into an Economic Crisis.

■ ■ ■

Chapter 4
WHAT HAPPENED: DERIVATIVES

I returned and saw under the sun that the race is not to the swift, nor the battle to the strong. Neither yet bread to the wise. Nor yet riches to men of understanding. Nor yet favor to men of skill. But Time and Chance happeneth to them all.
—*Ecclesiastes*

Okay. So maybe the race isn't always to the swift.
Or the battle to the strong.
But that's still the way to bet.
—*Damon Runyon*

A **Derivative** is a security whose value is based on (i.e., <u>derived from</u>) the value of a more senior asset (the **Underlying**) to which it's linked.

But Wall Street, in its hunger for more products to sell, sowed the financial landscape with a bewildering variety of Derivatives during the years leading up to 2008. Featuring all kinds of esoteric bells and whistles. Promising "fantastic returns" for "little or no risk." Too few of which traded on formal exchanges where actual prices reflect real market values.

So by 2008, large buyers of Derivatives (like banks, insurance companies, and pension funds) found themselves standing in a veritable minefield of unknown risks. With their portfolios stuffed full of possibly "**Toxic Derivatives**" that couldn't be valued objectively for balance sheet purposes because so few of them traded regularly in organized markets.

Naturally, these financial institutions panicked. Stopped buying Derivatives of any kind. Rushed to unload whatever they could. All at the same time. Which collapsed whatever secondary markets had existed for such Derivatives. Melting down the balance sheets of many financial institutions in the process.

Is it possible to make any sense of all this?

Yes. If we take things step by step.

■ ■ ■

How It All Began

The simplest example of a Derivative is something called a **FORWARD**, which dates back to Biblical times.

Each Forward involves a custom-tailored <u>Contract</u> between 2 parties covering the Price and Delivery Schedule for an Underlying Asset. Such as a farm crop.

For example, a Commercial Flour Miller agrees to <u>purchase</u> a Farmer's wheat crop, after it's harvested, for a set Price. The Farmer agrees to <u>deliver</u> his wheat crop to the Flour Miller for this Price once it's harvested. So he knows at planting time how much money he'll receive for his crop, regardless of what the market price may happen to be on Delivery Day.

The Farmer uses this Forward to protect himself against a possible <u>decline</u> in the market price for wheat. Thereby locking in a known Profit. While the Flour Miller uses the Forward to protect himself against a possible <u>rise</u> in the market price. Thereby locking in a known Cost.

This remarkable product of human ingenuity helped to make Agriculture an economically viable business. In fact, it was at least as important to the rise of civilization as the interesting deal made between human beings and feral cats. Whereby cats agreed to keep the (tasty) rodent population under control in food storage buildings in return for being treated with special consideration by humans.

(An historically unique phenomenon in the history of human/animal relationships. Because humans had to first capture and tame other animals like horses and cows before they could put them to productive work. While domestic cats remain untamed serial killers who made their own deal. No wonder they're so Arrogant.)

Since meaningful secondary markets don't exist for custom-tailored Forwards, they can't be traded in any reliable way. This makes them seem "obsolete." As they should be.

But they survive today (on too grand a scale) in many two-party Derivatives like **Credit Default Swaps**. Whose secondary markets are "exceedingly primitive" (to say the least).

This means there's no objective way to determine the actual market value of such Derivatives at any point in time. Which is very troublesome for those who hold them as assets on their balance sheets. No one really knows what they're worth.

The next step in the evolution of Derivatives was to create **FUTURES**. These are Forwards that have been "regularized" in <u>Structured Contracts</u> that have common specifications so they can be traded as formal **Securities** in organized secondary markets.

In fact, most Futures are created by formal Trading Exchanges like the **Chicago Board of Trade** (CBOT). These exchanges offer a host of Futures Contracts having <u>identical</u> specifications as to size, quality, and delivery dates.

- They "Make Orderly Markets" in Futures where they can easily be <u>bought and sold</u> by willing participants.

- They <u>publish</u> daily Market Prices at which Futures are being traded.

- They require traders to <u>demonstrate</u> their ability to fulfill their side of Futures Contracts by maintaining with the exchange **Margin Accounts** in cash. Whose necessary balances are determined by objective formulas that are "Marked To Market" each day.

- Plus, they offer other desirable benefits that make it possible to know a Futures Contract's "Actual Market Value" at any point in time.

<u>OPTIONS</u> are much like Futures except for one **Critical Difference**.

The owner of an Option has the **Right** (but not the **Obligation**, as with a Futures Contract) to **Exercise** it on (or in some cases before) the day it expires. This is an important benefit and one that has significant Market Value by itself.

In effect, this benefit <u>formalizes</u> a crucial aspect of the whole Options Concept (i.e., Voluntary Exercise by the owner) that exists—explicitly or implicitly—in virtually every financial transaction, whether or not the Buyer and Seller are consciously aware of it.

The **Second Important Benefit** that Options have is a "Mathematically Rigorous" formula to objectively determine an Option's "**Theoretical Value**" (i.e., what its market Price "<u>should be</u>"). This makes it possible (in theory) to spot Options that the secondary markets are "Overpricing" or "Underpricing."

This mathematical formula is the result of pioneering work done in the academic community in the 1960s and '70s by **Fischer Black, Myron Scholes,** and **Robert Merton** (and their many subsequent groupies). It's formally known today as the "**Black-Scholes-Merton Options Pricing Model**" and exists in a great many variations.

Recent critics insist that this model is conceptually oversimplified in certain important areas. And traders often find that it produces <u>theoretical</u> options values that are materially different from <u>actual</u> market prices. But the BSM

Model at least provides a usable Benchmark for what any particular Option "Should Be Worth."

Perhaps more importantly, the BSM Model provides a theoretical framework for constructing many different types of Options. Which are the whole basis for the explosion of Derivatives (for good or ill).

■ ■ ■

Options on Common Stocks

Probably the simplest example of a "plain vanilla" Derivative is a "**Call Option**" on the Common Stock of a publicly traded Corporation.

A Call Option gives the owner the <u>Right</u> (but not the <u>Obligation)</u> to **Buy** (or "**Call Away**") 100 shares of the corporation's stock for a specified price-per-share (known as the Option's "**Strike Price**") on or before the Option's specified **Expiration Date**.

In other words, a Call Option is a lot like an **Oil Lease**. Which gives the leaseholder the Right (but not the Obligation) to drill for oil on a specific parcel of land any time before the lease expires.

Suppose XYZ Corporation's stock has risen on the New York Stock Exchange to $25 per share and its Call Option's Strike Price is $20 per share (or $5 per share <u>lower</u>). If you own one of these Options, this means that you can **Exercise** your Right to buy 100 shares of XYZ for the below-market Strike Price of $2,000 ($20 times 100 shares). Then immediately turn around and sell these shares in the stock market at their current price of $2,500. Making yourself a nice profit of $500 (or 25 Percent).

Under these circumstances, your Call Option is said to have **Intrinsic Value** of $500 (or $5 per share)—equal to the immediate profit you can make by Exercising your Right to buy XYZ Corporation's stock at its "bargain" Strike Price and reselling it for the higher stock market price.

But your Option can also have additional value (called "**Time Value**") if enough buyers of Call Options believe that XYZ Corporation's stock price has a good chance of rising <u>further</u> than $25 per share before your Option's Expiration Date. In which case, you may prefer to sell your Option to one of these eager buyers for more than its Intrinsic Value (rather than simply Exercise it) in order to earn a higher profit.

All this is possible and even easy because so many Call Options for stocks trade on formal Exchanges like the **Chicago Board Options Exchange** (CBOE), which function much like the New York Stock Exchange. As we've seen, CBOE "Makes Markets" in the Call Options it lists. Matches buyers and sellers. Reports transaction prices on a continuous basis. Handles all the details for traders who want to Exercise the Call Options they own. And makes sure that each buyer or seller lives up to his commitment. So the Options trader never has to worry about (or even know the name of) the person he is buying from or selling to.

A Call Option has a "<u>mirror image,</u>" known as a "**Put Option**."

If you own a Put Option on XYZ Corporation's stock, you have the <u>Right</u> (but not the <u>Obligation</u>) to **Sell** (or "<u>Put</u>") 100 shares of the Corporation's stock you may own at the Option's **Strike Price** on or before the Option's **Expiration Date**. So if your Put Option's Strike Price is $20 per share, your investment in 100 shares of XYZ Corporation's stock is protected if its stock market price should fall below $2,000 ($20 times 100 shares) before the Option's Expiration Date. And no matter how low XYZ Corporation's stock price may fall, you <u>always</u> have the Right to sell your 100 shares for $2,000 until your Put Option expires.

Does this sound like the fire insurance policy a homeowner buys each year to protect himself from serious loss if his house should catch fire while he's away on vacation? Sure it does. Because the basic principle is the same. You pay a modest price to protect yourself from the possibility of a big loss while the insurance policy is in effect.

Put Options on the Corporation's stock trade on the same Exchange as its Call Options. So the Exchange handles all the details of buying, selling, and exercising the Put Option just as conveniently and transparently as for the Call Option.

So far, so good.

But now things start to get a little complicated.

■ ■ ■

Selling Options

The same exchanges that enable you to <u>buy</u> Call and Put Options on publicly traded stocks <u>also</u> enable you to <u>sell</u> (or "**Write**") these options **even when you don't own them**. Provided, that is, you're willing to deposit the required amount of "earnest money" (known as "**Margin**") with the exchange that lists the options in order to demonstrate your ability to deliver on your end of the transaction.

The ability to <u>Sell</u> options in this manner makes it possible for you to <u>place a bet</u> that a stock's price will **fall**. Just as the ability to <u>Buy</u> options makes it possible for you to place a bet that the stock's price will **rise**. And this has some interesting implications.

Suppose, for example, you <u>already own</u> 100 shares of XYZ Corporation's stock. You can sell a Call Option on these shares to a willing buyer. Then deposit the shares with the Exchange as Margin to guarantee your ability to deliver the 100 shares at the Option's Strike Price if the buyer should Exercise the Option because the stock's price has risen above the Call Option's Strike Price.

Why would you want to sell a Call Option on your 100 shares? In order to receive the Option's sale price (called "**Premium**") as income. And if XYZ Corporation's stock keeps trading in a narrow range that never rises above the Option's Strike Price, you can write one Call

Option after another as each one expires without being Exercised. Thereby earning yourself a **stream of income** (in the form of Premium Payments) from a stock that you continue to own. (Which is in addition to any Dividend payments you may receive.)

This investment strategy is known in the trade as "**Selling Covered Calls**" (whose sales are "Covered" by the fact that you already own the stock). It's regarded as a very conservative strategy, especially for income-oriented investors. In fact, some stock market investors choose which stocks to buy largely in order to earn income by selling Covered Calls on them.

Equally simple is the case where you like XYZ Corporation's stock as a possible buy at its current price of $25 per share. But you'd like it even more at $20 per share. Which you believe it may fall to at some point in the future because of general market conditions.

So you sell a **Put Option** with a $20 Strike Price on the stock. Then "Cover" yourself by putting up sufficient Cash Margin with the exchange to demonstrate your ability to buy 100 shares of XYZ Corporation for $2,000 ($20 times 100 shares) if the Option should be Exercised.

If this Option expires without being exercised (because the stock's price doesn't fall below $20 per share), you simply sell another Put Option. And another after that. Earning premium income from each one **even though you don't yet own the stock.** Which you remain willing and able to buy—at $20 per share. As you may actually do someday. Following which you may well turn around and start writing Covered Calls against your new shares to continue the income stream. Thereby earning yourself income from XYZ Corporation's stock both before and after you buy it. Which, over time, may generate a nice profit for you. Over and above any Capital Gains profit you may earn when you finally sell the stock.

All very nice indeed. But not quite as easy as it sounds. Because you must still do a great deal of tedious homework to identify good stocks for this investment strategy. Which (let's not kid ourselves) is Very Hard Work.

Especially since the **Financial Accounting Standards Board** (a private regulatory group that serves as the accounting profession's "Supreme

Court") insists that private corporations publish their financial numbers in the form of fairyland fictions known as "**Accruals**," rather than in cold hard <u>Cash</u>. So it often turns out that a corporation's **Cash Income** (which isn't shown on its Income Statement) is substantially <u>less</u> than its **Accrued Income** (which is what the Income Statement shows).

■ ■ ■

More Complicated Options

But the vast array of options on publicly traded stocks represents only the tip of the Derivatives iceberg. Because there are also options on:

- Various <u>stock market indexes,</u> like the S&P 500.
- Widely traded <u>bonds,</u> like those issued by the U.S. Treasury, foreign governments, and major corporations.
- <u>Interest rates</u> and <u>foreign currencies.</u>
- <u>Futures Contracts</u> for physical commodities like Crude Oil, Copper, Wheat, and the ever-popular Pork Bellies.
- <u>Futures Contracts</u> for interest rates, bonds, stock market indexes, and actively traded common stocks.

The list goes on and on. Limited only by the extravagant imaginations of Wall Street professionals hungry for more products to sell.

Note that the list mentions "<u>Options on Futures</u>." Since a Futures Contract is also a Derivative, such Options are "<u>Derivatives on Derivatives</u>" (known on Wall Street as **Derivatives Squared**). There are also "<u>Derivatives on Derivatives on Derivatives</u>"—known as "**Derivatives Cubed**." And Derivative Chains don't stop there.

Also, the **form** that options can take goes well beyond the simple Call and Put Options we've been looking at.

In his fascinating book *The Complete Guide to Options Pricing Formulas*, Espen Gaarder Haug describes more than 100 different options forms. Many of them so exotic as to boggle the mind. All designed to meet the real or imagined need for unique ways to exploit the special magic of options—which involves **Compressing Time** and **Transferring Risk** (for a price, of course).

But once we stray into the Deep Doo-Doo world of exotic options, life gets much more complicated. Because there are usually no formal exchanges like CBOE where they can be easily and safely traded. There may not even be any conventional **Over-the-Counter** markets for them. In many cases, the buyer and seller (accompanied by teams of lawyers) must meet in person to hammer out custom-tailored forms for these options. Which, it goes without saying, can't be regularly traded in anything resembling a normal Secondary Market.

■ ■ ■

What Determines an Option's "Fair Market Value"?

According to the theories taught in the nation's leading MBA schools, you can calculate this by using an appropriate version of the **Black-Scholes-Merton Options Pricing Model**. This model takes the form of an awesome-looking <u>Partial Differential Equation</u> into which you plug values for the independent variables. Following which it spits out the option's theoretical **Fair Market Value**.

This is actually easier to do than it sounds because you can use readily available computer software or suitably configured Excel spreadsheets to do the tough number crunching. Or even Hewlett-Packard's legendary 12C programmable pocket calculator.

For the record, Myron Scholes and Robert Merton won the **1997 Nobel Memorial Prize in Economics** for developing this model (Fisher Black having already died, and they don't give you Nobel Prizes after you're dead). This was after they had left the academic world to become founding partners in an elaborate hedge fund called **Long-Term Capital Management.** Which blew up catastrophically in 1998 when the wheels fell off their misplaced assumptions about "Market Efficiency," "Gaussian Risk Probabilities," and the "Power of Leverage." Swallowing up their seven-figure Nobel Prize money and much more besides. (See **Chapter 7** for the details of what happened.)

But the fact remains that the discovery of Options is one of the Great Intellectual Triumphs of financial history. As significant in its own way as the discovery of **Compound Interest.** Because Options have the seemingly magical ability to accomplish two very important things:

- **They can Collapse Time.** So we can treat a financial event scheduled to occur at some point in the future as if it were taking place today. And price it accordingly.

- **They can Transfer Risk.** This means that someone who wants to Avoid Risk (if the price for doing so is low enough) can transfer it to someone who's willing to Accept Risk (if the price is high enough).

That's why Options are embedded in virtually every financial transaction. Either directly or implicitly. Whether the participants realize it or not.

And so it's been ever since Biblical times when the Idea of Options emerged instinctively from the restless thickets of the Human Imagination.

Along with proto-markets for goods and services. And endless debates about the "One True God."

■ ■ ■

A Stroll through Wall Street's Harem of "Exotic Dancers"

Whatever its theoretical flaws, the mathematical model defining Options in objective (if highly theoretical) terms that Black, Scholes, and Merton published in the early 1970s fired the imaginations of enough gurus to produce a revolution in the kind and number of exotic new products Wall Street could sell.

Beginning with simple Options on common stocks we looked at earlier, these Derivative products blossomed like mad. Growing in complexity. Until many top managers in major financial institutions (preoccupied as they were by the usual high-level power struggles within their firms) had trouble understanding what the eager young MBA types who reported to them were actually selling.

And what their <u>real</u> implications might be.

But as long as the quarterly numbers kept improving . . . (You know how it is.)

Meanwhile, the fevered imaginations of those young MBA types kept boiling over with more ideas for irresistible new Derivatives. Whose links to the plain vanilla world of simple options on common stocks became increasingly remote.

Here's an example of how large portions of the Derivatives business work. (This happens to be a true story. Only the names have been changed to protect the guilty and avoid lawsuits.)

Charlie was an aggressive young MBA type working for the old-line investment banking firm of ***Whipsnade, Lascivine & Co.*** His year-end bonus was a highly lucrative multiple of his seven-figure base salary and reflected how much sales revenue he generated for his firm during the year. So he was always looking for glitzy new Derivative products to sell.

One of Charlie's favorite customer groups was the American insurance industry. These companies are always looking to invest their inflows of insurance premium cash in debt securities that provide regular payments of interest and principle. But any debt securities they buy must meet 2 conditions:

1. They must have **Investment-Grade ratings** (BBB or better).
2. They must be denominated in **U.S. Dollars.**

So Charlie started poring through his firm's vast inventory of debt securities to see what was available. And came across two groups of Mexican Government bonds that looked interesting.

- The <u>first group</u> of bonds was denominated in Mexican Pesos and **had a Triple A rating.** (No surprise. Because no matter what happens, the Mexican government can always meet payments of interest and principle on these bonds by simply printing more Pesos. (Printing money? Be patient. We'll see how this is done in **Chapter 7.**)

- The <u>second group</u> of bonds was **denominated in U.S. Dollars.** But these bonds were unrated.

After some thought, Charlie saw an exploitable angle. If he could find a way to blend the Peso bonds that had a top investment-grade rating with the unrated bonds denominated in Dollars, he'd have a debt security that could be sold to the insurance industry for a nice markup.

So he had his firm create a new, wholly owned subsidiary called **Pristine Beach Securities** in an independent Caribbean island nation with an easygoing government. And capitalize this subsidiary with both groups of Mexican bonds.

Next, he had his firm sign a contract with *Pristine Beach Securities* to **buy** both groups of Mexican bonds in return for **regular annual payments in U.S. Dollars.**

Then he had *Pristine Beach Securities* **issue new Class A Bonds** denominated in Dollars. For sale to the investing public, and secured by the annual Dollar payments *Pristine Beach* receives from *Whipsnade Lascivine* (which would underwrite the sale of these bonds for its usual lucrative fee).

Finally, he went to one of the major rating firms (like *Moody's*, *Standard & Poor's*, or *Fitch*) to seek an **investment-grade rating** for *Pristine Beach*'s new Class A bonds.

These rating agencies are private firms that earn their sales revenue from payments by debt issuers who want ratings for their securities. So they naturally lean over backwards to come up with ratings that meet their customer's needs.

In this case, the rating agency didn't have to lean backwards very far. After all:

- Dollar payments of interest and principle on *Pristine Beach*'s new Class A bonds were **secured by the annual Dollar payments** *Pristine Beach* received from *Whipsnade Lascivine* (which already had a Triple A rating).

- The Dollar payments from *Whipsnade Lascivine* were **partially secured by** *Pristine Beach*'s **delivery of its Mexican Peso bonds** in return for these payments. And these Mexican Government bonds already had a Triple A rating.

So it wasn't very surprising that the rating firm had little trouble giving *Pristine Beach*'s new bonds a Triple A rating. (For more detail about these interesting practices of rating firms, see Chapter 9 on Market Regulation.)

All of which gave Charlie the new product he was seeking to sell to the insurance industry at a nice profit for his firm. *Pristine Beach*'s new Class A bonds. Denominated in U.S. Dollars. Carrying an investment-grade rating. Which put him on a fast track for a year-end bonus of at least 5 times as much as his seven-figure base salary.

For the record, *Pristine Beach*'s new bonds are known as "**Derivative Debt Securities**" because they're ultimately based on ("derived from") the 2 groups of existing Mexican Government bonds that were imaginatively repackaged by Charlie.

So *Pristine Beach*'s bonds were quite different from more conventional "**plain vanilla bonds**" issued by industrial corporations to purchase new plant and equipment. And whose interest and principle are paid from the sales revenues these corporations earn by making and selling hand tools or plumbing fixtures or truck tires or other Real McCoy products.

But this distinction was of no concern to people like Charlie. Or financial institutions like *Whipsnade Lascivine*.

■ ■ ■

Credit Default Swaps

Here's another example of how exotic Derivatives can become.

Anthony grew up in a large brick house on a tree-shaded street in Brooklyn's Dyker Heights section and looked forward to a career in corporate management.

But two months after he received his MBA from Wharton, his father was killed in an automobile accident on the Belt Parkway. So Anthony had to take over the family business.

His father had made a nice fortune running money for one of New York's Five Families through a group of independent Loansharks who served some of Brooklyn's most lucrative personal loan territories. It was a simple enough business, and Anthony soon found that it took very little of his time.

Every Sunday, these Loansharks would meet Anthony in the backroom private office of a storefront insurance brokerage firm he owned on Eighty-Sixth Street. Each one bearing a plastic supermarket bag full of well-used cash. This cash was Anthony's cut of that week's interest payments the Loansharks had collected from their personal loan clients. For which Anthony supplied the loan capital.

Once the last Loanshark had left at the end of the afternoon, Anthony would divide the big pile of cash into bundles of slightly less than $1,000 each. Place each bundle into a heavy bank deposit envelope and fill out a deposit slip for it. Then walk half a block to the local branch of a well-known New York City bank and drop one-third of these envelopes in the big brass lockbox next to the front door. For deposit to a series of numbered accounts accessible by the Family's supervisor of its Brooklyn personal loan activities, who was the source of Anthony's loan capital.

The rest of the envelopes were Anthony's, and he deposited them in various accounts that carried the name of his insurance brokerage firm.

After about a year of watching the progress of this business, Anthony phoned one of his more intelligent Loansharks and suggested lunch at Gargiulo's Restaurant in Coney Island the following day.

"The personal loan business is dead in the water," Anthony said as soon as they were seated in a quiet corner of Gargiulo's high-ceilinged main dining room. "It's going nowhere fast."

The Loanshark's name was **Isaac**. He was a middle-aged Sephardic Rabbi and Talmudic scholar who'd learned years earlier that Loansharking paid a lot better than leading Sabbath prayers as a third-stringer in some back-street synagogue in Gravesend. And he blinked but said nothing in response to Anthony's comment.

"I mean, making 6-for-5 loans for a couple hundred bucks to tide working stiffs over to their next paycheck?" Anthony went on. "That's so Yesterday."

"It all depends on volume," Isaac said quietly.

"And the volume isn't growing. I've been tracking the number of loans per month you and the other guys have been generating. It's virtually the same as last year this time. We need a better angle."

"Do I get the idea you've already thought of a better angle?"

"Different, at least. You want to hear?"

"Sure."

"Suppose each loan could be for a couple thousand instead of a couple hundred? Think how much more cash you could generate from the same loan volume."

"But none of my clients could ever handle that kind of debt load."

"Right. But there are clients who can. Like retail stores."

"Retail stores?"

"The usual Mom and Pop places. They're all over the place. Thousands of them. And they have to restock their inventories every month or so. That costs them cash."

"But don't their distributors offer trade credit?"

"Sure. For a big price. Ever see the discounts store owners can get if they pay cash on delivery? We can offer them inventory loans so they can pay on delivery and get those discounts. And share a chunk of the savings with us. As the price of the loan."

"No 6-for-5, in other words."

"We don't need it. Not with loan values of a couple thousand each. The main thing is the amount of total cash we can generate."

"You can come up with enough loan capital?"

"No problem. My guy's been all over me to put more of his money to work."

"What about Security? I mean, a welcher on a couple hundred dollar loan is one thing. But if the loan's for a couple thousand . . . "

"How do you handle a welcher now?"

"Well, you know. I send a couple of guys around to see him."

"To break his knees?"

"Not right away. I want to keep him working so he can pay me off. But my guys are giant-size Russians from Brighton Beach. Very intimidating, if you know what I mean. One visit usually does the trick."

"You obviously can't do that with retail store owners. They're too friendly with local cops."

"So where does that leave us?"

"Very simple. I'll write insurance policies on every loan you make."

"Insurance policies?"

"If the store owner welches for any reason, the policy pays off in full."

"You can do that?"

"Sure. I can do it through my insurance brokerage firm. Do you see how it works?"

"Take me through the details."

"Okay. You lend a store owner, say, $3,000 to restock his inventory. He signs a contract promising to pay you back the $3,000 by such-and-such a date. Plus interest at a glatt kosher rate. Better than he could get from a bank. Plus the loan origination fee, which bumps up the effective interest rate. Plus the insurance policy premium. You with me so far?"

"Yes."

"You bring me the contract. And I'll write you an insurance policy for the full amount. So you're completely protected."

"And who backs the policy?"

"Don't worry. I'll get a respectable-sounding insurance company to put its name on every policy. My insurance brokerage writes a lot of business for those guys. So they owe me. The policies will look so kosher you'll even be able to sell them if you want."

"Sell them?"

"Right. Just like an over-the-counter stock. In fact, I'll even make a market in them. Match up buyers and sellers."

In other words, Anthony offered to <u>insure</u> Isaac and his other Loansharks against any **Risk** that the retail store owners to whom they made business loans would fail to repay on time.

The formal name for this kind of loan insurance policy is a **Credit Default Swap** (CDS). And they were by no means limited to backroom deals in Brooklyn's underground Loanshark industry.

In fact, during the years leading up to 2008, Credit Default Swaps became a <u>gigantic global business</u> among insurance companies, banks, and other financial institutions that got in the habit of swapping credit risks back and forth in pursuit of trading profits. Almost entirely on an **Over-The-Counter** basis (which could involve nothing more elaborate than a pair of Big Swinging Dick trader types haggling over price at opposite ends of a private telephone line or computer network).

In its Wall Street context, a "simple version" (hah) of a Credit Default Swap involves three parties:

- The <u>**Debt Issuer**</u>, who issues (let's say) $10 Million worth of bonds, each with a Face Value of $1,000. These bonds mature in 10 years and pay interest twice a year at an annual rate of Five Percent.

- The <u>**CDS Writer**</u>, who sells ("writes") one CDS for each of these bonds. Each CDS has a Face Value of $1,000 (same as each bond). And promises to pay this amount to the owner of the CDS if the Debt Issuer should <u>Default</u> (fail to make interest or principle payments) at any time prior to the bonds' maturity date. Plus the CDS Writer receives <u>regular payments</u> from the Buyer. All of which remains in effect until the bonds mature or a Default occurs.

- The **Original CDS Buyer**, who buys one (or more) CDSs in return for promising to make regular payments to the CDS Writer for as long as the CDS is in effect. If he owns one (or more) of the underlying bonds, he probably buys the CDS <u>primarily</u> to insure ("hedge") himself against the risk of the Debt Issuer defaulting. Just like a homeowner buys fire insurance on his house. But he isn't <u>required</u> to own any of the bonds. In such a case, buying a CDS means he's <u>placing a bet</u> that the market price of the CDS will <u>rise</u> and he can sell out later at a profit. A price rise means the market perceives that the Debt Issuer's **Credit Strength** is <u>declining</u>, thereby <u>increasing</u> the Risk that the bonds will default. Which <u>makes</u> the value of the protection offered by the CDS <u>more valuable</u>.

Clear so far?

Right. So what's the Big Deal?

Well, the Big Deal is in the <u>complications</u> that can follow. For example:

- There's <u>no limit</u> on the number of Credit Default Swaps that the **CDS Writer** can sell on this $10 Million bond issue. If he wishes, he can sell CDSs with a total Face Value of <u>$100 Million</u>. Thereby <u>increasing</u> the regular payments he receives from CDS buyers by <u>10 times</u>. And he doesn't have to stop there. Of course, he remains obligated to pay CDS owners the Face Value of <u>all</u> the CDSs he sells if the Debt Issuer should default.

- <u>Also</u>, the **CDS Writer** can <u>sell</u> (for a flat price in the open market) his **Right** to receive regular payments from the owners of any or all of the CDSs he's already sold. By (in effect) <u>selling his side</u> of the CDSs to **Secondary Buyers**. With these buyers taking over from the CDS Writer the Risk of having to pay out the Face Value of the CDSs if the Debt Issuer should default. The CDS Writer may sell at a profit if the market price of the CDSs has <u>risen</u> because of the perception that the Debt Issuer's Credit Strength has <u>declined</u>. While the Secondary Buyers believe that the market price of the CDSs will rise <u>still further</u> because of perceptions that the Debt Issuer's Credit Strength will <u>continue</u> to decline. Thereby giving themselves potential profit opportunity.

- <u>Similarly,</u> the **Original CDS Buyers** may sell their CDSs to Secondary Buyers if their market prices <u>rise</u> because of the same perceptions about the Debt Issuer's declining Credit Strength described above. And these Secondary Buyers may eventually resell these CDSs at a later date for a profit if market prices continue to rise.

- <u>Finally,</u> **CDS Writers, Original CDS Buyers,** and **Secondary Buyers** can <u>place bets</u> that CDS market prices will <u>fall</u> in the future because of perceptions that the Debt Issuer's Credit Strength is <u>increasing</u> (thereby <u>reducing</u> the Risk of default, so the protection offered by the CDSs becomes less valuable). They often do this by <u>temporarily borrowing</u> CDSs they don't own from CDS owners (for a fee) and selling them in the marketplace for <u>today's high prices</u>. In the hopes of being able to buy them back at <u>tomorrow's lower prices</u> and returning them to their original owners. (This is the age-old practice of **Short-Selling** and is by no means limited to Credit Default Swaps.)

In other words, Credit Default Swaps are <u>ideal</u> instruments to buy and sell in the kind of trading markets that the **Animal Spirits** of natural human instincts inevitably create for virtually <u>anything</u> whose market price can vary. Including Baseball Cards, Celebrity Autographs, Rare Comic Books, up to and including Big-Ticket items like Classic Ferraris.

An interesting variation of the basic Credit Default Swap was developed in 1997 by a team of Rocket Scientists at **JP Morgan**. They called it a "**Broad Index Securitized Trust Offering**" (or **BISTRO** for short).

Its main attraction to a commercial bank like Morgan was to provide an entirely kosher way to evade the burdensome capital reserve requirements imposed by federal regulators on the standard business loans such banks traditionally made (usually with their depositors' funds) to corporate borrowers like IBM, Ford, and Wal-Mart. The effect of these requirements was to <u>limit the amount of Leverage</u> (in the name of "minimizing Risk") the bank's Equity Capital was allowed to support. Thereby limiting the bank's Return on Equity to levels that were becoming increasingly uncompetitive with the returns offered by financial firms not subject to these federal regulations.

Here's how the original BISTRO worked:

- Morgan established an independent shell firm known as a "**Special-Purpose Vehicle**" (SPV). This SPV <u>was not</u> a commercial bank (in the sense of Taking Deposits). So it was <u>exempt</u> in the United States from any federal minimum capital reserve requirements that would limit its Leverage Ratios. Also, since it was an independent firm, the SPV's financial performance and balance sheet status would <u>never</u> have any impact on Morgan's.

- The SPV entered into a special Credit Default Swap with Morgan. This involved the SPV agreeing to <u>fully insure</u> Morgan against the default risk on $9.7 Billion worth of business loans to 307 different companies it was carrying on its books. In return, Morgan agreed to make regular payments to the SPV for this default protection.

- With all $9.7 Billion worth of these business loans now insured against default by the SPV, Morgan argued to the Feds that it should <u>no longer</u> be required to maintain capital reserves against these loans. So it should be allowed to use these capital funds for other purposes. Such as making <u>additional</u> business loans.

- Needless to say, the SPV had to maintain its own capital reserves so it could make good on its default insurance if the occasion should arise. It planned to create these reserves by selling notes to private investors and holding the proceeds in ultra-safe Treasury securities. But it contended that these reserves only needed to be a small percentage of Morgan's $9.7 Billion worth of insured loans. Because the probability was extremely small that more than a few would ever default. After much discussion with one of the rating firms (Moody's), the SPV agreed to sell notes worth about <u>Seven Percent</u> of Morgan's loans. And Moody's agreed to give two-thirds of these notes a much-prized Triple A rating.

Naturally, Wall Street firms rushed to design ever-more arcane variations of Credit Default Swaps. Most of which became little more than naked side bets for or against the credit strength of individual companies or industries. Which got peddled like cheaply repainted used cars to uncomprehending customers as ideal hedging tools. For a nice cut of the action.

So by 2007, the Face Value of outstanding Credit Default Swaps had reached the astonishing figure of **$62 Trillion**—or **15 Percent** <u>more</u> than the economic output of the <u>entire world</u> in that year. All of which were being traded in literally thousands of informal **Over-The-Counter** markets (many of the "here-today-gone-tomorrow" variety), since there were no organized exchanges for CDSs (as there are for Options on Common Stocks and many other types of financial securities). So there were no reliable sources of objective data about the current market price for any Credit Default Swaps.

This massive trading action was completely <u>unregulated</u> by any government agency. In fact, Congressional passage of the **Commodity Futures Modernization Act** in 2000 <u>deliberately excluded</u> Credit Default Swaps from being regulated by the Securities and Exchange Commission. Or by the Commodity Futures Trading Commission. Or by any state government (several of which had tried to regulate them under their gambling laws).

So no one really knew whether a party taking the guarantee side of any particular Credit Default Swap actually had the wherewithal to make good on its guarantee. Or what any CDS was <u>really worth</u>. Not that anyone seemed to care.

So goes life in the Fast Lane.

At least until the Summer of 2008, when the roof fell in. Because too many corporations discovered that their investment portfolios were stuffed full of "Monopoly Money" derivative securities that were impossible to value objectively for balance sheet purposes. Because no meaningful Secondary Markets existed where these securities could be bought and sold on anything like a regular basis.

More importantly, the Derivatives Boom had spread to the nation's Housing Markets. Where its subsequent meltdown brought the troubles of Wall Street to Main Street. With a vengeance.

■ ■ ■

Are Derivatives "Weapons of Mass Destruction"?

Not inherently.

Rather, they're <u>extremely useful tools</u> for **Transferring Risk** between willing buyers and willing sellers at mutually agreeable prices. And since the world is full of people who have different tolerances for Risk, Derivatives can serve a highly valuable economic purpose.

The catch is that buyers and sellers of Derivatives must be more than merely <u>Willing</u>. They must also be **Knowledgeable**. They must be aware of what Risk is really all about. And how <u>transferring</u> Risk doesn't make it <u>disappear</u>. Because Risk always remains a permanent **Fact of Life**. As Inexorable as the Sunrise. No matter how many times it's transferred. Or to whom.

It's astonishing how many so-called financial professionals have little understanding of what Risk is really all about. They too easily get carried away by the excitement of Trading. Let themselves believe they're participating in a no-lose game of higher profits with no downside.

Until they wake up one morning to find themselves drowning in huge losses. Being hurriedly pink-slipped by their equally ignorant bosses, anxious to cover their tushes. Reduced to driving cabs or waiting tables at restaurants where they were once fawned-over patrons.

While the rest of us were left holding the bag amid a shattered economy.

■ ■ ■

Risk Management

If we can put aside our natural sentimentalities for a moment, we might be able to recognize that <u>Three Basic Human Instincts</u> have largely been responsible for the rise of Civilization. They are:

- <u>FIRST:</u> **The Instinct to Trade.** Give any group of people <u>equal individual amounts</u> of various goods and see how quickly they begin trading these goods back and forth to reflect their personal preferences. Until it isn't long before the <u>allocation of goods differs</u> sharply from one person to another. This is how Markets naturally evolve. We will explore this in **Chapter 6** by seeing how such <u>Natural Markets</u> developed among Allied Prisoners of War during World War II in Germany's POW camps.

- <u>SECOND:</u> **The Instinct to Create Money.** Markets function more efficiently when the <u>Prices</u> of all goods can be expressed in terms of a <u>single good</u> that economists like to call the <u>Medium of Exchange</u>. In other words, **Money.** This is a natural human invention and one of the most important. **Chapter 6** shows how Allied POWs instinctively chose **Cigarettes** as their Money. But restless human nature is always seeking to make Money <u>more useful</u> as a device for trading in Markets. And the evolution of Money into more useful and sophisticated forms is detailed in **Chapter 7.**

- <u>THIRD:</u> **The Instinct to Gamble.** This involves the natural human willingness to take actions whose outcomes can't be known <u>for sure</u> in advance. In other words, these actions are "**Risky.**" And the more Risky you perceive a particular action to be, the <u>Higher its Potential Payoff</u> should be in order to justify your taking this action. As it happens, the Risk inherent in many actions can be roughly <u>Quantified</u>. This can give you approximate <u>Probability Percentages</u> of various actions paying off for you. So you can rank these actions by their estimated "Riskiness," compare them to each other and to their Potential Payoffs, and thereby make intelligent judgments about which (if any) actions to take. This is known as **Managing Risk**. And the widespread failure to Manage Risk in sensible ways is regarded as <u>a major reason</u> why the financial industry melted down so catastrophically in 2008. This is what we're going to look at in the pages that follow.

Many people insist that the financial industry and its many markets are simply a large collection of gambling casinos that offer investors a variety of "games" to bet on.

This is "almost right." But the "almost" is significant.

When you walk into a gambling casino in Las Vegas or Atlantic City or wherever, you face an immediate choice. Are you going to play the Slot Machines and various table games like Roulette and Craps like most suckers (er, "Customers")? Or are you going to seek out the Poker Rooms?

If you choose the slots or table games, you're highly likely to lose because you're <u>playing against the House</u>. And the payoffs of these games are structured (with the blessings of state gaming commissions) to give the House an edge that assures you'll lose in the long run. Which isn't like the situation in the financial industry.

But if you choose to seek out the Poker Rooms, <u>then</u> you have a chance of winning. Because you're playing against <u>other gamblers</u> like yourself. <u>Not</u> against the House. Which simply hosts the games (i.e., provides the space, tables and chairs, decks of cards, professional dealers, and so on). And takes a modest cut of the pot at the end of each hand for doing so. Which is a lot more like the situation you find in the financial industry.

If you're an experienced Poker player, you may sit down at one of the tables and join the game. Because you believe that your Poker skills will enable you to influence the outcome of most hands in your favor. In other words, you become a "Player" (which is like being a "Professional Investor" in the financial industry).

But you have another option.

In most casino Poker Rooms, "Side Betting" is a common practice. Players often place side bets among themselves about who's going to win the next hand (the outcome of which they can presumably influence with their Poker skills). Just like CEOs and other top management insiders of publicly traded corporations. Who can influence the movements of their firm's stock and bond prices by their control over its earnings (and the various accounting tricks they can use to manipulate these earnings).

Similarly, the people who visit casino Poker Rooms simply to watch the games ("Spectators") often place side bets among themselves about the winner of the next hand. But since they're unable to influence the hand's outcome (not being Players), their bets are basically "Pure Plays" in which their betting decisions simply reflect their estimates of the raw **Probabilities** (as in a straightforward "Heads or Tails" coin-flipping game). So they're in the position, as Bettors, of being "Outside Speculators," with no influence over who wins the next hand.

Let's suppose you choose to be a Spectator and sit down near one of the Poker tables where a "tournament game" of **Texas Hold'Em Poker** is in progress, and 6 Players are seated around the table. (In a tournament game, the Players buy their seats in advance for the same flat price. Start the game with each having the same dollar amount of chips in front of them. And can't leave the game until they've lost all their chips. So a single Player is going to end up as the Big Winner. Holding all the chips he and the other Players started with.)

Let's suppose further that you <u>don't recognize</u> any of these Players and know nothing about their Poker skills. So your <u>safest initial assumption</u> is that each Player has the same chance of winning the next hand—i.e., 1 chance out of 6. And the same chance of losing, or 5 chances out of 6. These chances translate into a <u>Win Probability</u> of about 16.7 Percent for each Player and a <u>Loss Probability</u> of 83.3 Percent for each Player.

This doesn't seem to offer you any opportunities for profitable bets.

<u>Unless</u>, that is, one of the other Spectators is willing to offer you highly favorable <u>Payoff Odds</u> if you bet on one particular Player. If these Payoff Odds are 10 to 1, for example, you can win $10 for every $1 you bet. Therefore, in raw terms, you have a 16.7 Percent probability of winning $10 if you bet on the designated Player vs. an 83.3 Percent probability of losing your $1. In other words, your **Expected Value** of a <u>win</u> (i.e., the dollar amount <u>times</u> its probability) is $1.67, while your Expected Value of a <u>loss</u> is only $0.83 (i.e., $1 <u>times</u> 83.3 Percent). So the Expected Value of your <u>profit</u> is $0.84 ($1.67 <u>minus</u> $0.83).

Depending on your personal <u>Risk Preference</u>, you may decide that this is a sufficiently profitable bet to be worth taking.

On the other hand, you'll want to ask yourself what <u>special knowledge</u> the other Spectator has that makes him willing to offer you such apparently favorable Payoff Odds.

Are there any ways you can refine your initial assumption about the win/lose probabilities?

Yes indeed.

One way is to simply watch half-a-dozen or so hands being played and see which Player (or two) seems to be dominating the action. Then make a subjective judgment about doubling, tripling, or whatever that Player's initial Win Probability (while reducing the Win Probabilities for the less-dominant Players). You can even write down the empirical rankings for all six Players in each of a number of hands based on how long they stayed in each hand, and do some fast computations with your pocket calculator.

Another way is to look at the relative sizes of the chip stacks in front of each Player. If one Player's chip stack looks to be roughly twice as large as the next largest, this can be evidence of that Player's superior Poker Skills relative to the other Players. So you raise his Win Probability accordingly.

But suppose you recognize at the outset that one of the six Players is **Doyle Brunson, Jennifer Harman,** or some other highly regarded <u>Poker Maven</u>. These Mavens tend to win a Significant Percentage of the hands they play. So you reflect this by assigning them a <u>higher</u> initial Win Probability and reducing the initial Win Probabilities for the other five Players accordingly.

Then you <u>refine</u> the Maven's Win Probability (up or down) by checking the relative size of his chip stack, seeing how well he does as subsequent hands are played, and so on. Writing everything down and making fast computations as you go.

And placing most of your bets on the Maven winning (which is usually the <u>safest</u> bet). But possibly adjusting the <u>size</u> of each bet by how well he's doing as the game proceeds and what kind of Payoff Odds you're getting from the other Spectators.

Now suppose the Poker Maven at the table is Jennifer Harman but her chip stack is the <u>smallest</u> of any of the Players.

Your knee-jerk assumption is that she's having a Bad Night and merits a low Win Probability.

But then you remember that Jennifer has an interesting habit of coming back from being low man on the chip count to end up as the game's Big Winner. So you watch her closely as the game proceeds to see whether she's going to start one of her famous "<u>runs-of-wins</u>" that progressively knock the other Players out of the game and turn her into the Big Winner. And if you see this start to happen, you immediately place a series of larger-than-usual bets that she'll win the next hand, and the next, and so on. While trying to get the other Spectators to give you more favorable Payoff Odds—to reflect her sub-par performance thus far.

So it goes.

Two points stand out about this little Poker example:

137

1. One Point is the <u>astonishing resemblance</u> of the monitoring and probability-adjustment techniques used by serious Poker game Spectators to those used by <u>Outside Speculators</u> placing bets on securities in the financial markets. This resemblance is no accident. Because the basic principles of betting on both types of "games" are the same. Except that, to an increasing extent, even so-called "amateur" Speculators in the financial markets use online PCs to automatically monitor in real time the price movements of financial securities, crunch the resulting numbers, and feed them into more or less sophisticated "automated models" to compute ever-changing win and loss probabilities.

2. The Second Point is the relatively <u>large numbers of variables</u> you have to keep track of. By monitoring how their inter-relationships and relative impacts are constantly changing. And accommodating the effect of unpredictable "qualitative variables" (like Jennifer Harman's habit of enjoying "runs-of-wins" when she seems to be having a bad night at the Poker table). This is especially true of the markets for financial securities. So during the years leading up to the beginning of 2009, many financial firms bowed to the temptation to "oversimplify" their "Value-at-Risk" models. If only to provide easily graspable "numbers" that their top managers could understand (or pretend to). With the result that too many of these models turned out to be less than worthless when the proverbial shit hit the fan. Contributing to the general meltdown they were supposed to warn people against.

■ ■ ■

"Value at Risk"

A major concern of most serious gamblers is their potential **Drawdown.**

This is the maximum portion of their gambling stakes they can expect to lose if they get stuck with a string of losing bets. So they devote a great deal of their attention to sensible <u>Money Management</u> in order to minimize Drawdowns.

In its most elegant form, Money Management uses various mathematical formulas to determine an "Optimal Bet." With "Optimal" being defined as that <u>percentage of their gambling stake</u> to devote to any particular bet. This <u>minimizes</u> their Drawdown risk while still enabling them to make money.

Math wizard **Edward Thorp** is the person most associated with this approach to Money Management in the gambling world. He's most famous for having developed a **Blackjack Card-Counting** technique during the 1950s that could give savvy players an edge over the casino. In 1962, he published a best-selling book describing it (titled *Beat the Dealer*), which made him unwelcome in all the world's casinos.

So he turned to Wall Street in 1964. Where he established a hedge fund using his (for those days) "sophisticated" Money-Management techniques. Which was very successful. Until he ran afoul of Federal Prosecutor **Rudy Giuliani's** racket-busting crusade in the late 1980s. And had to retire with a considerable fortune.

Needless to say, the issue of Drawdown became a matter of increasing concern to Wall Street managers as securities trading began accounting for an ever-larger share of their firms' profits. And this coincided with the arrival on Wall Street of the Rocket Scientists. Who could get up to speed very quickly in the new math-oriented theories emerging from the academic world.

So Wall Street managers responsible for trading operations (who may have been former traders themselves, or simply Power Players who had conned their way into high-paying management jobs, but in any case had no math literacy beyond Long Division) found themselves wondering:

"How much could our firm lose next week from all our outstanding trades?"

To which the Rocket Scientists responded that they could come up with new Value-at-Risk models to answer this question. Which they did with astonishing speed. Enabling them to say to the manager:

"We're 95 Percent confident that the firm <u>can't</u> lose more than $100 next week on its $10,000 in currently outstanding trades." (Except, of course, that the actual numbers were usually so much larger as to be mind-numbing to Normal People.)

This is another way of saying that *"the probability is <u>95 Percent</u> that the firm's maximum potential loss next week won't exceed <u>One Percent</u> of its outstanding trades."*

Or put even more clearly, *"There's only a <u>Five Percent chance</u> that next week's maximum potential loss will be greater than <u>One Percent</u> of the firm's outstanding trades."*

Numbers like this were very comforting to the manager. He could report to his boss that everything was under control in the trading room. Loss risks were no greater than One Percent. Too small to worry about. And maybe the firm should even consider laying on <u>more</u> and <u>larger</u> trades to take advantage of the potential for additional low-risk profits.

But if the numbers seemed a bit more worrisome, the manager could advise his boss that he was already planning to close out some trades so the firm could "get closer to home" (a phrase attributed to J. P. Morgan's **Dennis Featherstone**, an early and aggressive proponent of using such Value-at-Risk models to guide his firm's risk-management activities). All seemingly rational and prudent.

Value-at-Risk models became increasingly popular among Wall Street firms during the 1990s. Initially, Rocket Scientists in these firms based them on an academic concept known as **"Modern Portfolio Theory."** Which grocer's son and math-geek **Harry Markowitz** had developed during the 1950s as a dissertation subject for his Ph.D. in Economics at the University of Chicago. For which he shared the 1990 **Nobel Memorial Prize in Economics** with Merton Miller and William Sharp.

Markowitz's schtick was to develop a "mathematically elegant" way to construct Efficient portfolios of common stocks. With "Efficient" meaning that the portfolio as a whole would generate "the highest **Return** for a given level of **Risk.**" Or, conversely, would enjoy "the lowest level of **Risk** for a given **Return.**"

He did this by selecting stocks whose returns were Correlated with each other in such a way that any Loss in one stock would be automatically offset by Gains in one or more other stocks.

Needless to say, the computational challenges of crunching the vast array of numbers required to construct such portfolios were exceedingly heroic in those days. When computers were few and far between. Were large beasts powered by old-fashioned vacuum tubes. And had less memory and speed than one of today's lower-priced laptops.

So Markowitz had to make some extremely critical "simplifying assumptions" in developing Modern Portfolio Theory. Such as assuming that:

- **All relative changes in securities prices are Random, Unbiased, Independent of Each Other, and Perfectly Match the "Normal Distribution" of the Bell-Shaped Gaussian curve.**

Much empirical research done in the years since Markowitz published his model have established that the percentage price changes in most securities most of the time are none of these things. In the Real World, these changes tend to be mostly Non-Random, Biased, Dependent on Each Other, and Don't Fit the Normal Distribution.

But assuming that these fairyland shortcuts were true allowed Markowitz and Wall Street's Rocket Scientists to make use of the wealth of mathematical equations generated by several centuries of detailed work on <u>Gaussian Probability Theory</u> by a number of famous mathematicians.

• **Securities prices change "Continuously.**

In the Real World, of course, we know that securities prices at any given moment are the result of many discrete transactions made by individual buyers and sellers (often with middlemen greasing the wheels). Sometimes these transactions occur in big clumps that take place more or less simultaneously. Other times they occur one-by-one, separated by distinct periods of time. And most securities don't trade at all on weekends, holidays, and large portions of the normal trading day when their markets are closed. So the reality is that securities prices actually change "Discontinuously." By fits and starts.

But the assumption of "Continuous Change" enables Rocket Scientists to measure price changes with the mathematically convenient "Continuous Compounding" formula. Even though it shows relative price changes that rarely match the simple "percentage change" formula we learned in Junior High School.

• **The Best Measure of a security's "Riskiness" is the <u>Volatility</u> of its relative price changes, as computed by using the "Continuous Compounding" formula.**

We all know what "Risk" is. It's the chance of losing your shirt if you make the wrong bet. What could be simpler?

But Wall Street's Rocket Scientists want to be able to assign a precise "Probability Percentage number" to Risk. And it's mathematically easier to do this if you claim that "Risk" is the same thing as "the Volatility of continuous changes in a security's price" (like claiming that the Empire State Building is the "same thing" as Mount Whitney). With Volatility being measured by the price change's statistical <u>Variance</u>. Or its <u>Standard Deviation</u> (which is simply the Square Root of the Variance). Because <u>then</u> you can use the Gaussian probability tables in the back of statistics textbooks (or the probability functions conveniently built into Excel software) to quickly find a nice, neat probability Percentage Number to assign to Risk. Always assuming, of course, that the relative changes in question are Normally Distributed (which isn't true for most securities, but who cares?).

Also, if the probability of winning a coin-flip bet is the same as losing, then both outcomes are said to be "equally Risky." Which most Normal People feel lacks a necessary element of Common Sense.

- **A wealth of time-series data on historical daily prices exists for most securities, showing how they performed in good times and bad.**

This may be true for certain physical commodities like Cotton and Wheat that have been trading for a century or more. And for some old-line corporations, whose common stocks have traded for many decades.

But it certainly isn't true for the thousands of new **Derivatives** that became immensely popular as trading vehicles in the years leading up to 2008. This may be okay if you want to evaluate the historical default risk of a derivative like <u>Collateralized Mortgage Obligations</u> during the recent boom in housing prices. But you're pretty much out of luck if you're interested in their default risk when housing prices are falling. They're simply "too new" to have this kind of track record.

Be that as it may, Wall Street's Rocket Scientists had a field day coming up with Value-at-Risk models that could show trading managers (with simple numbers and in words of one syllable) whether their portfolios of bets on financial securities were free of any worrisome Time Bombs.

All reflecting the fairyland assumptions that Harry Markowitz had built into Modern Portfolio Theory. Which became known in the trade by the more elegant (if obscure) name of **"The Mean-Variance Model."** (With <u>Mean</u> referring to a portfolio's "Average Return" and <u>Variance</u> to its statistically computed "Risk"). Or, in simple terms, a **"Return-Risk Model"** (but you usually don't win Nobel Prizes by making things seem simple).

Needless to say, Wall Street's passionate embrace of Value-at-Risk models wasn't entirely free of criticism. But most of this came from radical academics. And other "non-mainstream" iconoclasts like **Nassim Taleb.** Who, with his well-honed talent for invective, labeled the whole thing as "*Charlatanism.*" Not that this mattered when Wall Street firms were making money hand over fist with the newfangled Derivatives.

So most of this intellectual carping over the shortcomings of Value-at-Risk models made little impression on Wall Street.

■ ■ ■

"The Model that Blew Up the World"

But the Rocket Scientists couldn't ignore the practical problem posed by lack of adequate historical data for new Derivatives. Especially when their increasing popularity as trading vehicles caused Wall Street's top managers to demand "effective risk models" to cover them.

Fortunately, a savior arrived in the person of a brilliant Chinese statistical mathematician named **David X. Li**. Who surfaced in 2000 as a researcher at **JPMorgan Chase**. When he published a landmark paper about a wildly esoteric statistical artifact known as a "**Gaussian Copula**," which he believed could be adapted to model Value at Risk for the new derivatives without requiring extensive historical data.

The underlying logic of Li's schtick mirrored the age-old debate about whether "**Fundamental Analysis**" or "**Technical Analysis**" was the best way to "pick winning stocks."

- **Fundamental Analysis** insists that the only way to determine whether a company's stock might be a "good buy" is to estimate its "Intrinsic Value" (i.e., what it should be worth). By studying its financial performance, capital structure, sales and profit trends, market strength, and a host of other fundamental information. If this Intrinsic Value is greater than the stock's current market price, then buy it and wait for other stock market investors to (inevitably) wise up. Pushing its market price up closer to its Intrinsic Value as a buying binge develops. Assuring you of a nice profit.

  (The acknowledged gurus of Fundamental Analysis are Ben Graham and David Dodd, two Columbia University

145

professors who codified it back in the 1930s in their book *Security Analysis,* whose current edition is the treasured Bible of Fundamentalist types. Graham and Dodd's most famous protégé is a guy from Omaha named **Warren Buffett.** Whose three-decade track record of stock market success isn't exactly what you'd call "unimpressive." But that's neither here nor there for our immediate purposes. Or, come to think of it, maybe it is.)

- **Technical Analysis** insists that all relevant "fundamental information" about a company is <u>already</u> reflected in the current price of its stock. So you should concentrate on the stock price <u>itself</u>. Monitor its movements. Study the typical patterns these movements form over time. Learn when they signal a buy opportunity that you can make money from. Etc. You get the idea.

(There's no shortage of books—and pricey "trading systems"—based on Technical Analysis and its many "indicators." This has led to at least a few wags insisting that *"more money has been made selling books and trading systems <u>about</u> it than has ever been made by actually <u>practicing</u> it."* But before you succumb to this facile cynicism, read a few books by technician **Larry Williams.** Then look at his trading record. Which may leave you wondering if Williams might not have made a private deal with **Satan.**)

Anyway, the point is that David Li used the basic logic behind Technical Analysis to argue that assessing the <u>Safety</u> of various **Collateralized Debt Obligations** <u>didn't require</u> detailed "fundamental analysis" of their underlying debt securities and default histories.

Instead, all you had to do was <u>monitor the trading prices</u> of the **Credit**

Default Swaps that supposedly <u>insured</u> these Collateralized Debt Obligations against defaults by their underlying debt securities.

So if the trading prices of these Credit Default Swaps <u>rose</u>, the markets were assuming <u>higher</u> probabilities of default by the debt securities backing the Collateralized Debt Obligations in question. Making the protection offered by their Credit Default Swaps <u>more valuable</u>. And vice versa.

In other words, the <u>market prices</u> of various Credit Default Swaps were <u>closely correlated</u> with the "relative safety" of their Collateralized Debt Obligations. Which made it a comparatively simple matter to use **Correlation Numbers** as reliable proxies for the <u>Risk Probabilities</u> of these CDOs.

And this approach would work for <u>any kind</u> of Collateralized Debt Obligation. Whether backed by pools of home mortgages (when they're known as Collateralized <u>Mortgage</u> Obligations). Or automobile loans. Or credit card balances. Or mortgages on office buildings and shopping malls. Whatever.

Li's groundbreaking paper backed up this logic with some mathematically elegant equations that quickly won the hearts of Wall Street Rocket Scientists. Leading to rapid development of new Value-at-Risk models based on the apparent correlation between <u>Credit Default Swap prices</u> and <u>Default Risk</u>.

Inevitably, these models caused Wall Street firms to focus increasingly on Credit Default Swaps themselves as "hot new financial products" with high-profit potential. So they worked overtime developing new issues of these Derivatives. Persuading Wall Street's rating firms to give them high safety ratings on the strength of their seemingly impressive Correlation Numbers. Selling them to a wide range of eager investors. And making active trading markets in them. Confident that their impressive Correlation Numbers assured that they were the next thing to being "Risk Free."

Until, by the end of 2007, the total <u>face value</u> of all outstanding Credit Default Swaps had grown to <u>$62 Trillion</u> (nearly <u>70 times</u> what it had been in 2001). While the face value of the Collateralized Debt Obligations they supposedly "insured" had grown a much more modest 17 times, to $4.7 Trillion in 2006.

From time to time, Li would caution people against "reading too much" into his Gaussian Copula concept. But he came across as such an "ivory tower math nerd" that few people paid any attention to these warnings.

At least, not until housing prices turned south in 2007. Causing defaults on vast numbers of the sub-prime mortgages backing Collateralized Debt Obligations to skyrocket (see **Chapter 5** for the details of this story). Which turned all those encouraging Correlation Numbers into so much chopped liver. Because it became apparent that their supposed <u>Stability</u> as risk proxies was a childish myth. So the market prices of these derivatives tanked.

This is what led to the enforced write-downs (described back in **Chapter 2**) by so many financial firms like Bear Stearns, Lehman Brothers, Merrill Lynch, and AIG in their huge portfolios of what became "toxic waste" derivatives. Precipitating the Financial Meltdown of 2008 and all that followed.

With David Li fleeing back to China, where he refused to say anything further about his Gaussian Copula model. Which might truly be called **"The Model that Blew Up the World"** (or at least lit the fuse).

It's tempting to imagine what a crowd-pleasing Hollywood suspense movie all this would make. With Li being secretly groomed as a "Financial Saboteur" by sinister counter-revolutionary forces in China (dreaming of a return to the days of Chairman Mao, perhaps). To ingratiate himself in Wall Street with his mathematical brilliance. Until he was in a position to "Wreck the American Economy" with his model and destroy its ability to continue as China's Number 1 export market. Thereby ending China's romance with Capitalism (known in Beijing as "Socialism with Chinese Characteristics") and bring about a return to Great Leap Forward days.

Even better would be to have this movie made by director Ang Lee, who's especially sensitive to the underlying "Mysticism" of such things. Causing him to convert the lead character into an enigmatic <u>female</u> Rocket Scientist whose math brilliance is exceeded only by her compelling beauty. Played by Hong Kong's glorious Michelle Yeoh, whose vast Asian eyes look as if they contain all the impenetrable secrets of Life itself. Flying away in the end, clad in appropriate martial arts robes. To disappear forever into the endless sunset beyond the South China Sea.

■ ■ ■

The Impact of Technology

Technology?

You mean, like those fancy Mechanical Robots that automatically handle, in a matter of seconds, complicated automobile assembly tasks that once took a gang of twenty sweaty guys armed with wrenches and welding torches five minutes to complete?

(So that, through the magic of free market capitalism, these twenty guys now ride herd over new collections of robots on the greatly expanded assembly lines needed to meet the rising demand for the higher-quality American automobiles produced at lower unit costs by this automated robot technology. Wearing pristine clean jumpsuits as they push buttons and monitor computer screens. While being paid a higher hourly wage that reflects their much higher productivity.)

Well, yeah.

But the impact of Technology isn't limited to making better products at a faster rate in modern factories. It's also revolutionized the World of Finance. By linking financial types together in a global Electronic Communications Web that lets every financial guy know in real time what every other guy is doing. Buying. Selling. Moving Money this way and that. Here. There. Everywhere.

Once upon a time, the trading rooms of Wall Street firms were fairly leisurely places. With traders sitting quietly at their rows of wooden desks, puffing away on cigars. Scanning pages of yesterday's securities prices typewritten overnight by the firm's typing pool. Periodically glancing at the Huge Blackboard covering the wall at the far end of the room. On which eager clerks wearing old-fashioned telephone headsets chalked up the latest transactions prices for securities their firm followed. Trying not to fall too far behind during sudden bursts of trading activity.

From time to time, a trader might notice an interesting price wiggle on the Blackboard for one of his securities. Note this on his yellow legal pad. Compare it with the typewritten page showing yesterday's prices for that security. See how it fit his copy of the security's hand-drawn price chart covering the last month. Wait for his experienced gut to tell him whether this price wiggle might signal the possibility of a buy or sell. Or simply wait for more information.

As he sits back in his desk chair to ponder all this. And relights his cigar.

But today, all this has changed. The world's (now smoke-free) trading rooms are all wired together in an elaborate Electronic Web. With each being instantly fed up-to-the-second data on the buy/sell activity of all other trading rooms. Not to mention constant alerts about the automated bets being placed by their firm's elaborately mathematical computer trading models that continually search the world for profitable price anomalies to exploit.

Today's gum-chomping or candy-munching traders sit with their eyes glued to banks of computer monitors on their desks. Watching the securities they follow being traded in Real Time. With their firms' trading models demanding permission to up the bets they've just placed by 10 or 20 times the programmed limit to fully exploit the latest trading opportunity.

So <u>now</u> you see it on a screen. <u>Now</u> you make a decision. <u>Now</u> you punch a few buttons on your keyboard. And it's <u>done</u>. With the rest of the trading world knowing in an instant what kind of bet you've just placed.

No time to think. Consult charts. Consider what your gut may be wanting to tell you. The world's turning much too fast for such old-fashioned lifestyles. Do it <u>Now</u>. Before this second passes into History.

And you miss this chance to fatten your year-end bonus.

Obviously, this revolution in Technology is here to stay. And it greatly magnifies our power to <u>Move Money</u> with maximum efficiency.

But it also magnifies our power to **Make Mistakes**. By something like 10,000 times. With consequences that can run into Trillions of Dollars.

In terms of sheer dollar losses, the "Fall of 2008" (along with the fall of so many other illusions) was probably the greatest financial disaster in world history. And its cost in wrecked human lives is still being counted.

Needless to say, it would be foolish to claim that this disaster was "caused" by New Technology. It had a number of causes, most of which got stuck together with the usual gluey mix of **"human greed and witlessness"** that have traditionally led to so much grief.

But the financial community's failure to appreciate the full implications of wiring itself together with the new Electronic Communications Technology surely made the disaster worse.

Just as during the first decade of the Twentieth Century. When Europe's Military Professionals failed to appreciate the full implications of Hiram Maxim's dramatic New Technology of the **Automatic Machine Gun**. Which enabled a single soldier to spray a battlefield with heavy lead bullets nearly one-third of an inch in diameter at the rate of 600 per minute. Greatly magnifying the terrible slaughter of World War I.

The implications of Maxim's technology may best be illustrated by the catastrophic **21 Percent one-day death rate** among the 100,000 British soldiers of Lord Kitchener's All-Volunteer army. Who went over the top against German machine guns on July 1, 1916 during the <u>First Day On The Somme</u>.

While another **36 Percent** lay bleeding and gasping for breath in the craters of No-Man's-Land by the end of the day. Whose numbers totally swamped the British Army's medical services. Resulting in still more deaths among the wounded.

As British Field Marshall **Sir Douglas Haig** continued to insist on the inevitable success of his battlefield strategy. Because it was divinely inspired by his "personal conversations with God" (possibly while imbibing too generously of his distillery family's famous Scotch Whiskey).

That sunlit day's overall **57 Percent casualty rate** broke the back of young British manhood (and the young British women who were left widows or lifetime spinsters) for decades to come. And started Imperial Britain on its downhill road to irrelevancy as a World Leader.

Was the **Fall of 2008** our generation's **First Day On The Somme?**

And can we learn something from it?

■ ■ ■

(Overheard late one night in a Lower Manhattan Designer Beer bar:)

"Hey. Did you hear about the investment banker's wife who found out he was painting plaster models of fruit slices to make them look real?"

"No. Tell me."

"She tried eating one of his orange slices."

"Yeah?"

"Turned her completely to stone."

"Must have been all the Vitamin C. So what did he do?"

"What else? Gave her a fresh coat of paint and put her on the shelf next to the other fruit slices."

■ ■ ■

Chapter 5
WHAT HAPPENED: HOUSING AND MORTGAGES

It's a white whale, I say. And his name is Moby Dick.
—Herman Melville

Those of you who've seen Frank Capra's classic 1946 movie *It's a Wonderful Life* (at least once, since it's been a Christmas Holiday perennial on television for decades) will remember one of its most famous sequences.

George Bailey (played by James Stewart) runs a one-horse **Savings and Loan** firm in the All-American town of Bedford Falls. And one day he's confronted by a group of his depositors who've come to withdraw their savings money because they've become nervous about its safety. So he must try to clue them in on the realities of the thrift business.

He explains that he doesn't keep their savings dollars lying idle in a safe in his back office. Instead, he's **invested** most of these dollars. By granting each one of them affordable mortgages on the homes they own.

So Sam's money is in Chuck's house. And Chuck's money is in Dick's house. And Dick's money is in Sam's house . . .

So it goes. With each of them able to own the homes they live in instead of having to pay rent to Old Man Potter, the hard-hearted villain who owns the leading commercial bank in Bedford Falls and most everything else worth owning in town.

■ ■ ■

153

George Bailey's Mortgage Model

What George was trying to describe to his nervous depositors is how the home mortgage business worked in the **"Good Old Days"** (or were they really so good?).

- A local Commercial Bank, Savings and Loan, or other thrift institution would encourage its customers to place their excess cash **"On Deposit"** in the institution to keep it safe from being lost or stolen.

- After setting aside a prudent reserve to cover normal everyday withdrawals, the institution would <u>invest</u> the rest of these deposit dollars. And in George's case, a significant portion of these investments took the form of **Home Mortgages** granted to his depositors. Who would make monthly payments of interest and principal on their mortgages to the institution until they were paid off. During which time, the institution would keep these mortgages on its balance sheet as **Assets**.

The pluses and minuses of this simple model are obvious enough.

In granting home mortgages, George's thrift institution was exposing itself to **Risk**. There was always the *"Possibility"* that a home buyer could, at some future time, become unable (for whatever reason) to keep making the monthly payments on his mortgage (known in the trade as **"Defaulting on the Mortgage"**). And since the institution kept the mortgage on its books as an Asset, it remained exposed to this Risk until the mortgage was paid off.

So it took steps to protect itself. By trying to make the *"Possibility of Default"* as small as possible.

- **First:** The institution would insist that any home mortgage be "**Secured**" by the house itself. This gave the institution the legal right to seize the house from an owner who Defaulted on his mortgage, through a process known as **Foreclosure**. The institution could then seek to recover all the money still owed to it on the mortgage by selling the house in the open market. With any excess cash from such a sale being turned over to the homeowner. But Foreclosure is a terrible nuisance that most lending institutions would rather avoid. So they sought to protect themselves in other ways as well.

- **Second:** The institution would require the home buyer to cover a significant portion (like 20 Percent) of the purchase price with his own cash—known in the trade as a "**Down Payment**." Therefore, the institution would be lending considerably less than 100 Percent of the house's current market value. Which increased the likelihood that the institution could recover through the foreclosure process all the money owed to it on the mortgage. Also, the institution believed that requiring the home owner to have some significant "**skin in the game**" would encourage the owner to make every effort to avoid ever defaulting on his mortgage payments.

- **Third:** The institution would obtain an appraisal of the house's **Current Market Value** from a qualified independent real estate appraiser. It would use this appraisal to determine that the house's purchase price was no greater than its market value, as further assurance of being able to recover the mortgage money due it through foreclosure and sale.

- **Fourth:** The institution would require the home buyer to maintain an adequate **Casualty Insurance Policy** on the house to assure that it could be fully repaired if damaged by fire, storm, or other destructive Acts of God.

- **Fifth:** The institution would require the home buyer to show proof of **Stable Family Income**. This would demonstrate whether he could afford the mortgage payments and other home ownership costs without undue strain.

- **Sixth:** To the extent feasible, the institution would seek to grant mortgages **only to its own customers** or to others with whom it had personal or business relationships so it could be confident that these home buyers were of good character and were safe credit risks.

Figure 5.1 shows a simple diagram of this traditional home mortgage model.

FIGURE 5.1. "GEORGE BAILEY'S" MORTGAGE MODEL

All well and good.

But once these local thrift institutions had invested all their available deposit funds, they couldn't grant any new mortgages until the total amount of their deposits increased or some of the existing mortgages they held were paid off. This placed a limit on mortgage availability at any given time. Which became a <u>ceiling</u> on the number of local families who could buy their own homes in any given year.

In purely economic terms, this had some negative consequences.

- When local thrift institutions <u>ran short of funds</u> for granting new home mortgages, the local market of families actively seeking to buy homes <u>became smaller</u> than it would otherwise have been.

- A <u>smaller</u> home-buying market forced local construction companies to build <u>fewer</u> new homes than they would have liked to.

- Since the construction of new homes is a <u>major component</u> of Gross Domestic Product, <u>less home construction</u> meant that the level of economic activity in the region was <u>lower</u> than it could otherwise have been.

- Less overall economic activity meant <u>less income</u> for the region's families. Who therefore bought <u>less</u> of other consumer products. Which caused private business firms making these consumer products to <u>produce less</u> than they could. So they hired fewer workers, leading to <u>less employment</u> in the region. And they also bought <u>fewer</u> raw materials and other supplies from private business firms that sell such goods. Causing <u>these</u> firms to hire fewer workers, leading to <u>still less</u> employment. Thereby (a classic example of **Circular Flow**) <u>further reducing income</u> for the region's families. And so it goes. Round and round.

- Since the nation's GDP is simply the total of all its local GDPs, less GDP at the local level inevitably meant less GDP at the national level. So the entire nation was "poorer" than it could otherwise have been.

Also, these ceilings clashed with something deeply embedded in the American Culture. Which is a **Grand Passion** for home ownership that's unmatched anywhere else in the world. And like so many Grand Passions, this one contained the seeds for major financial and social turmoil unless it was prudently regulated.

■ ■ ■

The New Deal's Mortgage Model

During the 1930s, the Roosevelt Administration's highest priority was to stabilize and stimulate the American economy in order to bring the nation out of the Great Depression.

One way to help accomplish this was to <u>increase</u> the level of new home construction activity, which has a <u>strong multiplier impact</u> on Gross Domestic Product. But this required making it possible for <u>more</u> American families to buy their own homes. Which, in turn, meant increasing the <u>availability</u> of home mortgages.

A clever way to increase the availability of home mortgages was to establish a strong **Secondary Market** for <u>existing</u> mortgages held by thrift institutions like George Bailey's.

- This Secondary Market would give such institutions the option of <u>selling</u> the mortgages they held for **Cash**, rather than having to keep them on their books until they were paid off.

- The institutions could then use this <u>fresh cash</u> to grant **new mortgages** to home buyers. And sell <u>these</u> new mortgages in the Secondary Market for still <u>more</u> fresh cash to grant still more mortgages. Thereby greatly increasing the availability of home mortgages. This would increase the number of American families who could buy their own homes and therefore stimulate new home construction.

In 1938, the federal government took the lead in creating such a Secondary Market for home mortgages. By establishing a commercial corporation called the **Federal National Mortgage Association** (popularly known as "**Fannie Mae**") as a wholly owned federal entity to <u>buy existing mortgages</u> from lending institutions. This worked so well that, in 1970, the federal government established a second such corporation for the same purpose. And called this one the **Federal Home Loan Mortgage Corporation** (or "Freddie Mac").

The federal government provided each corporation with its initial capital to buy existing home mortgages through direct grants. And it could have continued this subsidy process by providing more such grants at regular intervals.

But it had a better idea.

- The federal government authorized Fannie Mae and Freddie Mac to <u>issue their own bonds.</u> That were secured by payments of interest and principal on the home mortgages they'd bought from private thrift institutions and therefore owned. These bonds became known as **Collateralized Mortgage Obligations**. And as we saw in Chapter 2, they eventually became the equivalent of Scarlet Women.

- The cash generated by these mortgage-backed bond issues expanded the capital of Fannie Mae and Freddie Mac so they could increase their purchases of home mortgages without any further grants from the federal government. So they became, in effect, **Self-Funding Enterprises**.

- Their bonds were never intended to be **Legal Obligations** of the federal government. But over time, the perception grew in the bond market that the federal government would always stand behind Fannie Mae and Freddie Mac debt if push ever came to shove. Therefore, investors came to think of these bonds as "virtually as safe as regular U.S. Treasury securities," while paying slightly more interest. So they became very popular among risk-averse investors.

- By 1989, the self-supporting nature of Fannie Mae and Freddie Mac enabled the federal government to sell its entire ownership in them to the community of private investors. So they became wholly private commercial enterprises. But the perception that they were "**Implicitly Backed**" by the federal government remained unchanged.

Figure 5.2, on opposite page, shows a diagram of the "New Deal" mortgage model.

The success of Fannie Mae and Freddie Mac in establishing a thriving Secondary Market for home mortgages had four interesting consequences that played a major role in bringing on the Economic Crisis:

The **First Consequence** was that it gave rise to the concept of **Collateralized Debt Obligations** (or **CDOs**).

In their simplest form, CDOs were bonds issued by Fannie Mae and Freddie Mac that were secured ("collateralized") by the home mortgages

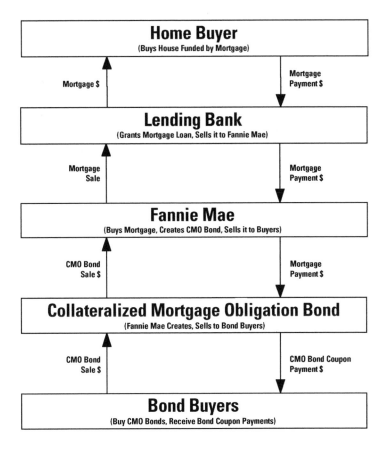

FIGURE 5.2. "NEW DEAL" MORTGAGE MODEL

they had bought from private thrift institutions. As such, CDOs were **Derivative Securities** because their value was "Derived From" the mortgages that secured them.

But beginning in the late 1980s, Wall Street (ever hungry for more products to sell) began to realize that CDOs could <u>also</u> be secured by other debt securities besides home mortgages. Such as corporate bonds. And automobile loans. And consumer credit card debt. And so on.

We'll look at the implications of this realization in a minute.

The **Second Consequence** of Fannie Mae and Freddie Mac's success was the <u>revolutionary change</u> it brought about in the basic business model under which thrift institutions made money in the home mortgage market.

- Under the <u>Old Model</u> that bankers like George Bailey followed, these institutions both **Originated** and **Invested In** home mortgages. So they received **Fee Income** from originating mortgages. Plus **Interest Income** from the mortgages they owned and therefore had much of their capital invested in.

- But the <u>New Deal Model</u> changed everything. Being able to sell the mortgages they originated in the Secondary Market meant that <u>Fee Income for originating mortgages</u> became much more important to these institutions. So the more mortgages they could originate (with the fresh cash they received from mortgage sales), the higher their Fee Income became. Until it more than replaced the Interest Income they lost by selling their mortgages. Thereby becoming an increasingly important source of revenue.

- <u>Also</u>, these thrift institutions earned **Mortgage Servicing Fees** on the mortgages they sold. They would receive payments of interest and principal from home owners and pass them on to the buyers of their mortgages—<u>after</u> subtracting their fee for "servicing the mortgages." This became another important source of revenue for these institutions.

So the new Business Model for thrift institutions became one of **originating as many home mortgages as possible** to maximize their Fee Income, and selling them off as quickly as possible (to maximize their Mortgage Servicing Fees). Even if this meant bending some of the traditional rules so more prospective home buyers would become eligible for mortgages. Just a little at first. Then more aggressively.

The **Third Consequence** of the New Deal Model was the increasing diffusion of traditional **Mortgage Risk.**

- As we've seen, thrift institutions incurred **Risk** in holding the mortgages they originated because of the possibility that some of these mortgages could **Default.** So the entire Mortgage Risk fell on the shoulders of these institutions.

- We saw how thrift institutions took a number of steps to minimize this Risk. Like ensuring that the price of the house being mortgaged was no greater than its assessed market value. Plus lending only a portion of this price to the home buyer (who had to cover the rest with his own cash in the form of a Down Payment). And making sure that the home buyer's monthly mortgage payments were a safely modest percentage of his documented family income. Not to mention restricting the mortgages they granted to their regular banking customers who were known to be of good character and safe credit risks.

- But once thrift institutions could sell the mortgages they originated in the Secondary Market, they <u>no longer had to be concerned</u> about Mortgage Risk. Sale of a mortgage meant that the <u>entire</u> Mortgage Risk passed automatically to the mortgage buyer.

- If the mortgage buyer assembled a pool of such mortgages and issued bonds secured by them (CDOs), the buyers of these bonds "functionally assumed" any Risk associated with the mortgages that secured them. Regardless of whether or not these bond buyers actually understood the nature and extent of the risk they were assuming.

- If these mortgaged-based CDOs were issued by Fannie Mae or Freddie Mac, they were assumed to be "implicitly guaranteed" by the federal government. So the perception grew that any risk associated with the mortgages securing Fannie Mae or Freddie Mac CDOs was actually the responsibility of the federal government.

Whenever credit risk becomes sufficiently diffused, it ceases to be perceived as "<u>true risk</u>" for practical purposes. Therefore, no one worries about taking any steps to protect himself against it. But perceptions are one thing. Reality is something else again. As we'll see in the next section.

The **Fourth Consequence** of the New Deal Model was how it changed the "<u>internal culture</u>" of Fannie Mae and Freddie Mac. Once they became privately owned underwriters of mortgage-backed securities and no longer expected to behave like green-eyeshade Washington bureaucracies, their internal cultures became little different from those of typical profit-maximizing Wall Street Big Swinging Dicks. And they (inevitably) began paying their top managers salaries typical of Wall Street rather than Pennsylvania Avenue. All of which (also inevitably) ultimately wrecked their finances and left them "wards of the Federal Government."

■ ■ ■

The Lascivines Run Wild

By <u>greatly increasing</u> the availability of home mortgages, the New Deal Model became a major factor in stimulating a huge rise in the home ownership rate among American families. Which soared from 44 Percent in 1940 to a peak of 69 Percent in 2005.

Also helpful were:

- <u>Favorable income tax benefits</u> for home owners (which amounted to federal subsidies).

- <u>Extra-cheap, no-down-payment mortgages</u> made available to millions of returning World War II veterans through the federal **G.I. Bill.** (Along with the Bill's generous income payments for attending college, these benefits had the effect of preventing returning veterans from swamping the nation's labor market during the immediate post-War period.)

- The <u>boost to metropolitan suburbanization</u> of the federal **Interstate Highway Program** during the 1960s and '70s. Many of these new highway links provided essential access to undeveloped suburban land for extensive new housing tracts.

- The <u>long-term rising trend of home prices</u>. Which made **Home Ownership** seem like a painless form of "family saving."

All these factors served to strengthen the passion for home ownership among the American public. But their impact was <u>greatly magnified</u> by the New Deal Model's revolution in home mortgage availability.

However, significant portions of the nation's population were excluded from participating in this revolution. Especially low-income "urban immigrants" from rural America and Puerto Rico seeking better economic opportunities. Who poured into the nation's central cities during the decades following World War II, as native-born urbanites with rising incomes fled to the new suburbs.

This led many mortgage lenders to **Redline** entire central city residential neighborhoods as "No-Mortgage" zones. And to impose penalty-level interest rates or fees that effectively excluded many lower-income families inside these zones from home ownership.

Yet the ethnically oriented nature of these home ownership exclusions was often more mindless than rational. Which had unrecognized costs for American prosperity generally.

(As illustrated by the so-called "**Decline of Central Cities**" during the 1970s and '80s. When large amounts of capital traditionally invested in urban housing fled to the suburbs. Leaving behind burned-out neighborhoods of abandoned residential buildings in places like New York City's South Bronx. Which had been surreptitiously "torched" by their owners for the insurance money.)

As it happens, one of the nation's most lucrative sources of export earnings from the rest of the world is **American Popular Music.** Which is almost entirely a product of the richly innovative culture of the **African-American Community.** Most of whose members now reside in the Black Ghettos of northern U.S. cities. But are descended from black slaves in the antebellum South (not to mention their white plantation owners like Colonial schnorrer Thomas Jefferson, who weren't exactly reluctant to practice widespread concubinage among the slave women they owned).

The roots of contemporary American Popular music in Rhythm & Blues, Jazz, and other generic African-American musical forms have given it a special zing that's made it the most popular kind of music in the world. So it would only be natural for a proverbial **Man From Mars,** after noticing the immense income this music generates, to assume that African-Americans must be among America's richest (and therefore most respected) ethnic groups.

But a classic feature of Capitalism is that the riches generated by innovative products too rarely flow to the "inventors" of those products. Instead, these riches tend to be monopolized by business-oriented types clever enough to exploit the commercial potential of such products.

This isn't an argument against just rewards for entrepreneurs. But it does suggest a certain caution in automatically assuming that members of low-income groups are "Indolent Natural Losers" in the American scheme of things, who produce nothing of value and therefore deserve their penury.

(Or have we been right all along in assuming that people who choose to squander their lives teaching children such irrelevancies as Reading and Arithmetic <u>deserve</u> to be paid only a miniscule fraction of the eight-figure incomes lavished on Wall Street types who create exotic new Derivatives for moving money from hand to hand?)

Be that as it may, the growing scope and power of the Civil Rights Movement caused the pervasiveness of these ethnically based home ownership exclusions to become a political issue that demanded corrective action. And since ethnically targeted actions were Constitutionally unacceptable, they had to be income targeted. So helping low-income families as a group achieve the All-American dream of owning their own homes became a political imperative that had to be addressed.

In theory, there were three ways to accomplish this:

- Follow the Western European practice of using direct government income subsidies and mechanisms like a much higher national Minimum Wage to <u>raise the incomes of these families to high enough levels</u> for them to qualify for home mortgages under existing regulations. (In effect, adopt capitalist hero Henry Ford's innovative approach for expanding the market base for his Model T automobiles. When he dramatically increased the wages of his assembly line workers so they could afford to buy the cars they produced.)

- Have government intervene in housing markets with down-payment subsidies and bargain-rate subsidized mortgages to <u>reduce actual out-of-pocket home ownership costs</u> for low-income families to levels they could afford under existing regulations. (Like an expanded version of the late-1940s federal program to support higher levels of private housing construction—by making it affordable for returning war veterans to buy their own homes through benefits provided under the G.I. Bill.)

- Bend existing regulations in imaginative ways so low-income families could qualify for mortgages with <u>no increases</u> in their existing incomes and <u>no reductions</u> in their out-of-pocket home ownership costs.

Needless to say, the first two possibilities seemed far too *Socialistic* to be seriously considered by Mainstream America. So the nation's only politically practical choice was to adopt the Third Way. And keep its collective fingers crossed that everything would somehow "work out." Or at least defer any problems to someone else's political watch.

Since American government is dominated by law school graduates, the inevitable result was an emphasis on Leninist-style "Command and Control" measures. This meant passing new laws to outlaw Redlining. To require banks to meet higher standards for "reinvesting in their depositor communities." And to impose other political directives that had the effect of corrupting the New Deal Model for home mortgages.

All this created three factors that helped to bring on the Economic Crisis:

THE FIRST FACTOR was an explosion of emphasis on the **Volume** of new mortgages being generated, because that's where the profits were. This greatly expanded the numbers of largely unregulated **Mortgage Brokers** (or Mortgage Bankers, depending on the state where you did business), whose middleman function was to match up home buyers seeking mortgages with lenders seeking to originate new mortgages to sell to Wall Street firms.

So thousands of slick salesmen, many exiled from back-alley used car lots by the proliferation of state anti-lemon laws, exchanged their checkered sports coats for conservative business suits. Filled out the one-page state applications for licenses as Mortgage Brokers. And started drumming up business among local real estate agencies (whose profits depended on the volume of home sales, and therefore easy mortgage availability) and hungry mortgage lenders.

If Frank Capra's *It's a Wonderful Life* were to be made today, its director would have to be an updated version of Capra's Poverty Row contemporary **Edgar G. Ulmer** (best known for his scathing 1946 low-budget film, *Detour*). Whose artistic soul had been hopelessly scarred by Central European cynicism.

So he would naturally turn George Bailey into a mortgage broker. A hungry lascivine willing and able to do anything to maximize his volume of mortgage originations.

Played to the smarmy hilt by a modern equivalent of shifty-eyed **Tom Neal.**

With George's impossibly "sweet-tempered" wife Mary converted into a reasonable facsimile of the terrifying **Ann Savage** (assuming such actresses still exist).

While Satan's glib-tongued angel Clarence (any current actor who can do a passable imitation of George Saunders) keeps goading George to fake his own suicide to escape the havoc he's sowing in the shattered Bedford Falls housing market. By fleeing in secret to Costa Rica with his ill-gotten fortune in mortgage fees.

Thereby assuring that the film's classic title will suitably impress intellectual audiences with its bitterly ironic tone.

Such a modern-day Edgar Ulmer would inundate us with a series of fast-paced sequences shot in George's cluttered office (to save money on sets). Showing us how he converts low-income home buyers with non-existent credit into qualified applicants for sub-prime mortgages. On houses he's arranged to have appraised at 20 Percent more than their sale prices (so they'll look like "bargains").

No money for a down payment?

"Not a problem," George reassures the applicant. "You can take out a small First Mortgage to cover the down payment. Then follow up with a larger Second Mortgage to cover the rest of the purchase price."

"But won't that mean high monthly mortgage payments?"

"Not with Adjustable-Rate mortgages that charge interest-only the first two years. At very low, 'pennies-per-day' rates. Giving you monthly payments lower than your current apartment rent."

"But after two years, when the much higher monthly payments kick in . . . ?"

"Nothing to worry about. The way house prices are skyrocketing these days, you'll be able to refinance with a single bigger mortgage to pay off both original mortgages. And give yourself enough extra cash to cover the monthly payments for at least two additional years. Maybe three."

"And after that?"

"As long as home prices keep going up, you'll be building more equity in your house. Which you can tap for ready cash through more refinancings."

"So the house keeps paying for itself?"

"That's what it amounts to."

"Sounds great. What's next?"

"Fill out the mortgage applications. We'll do it together right here on my PC. I know how to word the answers to give the banks what they're looking for. Here's a hard copy of the application form."

"Do I need documentation for my income?"

"Naw. It's all streamlined these days. You know, computerized. The banks run your applications against their crazy computer models to see if you qualify for the mortgages. And you will. I guarantee it. It's just a formality these days."

"A formality?"

"The banks are mainly interested in generating new mortgages to sell to Wall Street. Each mortgage they sell increases their servicing fee volume. That's where the profit is these days. So they want to approve as many applicants as possible."

"Oh."

"You brought the cash to pay me for the mortgage application fee?"

"Some of it."

"How much?"

"About half. I'll try to bring the rest next week after my wife gets her paycheck."

"Okay, look. Just to keep things simple, I'll add the balance of the fee to the amount of the First Mortgage. That way, I'll get paid at the closing. And you won't have to bring me any more cash."

"That's great. You're sure it's okay?"

"Of course. We do it all the time. I'll just add the usual deferred payment premium to the application fee."

"How much is that?"

"Only 10 Percent."

"Of the balance?"

"Of the total application fee. It's routine."

"Okay. As long as I don't have to come up with any more cash."

"Right. Now let's get these applications filled out."

Just then, George gets a phone call from Old Man Potter. Who's become George's hungriest lender for sub-prime mortgages that he can sell to his Wall Street buddies back East.

"Hi, Mister Potter," George says, leaning back in his desk chair with a big smile. "Just going to call you . . . Right. I'll have a new application faxed to you in another half hour . . . No, a First <u>and</u> Second Mortgage this time . . . Yeah, I thought you'd like that . . . Great. I'll see you at the Club around Six . . . "

Wonderful Life indeed.

■ ■ ■

Ditto "Good Gray Wall Street Bankers"

THE SECOND FACTOR that brought on the economic crisis, by wrecking housing, was the growing sophistication of Wall Street firms that bought mortgages from lenders to back the kind of new **Collateralized Debt Obligations** (CDOs) we looked at in **Chapter 4,** on Derivatives for sale to investors.

These firms became masters at creatively packaging various Prime and Sub-Prime mortgages in "pools" so they could offer different categories of CDOs to match the Risk Tolerance of different investors. For example:

- The "gilt-edged" category consisted of CDOs that had first call on the income generated by <u>all</u> the mortgages in the pool. These CDOs offered modest yields with a presumably high degree of "safety" to match the preferences of conservative investors like pension funds and life insurance companies.

- The next category consisted of CDOs that had second call on the income generated by all the mortgages in the pool. They offered somewhat higher yields with "reasonable" safety to investors willing to tolerate slightly greater risk in return for more income.

- The final category consisted of CDOs that depended on the pool's mortgage income available after the needs of the first 2 categories had been met. But the higher risk of these CDOs was supposedly offset by their much higher yields.

Which made them especially popular among hedge funds and other investment firms seeking high yields.

Wall Street firms would then seek investment-grade ratings (preferably Triple A) for all three CDO categories from private sector rating firms like Standard & Poor's, Moody's, and Fitch in order to boost their sales potential. While presenting the results of their sophisticated mathematical models to demonstrate that the overall Default Risk for all mortgages in the pool was low enough to justify investment-grade ratings for their CDOs.

In the old days of George Bailey's mortgage model, we saw that a lending institution granting a mortgage to a home buyer would keep that mortgage on its books until it was fully paid off. Therefore, the entire Default Risk of that mortgage was held by the lending institution. Which sought to protect itself by only granting mortgages to borrowers who were clearly creditworthy. Because they had stable and adequate family incomes to meet monthly mortgage payments. And because they were able to invest a significant portion of their own money in a down payment on the house.

But the New Deal Model changed that. It enabled lending institutions to sell off the mortgages they originated to other financial institutions (initially Fannie Mae and Freddie Mac). Which assembled these mortgages in pools to collectively back the CDOs they issued to investors, for which an active secondary market existed where investors could sell their CDOs if they wished. So Default Risk became diffused since no individual CDO was backed by a single identifiable mortgage whose safety could be assessed.

When only Fannie Mae and Freddie Mac issued such CDOs, this arrangement seemed copasetic enough. Both institutions set high safety standards for the mortgages they bought. Also, there was an active secondary market where investors could easily sell their CDOs if they wished. And since both institutions were originally owned by the Federal

Government, their CDOs were perceived as carrying implicit Federal guarantees.

But these protections disappeared during the pre-2006 housing boom.

- Previous lending standards went out the window, as hungry mortgage brokers and lending institutions corralled increasing numbers of fee-paying "warm bodies" with questionable credit standings to sign up for new mortgages. Which lenders quickly sold for fresh cash to numerous eager and unregulated Wall Street firms assembling mortgage pools to back the increasing numbers of CDOs they issued.

- The secondary markets for these CDOs were limited to chaotic, over-the-counter operations run by their issuing firms. Which found new profit opportunities in the widening spreads between buying prices (lower) and selling prices (higher) for these securities as they traded them back and forth like baseball cards. So it became increasingly difficult to determine anything like objective market values for the CDOs in an investor's portfolio. Or for an individual investor to have any assurance of finding buyers at reasonable prices for any CDOs he might wish to sell.

All this made the question of Default Risk for the mortgages in these pools at least a technical issue. Which the Wall Street firms attempted to address with their glitzy mathematical models.

Normal People know what **Risk** is. It's the chance of losing your shirt if you do something crazy. Like putting all your 401(k) money into a Hot Stock your talkative barber claims will fly you to the moon. And the greater the chance is, the More Risky that Hot Stock is. What could be more obvious?

But the numbers-obsessed Rocket Scientists developing mathematical models for Wall Street firms have a different definition of Risk. One based on theoretical thinking among ivory tower types about the price changes of securities being traded in financial markets like the New York Stock Exchange.

You ready for this?

According to Wall Street's Rocket Scientists, "<u>Risk</u> is equal to the <u>Standard Deviation</u> of a <u>Time Series</u> consisting of the <u>Natural Logs</u> of the <u>Daily Relative Changes</u> in the price (up <u>or</u> down) of a security like that Hot Stock." (Gasp.)

Wall Street types with MBAs in Finance like this definition because it gives them a precise number for expressing Risk. And with this number, they can use **Gaussian Statistics** to find the Probability of such a Risk actually materializing.

(Assuming, of course, that the relative price changes of the security in question fit that much-abused bell-shaped curve known as the **Normal Distribution**. Which they rarely do. But MBA types are taught to assume they do in order to make the math simpler.)

In other words, suppose your chances of winning the state lottery are the same as your chances of losing your shirt on that Hot Stock. Then Rocket Scientists insist that both are **Equally Risky**. Even though the first outcome can let you retire to a lavish seaside condo in Florida with a forty-foot sports fishing yacht tied up to your backyard dock. While the second may leave you eating dog food in a rundown mobile home somewhere in Florida's backwoods. Which represents a significant <u>qualitative</u> difference that Rocket Scientists choose to ignore.

It didn't require much imagination for Rocket Scientists to apply this kind of academic thinking to the task of developing the mathematical models their firms needed to demonstrate very modest **Default Risk** in their pools of mortgage-backed securities.

The unregulated rating firms may or may not have been impressed by the encouraging appearance of "low risk" these models showed.

But they were certainly impressed by the generous fee income they could earn by meeting their customers' needs for investment-grade ratings. Especially when doing so held out the promise of more business in the future from rating more and more CDOs. And they had the favorable results from those glitzy mathematical risk models to hang their hats on.

■ ■ ■

Not to Mention the Fed

THE THIRD DESTABILIZING FACTOR was the boom in housing prices encouraged by the low-interest-rate policies implemented by the Federal Reserve in the wake of the 2000 stock market crash, and the subsequent recession caused by the collapse of the Dot-Com bubble. (See Chapter 7 for an explanation of how the Fed influences interest rates.)

A climate of low interest rates reduces the cost of mortgages to prospective home buyers. This stimulates higher demand for houses, which usually leads to rising prices.

And a trend of rising prices leads to the perception that houses are more than just Consumer Goods (i.e., places to live). They're also seen as Investment Goods. Whose market value seems likely to keep rising in the years ahead (thereby increasing the homeowner's personal wealth).

Which further increases the demand for houses.

Stimulating further price increases.

Of course, China and similar low-wage countries weren't averse to helping the Fed keep interest rates low. By exploiting their non-union labor forces, they were able to keep reducing the prices of their exported consumers goods that Americans bought in ever-increasing numbers. And since we traditionally measure Inflation with the <u>Consumer</u> Price

Index (which excludes assets like homes and financial securities), a close-to-flat trend for this Index during the middle of the decade made it easy for the Fed to convince us that we should worry more about <u>De</u>flation than <u>In</u>flation. Which justified keeping interest rates low, as the Fed conveniently ignored accelerating inflation in the largely (and, in some cases, increasingly) unregulated markets for assets.

Naturally, China and other low-wage countries faced the problem of what to do with the burgeoning dollar profits they earned by selling bargain-priced consumer goods to the American public. Which they solved by the simple expedient of buying increasing amounts of U.S. Treasury debt that had to be issued to fund 2 expensive foreign wars after the Administration had hamstrung government revenues with large tax cuts.

So the nation found itself awash with capital (much of it debt based) seeking investments offering generous yields.

■ ■ ■

Chapter 6
IS MARKET CAPITALISM STILL ALIVE?

A crowd flowed over London Bridge, so many,
I had not thought death had undone so many.
Sighs, short and infrequent, were exhaled,
And each man fixed his eyes before his feet.
Flowed up the hill and down King William Street,
To where Saint Mary Woolnoth kept the hours
With a dead sound on the final stroke of nine.
—T. S. Eliot

Just as during the 1930s, the current Economic Crisis has created an explosion of opportunities for anti-capitalist types (closet or otherwise) in the news media and academia to loudly proclaim that so-called "Free Market Capitalism" has proved itself to be a costly fraud for the American people.

Here's a good example. Written by the redoubtable **Arianna Huffington.** Who posted it on her blog on December 22, 2008 (see http://www.huffingtonpost.com/arianna-huffington/laissez-faire-capitalism_b_152900.html for her complete article).

Laissez-Faire Capitalism Should Be as Dead as Soviet Communism

The collapse of Communism as a political system sounded the death knell for Marxism as an ideology. But while laissez-faire capitalism has been a monumental

178

failure in practice, and soundly defeated at the polls, the ideology is still alive and kicking.

The only place you can find an American Marxist these days is teaching a college linguistic theory class. But you can find all manner of free market fundamentalists still on the Senate floor or in Governor's mansions or showing up on TV trying to peddle the deregulation snake oil.

Take Sen. John Ensign, chairman of the National Republican Senatorial Committee, who went on <u>Face the Nation</u> and, with a straight face, said of the economic meltdown: "Unfortunately, it was allowed to be portrayed that this was a result of deregulation, when in fact it was a result of overregulation."

Or Gov. Mark Sanford, who told Joe Scarborough he was against bailing out the auto industry because it would "threaten the very market-based system that has created the wealth that this country has enjoyed."

If a politician announced he was running on a platform of "from each according to his ability, to each according to his need" he would be laughed off the stage. That is also the correct response to anyone who continues to make the case that markets do best when left alone.

It's time to drive the final nail into the coffin of laissez-faire capitalism by treating it like the discredited ideology it inarguably is. If not, the Dr. Frankensteins of the right will surely try to revive the monster and send it marauding through our economy once again.

The Market System's shattering loss of credibility is an especially compelling issue for those Americans who have lost their jobs. Lost their homes. Lost the investment value of their private savings for retirement or college for their children. Lost much of the hope they once had for a better future in a prosperous America.

All this is extremely troubling to those among us who've been hoping to harness the market's advantages in new programs to transform the nation's transportation systems and operate them more effectively. So we have to figure out how to roll with the punches.

In the process of doing so, it may help to keep a few things in mind.

■ ■ ■

Market Myths and Realities

Since the days of **Adam Smith,** more nonsense has been written about Capitalism than any subject other than Religion.

During the Nineteenth Century and the first half of the Twentieth Century, economists from **David Ricardo** to **Alfred Marshall** even raised the status of the Free Market (guided by its miraculous "<u>Invisible Hand</u>") to something like a beneficent secular priest that was supposed to rule our worldly lives.

And beginning in the 1960s, things got even worse.

Math-oriented ivory tower economists started developing a host of ostensibly "Rigorous" quantitative models that claimed to show how markets actually work. Tagged with such intimidating names as "*The Efficient Market Hypothesis,*" "*Modern Portfolio Theory,*" "*The Capital Asset Pricing Model,*" and "*The Black-Scholes-Merton Option Pricing Model,*" these models (expressed in obscure differential equations rather than clear English prose) focused primarily on the markets for common stocks and other financial securities that were assumed to represent the closest approximation to the Free Market ideal in the real world.

And guess what.

All these models were **Wrong**.

Because they were primarily based on a misapplication of **Gaussian Statistics** (epitomized by that overworked Bell-Shaped Curve, which supposedly demonstrates that female college students have less aptitude for math and science than males). Coupled with antiquated principles of **Newtonian Physics** that had long since been discredited by Albert Einstein and other clear-eyed thinkers.

But they still became **Mainstream Thinking** among Wall Street Rocket Scientists during the 1980s and '90s. Not to mention winning for several of their developers the **Nobel Prize in Economics** (which comes with an impressive gold medal and a nice seven-figure check). Despite the havoc they've brought to firms in the financial industry that actually tried to put them into practice.

It may come as a surprise to many people, but markets are by no means artificial hothouse entities invented by ivory tower Ph.D. types who like to munch on differential equations between meals. Markets are, in fact, entirely natural and instinctive products of everyday human pragmatism.

Nowhere is this more clearly illustrated than in the informal markets that developed among American and British bomber crews imprisoned in German prisoner-of-war camps during World War II after their planes had been shot down.

This story has been told many times. It's even been the basis for a fascinating article by British economist R. A. Radford titled "**The Economic Organization of a P.O.W. Camp**," which I had the good fortune to run across in graduate school in a book of readings on Economics.

More recently, Radford's article has been supplemented by the published experiences of American bomber pilots who were shot down during raids over Germany and spent the rest of the War in POW camps.

(In general, **World War II** was much better managed than **World War I**—especially by the Allies. But this didn't extend to the passion among U.S.

air force generals to "win the War on their own" with their cherished class-room concept of <u>Unescorted Daylight Precision Bombing</u>. This concept turned out to be a failure in practice, as demonstrated by the notorious **Second Schweinfurt** raid. This raid was the last attempt by the U.S. Army Air Force generals to make their "classroom concept" of Unescorted Daylight Precision Bombing work in practice. And produced horrendous casualty rates among American strategic bomber forces. Before the generals wised up and joined the **RAF** in burning down German cities. To punish German civilians so severely that they would <u>never again</u> support a national policy of making war against their neighbors in Europe, which had been a regular German passion for nearly a hundred years. And as European history since 1945 shows, <u>this</u> military initiative was a resounding success.)

Anyway, these thoughtful members of the Greatest Generation spent the rest of the War as German POWs. Then went to college on the **G.I. Bill** before building themselves highly successful careers. And their published experiences not only confirmed everything Radford covered in his article but added some interesting details of their own.

Including how the descriptions of markets in their college Economics courses bore little resemblance to the way natural markets <u>actually worked</u> in their POW camps.

■ ■ ■

How Free Markets Really Work

At the camps' peak, a typical camp housed about 11,000 American and British POWs in six large Compounds, each of which contained 15 barracks (for an average of about 120 POWs per barrack).

Fortunately for the POWs, these camps were run by Germany's elite Luftwaffe, rather than its more brutal Wehrmacht or militantly sadistic Gestapo. So camp guards and officers felt a certain sense of "brotherhood" for the Allied fliers in their charge.

This meant that POWs were never subjected to forced slave labor. Never tortured or otherwise abused. And generally left pretty much alone so long as they behaved themselves and didn't try to escape.

However, food was always a problem.

Luftwaffe camp managers tried to meet Geneva Convention standards for feeding POWs adequately. But growing food shortages throughout Germany made this increasingly difficult. So Luftwaffe-supplied food rations tended to be limited to twice-daily bowls of watery cabbage soup accompanied by black bread, occasionally supplemented by scraps of meat. Which fell short of meeting the recommended minimum daily calorie intake for POWs.

For the most part, this calorie shortfall was made up by weekly food parcels sent to each POW by the International Red Cross, based in neutral Switzerland. The contents of each parcel was identical, and typically included:

- Cans of Spam, corned beef, salmon, and liver pâté.
- Packages of powdered milk, sugar, dried raisins, instant coffee, graham crackers, and Vitamin C tablets.
- Jars of jam, peanut butter, margarine, and cheese.
- Several chocolate bars.
- Two bars of soap.
- 5 packs of cigarettes.

With lots of time on their hands and regular weekly deliveries of identical Red Cross parcels, the POWs inevitably began trading these goods among themselves according to their individual tastes.

For example, a confirmed chocolate freak might exchange his cans of corned beef for more chocolate bars. While a POW who preferred his coffee black might look for opportunities to exchange his powdered milk and sugar for more packages of graham crackers and jars of jam so he could enjoy something approximating a "traditional American break-fast" each morning. And so it went.

In a surprisingly short time, each barrack became a hotbed of infor-mal "Barter Markets" for the various goods in Red Cross parcels. With each POW trying to increase his supply of the goods he most preferred by trading off goods he considered less desirable. These activities soon expanded to include trading between barracks, and even featured "Bid and Offer" notes for various goods that aggressive POWs looking for trading action would pin to the bulletin boards in each barrack.

Such market activities are as old as human history and predate by many centuries the emergence of Economics as a recognized, degree-granting "Social Science" and the subject of many a learned tome. In fact, the instinct to trade seems to be as strongly hardwired into the human psyche as the instinct to reproduce (and has probably been the source of as much emotional and social turmoil—as we'll see).

However, the Barter System is an awkward way to conduct trading activity as its volume grows. Because the "Price" of each good has to be expressed in terms of all other goods being traded. And this becomes terribly cumbersome.

But natural human ingenuity quickly solves this problem. The solu-tion is to price all goods in terms of a **Single Good**, known formally as the "Medium of Exchange." In other words, **Money**. Another instinctive human invention that greatly simplifies market activity.

And which of the various goods in their Red Cross parcels did POWs instinctively choose as their "Money Commodity"? Why, **Cigarettes**, naturally.

Naturally indeed. Because even though it's traditional to think of **Gold** and **Silver** as classic forms of Commodity Money, **Tobacco** has an active history in this regard. Especially in the convenient form of cigarettes.

And since each Red Cross Parcel contained five packs of cigarettes, with twenty cigarettes in each pack, what could be simpler?

No wonder Cigarettes served as the most common form of money in all POW camps throughout Germany. And later became the "Standard Money" in the many underground markets that became the backbone of shattered Germany's economy during the two-year postwar Occupation by the Allies.

Once the POWs had a reliable and widely accepted form of Money, their trading activities increased by leaps and bounds. To become the most popular pastime among the camp's POWs, who had so much idle time on their hands. And could be neatly illustrated by the classic **Market Model** familiar to anyone who ever took Economics 101.

You can see this model displayed in Figure 6.1.

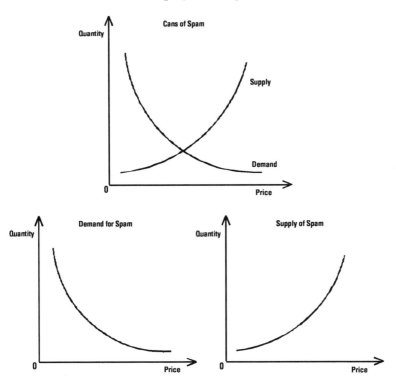

FIGURE 6.1. SUPPLY AND DEMAND I

The top diagram shows the standard Demand Curve/Supply Curve pattern found in all Economics textbooks. With Quantity on the Vertical Axis plotted as a function of Price on the Horizontal Axis. And the point where the 2 curves cross defining the "Market Clearing Price."

The lower-left diagram breaks out the Demand Curve separately. It illustrates the assumption that the Quantity of Demand among Buyers falls as the Price rises.

The lower-right diagram breaks out the Supply Curve separately. It illustrates the assumption that the Quantity of Supply provided by Sellers rises as the Price rises.

The top diagram in Figure 6.1 shows this classic model. For cans of Spam in this example. With the **Quantity** of cans of Spam being demanded and supplied depending on their **Price** in cigarettes. (In this diagram, we're following the standard mathematical convention of plotting Quantity— the Dependent Variable—on the vertical axis.)

Notice how the point where the Demand and Supply curves cross each other defines what's usually called the **Market Clearing Price**. This is the price at which Buyers can presumably purchase all the cans of Spam they wish to buy, while Sellers can presumably find purchasers for all the cans of Spam they wish to sell.

The two lower diagrams show the Demand and Supply curves separately in order to illustrate more clearly how they depend on Price.

In the lower-left diagram we see the classic assumption that the number of cans of Spam POWs want to buy depends on the **Price Per Can**. And as this price in cigarettes **Rises**, the number of cans POWs want to buy **Falls**. Clear enough in theory. (But as we'll see in a minute, the real world isn't always this simpleminded.)

By the same token, the right-hand diagram illustrates the classic assumption that the number of cans of Spam POWs are willing to sell also depends on the Price Per Can. But in this case, as the price in cigarettes **Rises**, the number of cans supplied to the market also **Rises**.

Meanwhile, the relatively few non-smokers among the POWs (this was the 1940s, remember, when virtually <u>every</u> male American smoked cigarettes) began looking for ways to use their growing hordes of cigarettes to do more than simply buy increasing amounts of other Red Cross parcel goods for their own consumption. And one of them (we'll call him "**Meyer**") came up with an interesting discovery.

Meyer noticed that the prices (in cigarettes) for these goods were at their <u>Lowest</u> immediately after new Red Cross parcels arrived, because of the sudden increase in the supply of goods available. But as the days passed and these goods were consumed, their supply diminished. So their prices <u>Rose</u>. Reaching a peak just before the next round of Red Cross parcels arrived.

So Meyer began using his horde of cigarettes to buy up as many of these consumption goods as he could when their prices were low. Then he would sit back and watch these prices rise day after day until they reached their peak. At which point, he would sell the goods he'd previously brought—for a nice profit. Which further increased his horde of cigarettes.

Meyer did this week after week. And in the process, he became quite "Wealthy" (as measured by the growing size of his cigarette horde).

Soon enough, other non-smoking POWS began doing the same thing. And eventually, even some smoking POWS joined the game. Forcing themselves to reduce their daily consumption of cigarettes in order to build up "Trading Capital." So they could buy Red Cross parcel goods when their prices were low in order to profit later by selling when prices had risen.

In time, the perceptions among POWS about the role of Red Cross parcel goods began to broaden. They were still regarded primarily as **Consumption Goods.** But to an increasing extent, they were <u>also</u> regarded as "**Investment Goods.**" In other words, goods that could be bought <u>not</u> to be consumed, but <u>solely</u> to be sold later at a profit.

This change in perception had some compelling implications that we'll look at in a minute.

But first let's consider the actions of those non-smoking POWs whose personalities were too conservative for them to be comfortable playing these trading games.

One of these conservative non-smoking types was named "**George.**" And he started a nice little business of <u>lending</u> his horde of cigarettes to other POWs. To be repaid a certain number of days later with <u>interest</u> ("*I'll lend you a pack of 20 cigarettes today. And you'll pay me back 22 cigarettes in 7 days.*").

In other words, these non-smokers like George became "**Cigarette Bankers.**" With their "Wealth" in cigarettes increasing in size from the "interest" they charged on the loans they made.

Needless to say, most of George's loan customers were heavy smokers who tended to run short of cigarettes before their receipt of new Red Cross parcels. So these customers were borrowing to help fund their daily cigarette consumption (just like their children and grandchildren decades later who were armed with Credit Cards).

But some loan customers were traders like Meyer. Who saw the benefit of being able to "**Leverage**" their trading capital with cigarettes they borrowed from bankers like George. Because this would enable them to make <u>larger</u> purchases of Red Cross parcel consumption goods when prices were low. And therefore be able to earn <u>larger</u> profits later (even after paying back—with interest—the cigarettes they'd borrowed) when prices rose and they sold these goods.

For example, suppose Meyer has 500 cigarettes of his own. If he borrows another 1,000 cigarettes from George, he'll be able to buy **three times as many** cans of Spam when prices are low than he would otherwise be able to. Therefore, he has **Leveraged** his trading capital by borrowing **Two** Cigarettes for each **One** Cigarette of his own.

And when the time comes to sell because the price per can has tripled, his gross profit will be **three times as large** as if his initial purchase had been limited to only 500 cigarettes' worth of Spam.

Of course, he'll have to pay back George the 1,000 cigarettes he borrowed—plus "interest" of 100 cigarettes (2 cigarettes for each pack of 20). But his net profit after paying off his debt to George will still be **45 Percent Higher** than if he'd only been able to buy 500 cigarettes' worth of Spam.

Achieving higher profits by using **Leverage** naturally increased the appetite among traders to borrow even more cigarettes ("further increasing the Leverage of their trading capital"). So they could make even larger purchases of Red Cross parcel goods when prices were low and therefore earn still-higher profits when they sold them later.

And just as naturally, bankers were eager to feed this increasing demand for cigarette loans by increasing their lending activity. Even to the extent of Leveraging their loan capital by borrowing cigarettes from the POW community at large. Offering to pay "interest" as an inducement (*"Lend me 20 cigarettes today and I'll pay you back 21 cigarettes in 7 days."*). Which they more than offset by the higher interest they charged on the loans they made. Thereby creating an increasingly robust "**Credit Function**" within the camp that fueled its increasingly active trading markets for Red Cross parcel goods.

Over the course of time, these markets came to be increasingly dominated by a growing volume of credit-fueled trading activities. To the point where this dominance caused a significant change to take place in one of the fundamental assumptions of the classic market model.

As we saw earlier, the classic model assumes that **higher prices** for any particular good **decrease the demand** for that good, and vice versa. Hence, the classic Demand Curve in Figure 6.1's lower-left diagram slopes **Downward to the Right**.

But the new credit-based "Trading Market Paradigm" dramatically changed this. Now the classic Demand Curve became **reversed** and began sloping **Upward to the Right**. Because now **higher prices** caused demand to **increase**. Due to the increasing perception among POWs that no matter how high today's price was for a particular good, tomorrow's price would inevitably be higher. And still higher the day after that.

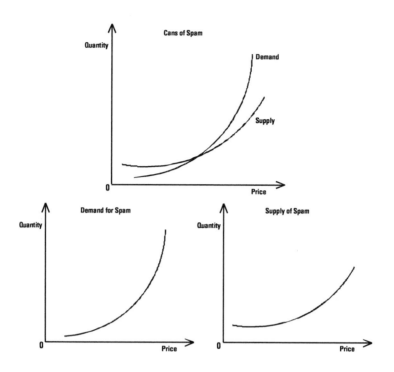

FIGURE 6.2. SUPPLY AND DEMAND II

Figure 6.2 shows the same Market Model we saw earlier in Figure 6.1. But there's been a shift in the Demand Curve. As we can see, the new **upward sloping** Demand Curve shifted the **Market Clearing Price** significantly to the **Right**. Making Demand **higher** for any given level of Supply.

So if you were a POW, you came to realize that you'd better buy the goods you wanted today. No matter how high the price. And even if you had to borrow the entire cost in cigarettes. Which, in any case, would be more than offset by the inevitably higher price tomorrow and in the days thereafter.

Does this sound suspiciously like the recent All-American **Housing Bubble**?

- When increasing numbers of homeowners ceased to regard houses simply as **Consumption Goods** ("places to live") but saw them as **Investment Goods** as well.

- Destined inevitably to command **higher prices tomorrow** than they did today.

- Therefore, worth taking out the **largest possible mortgages** to buy. Especially if these mortgages were easy to get and came with temporarily low "teaser rates."

- Because the inevitable **rise in housing prices** would always cover you, come what may.

Most economists take it for granted that the "Natural State" in which markets exist is a Static one of nearly constant "**Equilibrium.**" In which the Market Clearing Price is more or less fixed and can be depended upon. So the world as they see it is as simpleminded as a child's fairy tale.

But more sophisticated economists like Israel Kirzner (a leading theoretician of the "Austrian School" of market economics) reject this assumption of "Static Equilibrium." They insist that the natural state in which markets exist in the real world is a Dynamic one of nearly constant "<u>Disequilibrium</u>." In which the true Market Clearing Price is a moving target that buyers and sellers are forever chasing.

The assumption of Static Equilibrium is a key element in the **Efficient Markets Hypothesis** that underlies the math-oriented models for financial markets, like **Modern Portfolio Theory** and **The Black-Scholes-Merton Options Pricing Model**. Which have been taught by many Financial Moses types as something akin to "the Word of God" in the Mount Sinai classrooms of America's leading graduate business schools during the past 30 years.

According to these models, daily price changes in financial markets are entirely **Random** and **Unbiased**. With today's price having Zero influence on tomorrow's price.

Therefore, market price changes are (in theory) "**Normally Distributed**" and fit the standard bell-shaped curve that's at the heart of Gaussian Statistics ("*that Great Intellectual Fraud*," thundered iconoclastic risk maven Nassim Taleb in his 2008 book *The Black Swan*). This makes it easy to pontificate confidently that (for example) "*the probability of a daily price change exceeding X Percent is no greater than an infinitesimal 0.0000Y Percent.*" Which is why the more than 20 Percent decline in the S&P 500 Index on October 19, 1987 ("**Black Monday**") "couldn't really happen." Just like the Holocaust.

But take a look at the chart in Figure 6.3. It shows the daily closing prices for the S&P 500 during a fairly typical three-month period in 2005. With each day's price shown as a histogram to present its full range.

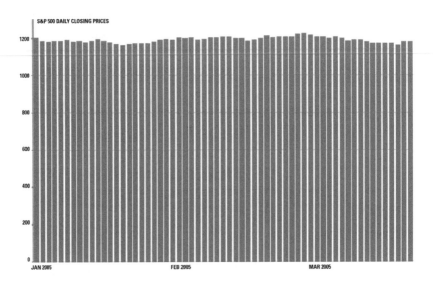

FIGURE 6.3. S&P 500 CLOSING PRICES

As we eyeball this chart, doesn't it appear that the most important factor by far in any given day's closing price is the <u>previous day's closing</u>

price? So doesn't this negate the popular academic theory that "**Prices Have No Memory**"?

Because the reality is that <u>Prices **don't** determine themselves</u>. They're determined by Buyers and Sellers. Who <u>always</u> know what the last Price was. Despite what all those mathematically intimidating market models that won Nobel Prizes for their developers would have us believe.

The obvious revelations from this simple exercise are further strengthened by more sophisticated analyses of actual price changes in financial markets.

For example, researchers have found that the **frequency** of these price changes in the tails of their actual distribution curves is **significantly higher** than the minimal frequency predicted by the Normal Distribution. This "Fat Tail" problem is known in the Statistics trade as "**Leptokurtosis**" (which sounds like a particularly unpleasant gum disease, but is far more serious). And it leaves Efficient Market fanatics mumbling helplessly that "*financial market price changes are <u>Almost</u> Normally Distributed.*"

The obvious conclusions we're bound to draw from these real-world price data tell us a great deal about how markets **Actually Work**. And they represent another way of demonstrating the truth of Kirzner's insights about the inherently **Dynamic Disequilibrium** in which all markets exist. For Investment Goods as well as for Consumption Goods.

This pervasive state of Market Disequilibrium creates opportunities for a critically important human action that savvy market mavens like Kirzner call "**Entrepreneurial Discovery.**"

In a full-scale economy that includes the <u>Production</u> of goods as well as their <u>Buying</u> and <u>Selling</u>, Entrepreneurial Discovery can include such actions as a sharp-eyed manufacturer spotting and adopting efficient new ways to produce goods at lower cost so they can profitably be offered in the marketplace at lower prices than previously.

But in the purely "Buy/Sell" economy of the prison camp, the process of Entrepreneurial Discovery tends to primarily involve the <u>heightened</u>

<u>sensitivity</u> of people like Meyer to the patterns of price changes.

<u>That's</u> why Meyer noticed that the prices of goods in Red Cross parcels were at their lowest on the day new parcels were delivered to the POWs. Then rose day by day as they were consumed. To reach a peak on the day before the next round of parcels was delivered. Which revealed to Meyer a **Profit Opportunity** that he proceeded to exploit.

The technical name for Meyer's trading activities is "**Arbitrage.**" ("*You buy goods when and where their prices are low. In the expectation of selling them at a profit when and where their prices are higher.*")

But because the famous white collar criminal and ex-convict **Ivan Boesky** engaged in Arbitrage as his principle business activity during the 1980s, it has come to have a bad smell. This is unwarranted, since Arbitrage is, at worst, "morally neutral" (Boesky's prison sentence came after he pleaded guilty to **Insider Stock Market Trading**, which is a Federal crime and has nothing to do with Arbitrage).

So Arbitrage doesn't automatically mean higher prices for buyers. In fact, it usually leads to <u>lower</u> prices overall by eliminating artificial price differences (between one POW barrack and another, for example) that prevent markets from functioning efficiently.

However, it's easy to see why some POWs may conclude that "too much" trading activity (through which Arbitrage is conducted) in markets for what are primarily consumption goods can raise their prices to buyers above what they would otherwise be. In other words, we confront the dreaded demon of **Inflation**.

This can be especially true when the <u>supply</u> of goods is, in practical terms, unaffected by market prices, but is determined instead mainly by forces that are external to the markets. Like the delivery of Red Cross parcels to POWs. Or the many months it takes to build new houses.

As the classic market model diagrammed in Figure 6.1 showed, higher prices theoretically motivate sellers to supply larger quantities of goods—which (again theoretically) can offset the impact of increased demand. Thereby helping to preserve price stability.

But to keep things simple, this Two-Dimensional model ignores the critically important Third Dimension of **Time** in market activity. It fails to reflect the fact that considerable time may pass before an increased supply of goods (in response to an increase in prices) actually reaches the market. So on this score, the classic model is grossly unrealistic and must be taken with a considerable grain of salt.

Also, we've seen that prices can rise when buyers develop the impression that prices "have nowhere to go but up." In such cases, buyers tend to lose their emotional awareness of the critical link between price and "fair value" (*"You'd better give me a binder check this afternoon because three other people are interested in this house."*), and therefore no longer behave rationally when responding to higher prices.

This is another factor that the classic model ignores. Further limiting its ability to serve as a meaningful guide to dynamic markets in the real world, whose natural state is to be <u>pursuing</u> Equilibrium rather than actually <u>enjoying</u> it.

What did POWs mean by "too much" trading activity? This isn't easy to pinpoint. But it was inevitable for some POWs to argue that the "optimal" amount of trading activity could best be defined as the volume that could be supported <u>only</u> by the total amount of "equity" trading capital held by all POWs in the camp. In other words, there should be no borrowing by traders to leverage their trading capital.

If most POWs accepted this constraint, then the growth of trading volume would be limited by the growth of the camp's total stock of equity trading capital. Which is assumed to be linked to the growth of total economic activity in the camp. Thereby helping to assure something close to the alleged nirvana of **"Price Stability."** So presumably everyone should be happy.

But obviously, traders like Meyer wouldn't be happy. They'd argue that their "economic freedom" was being arbitrarily and unfairly restricted by the prohibition against borrowing to fund trading activity. While cigarette bankers like George would voice the more sophisticated argument that Credit is the "life blood" of an economy. So any restrictions on its availability or use would only make all POWs "poorer" in the long run.

While this controversy ebbed and flowed without any progress towards resolution, the boom in the camp's trading activities grew by leaps and bounds. Until the early months of 1944. When external events involving the progress of the War began to change everything.

The most important of these external events was the growing effectiveness of the American and British strategic bombing campaigns against Germany.

Among other things, these campaigns began to severely disrupt Germany's railroad network and other transportation systems. This directly affected the schedules for delivery of Red Cross parcels, which became increasingly erratic. No longer could the POWs rely on weekly deliveries of their parcels. Sometimes a week or more would pass with no deliveries. Then a large group of parcels would arrive all at once. But as 1944 wore on, the overall pattern became one of fewer parcels per POW per month on average.

This became a great hardship for the POWs, who depended on the food goods in these parcels to supplement the meager daily food rations provided by the Luftwaffe camp managers. And it severely disrupted the camp's smoothly functioning trading economy. For two reasons:

- **FIRST:** It caused serious and unpredictable shortages of the goods being traded in the camp's various markets, as the regular delivery schedule for Red Cross parcels broke down. Accompanied by sudden and unexpected increases in Supply when several weeks' worth of parcels would arrive all at once. All of which led to increasingly severe Price Volatility in the camp's markets that discouraged POWs from trading in these parcels.

196

- **SECOND:** The growing shortage of cigarettes that came in Red Cross parcels meant that the camp's "Money Supply" shrank in an unpredictable manner as the months passed. Since a decline in any society's Money Supply causes prices to fall, this further discouraged POWs from buying and selling goods in the camp's markets. (*"Why buy today when prices will be lower tomorrow?"*) See **Chapter 7** for an explanation of why this happens.

Finally, at the beginning of 1945, these trading markets broke down completely.

A prolonged disruption in the delivery of Red Cross parcels left Meyer and the other aggressive traders holding large supplies of goods (bought primarily with borrowed cigarettes) as they gleefully watched prices soar out of sight.

Until the unexpected arrival one day of a month's worth of overdue Red Cross parcels caused prices to crash spectacularly as heavy supplies of goods flooded the markets.

This left traders like Meyer unable to pay off their cigarette loans to bankers like George. Who were left unable to pay back the cigarettes they'd borrowed from the other POWs to make loans to their trader customers.

All of which precipitated a **Social Crisis** that shattered the camp's trading economy. With POWs hurling charges of "bad faith" at each other and even engaging in fist fights. While marauding gangs of outraged POWs began looting the large stocks of Red Cross parcel goods held by traders like Meyer and distributing them freely throughout the camp ("All Power to the People"). Leaving their senior officers with no choice but to ban all trading in an effort to restore order.

It's possible (even likely) that normal trading would eventually have resumed after the social chaos induced by the Economic Crisis had run its course.

But at the end of January, with the Soviet Union's formidable Red Army approaching from the East, Germany's powers that be abruptly decided to evacuate the camp.

So they gathered Meyer, George, and the other POWs together on short notice and proceeded to march them several hundred miles west across Germany (during the worst European winter in a generation). To a new camp south of Nuremberg. Where they were liberated by advance forces of General Patton's American Third Army in April.

Thus ended the POWs' highly enlightening experiment with the market economies that naturally and inevitably emerge whenever human beings gather together in functioning societies.

From which we can learn a great deal about how markets Really Work in a world of full-blooded human beings.

■ ■ ■

Chapter 7
THE "SECRETS OF MONEY"

And when the money failed in the land of Egypt and in the land of Canaan, all the Egyptians came unto Joseph and said: "Give us bread. For why should we die in thy presence? For the money faileth."
—*Genesis*

By long tradition, economists have packaged up these "Secrets" into a branch of their so-called science known as **Monetary Theory**. And they've artfully spread the word to all and sundry that Monetary Theory is an <u>impossibly formidable</u> subject that Normal People can't be expected to understand. Presumably so the rest of us will be in awe of them for having mastered it.

But this is nothing less then a self-serving Con Job. Because there's nothing about the "Secrets of Money" that Normal People can't understand when they see it explained in down-to-earth terms.

Furthermore, we have an **obligation** to understand these so-called "Secrets." Because Money is the whole basis of a modern society. More so than any religion or legal code. It's something we develop instinctively to meet our pragmatic need to **"grease the functioning of the trading markets we naturally create"** in order to improve our daily lives by exchanging goods and services.

Therefore, Money is intensely **Mystical**. At least as Mystical as Sex. With which it's so often intertwined in the minds of the males of our species.

Money is what we work for in order to pay for the things we need to satisfy our daily consumption needs. And when we earn more Money than we need to pay these bills, we set aside the surplus and call it

Wealth. Which we can use as **Capital** to invest in activities that promise to make us and our societies **Richer** in the future.

Mystical indeed. In all its forms.

■ ■ ■

Commodity Money

This is the simplest form of Money. It's the first kind we instinctively create soon after we begin trading goods and services in fledgling "Barter Markets."

Because the "Price" of each good traded in a barter market has to be expressed in terms of all other goods being traded. And that turns out to be very cumbersome. So, in our infinite pragmatism, we choose **One** of these goods as our "**Money Commodity**" and express the prices of all other goods in terms of this one particular good.

We've already seen how American POWs in that German prison camp selected **Cigarettes** as their Money Commodity in order to make their trading markets for Red Cross Parcel goods function more effectively.

And they didn't need any Ph.D. economists from some Big Name consulting firm to tell them how to do this. They relied entirely on their natural human instincts. Just as they'd done to create trading markets in the first place.

As noted previously, Cigarettes (and other forms of Tobacco) have a proud history of serving as Commodity Money in many societies. But the commodities most traditionally associated with Money are **Gold** and **Silver**.

Figure 7.1 shows these three popular forms of Commodity Money. The **Cigarettes** at the top are typical of the standard American cigarettes supplied to POWs in their Red Cross Parcels. They were commonly used as Money in German prison camps during World War II and in the "underground markets" throughout war-shattered Germany after May 1945.

FIGURE 7.1. COMMODITY MONEY

Next is an **American Ten-Dollar Gold Coin** minted by the U.S. Treasury Department in 1896. It's one of a series of "Liberty Eagles" minted between 1838 and 1907, when U.S. currency was pegged to the international **"Gold Standard"** (as were most of the world's developed nations in those days, especially in Europe). The U.S. also circulated Twenty-Dollar Gold coins ("Double Eagles") during this period. Plus smaller Gold coins in denominations of $5.00 ("Half Eagles") and $2.50 ("Quarter Eagles").

This ten-dollar coin contains slightly less than half an ounce of the commodity **Gold** (48.375 Percent of an ounce to be exact, if melted down and the various impurities removed).

When the U.S. was on the Gold Standard, this meant that one dollar would buy approximately 4.84 Percent of an ounce of Gold. So one ounce of Gold was worth about **$20.67**. This relationship provided a theoretically objective way to estimate the value in Gold of any good or service priced in U.S. dollars.

At the bottom of Figure 7.1 is an **American Silver Dollar Coin** minted for the U.S. Treasury in 1903. It's one of a series of "Morgan Dollars" minted between 1878 and 1921, when U.S. currency was <u>also</u> on the international **"Silver Standard"** (typical of Asian nations like China in those days, when dollar-sized silver coins circulated widely as the basic Commodity Money). The U.S. also circulated smaller Silver coins in denominations of 50 Cents ("Half Dollars"), 25 Cents ("Quarters"), and 10 Cents ("Dimes").

This Silver Dollar contains slightly more than 3/4 of an ounce of Silver (or 77.34 Percent of an ounce), which was the amount of Silver that one dollar would buy when the U.S. was on the Silver Standard. So one ounce of Silver was worth a fraction of a cent more than $1.29.

■ ■ ■

"Warehouse Receipts"

Like Cigarettes in POW camps, Gold and Silver coins had "Commodity Value" in and of themselves (similar to jewelry) because of the precious metal they contained. Among other things, this made them popular as "game chips" in the Wild West Poker Games that were once a standard feature in so many Hollywood western movies.

But they were awkward to carry around in any quantity. And too easy to lose.

To overcome this problem, the U.S. Treasury Department (and its designated agent banks) followed a practice common in most nations using Commodity Money. It offered people possessing these coins the <u>option</u> of storing them free of charge in their vaults. Then issued **"Warehouse Receipts"** in the form of elaborately engraved and official-looking paper certificates to establish ownership of the coins. And clearly specified that these certificates were <u>legal proxies</u> for the precious metal coins. Therefore, the certificates themselves could circulate as Commodity Money.

FIGURE 7.2. WAREHOUSE RECEIPTS

Figure 7.2 shows <u>2</u> examples of such Warehouse Receipts. Specifically, a **Ten-Dollar Gold Certificate** and a **One-Dollar Silver Certificate** (each accompanied by its precious metal coin).

Note the wording on the front of the Ten-Dollar Gold Certificate:

Joseph M. Giglio

THIS CERTIFIES THAT THERE HAVE BEEN DEPOSITED IN THE TREASURY OF THE UNITED STATES OF AMERICA TEN DOLLARS IN GOLD COIN PAYABLE TO THE BEARER ON DEMAND

In other words, the U.S. Treasury is telling the world that anyone in possession of one of these Ten-Dollar Gold Certificates can exchange it at the offices of the Treasury (or one of its agent banks) at any time for $10 worth of Gold Coins. In the form of one Gold Eagle (shown here). Or two Gold Half Eagles. Or four Gold Quarter Eagles. Or any combination the bearer of the Certificate prefers that adds up to $10. No ifs, ands, or buts. And this legal pledge is signed by the U.S. Treasury Secretary and the U.S. Treasurer.

Because of this pledge, most people preferred to carry around these lightweight, easily foldable paper certificates in their wallets to use as Real Money for buying things.

But just in case a few people might have doubts about whether these pieces of paper were Real Money, the Treasury added the following words in the open space on the certificate to the left of the portrait:

THIS CERTIFICATE IS A LEGAL TENDER IN THE AMOUNT THEREOF IN PAYMENT OF ALLDEBTS AND DUES PUBLIC AND PRIVATE. ACTS OF MARCH 14, 1900, AS AMENDED AND DECEMBER 24, 1919.

In other words, if you owed me $10 and gave me one of these certificates as payment, I couldn't take you to court and claim you'd never paid me. Because "Big Daddy" (the United States Government) had passed laws stating that these certificates are Real Money. Just like the Gold Coins for which they can be redeemed.

The **One-Dollar Silver Certificate** shown just below the Gold Certificate (and accompanied by its precious metal coin) has the same redemption pledge printed on its face—though referring to "One Silver Dollar" in this case. And it also contains similar language to the left of George Washington's portrait, stating that Big Daddy has authorized the legal use of these certificates as Real Money. Just like the Silver Dollars for which they can be exchanged at any time.

For the record, these two certificates shown in Figure 7.2 are significantly larger than the small-sized paper currency we use today.

But we should resist the temptation to make snide cracks about how this demonstrates the "shrunken buying power" of the American Dollar during the years since large certificates were in circulation. The changeover to smaller bills was simply done in the interests of convenience.

In fact, during the early 1930s, when this changeover to small-sized bills took place, the United States experienced the worst period of **De-flation** in its history. With the average price for domestic goods and services falling by about **One-Third**. So the Dollar's buying power actually skyrocketed during these years. (Nice if you were owed money—and could collect. Not so nice if you were the one owing money.)

■ ■ ■

The (Not So) Good Old Days

Some people still cling to the antiquated notion that Commodity Money is "the best Money of all." They argue that linking a society's currency to a precious metal like Gold or Silver gives it an **Objective Value** that people can rely on. For example, Silver Dollar coins are always going to be worth the market value of the Silver they contain, no matter what happens. And this perception extends to their more convenient paper Warehouse Receipts, which can be exchanged for the actual Silver coins whenever you wish.

Therefore, linking a currency to Silver (or Gold) gives it a **Stable Value**. Which extends to the <u>Prices</u> for the goods and services bought and sold in the society using this currency. So we enjoy **Price Stability** and don't have to worry about our buying power being eroded by **Inflation**.

Well, sometimes maybe. But history shows us there are no guarantees.

For example, consider the case of **Spain** in the Sixteenth Century. When it was riding high as the world's Number 1 international power because of its conquest by armed force of what is now Latin America. And had a currency that was linked to **Silver**.

Ah Silver . . .

Spirit of the Moon Goddess . . .

The Thinking Man's Gold . . .

What Magic its name evokes . . .

No wonder the Spanish conquerors of Latin America got very excited when they discovered that **Peru, Bolivia,** and **Mexico** contained immense deposits of Silver ore. Which could be mined and refined at modest cost because of the large populations of Incas, Aztecs, and Mayans who could be pressed into slavery to do all the hard work.

So the Spanish conquerors couldn't resist exploiting to the max the inherent wealth of these vast gifts from the Moon Goddess and shipping huge amounts of refined Silver back home to Spain in their proud galleons.

Where the sudden and virtually non-stop increase in the <u>Supply</u> of coinable Silver available in Spain <u>far outpaced</u> any possible increase in the <u>Supply</u> of local Goods and Services. Which resulted in an <u>explosion</u> in the **Prices** for these Goods and Services. Destroying any hope for the **Price Stability** that fans of Commodity Money claim is one of its primary virtues.

During the Sixteenth Century in Spain, the **Average Price** level soared fivefold. And as Spanish Silver coins flooded the rest of Europe to pay for the imported goods that cash-rich Spaniards increasingly craved, these nations experienced equally destabilizing **Price Inflation**. Despite their currencies' link to Gold and Silver.

To help us understand all this, let's consider the following example of simple Algebraic logic:

Goods & Services Sold x Average Price = GDP = Money Supply x Circulation Rate

This expression tells us that the volume of **Goods & Services Sold** _times_ their **Average Price** per unit _equals_ **GROSS DOMESTIC PRODUCT** (which is a standard measure of a society's "Total Income"). However, **GDP** also _equals_ the **Supply of Money** _times_ the **Rate** at which this Money **Circulates**.

But we can simplify this expression to make it easier to play around with its key variables.

> **First:** The term "GDP" is simply an **Identity Term**. And since "two things equal to the same third thing are equal to each other," we can eliminate GDP.
>
> **Second:** The **Circulation Rate** of Money tends to be more or less fixed for practical purposes. Therefore, this term is an Algebraic Constant rather than an Algebraic Variable. So we can eliminate it too.

These two simplifications leave us with three key variables: **Goods & Services Sold, Money Supply,** and **Average Price**. And we can express any one of these variables in terms of the other two. Watch:

> (1) **Goods & Services Sold = Money Supply / Average Price**
> (2) **Average Price = Money Supply / Goods & Services Sold**
> (3) **Money Supply = Goods & Services Sold x Average Price**

These three expressions constitute the **Basic Model** for **Monetary Theory**. They're so intuitively obvious that any Normal Person can understand them with no difficulty. And can be forgiven for wondering why so many professional economists insist on making such a Fuss about Monetary Theory.

Expression Number 2 shows us the logic of what happened during the Great Inflation that overwhelmed Spain during the Sixteenth Century.

- Spain's Silver-based **Money Supply** increased by leaps and bounds as new coinable Silver flooded in from Latin America.
- But there was no material increase in the supply of **Goods & Services** to offset this <u>Money Supply increase</u>.
- So the **Average Price** of these Goods & Services had nowhere to go but <u>up</u>, as cash-rich Spaniards sought to buy more of these items in their marketplaces.

This illustrates one of the so-called "**Iron Laws of Economics,**" which goes by the name of *The Quantity Theory of Money*. It states that the **amount of Money in circulation is a major determinant of Price Levels**. So if the Money Supply is "Too Large" relative to the supply of things Money can buy, Price Inflation is inevitable.

But the flip side of this relationship is equally important.

If a society's Money Supply is "Too Small" relative to the supply of things Money can buy, then Price **Deflation** is inevitable.

We can see why this happens by looking again at **Expression Number 2**.

(2) **Average Price = Money Supply / Goods & Services Sold**

The logic of Algebra specifies that if a "Too-Small" Money Supply doesn't increase to the right size, then <u>either</u> the volume of **Goods & Services Sold** <u>or</u> their **Average Price** must shrink accordingly, so that both sides of the algebraic expression remain equal. And in the real world, it often happens that <u>both</u> right-hand variables end up shrinking.

In the POW camp, for example, we saw that the growing effectiveness of Allied bombing of Germany's transportation systems during 1944 disrupted normal weekly deliveries of Red Cross Parcels to POWs.

Among other things, this meant that the supply of **Cigarettes** (the camp's Commodity Money) couldn't be renewed as needed to offset the normal consumption of Cigarettes by smokers.

So the camp's Money Supply <u>shrank</u> day by day. Until it became "Too Small" to support the previous level of trading activities for Spam and other Red Cross Parcel items in the camp's markets. Therefore, the **Average Price** for these items had to <u>fall</u> day by day to compensate.

But as POWs became aware of this pervasive <u>Price Deflation</u>, they began postponing their purchases of Red Cross Parcel items ("*Why buy cans of Spam today when their price will be lower tomorrow?*"). And through the inevitable process of **Feedback**, these decisions to postpone purchases resulted in a decline in the daily demand for Red Cross Parcel items in the camp's markets. Which led to further declines in prices that accelerated the process of **Price Deflation.**

However, this Price Deflation caused POWs like Meyer, who had normally been the markets' primary suppliers of these items, to cut back on the Red Cross Parcel items they were willing to offer for sale. This reduction of the **Supply** of Spam and other items in the markets caused the **Volume** of market trading activity to <u>decline</u>. And since market trading was the camp's principle economic activity, this meant that its overall economy <u>shrank</u> until it became virtually moribund. With all the negative social consequences that inevitably followed.

As noted earlier, probably the most spectacular example of this Price Deflation phenomenon occurred in the United States during the early 1930s. When it helped turn a moderately severe business recession into the socioeconomic calamity of the Great Depression. Which brought the nation dangerously close to coming apart at the seams.

■ ■ ■

Paper Money

Let's consider the case of a society whose democratic government has been traditionally run by a political party of **Old Guys.**

These Old Guys are great believers in "prudent government." And their definition of prudence includes having the government spend no more than it takes in from tax revenues. Therefore, the government has always had "balanced budgets." So Spending never exceeds Revenues.

But along comes a group of ambitious **New Guys** whose goal is to win control of the government in the next election. So they form their own political party and begin campaigning aggressively. And their campaign strategy involves discrediting the competence of the Old Guys to run the government.

"Look at the terrible condition of our unpaved roads," the New Guys thunder away in their campaign speeches. *"The people of our society deserve modern paved roads so they can travel more safely and easily. But the incompetent Old Guys running our government won't lift a finger to give us the paved roads we need."*

To which the Old Guys calmly reply:

"If the people of our society really want paved roads, then the government should certainly provide them. But paving our roads will cost money. And the people will have to pay this cost. Which will require a tax increase."

"What nonsense," the New Guys respond confidently. *"Everybody knows the government is riddled with Waste, Fraud, and Abuse. Elect us and we'll get rid of all that Waste, Fraud, and Abuse. That will free up more than enough money to pave our roads. With no need to increase taxes."*

Needless to say, the voters can't help being impressed by what the New Guys are saying. They're promising to have the government pave the roads without making the people pay more taxes. Something for nothing, in other words. Which is very hard to resist.

So on Election Day, the voters hand the government to the New Guys with a solid majority.

But not long after the New Guys take control of the government, they come face to face with two awkward realities:

- The **total cost** of Waste, Fraud, and Abuse in the government isn't nearly as great as they expected. And is much less than the cost of paving the roads.

- The **extra administrative cost** of eliminating most of the actual Waste, Fraud, and Abuse is going to be considerably greater than the total savings from doing so.

These two all-too-common realities put the New Guys in a real bind.

They can't cover the cost of paving all the roads with savings in other government expenses. Which have turned out to be illusory.

They don't want to borrow the necessary money from local banks because this would add a new expense for debt service to the government's budget in future years. Which might require a tax increase to cover if the budget is to remain balanced.

But they feel committed to delivering on their campaign promise to pave the roads before the next election.

So what are they to do?

Many governments have faced this problem down through the ages. And a common solution is the one presented by a super cool and clever New Guy who's working for the government's Treasury Department and is definitely on the make.

"Here's our solution, Mister Secretary," the clever New Guy says to his boss the Treasury Secretary as he lays the following picture on his boss's desk.

FIGURE 7.3. WAREHOUSE RECEIPTS AND "PAPER MONEY"

"Yeah. It's a picture of our regular Dollar Bills," the Treasury Secretary says. "So what?"

"Notice the second bill, Mister Secretary. Right under the top one," the clever New Guy says. "I had it printed up to illustrate our solution. See the difference?"

"They both look pretty much the same to me."

"That's the whole idea. People will <u>think</u> they're the same. But there's a slight difference in the wording."

"What wording?"

"The Silver Certificate on top promises to pay the bearer One Silver Dollar on demand."

"Yeah. So?"

"But the second bill simply promises to pay the bearer One Dollar, period. And it doesn't say in what form."

"Oh. But wait a minute. Isn't all our currency supposed to be backed by Silver?"

"It is now, Mister Secretary."

"Then how does this solve our road paving problem?"

"Look at it this way, Mister Secretary. One way to pay for road paving is to issue more currency to cover the cost."

"Okay."

"But if the extra currency we issue takes the form of regular Silver Certificates, we'll have to buy more Silver to back them. That's a new budget expense. So we won't be generating any new money to pay for road paving. On the other hand, if the extra currency we issue takes the form of these new bills . . . "

"Which aren't specifically backed by Silver?"

"That's the idea, Mister Secretary. So we don't have to buy more Silver. Our only cost is printing the bills. A few cents each."

"In other words, you're saying we can pay for road paving simply by issuing enough of these cheap new bills to cover the cost?"

"It could be the perfect solution, Mister Secretary."

"But can we get away with such a thing? I mean, what will people think if we issue currency they can't redeem for Silver Dollars?"

"Mister Secretary, people have been carrying around Silver Certificates for years. So they're in the habit of thinking of those engraved pieces of paper as Money. And they rarely exchange them for Silver Dollars. When was the last time you saw any of your friends carrying Silver Dollars?"

"You may be right. This second bill certainly <u>looks</u> like a Silver Certificate."

"Absolutely. And we've covered ourselves in another way."

"What way?"

"Look at the second bill again, Mister Secretary. Specifically, look at the words printed in blue just to the left of the portrait."

"Where?"

"Right here, Mister Secretary."

"Oh. You mean the thing about 'this note is a legal tender . . . ' and so forth?"

"Yes. It's basically the same as what's printed in the same place on the Silver Certificate. I checked it out with Legal. In effect, both bills are Real Money because the government <u>says</u> they're Real Money."

"Yeah. Yeah, I see what you mean."

Just then, the Treasury Secretary's phone rings. He holds the receiver to his ear and listens for a moment.

"Yes, put him on . . . " he tells his secretary. "Hello General. We're still on for golf at three. . . ? Good. I may have a solution for that road problem we talked about last week . . . Right. One of my guys came up with an interesting angle . . . Yes, I'll fill you in as soon as we tee off . . . Okay, General. See you at three."

The Treasury Secretary hangs up his phone and turns back to the super cool and clever New Guy.

"I'd like you to pursue this further," he says. "Keep me informed. But don't talk to anybody else about it for the time being."

"Yes, Mister Secretary."

Variations of this scene have been played out in government offices since the proverbial dawn of history. And it illustrates the **Big Problem** with Commodity Money. A problem so big, in fact, as to constitute what amounts to a **Fatal Flaw**.

To put this problem in the right perspective, let's take a look at **Expression Number 1** again.

Goods & Services Sold = Money Supply / Average Price

It's an unavoidable fact of life in most societies that their populations increase over time. So the supply of **Goods & Services** must increase at least as fast as the population to avoid a decrease in the society's overall **Standard of Living** (and preferably to increase it).

The simple algebraic logic of Expression Number 1 states that we can increase the supply of **Goods & Services** available to be sold <u>either</u> by increasing the **Money Supply** <u>or</u> by decreasing the **Average Price** at which these goods & services are sold.

But the logic of the Real World is more complicated than the logic of Algebra. For as we've seen, decreasing the **Average Price** can <u>decrease</u> the supply of **Goods & Services**. Therefore, we're stuck with increasing the **Money Supply** as the only practical way to increase the supply of **Goods & Services**.

However, the only way to increase the supply of Commodity Money is to increase the <u>stock of the Money Commodity</u> (Gold or Silver, or Cigarettes in the case of the POW camp) that constitutes the society's money.

But increasing the stock of Gold or Silver can be an expensive undertaking. In the sense that some portion of the available supply of **Goods & Services** must be diverted to accomplishing such an increase (Gold and Silver aren't cheap to mine and refine unless, like the Spaniards in Sixteenth-Century Latin America, you have enough slave labor available). And this diversion generally reduces the amount of **Goods & Services** available to most other people in a society.

In practical terms, the <u>gross</u> increase in the **Money Supply** may have to be significantly larger than the <u>net</u> increase you're seeking.

On the other hand, **Paper Money** is very cheap to produce. As that super cool and clever New Guy explained to his not-overly-bright Treasury Secretary in the scene we just saw played out.

So is it any wonder that Commodity Money inevitably gives way sooner or later to Paper Money in most societies?

Of course, Paper Money has its own disadvantages. Not the least of which is the unavoidable temptation for governments to pay increasing portions of their ongoing expenses by simply "Printing More Money." Which, if carried too far, can increase the **Money Supply** to a level that overwhelms the supply of **Goods & Services**. Causing **Average Prices** to rise until the society thus affected experiences severe **Inflation**.

Just as happened in Sixteenth-Century Spain, when its supply of

Silver-based money skyrocketed because of the huge influx of fresh coinable Silver from Latin America.

■ ■ ■

Bank Money

In many ways, this is the most interesting form of Money. And probably the most Mystical.

We saw in the POW camp that non-smokers like George found an interesting use for their increasing hordes of **Cigarettes** from weekly Red Cross Parcels.

They would **lend** these cigarettes to other POWs. To be paid back a week later "**with interest**" (in the form of 2 additional cigarettes for each pack of 20). So they developed profitable businesses as **Cigarette Bankers.**

This is an entirely natural process that quickly develops in all human societies. Some entrepreneurs prefer to make short-term business loans with their capital. As opposed to using it to buy equipment, raw materials, and labor services so they can "make things" to sell in the marketplace.

Such "Banker Entrepreneurs" provide an essential **Credit Function** that enables "Producer Entrepreneurs" to flourish. Because their lending activities bridge the inevitable gap between the time when Producer Entrepreneurs must spend money to acquire the resources needed to make things, and the time when they receive money by selling these things to customers.

Meanwhile, the members of society have gotten into the habit of carrying their folding money around with them or hiding it at home in (hopefully) safe places. In the absence of any alternatives, people manage to live with this. But they don't find it all that convenient.

So it isn't long before a few especially perceptive bankers see a new profit opportunity.

Bankers can offer people the opportunity to store their money (i.e., **Deposit it**) for safekeeping in the bank's secure vaults. Where they can have access to it (i.e., **Withdraw it**) any time they wish.

And the bankers go one step further. By offering their **Depositors** a more convenient way to pay their bills.

For example, suppose Moe owes Larry $100. Obviously, Moe can go to his bank. Withdraw $100 in cash from his **Deposit Account**. Then go to Larry's house and hand him the cash. And Larry can take this cash to his bank and deposit it in his account.

But all this takes time and isn't very convenient.

So suppose Moe's bank lets him write a little note directing the bank to pay Larry $100 from his Deposit Account. He signs this note and mails it to Larry. Who takes it to his bank and deposits it directly into his account. And the two banks handle the details of transferring the $100 from Moe's account to Larry's.

What could be simpler?

The banks even supply their deposit customers with printed forms to make writing these notes easier, as seen in Figure 7.4.

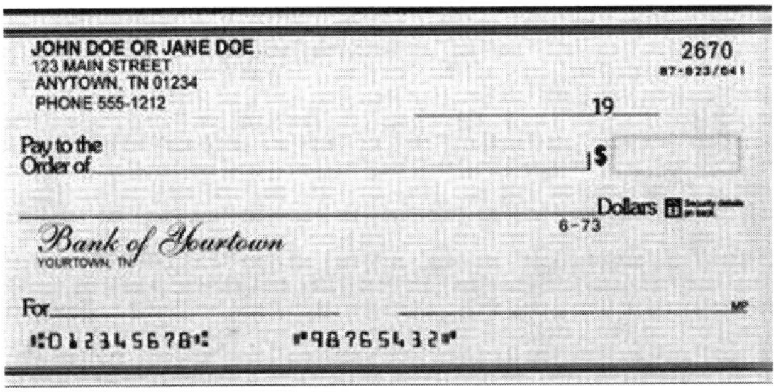
JOHN DOE OR JANE DOE
123 MAIN STREET
ANYTOWN, TN 01234
PHONE 555-1212

2670
87-623/641

19

Pay to the Order of $

Dollars

6-73

Bank of Yourtown
YOURTOWN, TN

For

⑆0123456789⑆ ⑈987654321⑈

FIGURE 7.4. STANDARD CHECKING ACCOUNT PAYMENT FORM

These printed forms are known as **Checks**. Which is why the Deposit Accounts of Moe, Larry, Curly, and other people who use this process are called **Checking Accounts.** And which many professional economists refer to by the less obviously descriptive name of "**Demand Deposits.**"

All of which is so convenient that it isn't long before most people and business firms in the society keep the bulk of their money in Checking Accounts. Holding only a small portion in their pockets as daily "walking-around money."

So the largest component of the society's **Money Supply** now consists of Checking Accounts held in banks (which we can call "**Bank Money**"). With only a small amount consisting of circulating cash in the form of folding money that people carry in their pockets.

But now something truly astonishing occurs.

So watch carefully as we step our way in the next section through the amazing process by which banks "**Create New Money.**" Seemingly out of Thin Air.

■ ■ ■

How Banks "Create Money"

Commercial bankers soon get in the habit of keeping careful records of each day's Deposits and Withdrawals. And it isn't long before they notice something Very Interesting.

During periods of normal economic growth, <u>the amount of new money that customers are depositing</u> in their Checking Accounts each day <u>exceeds the amount of money being withdrawn</u> from these accounts each day as checks come in to be paid.

In other words, daily Deposits are covering daily Withdrawals by a significant margin. Which means that the **Total Balances** of the Checking Accounts held by each bank are **growing steadily**. And since these Total

Balances held in all banks constitute most of the society's Money Supply, this means that the Money Supply is **increasing**. To fuel more economic activity, as measured by the volume of Goods & Services Sold. Just as Expression Number 1 implies.

(1) **Goods & Services Sold = Money Supply / Average Price**

Obviously, bankers are going to look at these growing Checking Account Balances that are, in effect, "lying idle" for the most part and start asking themselves whether they couldn't be put to work as the basis for making new loans to customers. Which would increase the bank's interest income. And the more they think about this, the more compelling its logic becomes.

So they decide to give it a try. In the following manner:

- Just to be on the safe side, bankers set aside a certain portion of their Total Checking Account Balances as a **Reserve** against the possibility of any unexpected upticks in daily Withdrawals. To keep the arithmetic simple and intuitive, we'll assume that the **Reserve Ratio** they choose is a nicely prudent 20 Percent.

- The rest of these Balances (i.e., the remaining 80 Percent) they use as the basis for making new loans to their customers.

- And they do the same thing with the New Deposits customers make each day to their Checking Accounts. That is, they set aside 20 Percent of each day's New Deposits to increase their **Total Reserves**. And use the remaining 80 Percent as the basis for further New Loans.

Of course, when a bank makes a loan to one of its customers, it usually doesn't hand him cash from its vaults. Which the customer would most likely take to a teller's window and deposit in his Checking Account.

Instead, the bank simply <u>increases</u> the balance of the customer's Checking Account by the amount of the loan. With a few strokes of a pen in its ledgers (or, these days, a few clicks on a computer keyboard).

But this <u>increase</u> in the balance of the customer's Checking Account represents a <u>New Deposit</u>. Which, after the bank subtracts the usual 20 Percent to add to its Total Reserves, becomes the basis for making more new loans to other customers in the same manner.

This whole process is known as **"Fractional Reserve Banking."** And its ability to increase a society's **Total Checking Account Balances** (and therefore its **Money Supply**) is nothing less than breathtaking.

To see how this works, let's walk through the process step-by-step. To keep things simple, we'll temporarily assume that the society's banking system consists of a single large bank where all individuals and business firms keep their Checking Accounts. And we'll continue to assume a **Reserve Ratio** of 20 Percent. Which, as we'll see in a minute, has the effect of enabling each New Deposit to ultimately <u>increase</u> Total Deposits by a **multiple of 5** (the reciprocal of the Reserve Ratio—or 1.00 divided by 0.20 in this case).

Sam returns from a business trip bearing a <u>one-thousand-dollar check</u> payable to his manufacturing firm for widgets he sold to customers during the trip. He immediately deposits this check in his firm's Checking Account at the bank.

- The bank adds to its Total Reserves <u>$200</u> of this $1,000 increase in the Checking Account balance of Sam's firm. And uses the <u>remaining</u> $800 to make a new inventory loan to **Eli's wholesale supply firm** so it can increase its stock of the raw materials it sells to manufacturing firms like Sam's. The bank makes this loan through a standard bookkeeping entry to <u>increase</u> the Checking Account Balance of Eli's firm by $800.

- The bank then adds to its Total Reserves <u>$160</u> (or 20 Percent) of the <u>increase</u> it just made to the Checking Account Balance of Eli's firm. And uses the <u>remaining $640</u> (or 80 Percent) to make a new accounts receivable loan to **Mike's trucking firm** so it can extend normal trade credit to more firms like Eli's and thereby serve more customers. Again using the standard procedure of making a bookkeeping entry to increase the Checking Account Balance of Mike's firm by $640.

- Following which, the bank adds to its Total Reserves <u>$128</u> (again 20 Percent) of the <u>increase</u> it just made to the Checking Account Balance of Mike's firm. And uses the <u>remaining $512</u> (again 80 Percent) to make a new inventory loan to **Julie's retail dress shop** so it can buy more dresses to sell to her customers. By making the usual bookkeeping entry to increase her firm's Checking Account Balance by $512.

- Whereupon the bank adds to its Total Reserves <u>$102.40</u> (still 20 Percent) of the increase it's made to the Checking Account Balance of Julie's firm. And uses the <u>remaining $409.60</u> (still 80 Percent) to make a new loan to **Charlie's firm.**

- And so it goes. Round after round. With each round increasing the bank's Total Deposits, therefore its Total Reserves, and thus its Total Loans, by gradually decreasing amounts.

By the time these successive rounds of **Deposit Expansion** finally exhaust themselves (after 62 rounds in this example), Sam's <u>original $1,000 deposit</u> of that check has <u>increased</u> the bank's **Total Deposits** by <u>$5,000.</u>

221

So the society's **Money Supply** has increased by **$5,000**. This can support a **$5,000 increase** in the total volume of economic activity. In the form of **Goods & Services Sold** to and by numerous business firms like Eli's, Mike's, Julie's, and Charlie's, and by the people who earn their livings working for them.

■ ■ ■

Managing the Money Supply: The General Idea

Now wait just a second, you're saying to yourself.

All those people and business firms brought their money to the banks and left it on deposit in checking accounts. Right?

Right.

They did so on the understanding that they could withdraw it whenever they wanted to?

Of course.

And the banks encouraged them to believe this?

Naturally.

But the banks actually used most of this depositor money to make new loans?

Correct.

So weren't the banks engaging in a Con Game? Just like Bernie Madoff? Promising to give depositors their money back whenever they asked for it? Even though the banks were using most of that money to make new loans? Which meant that it wasn't available to give back to depositors?

Not exactly.

Then how . . . ?

Remember. Each day's **New Deposits** usually <u>exceed</u> each day's **Withdrawals** by a considerable margin. And under the standard **Fractional Reserve Banking Mechanism**, a bank adds a portion of each day's New Deposits to its **Reserves**. Just to be on the safe side.

So if a depositor should get "nervous" for any reason about the safety of his money, he can go to his bank to withdraw all the money in his checking account. And be paid in cash on the spot from the bank's Reserves.

This calms the depositor's nervousness. Usually causing him to immediately re-deposit the cash in his checking account for safekeeping. And tell his friends that he had absolutely no problem getting his money back from the bank. This builds confidence among his friends that the bank is a safe place to keep their money.

So everything's okay.

But suppose, for some reason, <u>all</u> the bank's depositors should get "nervous" on the same day and show up at the bank to withdraw all their money from all their checking accounts at the same time? (This is the problem George Bailey faced in that sequence from Frank Capra's movie *It's a Wonderful Life*.)

Such a "**Run On the Bank**" would obviously cause it serious problems.

Maybe the bank could arrange Emergency Cash Loans from the other banks in town to cover this unexpected burst of withdrawals. Otherwise, in a totally unregulated banking system, the bank would have to turn away its depositors and close its doors. And the bank would be said to have "<u>Failed</u>." Leaving its depositors holding the bag.

Such **Banks Failures** were all too common in the United States during the Nineteenth Century, and even during the early decades of the Twentieth Century. The nation's banking system was largely unregulated. And many banks found it very tempting to cut corners when it came to maintaining adequate Reserves to meet mass withdrawals (lower Reserves freed up more depositor money to make new loans—and therefore enabled the banks to earn more interest income).

In some cases, a run on one bank would precipitate runs on a number of other banks. Until large portions of the nation's banking system were in trouble. Such events were called **Bank Panics** and often led to Economic Recessions.

The most famous of these panics was the **Panic of 1907**. Which was resolved when New York City banker J. Pierpont Morgan took it upon himself to organize a temporary consortium of Very Large Banks to provide emergency loans to bail out the nation's banking system.

In other words, a Fractional Reserve System of banks that are as unregulated as neighborhood grocery stores may work well enough most of the time. But when problems arise (as they inevitably will), something better is needed.

One obvious safety mechanism is to have government insure the deposit balances of all checking accounts up to a certain maximum. In the U.S., this is done by the **Federal Deposit Insurance Corporation**. It insures bank deposits up to a maximum of $100,000. So individual depositors have their Checking Accounts protected if their banks should fail for any reason.

But a more comprehensive approach is to establish a **Central Bank** (quite literally, a "**Bank for Bankers**") and give it the responsibility of preventing banks from getting into trouble in the first place.

In the United States, the Central Bank is known as the **Federal Reserve System**. It's called a "System" because it actually consists of 12 regional **Federal Reserve Banks** in different parts of the country. Plus a **Federal Reserve Board** in Washington to "coordinate things."

This follows the typical American practice of leaning over backwards to make things as complicated as possible. (Witness the recent proposals of mind-boggling complexity for providing the U.S. with comprehensive medical care for all its citizens. Which other industrial nations have long since done through the simple and efficient expedient of a government-administered "Single Payer" system. Equivalent to "Medicare for Everybody.")

A Central Bank attempts to keep a Fractional Reserve banking system out of trouble by implementing the following kinds of mechanisms:

- The Central Bank sets the **Reserve Ratio** that all banks must adopt for their New Deposits. This may change from time to time as circumstances warrant.

- The Central Bank requires all banks to deposit their **Total Reserves** with it so they can be monitored on a daily basis to make sure that commercial bankers aren't succumbing to their knee-jerk instinct to pursue every last possible dollar of interest income from new loans.

- The Central Bank maintains an **Emergency Loan Window** from which any bank can borrow if it should get into trouble. In effect, the Central Bank becomes a society's formal "**Lender of Last Resort**" for its commercial banking system.

With these regulatory safeguards in place, the logical next step is to give the Central Bank explicit responsibility for "**Managing Society's Money Supply.**" And to set the overall goal for this management responsibility as one of assuring that the Money Supply:

- Is **always large enough** to support society's potential volume of **Goods & Services Sold** (i.e., its **GDP**).

- **Grows at a prudent rate** over time to support the economic growth needed to provide an adequate supply of goods, services, and jobs for a growing population.

- **Never grows so fast** that it swamps the available supply of Goods & Services. Which could unleash the kind of severe

Inflation that destabilized Spain's economy in the Sixteenth Century. When its Silver-based Commodity Money Supply was exploded by unmanaged imports of monetary Silver from the mines of Latin America.

All of which seems entirely reasonable.

Certainly a lot more reasonable than leaving the size of the Money Supply to be determined by unpredictable increases or decreases in each year's volume of new Gold or Silver produced by the metal mining industry (or the arrival of Red Cross parcels in our POW camp, with their new packs of Cigarettes). As happens with a Commodity Money system.

Or allowing governments to pay their bills by simply <u>printing</u> more low-cost Paper Money, in lieu of raising taxes.

Instead, we rely on one of the Great Talents we human beings possess. Which is to observe the world around us with critical eyes. Figure out how it works. And come up with responsible ways to exploit this understanding to improve our societies.

For in the last analysis, this is our **Most Powerful Weapon** in the never-ending battle with Fate, the Invisible Hand, Ma Nature, or God (take your pick) for dominion over our lonely blue planet.

■ ■ ■

Managing the Money Supply: How It's Actually Done

Yes, fine.

But exactly <u>how</u> do Central Banks control the size of the Money Supply?

The answer lies in that interesting wrinkle we looked at in the mix of regulatory mechanisms Central Banks impose on the banking system.

Specifically, the mechanism that requires commercial banks to deposit their **Total Reserves** with the Central Bank.

Suppose a Central Bank should, through a simple accounting entry, increase the balance of a particular bank's Total Reserves account. To the tune of (let's say) $200.

This immediately means that the bank in question now has $200 worth of "**Free Reserves**"—the amount in excess of what it's required to have on deposit with the Central Bank that day.

- But isn't this the same as if the bank suddenly received a **New Deposit** of $1,000 from one of its Checking Account customers?
- From which it would have to set aside $200 (assuming the same 20 Percent Reserve Ratio we used in our earlier example) to increase its **Total Reserves**?
- Therefore leaving it free to make $800 in **New Loans** to its customers?
- With these new loans increasing the **Checking Account Balances** of these borrowing customers by $800?
- Which would translate into an immediate $800 increase in the **Money Supply**?
- And an ultimate Money Supply increase (after the **Deposit Expansion Process** has fully worked its magic) of $5,000?
- Okay.

But why would the Central Bank arbitrarily increase the balance of a commercial bank's Total Reserves account?

Well, suppose (purely for the sake of illustration) the Central Bank decided to buy $200 worth of secondhand office furniture from the commercial bank. But instead of writing a check for this amount, the Central Bank paid the commercial bank by increasing the balance of its Total Reserves account by $200.

Needless to say, Central Banks aren't normally in the business of buying secondhand office furniture. But they <u>are</u> in the business of buying secondhand debt securities issued by the government—especially securities that mature in less than a year.

The secondhand (i.e., "**Secondary**") markets for government debt securities are enormous. Patronized by many thousands of buyers and sellers. So they're very active. And they're therefore "Very Liquid" (which means modest spreads between the prices buyers are offering and the prices sellers are asking).

So participating in these markets is an excellent and efficient way for a Central Bank to manage the size of the Money Supply. By the <u>daily rate</u> at which it purchases short-maturity government debt securities. A <u>high</u> daily purchasing rate causes the Money Supply to <u>grow faster,</u> while a <u>lower</u> rate causes it to grow <u>more slowly.</u> (And on rare occasions when the Central Bank wants to <u>shrink</u> the Money Supply, it can do so by <u>selling</u> government debt securities.)

This process is known in the trade as "**Open Market Operations.**"

In the United States, overall policy governing Open Market Operations is normally set at meetings of the **Federal Open Market Committee,** composed of top officials of the **Federal Reserve Board** and the twelve regional **Federal Reserve Banks.**

These policies are actually carried out by the **Federal Reserve Bank of New York.** Which occupies an appropriately magnificent Florentine palace on Liberty Street in Lower Manhattan's Financial District. And which (not so coincidently) is also the <u>world's largest storehouse</u> of **Monetary Gold.** Kept safely in its basement vaults in the form of some 5,000 metric tons of thirty-pound Gold Ingots. Each engraved with its own serial number to facilitate keeping track of the ingots' circulating ownership among the world's Central Banks. (One more reason why arrogant New Yorkers believe their home town to be the "Center of All that Really Matters in the World.")

In actual fact, most Central Banks look at the <u>Effect</u> of Money Supply changes rather than their <u>Magnitude</u> to guide the rate at which they buy government securities. Because the Effect is easier to monitor than the Magnitude—by watching variations in the **Interest Rate** in the over-the-counter trading market where commercial banks buy and sell Total Reserves among themselves.

In the course of a normal business day, a commercial bank's Total Deposits and Total Reserves are <u>constantly changing</u> as customers deposit and withdraw funds, and new loans are made while old loans are paid off. As the end of the day approaches, some banks find that their Total Reserves are <u>larger</u> than the Central Bank requires, while other banks see that their Total Reserves are going to end up being <u>too low</u>.

So banks with **Excess Reserves** will <u>lend</u> them overnight to banks whose Reserves are falling short. And the **Interest Rate** at which these loans are made reflects the Supply and Demand among these banks for Reserves in this highly transparent over-the-counter market. <u>Plus</u> (a very important plus) the rate at which the Central Bank is <u>adding</u> Total Reserves to the entire banking system through its daily purchases of government securities.

In the United States, this overnight interest rate is known as the "**Federal Funds Rate.**" It's the "**Basic Interest Rate**" against which all other interest rates are determined. And the Federal Reserve System uses it as its **Formal Target** for managing the nation's Money Supply.

So the **Federal Open Market Committee** expresses its policies for the **rate of Money Supply growth** by announcing its <u>Target</u> for the **Federal Funds Rate** (a <u>lower</u> rate target implying <u>faster</u> Money Supply growth and a <u>higher</u> rate target meaning <u>slower</u> growth). And the **Federal Reserve Bank of New York** implements these policies by keeping the Federal Funds Rate within an eyelash of this target though the rate at which it buys short-maturity Treasury securities.

That's basically all there is to **Monetary Theory**. A fair amount of detail perhaps. But not so much as to be incomprehensible to Normal People. Especially since it's all quite logical.

So you may be forgiven for wondering why professional economists make such a Forbidding Fuss about all this. Because you now have a better and more practical understanding of Monetary Theory than the average Economics Ph.D. candidate showing up for his Oral Exams.

But now let's look at two examples of how Monetary Theory has actually been practiced in the real world. One example illustrating Intelligent Money Supply Management. The other Not-So-Intelligent Money Supply management.

■■■

Managing the Money Supply: Giannini's Miracle

At 5:12 in the morning on April 18, 1906, San Francisco was struck by a Severe Earthquake estimated at a Moment Magnitude of 7.8 (within shouting distance of the great 1960 earthquake in Chile, which was the most powerful earthquake ever recorded and actually caused the earth to wobble on its axis).

The San Francisco quake devastated a great many of the city's buildings and generated fires that burned for four days. At the end of which more than 80 Percent of the city's built-up area had been destroyed. Over 3,000 people lay dead. And three-quarters of the survivors were homeless.

This was a catastrophe equal (in relative terms) to the 5 B-29 fire raids in 1945 that destroyed Tokyo, which had been the world's Third Largest City. So the West Coast's most important ocean shipping port and commercial center had effectively ceased to function. Or so it seemed.

But while the fires were still burning, **Amadeo P. Giannini** was aggressively seeking out his **Bank of Italy**'s small-business customers whose firms had been wiped out by the disaster. Even though his bank's storefront headquarters in North Beach had been devastated by the quake and fire.

Working from a salvaged plank placed across 2 barrels in the middle of a North Beach street, Giannini helped each one of his customers estimate how much it would cost to restart his business. Noted the amounts next to their names in his black pocket notebook. And told each one that the Bank of Italy was granting him a loan for the full amount. Which he could begin drawing on the next morning.

Giannini's gutsy entrepreneurial actions (which soon extended to small-business owners who hadn't previously been Bank of Italy customers) effectively shamed the leaders of San Francisco's larger and more aristocratic banks to cease their paralyzed hand-wringing. And get to work making increasing numbers of new loans to their own business customers.

The result was a <u>massive expansion</u> in San Francisco's Money Supply. This free-flowing liquidity fueled a burst of new business activity. Hiring San Francisco's homeless residents to clear away the debris. Starting construction of new buildings to house its people and business firms. On what amounted to a non-stop basis.

By the opening of San Francisco's Panama-Pacific International Exhibition (and world's fair) in 1915, the city had been totally rebuilt and few signs remained of the 1906 disaster. Indeed, monthly time-series data for San Francisco's economic activity for the 1900–1920 period show only a minor downward blip for the last half of 1906 amid a general trend of healthy growth.

San Francisco's quick-march reconstruction shows what intelligent management of a society's Money Supply can accomplish when the chips are really down. Especially under the sleeves-rolled-up leadership of a savvy banker like that son of Italian immigrants. Whose Bank of Italy grew into today's giant (and recent Federal Bailout recipient) **Bank of America.**

Amadeo Giannini is surely one of the nation's Greatest Capitalist Heroes. Whose influence on the take-charge actions by New York City's J. P. Morgan during the Panic of 1907 is greater than most people realize.

Yet his name is largely unknown to most Americans. Why?

Is this evidence of the too-long lingering All-American tradition that "Italians don't get no respect"?

It's interesting to note that books on the history of Organized Crime go out of their way to remind readers that the ultimate mental befuddlement of people like Chicago's **Al Capone** and New Jersey's **Willie Moretti** can be attributed to **Syphilis**. Which is a classic symbol of presumed Southern European moral weakness in the face of sexual desire. (We can be forgiven for wondering if their mental deterioration would be attributed, more politely, to **Alzheimer's Disease** or **Senile Dementia** if they hadn't been Italian.)

As a nation, we continue to be imprisoned by foolish myths and enchantment tales about "Immigrants," "Foreigners," and others, like Giannini, who lack the names and physical features of "good Yankee Americans." Thereby robbing ourselves of their talents and drive when we most need them.

Which inevitably costs us. Big Time.

■ ■ ■

Managing the Money Supply: Greenspan's Folly

Alan Greenspan was appointed Federal Reserve Chairman by President Reagan and took office in August 1987.

Because of his business background and admitted "Libertarian Republican" ideology, he was expected to continue emphasizing the low-inflation policies of his predecessor, Paul Volker. Who had towered (both physically and intellectually) over the economic world like an NBA Center and is credited with having broken the back of the virulent 1970s inflation spiral by choking off Money Supply growth (which also produced the sharp recessions of 1980 and 1982).

But within months of taking office, Greenspan was confronted by **Black Monday.** The catastrophic crash of more than 20 Percent in U.S. stock markets on October 19, 1987. This was a one-day decline that the "Efficient Markets Theory" financial gurus, bewitched by their conviction that stock price changes follow the Gaussian Normal Distribution, had insisted was "too large ever to happen in the lifetime of the Universe."

(This is why Nassim Taleb regards Black Monday as a prime example of a **"Black Swan Event"**—something whose so-called "probability" might be very low according to Gaussian Statistics but whose consequences can be enormous. And why Taleb freely admits that his trading career's "most profitable day" came on Black Monday. When he found himself holding, by sheer chance, a portfolio of in-the-money Put Options that had become extremely valuable.)

Black Monday's disaster is mainly attributed to something called **"Portfolio Insurance,"** a presumably "no-lose" hedging mechanism that had become extremely fashionable in the financial community during the 1980s.

It was originally developed during the 1970s by Californians **Hayne Leland** and **Mark Rubinstein** and drew heavily on theoretical work done by **Fisher Black, Myron Scholes,** and **Robert Merton** for their famous (if flawed) **Black-Scholes-Merton Options Pricing Model.**

But its wheels came off with a vengeance on October 19, 1987.

The main schtick of Portfolio Insurance involved hedging a stock portfolio by selling <u>S&P 500 Index Futures</u> to establish a "stock price floor" in the event of market declines. Its secondary schtick was to <u>automate</u> the buy/sell process for constantly optimizing the balance between portfolio holdings and futures hedges. By having suitably pro-grammed computers place transaction orders according to built-in algo-rithms that required no direct human action. In theory, this should work fine. For individual portfolios in normal markets.

But it breaks down when everyone is running for the exits at once. Just like in the panic that overtook the patrons jamming Chicago's brand new **Iroquois Theater** on the night of **December 30, 1903**. When a sud-den fire on stage sent them fleeing for the exits in a huge mob. Leaving 575 dead bodies piled up around the blocked exits. In the greatest the-ater fire disaster in American history.

This is basically what happened on Black Monday. Cascading vol-umes of automated sell orders found no buyers. So stock prices went into free fall. Wiping out Billions of Dollars in stock values throughout the shattered markets of the U.S. and Europe by the time the carnage was over.

Greenspan's response to the panic of Black Monday was to flood the banking system with "Emergency Liquidity." That is, he directed the New York Fed to buy Treasury securities like there was no tomorrow to expand the banking system's Total Reserves. Then made it clear to bankers that they were expected to use these fresh reserves to aggres-sively increase their lending to the financial community as if Black Mon-day had merely been a bad dream.

This bold action pumped up the banking system's Total Deposits and therefore the nation's Money Supply (just as Giannini did after the San Francisco earthquake). With the result that the major stock markets re-covered their Black Monday losses in a matter of months, and Wall's Street's bloodbath never touched Main Street. So is it any wonder that Greenspan subsequently made the cover of *Time Magazine* as the "Man Who Saved the World"?

In retrospect, some analysts have argued that Black Monday was an **Early Warning** of the increasing turmoil that took over the financial world and climaxed in the current Economic Crisis. Which we could have headed off by doing sensible things. But instead chose to ignore.

These analysts like to use "hard numbers" to show that Main Street's economy has become progressively "Less Risky" during the past half century. With this "Risk" being measured by shrinking year-to-year variations in GDP. While Wall Street's markets have become progressively "More Risky" during the same period. Measuring "Risk" by the escalating variations in securities prices.

(But let's remember that numbers-oriented financial analysts typically define "Risk" as the **Standard Deviation of Relative Changes in Price or Value**—up as well as down. Because this facilitates computing the numerical probability of a "Risky Event" occurring. Therefore, if winning your state's lottery by purchasing a dollar ticket has the same numerical probability as getting your head handed to you by taking a flyer on a hot stock, both are "Equally Risky." Needless to say, this quirky definition is totally at odds with what Normal People regard as "Risk." Which is understandably concerned only with getting your head handed to you.)

From a more qualitative (i.e., "Realistic") perspective, analysts cite various "Problems" as evidence of how Wall Street got turned on its ear and caused such problems for the rest of us. These include:

- **The increasing proliferation of highly complex Derivatives during the 1990s and the current decade.**

  We saw in **Chapter 4** how the basic **Options** concept can be twisted into mind-boggling shapes to give Wall Street financial firms highly profitable new products to sell in the burgeoning markets for "exotic" home mortgages and other debt-based securities. Many of these products were so complex that few top managers in these firms really understood the dangers they posed, especially in an unregulated environment. And didn't care so long as higher profits kept rolling in.

While Fed Chairman Alan Greenspan kept <u>opposing</u> proposals to regulate these products and the new markets that sprang up to accommodate them. Arguing that "free markets are inherently self-regulating" (like "foxes are inherently the best guardians of chickens"?).

- **The Meltdown of hedge fund Long-Term Capital Management in 1998.**

LTCM was founded in 1994 by **John Meriwether,** the former Vice Chairman and head of bond trading at the investment banking firm of Salomon Brothers (until he was forced out in the wake of a bidding scandal involving U.S. Treasury securities).

Other founding partners included **Myron Scholes** and **Robert Merton,** academic quants fresh from their much-praised work in helping to develop the popular **Black-Scholes-Merton Options Pricing Model.** Plus **David W. Mullins Jr.,** former Vice Chairman of the Fed and leading candidate to (eventually) succeed Alan Greenspan as Fed Chairman.

LTCM's basic schtick was to turn its powerful computers loose on the world's financial markets to spot "<u>Mispricing Opportunities</u>" (i.e., securities whose prices had temporarily gotten out of whack with their traditional relationships to the prices of certain other securities). Then placing <u>arbitrage bets</u> on these anomalies quickly disappearing. By purchasing the "<u>Underpriced</u>" securities and selling short the "<u>Overpriced</u>" securities.

While the profits per bet were small in dollar terms, the return on LTCM's equity could be enormous if it placed many Very Large Bets with mostly borrowed funds (typically with debt-to-equity ratios in the 25-to-1 range). During LTCM's early years, this strategy produced annualized returns of over 40 Percent (net of its hefty management fees) for its so-called "sophisticated" investors.

But LTCM's strategy began coming apart in the wake of the 1997 East Asian financial crisis. And shattered completely when Russia defaulted on its government bonds in August and September 1998.

These events caused the "temporary price anomalies" on which LTCM had placed huge bets to diverge further, instead of converging, as expected. Forcing LTCM to close out its heavily leveraged positions for large loses that dramatically shrank its equity capital.

Spooked by concern that the possibility of further sizable loses to LTCM's creditors (mainly large Wall Street banks) would cause the credit markets to freeze up, Alan Greenspan worked behind the scenes to have the Federal Reserve Bank of New York orchestrate a bailout of LTCM by these banks. In effect, these banks took over control of LTCM from its founding partners, injected nearly $3.7 Billion in temporary capital, and proceeded to unwind the rest of its bets in an orderly fashion. With the Fed pumping up the Money Supply to push down interest rates, thereby making life easier for the banks.

LTCM closed down completely in early 2000, after the

bailout banks had recovered all their money. But there were devastating after-effects for some of those concerned.

Such as LTCM's founding partners losing their entire equity stakes. Scholes and Merton having to virtually go into hiding as their super-quant reputations took a public beating. David Mullins seeing his future as a star of the Fed evaporate. And Goldman Sachs CEO Jon Corzine (heavily involved in bankrolling LTCM) losing a boardroom coup to Henry Paulson and ending up ultimately losing his re-election bid for Governor of New Jersey.

• The Dot-Com Bubble.

This was one of the most classic bubbles in stock market history. With speculators and the usual suckers paying outrageous prices for fresh-faced companies whose names implied some kind of connection with the increasingly fashionable Internet, but which had yet to earn a dime in profits. Justifying their self-perpetuating actions with the old saw that *"no matter what I pay today, there'll always be some Greater Fool to take the stock off my hands tomorrow at a nice profit."*

Nothing new really. The same thing happened with **Railroads** in the 1840s.

Automobiles and Radio in the 1920s. **Transistor Electronics** in the 1950s. **Mainframe Computer Time-Sharing** in the 1960s. **Home PCs** in the 1980s. There've always been plenty of Greater Fools waiting in the wings to fuel the next bubble. And sharp-eyed financial entrepreneurs ready to take their money.

So with Alan Greenspan's Fed keeping interest rates comfortably low during the last half of the 1990s, restless venture capitalists sought out hordes of tech-oriented Silicon Valley types with what could pass as "<u>the next Great Idea for exploiting the Internet</u>." Gave them enough start-up money to organize what looked like bona fide companies with properly glamorous "Dot-Com" names. Helped them create attractive Business Plans based on extreme versions of the Japanese schtick to "<u>build market share first and worry about profits later.</u>" Arranged quickie Initial Public Offerings with hungry broker-dealers to give these start-ups enough cash to support their Let's Pretend act of running "real businesses" for a while. Then stepped back to let the "<u>All-Knowing Stock Market</u>" pick the ultimate winners.

The bubble peaked in early 2000 when the tech-heavy **NASDAQ Index** topped out on March 10 at more than twice its value of a year earlier. Followed by the more diverse **S&P 500**'s last-gasp hiccup on March 24.

After that came the **Great Whoosh**, as the bubble deflated with the usual speed. Wiping out more than $5 Trillion (that's "T" as in "Trauma") in stock market value among tech companies by the end of 2002. Helped along by the astonishing terrorist attack on Lower Manhattan's World Trade Center on 9/11/01.

What caused the stock market's Great Whoosh?

Well, some commentators think it was due to <u>abrupt spending cutbacks</u> by American industry. Which had overinvested in backup communications capacity in the run-up to highly publicized **Y2K problems** that never materialized.

Others point to Greenspan's uncharacteristic experiment with a series of <u>interest rate increases</u> in 1999 (which he quickly reversed after 9/11).

Not to mention the <u>accounting scandals</u> that blew apart tech companies like **WorldCom** and **Global Crossing**. Whose financial managers exploited the numerous opportunities for outright fraud in the <u>Alice-In-Wonderland accounting practices</u> imposed on American corporations by the meshugas of the private sector's **Financial Accounting Standards Board**. Or the realization that the January 2000 acquisition of media giant **Time Warner** by dot-com darling **America Online** was destined to become the <u>most disastrous merger</u> in American corporate history.

The list goes on and on. And none of it really matters. Financial bubbles are always destined to pop sooner or later. Enriching a few sharp speculators who cash in their chips at the Casino window at the right time. While the rest of us are left holding the bag, licking our wounds in bewilderment (and other standard clichés).

But at least it gave Alan Greenspan plenty of excuses for pumping up the Money Supply during the current decade to keep interest rates comfortably low. Which opened wide the door for the housing and derivative booms we looked at earlier.

Notice how often Alan Greenspan pops up in these events. <u>Opposing regulation</u> of the financial markets. <u>Arranging bailouts</u> when they get into trouble. Keeping interest rates <u>too low</u> at the wrong times. Generally taking the Fed in a direction quite different from the previous ruling guideline expressed by William McChesney Martin, Fed Chairman from 1951 to 1970, who's famous for supposedly having said:

"The Fed's job is to take the punch bowl away just when the party's going good."

(Or words to that effect. Sources vary as to the actual words Martin used in expressing this metaphor. But they all mean the same thing.)

So when it comes to managing the Money Supply, the Fed is supposed to "lean against the wind" (another facile metaphor that means less than it says). That is, the Fed should presumably grow the Money Supply <u>more slowly</u> during good economic times and <u>more rapidly</u> during recessions.

But under Greenspan, there's a growing sense that this overall guideline became:

"Keep the party going full blast with generous bowls of vodka-spiked punch. Until the guests are staggering drunkenly around the room. Stumbling into the furniture. Singing bawdy songs. Knocking over floor lamps. Throwing up on the carpet and each other. Then bring in the Fed to clean up the mess."

This approach to Monetary Policy became known as **"Greenspan's Put."** (Remember from **Chapter 4** how the owner of a common stock **Put Option** has the contractual right to sell his shares at a predetermined price, thereby greatly limiting any losses if the market should tank. So it's less risky for him to take a flyer on a hot stock tip from a voluble barber or taxi driver.)

So we had to witness the sad spectacle of bewildered testimony by (then-retired) Greenspan during an October 23, 2008 Congressional hearing. When, in response to questioning by California's go-for-the-jugular Congressman Henry Waxman, he admitted:

"Those of us who have looked to the self-interest of lending institutions to protect shareholder's interests—myself especially—are in a state of shocked disbelief . . . I have found a flaw. I don't know how

significant or permanent it is. But I have been very distressed by that fact . . . Because I have been going for 40 years or more with very considerable evidence that it was working exceptionally well."

By any objective measure, Alan Greenspan easily merited the title of **"History's Most Qualified Central Banker"** when he was named Fed Chairman. He was, after all, no ivory tower academic lost in the stacks of some dusty university library with no hands-on experience in how the world really worked. In fact, his vast and varied range of colorful life experiences truly made him a quintessential **Man of the World.**

- As an undergraduate during the 1940s, he majored in the Clarinet at the Julliard School of Music in Manhattan.

- Thereafter, he toured the country as a Saxophonist in a popular night club jazz band. During which he developed an interesting sideline preparing income tax returns for his fellow musicians. Which gave him an understanding of basic accounting.

- He then enrolled in New York University to study Economics. And became a member of an informal discussion group led by **Ayn Rand,** the famous libertarian philosopher who was instrumental in resurrecting Free Market Economic Theory through her best-selling novels *The Fountainhead* and *Atlas Shrugged.*

- After NYU, he went to work for an economics consulting firm whose clients included Blue Chip corporations in the Fortune 500. Eventually, he became the firm's owner and CEO (so he knew what it was like to be a real businessman and "have to meet a payroll") and made himself a nice fortune in the process.

- During the 1970s, he had his first round of experiences as a Federal official. By serving as Chairman of the President's Council of Economic Advisors in the administration of Gerald Ford. After which he returned to his consulting firm.

- In 1987, President Reagan named him Chairman of the Federal Reserve Board to succeed the legendary Paul Volker. And almost immediately, he was confronted by the massive stock market crash of October 1987. To which he responded by flooding the financial markets with liquidity. Which prevented the Wall Street crash from becoming a Main Street recession.

- During all these years, he led an exceedingly full life as an active pursuer of interesting women. His many romantic targets included such celebrities as **Barbara Walters** and NBC's **Andrea Mitchell** (who became his second wife while he was Fed Chairman).

So how could such an intellectually gifted, highly educated, worldly Renaissance Man screw up so badly during his years as Fed Chairman while the nation's economy was careening towards a cliff?

Some cynics like to argue that the United States is inherently a nation of crooks and scoundrels (in the best "Wild West" tradition) who can't be trusted to act responsibly in the social sense. Especially where **Money** is concerned. So their behavior must be tightly controlled by sophisticated laws, regulatory codes, and aggressive government policing agencies to prevent them from bringing the nation to grief.

Others insist that Americans are fundamentally decent, moral, and innovative (if childlike) people. But the many shortcomings of the nation's sports-obsessed and hamstrung-by-Religion public education systems have left Americans woefully ignorant in such critically important areas as science, economics, and finance.

This prevents them from making sensible decisions through the democratic process about matters that affect the nation's future. Therefore, such decisions should be left to an **"Educated Elite"** in Washington. Building on the highly effective **"Central Planning"** tradition that enabled the United States to defeat Germany and Japan in World War II.

Go figure.

■ ■ ■

Chapter 8
WHO ARE THE VILLAINS?

Batter my heart, three personed God. For you
As yet but knock, breathe, shine, and seek to mend.
That I may rise and stand, o'erthrow me, and bend
Your force, to break, blow, burn, and make me new.
I, like an usurped town to another due,
Labor to admit you. But oh, to no end.
Reason your viceroy in me, me should defend.
But is captived and proves weak or untrue.
Yet dearly I love you, and would be loved fain.
But am betrothed unto your enemy.
Divorce me. Untie or break that knot again.
Take me to you. Imprison me. For I
Except you enthrall me, never shall be free.
Nor ever chaste, except you ravish me.
—John Donne

Well, one thing is certain. They <u>don't</u> include the **Free Market Ideal** itself.

Whatever their shortcomings, Free Markets still remain the <u>best source</u> of Prosperity for human society. A <u>Natural Triumph</u> of human instinct. The <u>underlying basis</u> for everything Worthwhile that Civilization is capable of producing.

Oh come on. Isn't that overdoing it a little?

Think so?

Then pay a visit to one of the places where Free Markets flourish in something close to their Pure Form.

Like **Canal Street** in Manhattan's teeming Chinatown. Lined on either side by open-air stalls selling Chinese-made "Reproductions" of well-known luxury goods. Rolex wristwatches. Mont Blanc pens. Louis Vuitton handbags. Bottles of "Designer Label" perfume. The choices seem endless.

No wonder the sidewalks in front of these stalls are jammed with people (including savvy tourists from Germany and Scandinavia). All clutching Twenty-Dollar bills. Eager to hondel the stall operators for the Best Deal.

This isn't Schlock Merchandise we're talking about. Many of these "Reproductions" are stunningly accurate. And far better values than the Originals selling for 10 times as much Uptown.

Example? On Canal Street, you can buy a Chinese Reproduction "Breitling Chronograph" wristwatch for about $75 or so. In a Madison Avenue jewelry store uptown, the Original goes for maybe $5,000. Put the two side-by-side, and even an experienced jeweler is hard-pressed to tell the difference.

But there is a difference. And an important one.

The Chinese Reproduction Breitling is powered by an inexpensive mass-produced Quartz movement. While the Madison Avenue Original contains a beautifully complicated mechanical movement made with lots of expensive custom hand labor.

But even the cheapest Quartz movement is a far more accurate time-keeper than the finest mechanical movement. And isn't the Number One requirement of a watch that it keep time accurately? (Unless you just want to show the world "how Filthy Rich you are" and don't mind being late.)

So in a lot of cases, the Best Value is to be found in Canal Street's thriving Free Markets. Where even the usual language barriers don't matter. (The stall operators enter their asking prices on cheap calculators. While you respond by entering your much lower offering price on the same calculator. And so on, back and forth, until the two of you get together.)

Spend an hour or so on Canal Street bargaining with the stall operators. And see if you don't come away with a much more realistic perspective on what Free Markets are <u>really all about</u>.

Not villains at all. But **Liberators.**

■ ■ ■

Oh Really?

Well, maybe not if <u>Popular American Television Crime Shows</u> are to be
believed.

An underlying schtick of these shows seems to be that **Capitalist
American Business Corporations** are the most <u>reliable and credible
sources</u> of Murder, Theft, Extortion, and other Terrible Crimes committed against decent Americans. From which brave and resourceful government civil servants (i.e., Cops of one kind or another) are constantly
fighting to protect the rest of us.

Typical examples of these shows include the long-running *CSI: NY* on
CBS. Plus the three even longer-running *Law and Order* shows on NBC.
Not to mention hit shows on the (otherwise militantly pro-business) Fox
Network like *24* and *Prison Break*. Just to name six of the best known.

There are two more or less interchangeable versions of this underlying
schtick.

- **Capitalist American Business Corporations** may be basically "decent organizations" for the most part. But <u>too
many of them</u> get taken over by <u>Shameless Lascivines</u>. Who
corrupt them into committing Terrible Crimes against innocent Americans. Simply to <u>Make More Money.</u>

- **Capitalist American Business Corporations** are <u>Inherently Evil</u> because of their single-minded pursuit of Profits. So they can corrupt the most morally upright Boy Scout Leader types among their employees into committing Terrible Crimes against the American People.

Are these shows well-funded propaganda pieces supported by elaborate foreign conspiracies (possibly Islamic terrorist groups) to undermine support for Capitalism among American television viewers?

Far from it.

- The **CBS Corporation** is controlled by leading American capitalist **Sumner Redstone** though his 80 Percent owned **National Amusements Inc.**

- **NBC Universal** has long been a unit of the huge capitalist icon **General Electric Corporation** (but now seems on the verge of being sold to Comcast).

- The **Fox Broadcasting Company** is owned by the **Fox Entertainment Group,** which is a unit of hands-on capitalist investor **Rupert Murdoch's News Corporation** (which also owns *The Wall Street Journal*).

In which case, <u>why</u> do these private business corporations support television shows whose underlying message seems to be that too many Capitalist American Business Corporations are major sources of <u>Evil Crimes</u>?

The clearest answer seems to be that the <u>business goal</u> for these shows is simply to maximize the revenues their owners can earn by selling commercial airtime on television to <u>other</u> American Corporations wishing to advertise their consumer products. And the shows can do this best by attracting the <u>maximum number</u> of television viewers. Which is easiest to accomplish by playing to the <u>instinctive biases</u> of these viewers. Who are assumed to harbor grave suspicions that America's Capitalist Business Corporations are <u>sources of major crimes and other evils</u>.

In other words, Capitalist Ideology is a fine thing and well worth supporting. Just so long as it doesn't get in the way of anything <u>Really Important</u> (like the capitalist imperative of <u>Making Money</u>).

Want proof?

Then let's listen in on a typical "story conference." Where a TV Writer for one of the most popular crime shows is pitching his story outline for an upcoming episode to a Representative of the Television Network that carries the show and funds its production costs. Backstopped by the show's Producer.

" . . . so to grab viewers right off the bat, we open with an attractive American businesswoman arriving home after work to her modern apartment on Manhattan's Upper East Side . . . " the Writer says eagerly.

"Blond?" the Network Rep interrupts.

"Right," the Writer says. "But, you know, not Show Biz Blond. Or even Trophy Blond. Definitely upscale WASP blond. Mid-thirties. Wearing a dark business suit. Probably from Wisconsin or Minnesota. With an MBA from a top business school . . . "

"That's good," the Network Rep says. "Our audience research shows viewers relate well to that kind of businesswoman. Especially if she's a Crime Victim."

"Oh she's definitely a Victim, Frank," the Producer says. "Tell him, Ira."

"She opens her hall closet," the Writer says. "And an <u>Intruder</u> immediately leaps out and begins attacking her."

"What does the Intruder look like?" the Network Rep says.

"Big and powerful," the Writer says. "Late 20s. Short black beard. Dark skin . . . "

"Mexican maybe?" the Network Rep says. "An Illegal Mexican Immigrant?"

"You've got the whole picture, Frank," the Producer says quickly. "Attractive WASP businesswoman attacked in her apartment by a dangerous-looking Illegal Mexican Immigrant intruder."

"The Mexican angle is key," the Network Rep says. "Our research numbers show a big proportion of viewers think Illegal Mexican Immigrants are a major source of violent crimes. Right behind Islamic Terrorists."

"As a matter of fact, the Mexican also turns out to be an Islamic Terrorist," The Producer says.

"That's great," the Network Rep says. "Looks like you guys are covering all the bases."

"You'll see how in a minute," the Producer says. "Go ahead, Ira."

"Anyway, the woman tries to fight off her attacker. The Mexican," the Writer says. "Manages to break free and runs into the living room. With the Mexican right behind her. He catches her. Smashes her in the face several times. She falls onto the glass coffee table. Which shatters. The Mexican grabs a heavy floor lamp and starts beating her in the head with it. Again and again. So we can show lots of blood-spatter on the beige sofa. And we cut to the show's Title Break."

"Great opening," the Network Rep says. "Real audience-grabber."

"You see what we've done, Frank," the Producer says. "We've given viewers the impression that the Mexican was burglarizing the woman's apartment when she unexpectedly walked in on him. So he attacked her. Beat her to death with that floor lamp. And escaped. So viewers think this is just a standard Burglary-Turned-Murder crime."

"But viewers who know the show are going to wonder if there's more to it than that?" the Network Rep says.

"Right. Tell him, Ira," the Producer says.

"Okay," the Writer says. "Anyway, after the Title Break we do the usual Police Procedure routines. Our two NYPD Detectives and the Crime Lab people go through the Crime Scene carefully. And find clues that seem to confirm the expected Burglary-Turned-Murder pattern. Like the apartment being ransacked. The woman's credit cards missing from her empty purse. Maybe some of her jewelry missing from the bedroom. Plus good footage from the apartment building's security cameras showing the Mexican entering the building, and rushing out later. And a description from the building's doorman of the Mexican leaving in a rush. All leading to the obvious conclusion . . . "

"Jump ahead to the Payoff, Ira," the Producer interrupts. "We can go back to the middle story details after that."

"Right, right," the Writer says. "Actually, the Payoff starts when our Detectives do a routine check into the woman's background. She worked for a major Pharmaceutical company. Had a high-powered career going for herself. But several of her closest associates tell our Detectives about growing tension between her and her boss. A Company VP who'd always regarded her as a star player. But recently, there were problems. And her associates wonder if she and the Company VP were having a secret love affair that had fallen apart . . . "

"Bottom line, Frank. The woman was going to blow the whistle on the Pharmaceutical Company," the Producer breaks in impatiently.

"A Whistle Blower?" the Network Rep says.

"Absolutely." the Producer says. "She accidentally stumbled across information that the Pharmaceutical Company was paying off doctors to prescribe its new Wonder Drug to their cancer patients. Which turned out to do nothing. Safe enough, but totally ineffective. So she tried to persuade the Company VP to pull it from the market."

"But the Company VP refused. Because they were making enormous profits on it," the Writer quickly adds. "So she threatened to go to the FDA."

"And the Company VP hired an Assassin to kill her and make it look like a standard Burglary-Turned-Murder," the Producer says.

"The Mexican?" the Network Rep says with a pleased smile.

"He was working for one of the big Mexican drug gangs," the Writer said. "They sent him to Afghanistan to be trained as a Professional Assassin by an Islamic Terrorist group. The Mexican drug gangs have a lot of work for Assassins."

251

"But how did the Company VP hook up with the Mexican?" the Network Rep asked.

"One of the units the VP ran was a Central American Subsidiary that sold supposedly kosher opium derivatives through local medical groups," the Writer says. "The Subsidiary got its products from the Mexican drug gang. Which got its opium from Afghanistan. So when the VP needed an Assassin . . . "

"Do you see how the Payoff Chain works, Frank?" the Producer says.

"Take me through it, so I'll be clear," the Network Rep says.

"NYPD catches the Mexican and charges him with Murder," the Producer says. "But he negotiates a plea deal in return for fingering the Company VP. So NYPD arrests the Company VP and charges him with Conspiracy to Commit Murder. Who negotiates his own plea deal. To finger the Pharmaceutical Company's CEO. Ready to testify that the CEO gave him direct orders to 'eliminate the woman' as a Whistle Blower. Leaving the CEO with nothing to negotiate for when NYPD arrests him."

"Great. Just great," the Network Rep says. "You link what originally looks like a simple Murder to major crime by that Pharmaceutical Company. Our viewers will love it. The numbers clearly show how convinced they are that Big Corporations are all crooks."

Fanciful?

Well, maybe in Real Life. But you watch enough television to know how popular these fanciful "Big Business Conspiracy" stories are in crime shows. Pulling in viewers by the Millions. So the TV corporations can sell more top-dollar commercial air time. Make More Money.

And never mind any collateral damage to the whole concept of American Capitalism.

■ ■ ■

Psychopaths and Schnooks

Of course, many people believe that the "Real Villains" behind the Economic Crisis were a relatively few individuals. On Wall Street. In banks and other financial institutions. On the faculties of the nation's leading graduate business schools. Running large industrial corporations. Writing ideological papers for small-circulation journals. Setting policies in the West Wing of the Bush White House and on Alan Greenspan's Federal Reserve Board.

The popular view is that these Individuals hijacked the Free Market Ideal because it seemed to be Readily Available. Highly Popular. And as Distinctively <u>American</u> as hand guns. Then proceeded to twist it out of shape to serve personal agendas that turned out to be at odds with the public welfare. At great cost to the rest of us.

Admittedly, some of these hijackers could have been hopeless psychopaths. Whose brains were wired in such a screwed-up manner they actually got more pleasure scamming ten dollars from the usual "widows and orphans" through elaborate Times Square shell games than by honestly earning a hundred dollars selling Bibles door-to-door.

Presumably, the only defense against such psychopaths is to spot them before they can do too much damage and isolate them from the rest of America. For our own safety.

But the overwhelming majority of those who are assumed to have corrupted the Free Market Ideal and turned it into a rip-off of the American public probably started out as fundamentally decent individuals. As Morally Straight as church deacons. Subscribing without question to the best of singsong "American Family Values."

So how did these Boy Scout Leader types go wrong? What turned them into Shameless Lascivines eager to sell their mothers ten times over for a fast buck?

In metaphorical terms, the answer's clear enough to anyone who's ever been bedazzled by **Billy Wilder**'s corrosively breathtaking 1944 move *Double Indemnity*. With **Barbara Stanwyck**'s pathologically definitive *Scarlet Woman* promising poor schnook **Fred MacMurray** riches and sexual ecstasies beyond his wildest dreams. If only he'll bend a few rules.

Just a little.

For a short time.

Far too many middle-aged men know (to their sorrow) how hopelessly tangled Money and Sex are in the male consciousness.

So when a Scarlet Woman strutting in Capitalism's strapless red gown turns her wet-lipped allure loose on us and moves in close enough to fill our lungs with her dizzying perfume, what Boy Scout Leader among us is strong enough to resist her? Or even care much when our homes and hearths and panoply of family values go rushing down the drain?

And if worst comes to worst, we can always stand up in court and plead the equivalent of **Adam's excuse** when God scolded him for having eaten the **Forbidden Fruit** (*"the Woman made me do it."*). Which always plays well among male editors of the tabloids.

Barbara Stanwyck's definitive portrayals of Scarlet Women in so many films throughout her long career makes these performances <u>especially</u> <u>relevant</u> in helping us appreciate why so many men in our male-dominated society remain "confused little boys" who get Sex and Money all mixed up in their minds. Becoming ready prey for real-life "Stanwycks." And all too eagerly sacrificing their careers, families, and very lives for the promises implicit in her eyes.

Apart from *Double Indemnity*, some of Stanwyck's other memorable Scarlet Women fire our imaginations in *The Strange Love of Martha Ivers* (1946), *Sorry, Wrong Number* (1948), and *The File on Thelma Jordan* (1949).

But don't overlook Preston Sturgis's great comedy *The Lady Eve* (1941). With Stanwyck artfully satirizing her Scarlet Woman character, giving it a revealing new perspective. And Frank Capra's masterpiece

Meet John Doe (1941). Where Stanwyck's fledgling Scarlet Woman turns out to be simply an aggressive career gal's defensive "masquerade" (no doubt learned from seeing "too many movies").

To our good fortune, DVDs are becoming available of Hollywood's raunchy "Pre-Code" exploitation films from the early 1930s, where Stanwyck got her start. So be on the lookout for her early Scarlet Woman performances in *Ladies of Leisure* (1930), *Illicit* (1931), *Ladies They Talk About* (1933), *Baby Face* (1933), and *Gambling Lady* (1934, Warner Brothers). Plus Frank Capra's mesmerizing *The Bitter Tea of General Yen* (1933), with Stanwyck as an "emotionally repressed" Scarlet Woman who still manages to seduce and destroy the Chinese warlord who kidnaps her.

Stanwyck's only serious rival for portraying Scarlet Women was **Joan Bennett** (after she became a brunette) for a few years in the 1940s. Bennett's ability to combine skin-deep sexual elegance with the faint suggestion that her ankles might be "slightly dirty" made her totally convincing as a woman even the most respectable of men would throw their lives away for. Best illustrated in the two films she made for director Fritz Lang—*The Woman in the Window* (1944), and *Scarlet Street* (1945). Both with **Edward G. Robinson** as the poor schnook her character victimizes.

A very different (but equally compelling) take on the money/sex theme is the Michael Curtiz 1945 classic *Mildred Pierce*.

Single mother and classic schnook Mildred (**Joan Crawford** striding 10 feet tall in her most iconic role) is driven by a hunger for Money to turn herself into a "traditional go-getting male Entrepreneur" and builds a highly successful restaurant business. All to win the approval of the Great Love of her Life. In the person of her adolescent "Scarlet Woman" Daughter-from-Hell (chillingly played by the usually sweet and innocent **Ann Blyth**). As everything explodes in a climax of Bankruptcy and Murder. With an emotionally shattered Mildred returning in the end to her schlubby ex-husband. As a ragged dawn silhouettes the two of them on the marble steps outside Police Headquarters (one of cameraman Ernest Haller's many unforgettable "noir shots" in this superb and haunting film).

Nothing beats Hollywood movies from the classic "Noir Era" when it comes to providing us with psychological insights into why so many Americans are driven to behave like schmucks.

Or at least offering some convenient and reassuring explanations.

■ ■ ■

The American Public?

That includes the rest of us.

Innocent victims all?

<u>Morally Blameless</u> for what happened? Just like Fred MacMurray's poor schnook in *Double Indemnity*? Totally victimized by Barbara Stanwyck's pathological Scarlet Woman?

Sure.

But <u>why</u> was MacMurray's schnook so easily victimized?

Did it have something to do with his uncontrollable <u>Sexual Greed</u>? Presumably programmed into his male psyche by God with what can only be called malicious intent? Leaving him <u>unable</u> to resist the temptations of Stanwyck's Scarlet Woman as she lured him to Perdition with her mezzo-voiced caressings?

In which case he's obviously <u>morally blameless</u>.

<u>Or</u>, did he make what amounted to a classic Judeo-Christian <u>Moral Decision</u> on his own to become her Partner in Murder and Larceny?

In which case . . . ?

Well, watch *Double Indemnity* and the other films a few more times and see if you can guess the answer. Or (for that matter) read the right parts of the Talmud or the Christian Gospels.

Meanwhile, on what may seem like a more prosaic note, let's look at the All-American **Stock Market Investor** and see what that tells us.

As we saw in **Chapter 2**, ivory tower theorists insist that the millions of stock market investors are all super-rational "**Mister Spock**" types. Possessing complete information about all the corporations whose stocks trade in the nation's stock markets. Knowing everything there is to know about the ins and outs of Accounting and Finance. And basing their daily <u>Buy/Sell/Hold</u> decisions on the classic **Graham-Dodd** mantra of calculating objective "**Risk/Reward**" ratios. (That's why these theorists believe that changes in stock prices are as **Random, Independent,** and **Patternless** as flips of an unbiased coin. And therefore fit the **Bell-Shaped Probability Curve** of Gaussian Statistics.)

But more recent information from interesting fields like **Chaos Theory** and **Behavioral Economics** suggests that Reality is quite different.

The Buy/Sell/Hold decisions of stock market investors are <u>more likely</u> to be driven by what Lord Keynes called "**Animal Spirits.**" Such basic instincts as **Fear, Greed, Hunger,** and the **Actions of the Herd,** for example. Which can be <u>anything</u> but rational. Leading to changes in stock prices that <u>don't fit</u> the popular Bell-Shaped Probability Curve.

These millions of investors tend to group themselves into certain categories. For example:

• Some are the usual **Naïve Sucker Types** looking for the next hot stock that can fly them to the moon in the blink of an eye. Promising them <u>Easy Money</u> they don't have to work for.

So they rely on "tips" from the velvet-voiced Registered Reps at retail brokerage firms trying to unload their firm's bloated inventories of certain stocks.

Or fast-talking "analysts" on cable TV who have an alarming tendency to underperform the S&P 500 on a regular basis.

Or overpriced newsletters claiming to offer new, proprietary, top-secret, computerized software for picking can't-miss stocks. Which usually consist of repackaged "Technical Indicators" that haven't worked for years.

Or cocktail party chatter with fellow dentists, podiatrists, insurance salesmen, real estate agents, and other obvious "market experts." Including the ever-trusty shoeshine guy in the lobby of their office building who claims to have an inside track to the New York Stock Exchange trading floor.

• Others are presumably committed to **"Buying Stocks for the Long Haul."**

Which too often means buying near market tops, because that's what everyone else seems to be doing. After careful study of annual reports, multi-colored stock charts, and company stories in *The Wall Street Journal* or *Forbes*.

Then riding the stocks they've bought down to market bottoms. At which point they become discouraged and sell out. Thereby turning their "paper losses" into actual dollars down the drain.

• Still other investors are so-called **"Market Professionals."** Who work for various financial institutions, like mutual fund companies, and trade the markets with their firm's capital.

They're often armed to the teeth with elaborate, computer-ized, **Mathematical Models** of market behavior and risk man-agement. Most of which are based on outdated principles of Newtonian Physics and Gaussian Statistics, and are worthless when the chips are really down (like during the 40 Percent plus Market Meltdown in the Fall of 2008).

- Then, of course, there are those investors who base their buy and sell decisions on so-called **"Inside Information"** that's not yet generally available to the investing public.

Trading on Inside Information is technically illegal. But scarcely uncommon. Especially among top business executives who've awarded themselves generous stock options in the firms they manage as part of their lavish compensation packages. And are able to manipulate their firms' stock price by clever use of accounting tricks to inflate its latest earnings report.

- Finally, there are the all-too-few **Warren Buffett** types. Who have the skill and patience to uncover "hidden value" in often neglected companies. Make large buys at bargain prices. And often make out like bandits.

But don't kid yourself. This can't be done as a weekend hobby. It's a full-time job and requires plenty of resources. (How large a staff do you think Warren Buffett has?)

All this may sound fashionably cynical and designed to wow left-of-center trophy blonds at wine and cheese parties in the art galleries of Manhattan's Soho. But It contains more than a few grains of truth.

And doesn't it remind you of people who bought houses they couldn't afford during the housing boom? In the hope of being able to make

Quick Profits by flipping the house to the next Greater Fool? Because house prices (like stock prices) were destined to <u>rise forever</u>?

Or people with old-fashioned fixed-rate home mortgages. Who let themselves be tempted into refinancing with glitzier mortgages in order to pocket the cash equity bonanza in their houses that had ballooned like crazy during the housing boom. Which they could use to buy a new SUV or vacation home. Or maybe even invest in the ever-hot stock market.

Or supposedly "prudent and responsible" heads of private charities, non-profit cultural institutions, and the like. Who begged Bernie Madoff to accept a chunk of their endowments to manage. Without doing any basic homework first. Because "everybody" was saying that Bernie was an "investment genius." Able to boost the asset value of their endowments high enough to impress their Boards of Directors and win them a nice raise.

The list goes on . . .

And doesn't this suggest that maybe those millions of irrational stock market investors have nothing on the rest of us when it comes to indulging our Animal Spirits?

In other words, <u>aren't we all to blame</u> for the Economic Crisis? At least a little? Maybe just around the edges?

Let's not forget that Fred MacMurray's supposedly hapless schnook was <u>instinctively hunting</u> for Barbara Stanwyck's ultimate Scarlet Woman. And never mind the consequences.

■ ■ ■

Myths and Enchantment Tales

Meanwhile, let's keep in mind some of the popular myths and enchantment tales about Markets that have brought us so much grief:

- *"Markets exist in a natural state of **Static Equilibrium**. Where the amount of goods and services Consumers are willing to buy at the so-called 'Market Price' always equals the amount Producers are willing to sell."*

WRONG!

Empirical evidence indicates that the natural state of Markets in the Real World is one of **Dynamic Disequilibrium**. With Buyer-and-Seller pairs forever chasing transaction prices that coincide just long enough for them to strike deals. Prices that may be different from those for deals struck at the same instant on the other side of the "trading room."

This should come as no surprise to anyone who's ever bought a "Chinese reproduction" of a Rolex wristwatch or Mont Blanc pen or Vuitton handbag at a bargain price from one of those sidewalk stalls lining Manhattan's **Canal Street**. Where the sweaty reality of Free Markets truly flourishes.

- *"Markets are **Perfectly Efficient** because all decisions to buy and sell are made by coldly rational androids who possess complete information. Have absolute freedom to enter into transactions or to pass on them. And seek only to maximize their personal satisfaction in objective ways.*

WRONG!

Once again, real-world evidence shows us that Markets are primarily **Chaotic**. With the average buyer or seller trying to guess what "<u>all other</u>" average buyers and sellers think is the Right Price.

Not to mention those forced by circumstances to rent that motel room at whatever price the landlord demands—or leave their families standing in the rain after being burned out by a fire in their apartment building. Or sell their inventory of fresh fish at the end of the day for whatever price the manager of a restaurant chain offers—because it'll spoil overnight.

In which case, all thoughts of "maximizing personal satisfaction in objective ways" fly out the window. (Granted, the level of Chaos in many markets is low enough much of the time to provide the "**Illusion of Efficiency**." But illusions are too costly to live by.)

• *"Market price changes are entirely **Random** and **Independent** of each other, just like consecutive tosses of a balanced coin. So they perfectly fit the popular Gaussian bell-shaped curve known as the **Normal Distribution**."*

WRONG!

This goes well beyond the convincing statistical evidence of "Fat Tails" in real-world distributions of price changes (and Nassim Taleb's warnings of potentially catastrophic "Black Swans" like 9/11). Because Normal People know instinctively that prices are determined by full-blooded human beings. Who always start their Bid/Ask negotiations by knowing what the last transaction price was. Random and Independent? Fairyland. The real world is full of **Patterns** and **Dependencies**. Like an unbalanced roulette wheel.

• *"Markets work best when they're not subject to any **Meddling** by external institutions like Government."*

<u>**WRONG!**</u>

This last myth is especially important to those of us who would like to harness the benefits of markets to better serve the public in areas like Transportation.

So let's see what this looks like in real life.

■ ■ ■

The Role of the Government

As I watched the Federal Government's attempts to deal with the **Great Meltdown of 2008**, I was often reminded of the little note my grade school teachers scrawled on too many of my report cards:

"Could have done better."

To help put this in perspective, here's a chronology of Key Events in the evolution of the federal government's Big Daddy transformation.

<u>**Reader Advisory**</u>: This is a <u>very long and detailed list</u> covering the critical period from August 2007 through September 2009 (when many people were claiming that "the Recession was over"). But it can actually be skimmed through relatively quickly.

Its <u>main purpose</u> is to give you a fairly comprehensive picture of how the Federal Government finally got its act together and went on to save the nation from a **Financial Apocalypse** that probably would have destroyed it.

Plus, to show you the truly enormous and multifaceted scope of the Federal Government's rescue actions.

And to fill in some of the blanks surrounding the stories of Bear

Stearns, Lehman Brothers, Merrill Lynch, and AIG that were detailed in **Chapter 2.**

It's one thing to talk in grand and stained-glass tones about "Federal Rescues." But seeing how such things are <u>actually done</u> brings it all home. So dig in. And watch the world change before your eyes.

- **August 2007:** In the wake of the July 31 bankruptcy of the 2 Bear Stearns hedge funds, the **Federal Reserve** makes several announcements during August to remind people that it's ready, with its usual tools, to provide reserves to the banking system "as necessary" and to keep the mortgage crisis from getting out of control.

- **October 9, 2007:** The **S&P 500 Index** reaches an inter-year high of **1565**. This marks the Stock Market Top. After that, everything goes downhill.

- **October 10, 2007:** Bush Treasury Secretary **Henry Paulson** announces the **Hope Now** outreach initiative to help financially pressured homeowners remain in their homes. This is a cooperative alliance of various private sector firms already active in the home mortgage markets, formed with the blessings of the **Treasury Department** and the **Department of Housing and Urban Affairs.**

- **December 12, 2007:** The **Federal Reserve** creates a new **Term Auction Facility** to auction off term loans to commercial banks against a wide variety of collateral. It also establishes "temporary" currency swap arrangements with the **European Central Bank** and the **Swiss National Bank.**

Coincidently (or perhaps not), the Powers That Be subsequently determine that December marked the beginning of the **Recession of 2007–2009**.

- **February 13, 2008**: The **Economic Stimulus Act of 2008** is signed into law by **President Bush**. Consistent with classic GOP ideological principles for "fighting recessions," the Act provides for income tax rebates to individuals ("to stimulate Consumer spending") and tax incentives for business firms to increase their capital investments in new plant and equipment.

It's now generally accepted that individuals used their tax rebates mainly to pay down credit card debts and rebuild their savings accounts, rather than to increase their Consumer spending. While business firms continued to hoard cash, postpone investment outlays, and lay off workers in response to continuing declines in Consumer spending. Therefore, the roughly $150 Billion cost of the Act had no material impact on the Recession.

- **March 11, 2008**: The **Federal Reserve** creates the **Term Securities Lending Facility**. Under this new mechanism, the Fed will lend up to $200 Billion to major investment banks (as opposed to lending only to deposit-taking commercial banks). And will accept a wide variety of securities (including those backed by home mortgages) as collateral for these loans.

The Stock Market responds by rising sharply, with the **S&P 500 Index** rising a whopping 6.7 Percent by the end of the day. But the markets have a change of heart overnight and give back most of these gains the next day.

In subsequent weeks, the **Federal Reserve** continues its rapid process of cutting short-term interest rates on Treasury securities to boost the nation's **Money Supply** as a way to fight the Recession. (**Chapter 7** explained how all this works.)

- **March 24, 2008**: The **Federal Reserve Bank of New York** announces that it will provide term loans to **JPMorgan Chase** for its emergency acquisition of **Bear Stearns**. (See "The **Bear Stearns Story**" in **Chapter 2** for the details.)

- **July 30, 2008**: The **Housing and Economic Recovery Act of 2008** is signed into law by **President Bush**. This authorizes the **Federal Housing Administration** to guarantee $300 Billion in new thirty-year fixed-rate mortgages to sub-prime borrowers. But only if their lenders reduce outstanding balances on existing mortgages to 90 Percent of currently appraised value.

- **September 7, 2008**: The **Federal Housing Finance Agency** (backstopped by the **Treasury Department**) "nationalizes" **Fannie Mae** and **Freddie Mac**. As **Chapter 5** explained, these were the nation's two largest buyers of home mortgages from lending institutions. But they were on the verge of bankruptcy despite the credit line increases extended to them by the Treasury Department on July 15 and despite additional support provided for them in the Housing and Economic Recovery Act of 2008.

- **September 15–19, 2008**: As we saw in **Chapter 2**, this is the **Week of Long Knives** that forever changes the role of the Federal Government.

On September 15, **Lehman Brothers** files for Chapter 11 Bankruptcy after the Federal Government refuses to provide financial assistance. Panic immediately grips the financial markets, with the **S&P 500 Index** plunging 5 Percent for the day. And the nation's largest **Money Market Fund** is forced to cut its per-share value below the "sacred level" of One Dollar because a major portion of its portfolio invested in short-term debt issued by Lehman is now frozen in Bankruptcy Court. This brings the problems of Wall Street home to Main Street with a bang by undermining the confidence of millions of small investors in the previously unquestioned "safety" of the nation's huge money market fund industry as a place to park their savings.

But later on September 15, in a dramatic change of heart, the Federal Government opens its checkbook wide to support **Bank of America**'s $50 Billion acquisition of **Merrill Lynch**.

And on September 16, the Federal Government rushes forward with an initial $85 Billion in taxpayer cash to bail out **AIG** (the nation's largest insurance company). Which had mismanaged itself to the verge of bankruptcy by stuffing its portfolio full of "high yield" Credit Default Swaps whose value has collapsed. And is "elaborately interconnected" with so many other financial institutions as a borrower, lender, and credit insurer that its failure would be like the explosion of a high-megaton Nuclear Bomb.

On September 17, the **Treasury Department** announces a series of "supplementary" short-term debt issues to provide the **Federal Reserve** with extra cash for these emergency financial assistance measures.

(Gasp.)

• <u>September 21, 2008</u>: The **Federal Reserve** approves requests by investment banks **Goldman Sachs** and **Morgan Stanley** to convert themselves into "bank holding companies."

This makes them eligible to borrow emergency cash from the Federal Reserve when necessary (just like deposit-taking "commercial banks"). But they have to submit to the much lower commercial bank limits on "**Leveraging**" their Equity Capital with borrowed funds to enhance profitability.

• <u>September 29, 2008</u>: The soon-to-be-lame-duck **House of Representatives** arbitrarily <u>votes down</u> the Bush Administration's $700 Billion **Troubled Assets Relief Program** to invest taxpayer capital in troubled banks by purchasing their mortgage-backed securities and other "distressed assets." This action seemed to be based on the three-page memo summarizing the Program that Treasury Secretary **Henry Paulson** has submitted, rather than on a careful reading of the actual legislative bill.

Needless to say, the Stock Market reacts with panic to this "failure of democratic government" and suffers one of its worst single-day price declines. With the **S&P 500 Index** plunging a horrendous <u>8.8 Percent</u> by the end of the day.

• <u>October 3, 2008</u>: Rattled by the Stock Market's obvious panic, Congress passes the **Emergency Economic Stabilization Act of 2008**—which includes a cosmetically revamped **Troubled Assets Relief Program**.

But the Stock Market seems too discouraged by the La-La-Land week of Congressional dysfunction in the face of the

Financial Crisis and resumes its decline. As the **S&P 500 Index** falls another <u>18 Percent</u> during the next five trading days.

- <u>October 7, 2008</u>: The **Federal Reserve** creates the **Commercial Paper Funding Facility** to buy short-term debt from large corporations that depend on this kind of borrowing to smooth out normal fluctuations in their operating cash flows.

- <u>October 13, 2008</u>: The **Treasury Department** announced that it will make available <u>$250 Billion</u> in new, taxpayer-funded Equity Capital to financial institutions. By October 28, 9 large banks have sold $125 Billion in new dividend-paying **Preferred Stock** to the Treasury Department.

  Preferred Stock is a special form of Equity Capital whose dividends must be paid in full <u>before</u> any dividends can be paid to the owners of Common Stock.

  So in effect, American taxpayers are given a reasonably secure <u>dividend income stream</u> in return for investing their capital. Just like Warren Buffett and other deep-pocket investors who buy into **Goldman Sachs** and certain other financial institutions during the Meltdown.

  And the banks have the option of <u>buying back</u> this Preferred Stock from the Treasury Department for its original price whenever they wish to restore <u>full dividend rights</u> to the owners of their Common Stock. Thereby (in effect) returning these funds to American taxpayers, who will have earned dividend income on them in the meantime.

- <u>October 21, 2008</u>: The **Federal Reserve** creates the **Money**

Market Investor Funding Facility in an effort to restore the confidence of Main Street's small investors in the safety of the nation's Money Market Fund industry.

As mentioned above, this confidence has been badly shaken in the wake of the Chapter 11 Bankruptcy filing by **Lehman Brothers** on September 15. This action has (among other things) temporarily frozen payments of interest and principal on short-term debt issued by Lehman. Since some Money Market Fund companies hold significant amounts of this Lehman debt, their ability to maintain their "sacred value of $1.00 per share" is threatened.

- **November 4, 2008**: **Barack Obama** wins the Presidential election. And the **Democrats** win control of both the Senate and the House of Representatives. To which the Stock Market responds by continuing its Autumn decline. With the **S&P 500 Index** falling another 25 Percent after Election Day to its Autumn low on November 20.

One reason for the Stock Market's negative response may be its awareness that the U.S. Constitution continues to assume that all travel to Washington is still by horseback. So President-Elect Obama and the members of the newly elected Congress aren't permitted to take office and begin running the Federal Government until **January 20, 2009.**

Therefore, lame-duck President Bush and lame-duck members of the old Congress remain Officially In Charge for more than two months following the election. This delay wastes much valuable time during one of the most critical periods in American history.

(For the record, the **S&P 500 Index** doesn't reach its final Recession low until March 9, 2009. After falling <u>33 Percent</u> since Election Day. Not to mention falling <u>47 Percent</u> since September 1, 2008. And falling <u>57 Percent</u> since the Market's cyclical top on October 9, 2007.)

• <u>**November 10, 2008**</u>: With the approval of the **Federal Reserve, American Express** follows the earlier example of **Goldman Sachs** and **Morgan Stanley** and converts itself into a Bank Holding Company.

<u>**Also,**</u> the **Federal Reserve** and the **Treasury Department** announce a "restructuring" of the **AIG** bailout.

The **Treasury Department** will buy <u>$40 Billion</u> of new, dividend-paying Preferred Stock from AIG, using taxpayer funds from the **Troubled Assets Relief Program.** In return, the Federal Government (i.e., "taxpayers") will <u>own 80 Percent</u> of AIG. With the power to make management changes.

AIG will use <u>$25 Billion</u> of the funds it receives from this sale of Preferred Stock to <u>pay back</u> a portion of its <u>original $85 Billion loan</u> from the **Federal Reserve**. Repayment of the remaining <u>$60 Billion</u> will be extended to <u>5 years</u> at a <u>lower interest rate</u>.

The **Federal Reserve Bank of New York** is authorized to <u>lend $23 Billion</u> to a new, government-owned Limited Liability Company (**Chapter 7** explained the <u>special role</u> of the Federal Reserve Bank of New York within the Federal Reserve System). This company will use these loan funds to <u>buy from AIG</u> Collateralized Debt Obligations backed by home mortgages.

In Addition, the **Federal Reserve Bank of New York** is authorized to <u>lend $30 Billion</u> to a <u>second</u> government-owned Limited Liability Company. This company will use its loan funds to <u>buy from AIG</u> other Collateralized Debt Obligations <u>not</u> backed by home mortgages (i.e., those backed by automobile loans, credit card balances, etc.).

In other words, <u>total taxpayer funds</u> invested in the AIG bailout have now grown to <u>$153 Billion</u>. In return, American Taxpayers now <u>own 80 Percent</u> of AIG. Plus receiving <u>dividend income</u> on AIG's Preferred Stock and <u>interest income</u> from the various loans in the package.

- <u>November 12, 2008</u>: Lame-duck Treasury Secretary **Henry Paulson** announces that the **Treasury Department** has decided <u>not</u> to use funds from the **Troubled Assets Relief Program** to buy toxic mortgage-backed securities from financial institutions. <u>Instead,</u> Treasury will use these funds to make <u>direct capital investments</u> in these institutions. (The Treasury Department has legal authority to do this under obscure wording in the 1,200-page legislation creating the Troubled Assets Relief Program, which few members of Congress have bothered to read.)

- <u>November 17, 2008</u>: Three large life insurance companies announce their intention to take the necessary actions to "qualify" for financial assistance from the **Troubled Assets Relief Program**.

- <u>November 18, 2008</u>: Top managers of **General Motors, Chrysler,** and **Ford** testify before the lame-duck Congress to request "Billions of dollars" in financial assistance under the **Troubled Assets Relief Program**. These executives fly to Washington in their <u>luxury corporate jets</u>. Needless to say, members of Congress and the media have a field day with this astonishing demonstration of how totally clueless these highly paid executive klutzes are about the Real World.

- **November 23, 2008:** The **Treasury Department**, the **Federal Reserve,** and the **Federal Deposit Insurance Corporation** announce a <u>$326 Billion</u> package of taxpayer-funded financial aid to ailing giant **Citigroup**. The Treasury Department and the Federal Deposit Insurance Company will provide Citigroup with a <u>Federal Guarantee</u> against losses on a <u>$306 Billion</u> pool of securities held by Citigroup, which are backed by residential and commercial mortgages.

  Also, the Federal Reserve will provide an interest-paying Credit Line to backstop Citigroup against any <u>further losses</u> in this asset pool beyond its $29 Billion deductible.

  Finally, the Treasury Department will invest an <u>additional $20 Billion</u> in Citigroup. Using taxpayer funds from the **Troubled Assets Relief Program** and receiving dividend-paying Preferred Stock in exchange.

- **November 25, 2008:** The **Federal Reserve** agrees to purchase <u>$100 Million</u> worth of home mortgages held by **Fannie Mae** and **Freddie Mac**. The practical effect of this is to <u>reduce</u> interest rates on thirty-year home mortgages from 6.3 Percent to 5.5 Percent. This is intended to provide a welcome boost to the home mortgage market. These purchases begin on January 5, 2009.

- **December 16, 2008:** The **Federal Reserve** establishes a <u>target range</u> for the all-important <u>Federal Funds Rate</u> at between Zero Percent and 0.25 Percent and makes certain other technical changes. These actions are designed to induce the banking industry to make <u>more</u> loans to business firms and consumers, in an effort to help revive the nation's economy.

(As **Chapter 7** explained, the **Federal Funds Rate** is the interest rate at which commercial banks lend "excess reserves" to each other in the overnight market. Therefore, it's the nation's <u>basic short-term interest rate</u>. In effect, the <u>benchmark</u> that determines all other interest rates.)

- **December 29, 2008:** The **Federal Reserve** announces that it will make a <u>$5 Billion equity investment</u> in the **General Motors Assistance Corporation** (GMAC), as part of its program to assist the domestic automobile industry.

<u>Also</u>, the **Treasury Department** agrees to <u>lend $1 Billion</u> to **General Motors** so it can participate in GMAC's reorganization as a bank holding company.

- **January 2, 2009:** The **Treasury Department** issues to cash-strapped **Chrysler Corporation** an interest-paying <u>$4 Billion</u> emergency loan from the **Troubled Assets Relief Program** so Chrysler can pay its suppliers and meet payroll while it negotiates a complicated restructuring of its debt.

- **January 12, 2009:** Lame-duck **President** Bush asks Congress to release the remaining <u>$350 Billion</u> in funds from the **Troubled Assets Relief Program.** This is done at the request of **President-Elect Obama,** whom the U.S. Constitution <u>still</u> won't allow to take formal command of the Federal Government. Even though he'd been elected to do so by America's voters <u>two months earlier.</u>

- <u>January 16, 2009:</u> The **Treasury Department**, the **Federal Reserve**, and the **Federal Deposit Insurance Corporation** announce a <u>$138 Billion</u> package of financial assistance for **Bank of America** (which, on September 16, had agreed to acquire **Merrill Lynch** at the urging of the Federal Government).

The Treasury Department and the Federal Deposit Insurance Company will enter into a <u>loss-sharing arrangement</u> with Bank of America for its <u>$118 Billion</u> portfolio of loans, securities, and other assets after it has absorbed the first <u>$10 Billion</u>. In return, the Federal Government will receive <u>$24 Billion</u> in new dividend-paying Preferred Stock from the Bank.

<u>Also,</u> the Federal Reserve will provide Bank of America with a backstop <u>Line of Credit</u> (similar to Citigroup) to cover any <u>additional</u> losses in this portfolio.

<u>Finally,</u> the Treasury Department will <u>buy</u> an additional <u>$24 Billion</u> in dividend-paying Preferred Stock from Bank of America, using taxpayer funds from the **Troubled Assets Relief Program.**

<u>On the same day,</u> the Treasury Department announces that it will <u>lend $1.5 Billion</u> to a new entity established by **Chrysler Financial** (the Chrysler Corporation's consumer financing arm). The sole purpose of this loan is to finance <u>new consumer auto loans</u> for Chrysler customers. In return, Chrysler

Financial will have to meet new federal restrictions on executive compensation and other governance issues.

- **January 20, 2009**: **Barack Obama** is <u>finally</u> inaugurated as President, on the date prescribed by the U.S. Constitution. So the man elected President by the voters way back on November 8 <u>at last</u> takes command of the Federal Government.

- **January 28, 2009**: The **National Credit Union Administration** announces that it will <u>guarantee</u> all shares in <u>corporate</u> credit unions through February 9. And will establish a <u>voluntary</u> guarantee program for shares in <u>retail</u> credit unions until the end of December 2010. <u>Also</u>, it will make a <u>$1 Billion capital investment</u> in the **U.S. Central Corporate Federal Credit Union**.

(<u>Corporate</u> credit unions provide financing, check-clearing, and other support services to <u>retail</u> credit unions that serve consumers. Retail credit unions are similar to commercial banks but are owned by their <u>depositors</u> rather than by private investors. They're an important source of automobile loans and other forms of consumer credit.)

- **February 6, 2009**: The **Federal Reserve** announces <u>additional</u> terms and conditions for the **Term Asset-Based Securities Loan Facility.** Originally established on November 25 and scheduled to get under way during the first week of March.

<u>Most important</u> is that the **Federal Reserve Bank of New York** will provide up to <u>$200 Billion</u> in interest-paying loans to eligible owners of Triple A securities backed by new and recent automobile loans, credit card loans, student

loans, and business loans that were guaranteed by the federal **Small Business Administration.**

• **February 10, 2009:** The Obama Administration's new Treasury Secretary, **Timothy Geithner,** announces a new **Financial Stability Plan** that involves four significant actions:

First: The **Treasury Department** will <u>buy</u> dividend-paying Convertible Preferred Stock in eligible banks. (<u>Convertible</u> Preferred Stock gives its owner the <u>option</u> of exchanging it later for regular Common Stock for a specified price.)

Second: A new **Public-Private Investment Fund** will be created to <u>buy</u> troubled loans and other assets from financial institutions.

Third: The **Federal Reserve's Term Asset-Backed Securities Loan Facility** will be expanded further.

Fourth: New initiatives will be implemented to stem <u>foreclosures of home mortgages</u> and to expand <u>loans to small businesses.</u>

But the devastated Stock Market responds to this announcement by continuing its long decline. The **S&P 500 Index** fell another <u>5 Percent</u> by the end of the day.

• **February 17, 2009:** President Obama signs the American Recovery and Reinvestment Act, which Congress had passed on February 11, 2009.

This $787 Billion economic stimulus program will provide $288 Billion (37 Percent) for tax relief. Plus $48 Billion

(6 Percent) in direct Federal grants for road and bridge construction and other infrastructure projects. And $451 Billion (57 Percent) in Federal dollars for various other counter-recession measures.

- **February 18, 2009**: **President Obama** announces the creation of the **Homeowner Affordability and Stability Plan.** This will allow the refinancing of home mortgages owned or guaranteed by **Fannie Mae** or **Freddie Mac** if their balances exceeded 80 Percent of the currently assessed value of the homes in question.

The Plan also establishes a $75 Billion Homeowner Stability Initiative to reduce monthly payments on eligible home mortgages.

Plus, the **Treasury Department** will increase by **$200 Billion** its commitment to buy dividend-paying Preferred Stock from Fannie Mae and Freddie Mac. As well as increasing the limits of the size of their portfolios to $900 Billion.

(But the Stock Market merely yawns.)

- **February 25, 2009**: The **Federal Reserve**, the **Federal Deposit Insurance Corporation**, the **Office of the Comptroller of the Currency**, and the **Office of Thrift Supervision** (all of which have regulatory control over banks) announce that they will conduct detailed "Stress Tests" of major bank holding companies, to be completed by the end of April.

The purpose of these Stress Tests will be to identify the range of potential losses these companies might incur during the next two years. And to assess the size of their resources to absorb such losses.

- **February 26, 2009**: **Fannie Mae** (which had been "nationalized" by the Federal Government on September 7, 2008) reports a $59 Billion loss for the year 2008. With 43 Percent of this loss occurring during the year's final 3 months.

  Also, Fannie Mae announces that the **Federal Housing Finance Agency** submitted a request to the **Treasury Department** the previous day to buy $15.2 Billion in dividend-paying Preferred Stock from Fannie Mae. This purchase will be made under the terms of the **Senior Preferred Stock Purchase Agreement** and will eliminate Fannie Mae's negative equity balance (i.e., the amount by which its Total Liabilities exceeded its Total Assets on its balance sheet).

- **February 27, 2009**: **Citigroup** announces that the **Treasury Department** will convert $25 Billion of its previously purchased Preferred Stock into a 36 Percent Common Stock ownership stake in the bank holding company.

  This will make the Federal Government (on behalf of taxpayers) the largest single shareholder in the company. And could dilute the value of Common Stock held by other shareholders by as much as three-quarters.

  In other words, the Federal Government will effectively hold decisive power in this deeply troubled financial giant and be able to ride herd on its efforts to slim itself down so it can become profitable again. (At which point, hopefully, Citigroup's common stock price will rise and the Federal

Government can sell its shares at a profit for taxpayers.)

The Treasury Department immediately begins exercising its ownership clout by telling Citigroup to suspend all dividend payments to conserve cash, and to revamp its board of directors. But it allows Citigroup's CEO to remain in his job.

- **March 2, 2009**: The **Treasury Department** and the **Federal Reserve** announce <u>another</u> restructuring of their financial assistance to gravely ill **AIG**. This brings the <u>total investment</u> of taxpayer funds to rescue this mismanaged life insurance giant to more than <u>$170 Billion</u>.

  <u>Now</u>, AIG will receive up to <u>$30 Billion</u> in fresh capital in the form of a new Credit Line from the **Troubled Assets Relief Program**. In return for issuing an <u>additional</u> $30 Billion in Preferred Stock to the Treasury Department.

  <u>Plus</u>, the Treasury Department will exchange its <u>existing $40 Billion</u> in AIG Preferred Stock for <u>new</u> Preferred Stock of the same dollar value, tailored to more closely resemble Common Stock (i.e., <u>not</u> paying dividends unless each such payment is specifically declared by AIG's board of directors to come from actual profits).

  <u>Also</u>, AIG's <u>Revolving Credit Line</u> with the **Federal Reserve Bank of New York** will be <u>reduced</u> to not less than $25 Billion, and its terms modified, to enable AIG to conserve cash by saving up to $4 Billion in interest payments.

  In return, the New York Fed will receive Preferred Stock in two <u>Special-Purpose Vehicles</u> (i.e., independent corporations) established to hold the Common Stock of two AIG life in-surance subsidiaries. The New York Fed will determine the <u>dollar value</u> of this Preferred Stock based on its estimate of the market value of the two Special-Purpose Vehicles.

<u>Finally</u>, as required by the Revolving Credit Line Agree-ment, AIG will issue Preferred Stock convertible into a <u>78 Percent ownership interest</u> in itself. This Preferred Stock will be issued to an <u>Independent Trust Fund</u> for the sole benefit of the Treasury Department.

In other words, the Federal Government will <u>functionally own</u> more than **three-quarters** of AIG. In return for having invested <u>$170 Billion</u> worth of taxpayer funds in this sick (but potentially valuable) giant. While staving off financial ruin for a host of private companies that held securities is-sued by AIG.

Meanwhile <u>on the same day</u>, AIG reports that its loss for the year 2008 was <u>$99 Billion</u>. With <u>62 Percent</u> of this loss incurred during the year's final 3 months.

- **<u>March 9, 2009</u>:** The Stock Market <u>finally</u> reaches its **Re-cession Low.**

The **S&P 500 Index:**

> ➤ Has fallen <u>16 Percent</u> since President Obama was in-augurated on January 20.

> ➤ Has fallen <u>33 Percent</u> since Election Day 2008, when voters chose Obama as their new President. But the U.S.

Constitution wouldn't allow him to take office until January 20, 2009, more than <u>two months later.</u>

➤ Has fallen 47 <u>Percent</u> since August 29, 2008, when the Recession's decline started turning Really Ugly as the financial industry's meltdown began to assume critical proportions.

➤ Has fallen 57 <u>Percent</u> since the Market's last cyclical high on October 9, 2007.

But at last the **Animal Spirits** of Stock Market investors turns <u>positive.</u> Whether because of the recent flurry of Recession-Fighting activity by the new Obama Administration. Or simply because investors have gotten all the Selling Sentiment out of their systems (take your pick).

So the Stock Market <u>roars upwards</u> with encouraging enthusiasm. With the S&P 500 Index shooting above the psychological barrier of its Two-Hundred-Day Moving Average on June 1. Having risen <u>39 Percent</u> since its March 9 Recession Low. Bounces around for several weeks to catch its breath. Then resumes its strong advance.

• <u>**March 10, 2009:**</u> In a virtual repeat of the February 26 announcement by Fannie Mae, **Freddie Mac** reports a <u>loss of $50 Billion</u> for 2008. With <u>48 Percent</u> of this coming in the last 3 months of the year.

Continuing the dreary rerun, Freddie Mac also reports that the **Federal Housing Finance Agency** has asked the **Treasury Department** to <u>buy</u> another $31 Billion in dividend-paying

Preferred Stock from Freddie Mac under the terms of the **Senior Preferred Stock Purchase Agreement.**

• **March 14, 2009:** Howls of protest arise in the media and Congress when reports surfaced that **AIG** plans to award $165 Million in bonuses to its managers. Presumably to comply with agreements made before the Federal bailout that became necessary after these executives had mismanaged AIG into Deep Doo-Doo.

Two days later, **President Obama** announces that he will "pursue every single avenue" to block payment of these bonuses.

Well, the bonuses get paid on schedule. But five days later, the **House of Representatives** passes a bill imposing a 90 Percent tax on bonuses paid to executives of companies that have received taxpayer dollars. So 15 of AIG's 20 highest-paid executives wise up and give their bonuses back.

• **March 19, 2009:** The **Treasury Department** announces the establishment of the **Auto Supplier Support Program** to provide up to $5 Billion in financial assistance to the suppliers of auto parts to automobile manufacturers.

The Program will give financial protection to selected suppliers of auto parts for cash payments they are owed by **Detroit's Big 3.** Plus enable these supplier firms to immediately borrow cash on favorable terms secured by these unpaid bills.

• **March 23, 2009:** The **Federal Reserve** and the **Treasury Department** jointly announce the "appropriate roles" for each agency during the financial crisis and beyond.

<u>First</u>: Both agencies will continue their cooperative efforts to improve the functioning of credit markets and to foster financial stability.

<u>Second</u>: The Federal Reserve will avoid actions that worsen credit risks or allocate credit, since these are the responsibilities of the Treasury Department.

<u>Third</u>: The Federal Reserve's actions to pursue financial stability will not interfere with its Congressionally mandated role of fostering both full employment and price stability.

<u>Fourth</u>: There is a need for some kind of "Comprehensive Resolution Regime" for critically important financial institutions.

<u>Fifth</u>: The Treasury Department will seek to remove certain "special-purpose financial aid entities" from the Federal Reserve's balance sheet.

(If all this sounds like a soothing bureaucratic commitment to "Motherhood and Turf Protection," it is probably no accident. But at least it gives the media something to chew over on an otherwise slow-news Monday.)

- **<u>March 24, 2009</u>**: Treasury Secretary **Geithner** announces the details of his **Public-Private Investment Fund** to remove up to <u>$1 Trillion</u> worth of toxic mortgage assets from banks. This is part of the **Financial Stability Plan** that Geithner originally unveiled on February 10.

- **<u>March 24, 2009</u>**: The **Treasury Department** proposes legislation to grant the Federal Government authority to place certain financial institutions into "receivership" (a form of bankruptcy) if their potential insolvency poses risks to the financial system.

In effect, this will extend to <u>non-bank</u> financial institutions (like AIG) the same government supervisory powers <u>already</u> held by the **Federal Deposit Insurance Corporation** with respect to commercial banks. And by the **Federal Housing Finance Agency** with respect to "Government-Sponsored Enterprises" like Fannie Mae and Freddie Mac.

- <u>**March 31, 2009:**</u> Four small bank holding companies announce that they have <u>bought back $338 Million</u> in Preferred Stock they had previously sold to the **Treasury Department** under the **Troubled Assets Relief Program.**

- <u>**April 2, 2009:**</u> At the urging of the Federal Government, the accounting profession's **Financial Accounting Standards Board** (FASB) provides new guidelines for reporting the <u>fair value</u> of certain securities held by banks and other financial institutions.

Previously, securities like Credit Default Swaps and Collateralized Debt Obligations had to be valued at their <u>current market prices</u>. But active trading markets for many of these securities have disappeared (if they ever really existed). So market price valuation is clearly impractical.

Therefore, FASB's new guidelines allow financial institutions to use <u>theoretical models</u> to estimate what the fair value of these securities <u>should be</u> if markets for them actually existed. Under the circumstances, this is the only practical alternative.

- <u>April 30, 2009</u>: The **Obama Administration** announces that the now-bankrupt **Chrysler Corporation** will be acquired by Italy's **Fiat Corporation**, with "substantial Federal Government assistance."

This assistance will include a <u>$3.3 Billion loan</u> to "Old Chrysler" to help it complete its Chapter 11 process.

<u>Plus</u> a <u>$6 Billion loan</u> to "New Chrysler" (post-bankruptcy). New Chrysler will use <u>$2 Billion</u> of this loan cash to buy Old Chrysler's assets from its debt holders—at a price that represents a <u>$4.9 Billion loss</u> to debt holders on the theoretical "fair value" of these assets.

In return, the **Treasury Department** will receive an <u>8 Percent</u> ownership stake in New Chrysler and the right to name the 4 initial members of the company's Board of Directors.

NOTE: The **Ford Motor Company** is the "least sick" of Detroit's Big Three and is able to get through this period of turmoil <u>without</u> requiring any financial assistance from the Federal Government. But this may be at least partly because of the **Special Factor** at work in Ford's case.

Its <u>functional ownership</u> rests with the <u>Ford Family</u> itself. These many descendents of the legendary Henry Ford have an emotional concern for the welfare of the "Family Firm" that transcends the usual grubby financial considerations. This enabled board chairman **Chris Ford** to do many intelligent things to keep the company solvent and turn it around that were beyond the capability of the hired-gun top managers at General Motors and Chrysler (assuming they could even have thought of them).

Maybe there's a lesson here about the larger "social value" of the Old- Fashioned model of hands-on **Owner-Managers,** even for very large corporations. (For the record, several of Ford's current automobiles actually have <u>higher quality ratings</u> than their counterparts at Toyota. No kidding.)

• <u>May 7, 2009</u>: The **Federal Reserve** releases the results of its "Stress Tests" on the nation's <u>19 largest bank holding companies</u>. (On April 24, the Federal Reserve had published a report describing the methodologies it used for these estimates.)

The Stress Tests found that these 19 companies could potentially lose a collective total of <u>$600 Billion during 2009 and 2010</u> if the nation's economy followed the relatively grim scenario assumed for these estimates.

<u>Also,</u> 9 of these 19 companies (roughly 47 Percent of them) were found to already have <u>6 Percent more total capital</u> than they would need to deal with these losses. As well as having <u>4 Percent more equity capital</u> than they would need.

But the remaining 10 companies (about 53 Percent) would need to <u>add $185 Billion</u> to their total capital to adequately protect themselves. However, after allowing for revenues and other transactions occurring since the beginning of 2009, these necessary capital additions netted out to an actual <u>$75 Billion.</u>

287

Bank holding companies needing to augment their capital to ensure adequate protection against potential losses would be required to develop detailed plans within 30 days to acquire sufficient capital. And to actually secure this capital by November 2009.

Some critics dismiss this whole exercise as a "whitewash," which is probably understandable. But most people seem to find some comfort in the Federal Reserve's results.

• <u>May 8, 2009</u>: **Fannie Mae** reports a <u>loss of $23 Billion</u> during the first 3 months of 2009.

Its "overseer," the **Federal Housing Finance Agency**, asks the **Treasury Department** to <u>buy $19 Billion</u> in new Preferred Stock from Fannie Mae to cover its shortfall in Assets relative to Liabilities. Just as it had done back on February 26. (To be considered "solvent," a firm's Assets must be worth <u>at least</u> as much as its Liabilities—and preferably more. Any Assets in excess of Liabilities are called "Net Worth" or "Owners' Equity.") As before, this action is covered by the **Senior Preferred Stock Purchase Agreement**.

At the same time, the Federal Housing Finance Agency and the Treasury Department amend this Agreement to <u>double</u> the size of Treasury's funding commitment to Fannie Mae, to <u>$200 Billion</u>. Plus, to increase the allowed size of Fannie Mae's home mortgage portfolio to <u>$900 Billion</u>. And finally, to increase the limit on Fannie Mae's outstanding debt to <u>$1.1 Trillion</u>.

(Does all this sound familiar?)

- **May 12, 2009:** Not to be left behind, **Freddie Mac** reports a loss of $10 Billion during the first 3 months of 2009. Plus a $6 Billion shortfall in its Assets relative to its Liabilities as of March 31.

  So the **Federal Housing Finance Agency** (Freddie Mac's "federal overseer") asks the Treasury Department to buy $6 billion worth of new Freddie Mac Preferred Stock to cover this shortfall. Consistent with the terms of the **Senior Preferred Stock Purchase Agreement.**

  A week earlier, the Federal Housing Finance Agency and the Treasury Department had amended this Agreement to double the total amount of Preferred Stock (to $200 Billion) that Treasury would buy from Freddie Mac. Plus increase the allowed size of Freddie Mac's home mortgage portfolio to $900 Billion. As both had been done for Fanny Mae.

- **May 13, 2009:** The **Treasury Department** proposes amendments to the **Commodity Exchange Act** and other securities laws to provide for Federal Government regulation of the so-far unregulated "Over-the-Counter" markets for **Derivatives,** like Credit Default Swaps and Collateralized Debt Obligations. (Over-the-Counter markets can be as "informal and ephemeral" as 2 traders hondeling over a particular security's price at opposite ends of a telephone line.)

  Treasury's proposals include requirements that all tradable Derivatives be in the form of "standardized contracts." Just like the Futures Contracts described in **Chapter 4.**

<u>Plus</u>, that such Derivatives be traded and cleared through <u>Organized and Regulated Central Exchanges</u> (equivalent to the New York Stock Exchange).

<u>Plus</u>, that all <u>securities dealers</u> and <u>other firms that actively trade Derivatives</u> be required to <u>maintain</u> standardized documentation of their trading activities and <u>regularly submit</u> such documentation to federal regulators. And be subject to "<u>prudent supervision and regulation</u>" by the Federal Government.

<u>Finally</u>, that the authority of the federal **Commodity Futures Trading Commission** be expanded so that it can <u>regulate Derivatives trading</u>.

While he was Federal Reserve Chairman, **Alan Greenspan** <u>opposed</u> any such regulation of Derivatives. And his views gained sufficiently wide support to result in 1998 Congressional legislation that <u>expressly prohibited</u> the Federal Government and any state government from regulating these securities.

But the <u>collapse</u> of the unregulated Derivatives markets during the **Financial Meltdown of 2008** brought so much grief to so many firms that sentiment quickly changed. There were increasing calls in many circles for the Federal Government to regulate Derivatives. This finally led to the Treasury Department's proposals.

However, most firms in the financial community <u>continued to oppose</u> such regulation and set their highly paid K Street lobbyists to work pressuring Congress to shelve any legislation along these lines. Convincing many critics that the financial community's only concern was to "**privatize profits**

and socialize losses." With any sense of responsibility governed by the **IBG** ("*I'll be gone*") principle.

- **May 19, 2009:** The **Federal Reserve** announces that (beginning in July), certain "high-quality" securities backed by commercial mortgages issued before 2009 (dubbed "Legacy Securities"), and rated Triple A by at least 2 major rating firms, can be used as collateral for government loans made under the **Term Asset-Backed Securities Loan Facility.**

The Federal Reserve's objective was to restart the trading markets for these securities by easing balance sheet pressures on financial institutions in an effort to stimulate new credit activity.

- **May 20, 2009**: **President Obama** signs the **Helping Families Save Their Homes Act of 2009.**

One of its most important provisions temporarily raises federal insurance coverage on bank deposits to $250,000 per depositor. This provision will expire on January 1, 2014, when the coverage limit will revert back to the standard $100,000 per depositor. Except for IRAs and certain other retirement accounts.

- **June 1, 2009: General Motors** and 3 of its American subsidiaries file for Chapter 11 Bankruptcy.

This reflects an understanding with the Federal Government to pave the way for a financial restructuring of GM, which has effectively "run out of operating cash."

The restructuring will include <u>$8.8 Billion</u> worth of taxpayer investments and loans from the **Troubled Assets Relief** Program. In exchange for a <u>60 Percent</u> federal ownership share of GM.

Meanwhile, GM continues running TV commercials and print ads promoting its **Chevrolet Cobalt.**

Cobalt? As in **"Cobalt Bomb"**? The Doomsday Weapon in Stanley Kubrick's 1964 movie *Doctor Strangelove.* That would wipe out all life on earth if it was detonated.

Are GM's managers planning to roll out a "Chevy Polluter" next? Or a "Chevy Clunker"? Or a "Chevy Cramped"?

How far and wide would we have to search in the offices of Government to find bureaucratic drones capable of making such a hopelessly idiotic Marketing Boo-Boo?

- <u>June 9, 2009</u>: The **Treasury Department** announces that 10 of the largest American financial institutions participating in the **Capital Purchase Program** <u>now meet the requirements</u> established by their primary bank supervisors for being allowed to "repay" the taxpayer funds they received under the Program.

  If all 10 firms choose to repay these funds, Treasury will receive <u>$68 Billion</u> on behalf of American taxpayers.

- <u>June 24, 2009</u>: The U.S. **Securities and Exchange Commission** proposes rule amendments to strengthen the regulatory framework for **Money Market Funds.**

The amended rules would <u>reduce risk</u> in Money Market Funds by establishing higher cash-on-hand requirements. By reining in the average maturities of the debt securities the Funds hold. By increasing the credit quality of these securities. And by requiring monthly reporting of all securities each Fund holds.

<u>Also,</u> any Fund would be allowed to suspend redemptions by its shareholders if it developed financial problems that caused its value-per-share to fall below the sacred level of $1.00 (i.e., to "Break the Buck").

- <u>**June 25, 2009**</u>: **AIG** announces that it has entered into an agreement with the **Federal Reserve Bank of New York** to <u>reduce by $25 Billion</u> its debt to the New York Fed.

  <u>Also,</u> the Federal Reserve Bank of New York will receive dividend-paying Preferred Stock, worth $25 Billion, in 2 **Special-Purpose Vehicles** created to hold the <u>Equity Ownership</u> of **American International Assurance Company** and **American Life Insurance Company** (two of AIG's insurance subsidiaries).

- <u>**July 8, 2009**</u>: The **Treasury Department**, the **Federal Reserve**, and the **Federal Deposit Insurance Corporation** announce the details of the **Legacy Securities Public-Private Investment Program**.

  The Treasury Department will invest up to <u>$30 Billion</u> in taxpayer funds to <u>buy</u> "Legacy Securities," in partnership with private sector fund managers and private investors. (Legacy Securities are mortgaged-backed securities issued before 2009 that were originally rated Triple A by 2 or more major rating firms.)

293

- <u>July 21, 2009</u>: Federal Reserve Chairman **Ben Bernanke** presents to Congress the Federal Reserve's latest semi-annual **Monetary Policy Report.**

(The U.S. Constitution gives Congress the power to manage the nation's Money Supply. Congress, in turn, has delegated this responsibility to the Federal Reserve, with the guideline that the Money Supply should be managed in such a way as to achieve high employment and stable prices. The Federal Reserve is required to report to Congress twice a year on how well it's doing.)

In his Congressional testimony, Bernanke notes that *"the extreme risk aversion of last Fall has eased somewhat, and investors are returning to private credit markets."* Most people regard this as Fed-speak for "<u>the Recession is nearly over.</u>" Which subsequently turned out to be the case. The Stock Market seems encouraged by this and resumes its strong rise. By August 3, the **S&P 500 Index** has closed above its psychologically important "1000 level." Having risen <u>48 Percent</u> since its Recession Low on March 9.

- <u>October 19, 2009</u>: The Federal Government's **Commerce Department** announces that the nation's longest post-World War II recession appears to <u>have ended</u>. Data for the 3 months ending September 30 show that inflation-adjusted (i.e., "Real") Gross Domestic Product has <u>risen</u> at an annual rate of <u>3.5 Percent</u>. Breaking a string of 4 three-month quarters during which Real GDP had fallen.

The stock market responds positively to this news. With the S&P 500 rising a nice <u>2.3 Percent</u> for the day.

But there is concern in many quarters that much of the GDP's encouraging increase is due to Federal Government <u>stimulus measures</u> that are running out. Not to mention the fact that <u>Job Losses</u> are continuing. And average Americans regard Unemployment as the <u>most important indicator</u> of the nation's economic performance.

So there's new debate over the question of whether a <u>new round</u> of Federal stimulus measures is needed. With liberal Democrats and their favorite economists insisting that this is <u>critically important</u> to keep the recovery going. While most Republicans and their economists argue that anything like this is "out of the question" because of "record high Federal deficits and borrowing needs."

Most people expect this debate to remain a front-burner issue for the foreseeable future.

■ ■ ■

Implications of the Federal Bailout

We should keep in mind <u>Four points</u> in considering the Federal Bailout activities described above:

- **<u>POINT 1</u>**: The <u>$11 Trillion</u> in taxpayer funds committed as of September 2009 to bailing out private sector business firms that had mismanaged themselves into serious financial trouble <u>should not</u> be thought of as "free money" handed out as a "reward" for royally screwing up.

In other words, these funds are <u>in no way</u> like **Federal Grants** given to **State Governments** from the **Transportation Trust Fund** to support roadway and mass-transit construction projects. Grants that these State Governments <u>never have to pay back</u>.

<u>Instead</u>, these taxpayer funds are more properly regarded as <u>Emergency Investments</u> made on behalf of the <u>American People</u> to save the nation from a **Financial Apocalypse** of truly Biblical proportions. <u>All</u> these investments have taken the form of purchases of dividend-paying Preferred Stock. Or purchases of Common Stock with full voting power. Or interest-paying commercial loans (often secured by specific assets of the borrower). And they're expected to be <u>fully repaid</u> by their private sector recipients in due course.

While earning a <u>reasonable profit </u>for taxpayers in the meantime.

(No doubt you've heard stories about how New York's Five Families gain control of financially ailing private firms by extracting bargain-priced majority ownership in return for desperately needed cash. The parallels here may not necessarily be all that coincidental. Anyway, it's nice to have the Feds on <u>our</u> side.)

<u>Even so</u>, there are people who <u>oppose</u> such actions by the Federal Government as a matter of **Sacred Principle**. Many such people claim to be "**Economic Libertarians**" (even if

they've never actually read Ludwig von Mises, or even Ayn Rand). They insist that 'the greater good" in a capitalist society is best served by <u>allowing</u> business firms that get themselves into financial trouble <u>to fail</u> (just like Lehman Brothers). As a <u>warning</u> to other business firms to manage their financial affairs <u>more prudently</u>. And to <u>demonstrate</u> that the nature of their businesses obviously involved an <u>economically wasteful use of scarce resources</u> that could be put to more profitable use elsewhere.

This kind of "reasoning" reflects the concept of "**Creative Destruction**," usually associated with an early-Twentieth-Century Austrian economist named **Joseph Schumpeter**. He argued that this was the <u>healthiest</u> way for Capitalism to <u>renew itself</u>.

In many respects, Schumpeter's concept is like the idea that a municipal fire department <u>should never</u> try to put out a fire in your house (or any other house in the neighborhood). Instead, the fire should be allowed to <u>burn itself out</u> naturally. Even if this means that your house and everything in it is <u>totally destroyed</u>. Because this will warn <u>other</u> homeowners in the neighborhood to act more "vigilantly" in terms of fire prevention. While freeing up the land on which your house stood for "new construction."

Such "logic" ignores the possibility that your house may have caught fire due to a lightning strike, or some other virulent **Act of God** over which you had no control. Or that the fire in your house may have been ignited by a fire raging in the <u>house next door</u>, which the fire department was allowing to burn freely.

Obviously, Normal People have little patience with such ivory tower nonsense. That's why they universally revere their municipal fire departments. And the dedicated fire-fighters who <u>lay their lives on the line</u> without hesitation to save life and property from the **Fire Demon**.

It was in this spirit of instinctive human pragmatism that most Americans (<u>just barely enough,</u> as it turned out) came to generally support the Federal Government's emergency financial assistance measures to save the nation's capitalistic system from a Fire Demon of terrifying proportions. And now find themselves able to hope for better days.

This wasn't the <u>first time</u> the Federal Government had done such a thing. Best known (and most comprehensively studied—especially by Fed Chairman Bernanke) was during the 1930s, when President Roosevelt's **New Deal Administration** rose up to defend the country against being destroyed by the **Great Depression**.

But there's another example that was equally dramatic and perhaps more telling. This was the so-called "*Federal Bailout of New York City in 1975.*" When the **Treasury Department** implemented its **Seasonal Loan Program** to make short-term loans with taxpayer cash to the city's huge municipal government (the nation's Second Largest "Full Service Government"). After a series of severe budget problems had shut the city's government out of the normal short-term credit markets and threatened it with **Bankruptcy** (just as happened in 2008 to Lehman Brothers).

At the time, very few people realized that this threat was no mere "local problem." It was, in fact, an <u>International Crisis</u> of the most serious kind. Because the **OPEC** oil-producing nations were keeping their enormous receipts of cash from petroleum sales in overnight deposits in American banks.

We now know that bankruptcy by America's commercial and cultural capital would have shattered the confidence of OPEC nations in the United States as a "safe haven" for their funds. So they would have immediately yanked these funds from the banks and invested them in **Gold**. This would have caused a horrendous "run on the banks" that would have blown the American banking system out of the water. Destroying the banking systems of Europe and Asia in the process. Leaving the U.S. Dollar and all other currencies in the developed world virtually worthless. As the price of **Gold** sky-rocketed to something like <u>$15,000 per ounce</u>. And all Western economies lay moaning in the weeds. Or (to use the quaint British phrase), *"the end of Civilization as we know it."*

Astonishingly enough, it was touch-and-go right up to the final hour. Because **President Gerald Ford** initially <u>refused</u> to approve the Seasonal Loan Program. Preferring instead to make speeches (including one in <u>Yugoslavia</u> of all places) about how *"New York City's Jews should be punished for their Sins of Profligacy."* (So Woody Allen was right all along.)

Fortunately, a break came at virtually the Eleventh Hour. When West German Chancellor **Helmut Schmidt** arrived in Washington on a previously scheduled State Visit. Schmidt was a well-educated and savvy political leader who realized that West Germany's financial fate was also at stake. So he

immediately took President Ford aside and explained the
Facts of Life to him in what are said to have been "Very
Blunt Terms." After which Ford withdrew his opposition
to the Seasonal Loan Program and allowed it to proceed.

So New York City was able to avoid bankruptcy at the last
minute, as the Treasury Department rushed to start the flow
of short-term loans. All of which the city's government repaid
on time (or ahead of time). With <u>interest</u>, so American taxpayers "made a profit." And in the course of time, New York
City's government got its act together and became widely ad-
mired for its "responsible and prudent financial management."

Those among you who appreciate the ironies that History
likes to throw at us may appreciate this interesting wrinkle
that arose from the 1975 Fiscal Crisis.

New York City is (among other things) the world's largest
and most important <u>Jewish city</u>. But in 1975, due to an especially ironic turn of events, it ended up owing its financial
salvation to . . . a **German**.

Thus does Fate like to taunt us with its little jokes.

• <u>**POINT 2**</u>: Even so, investing taxpayer dollars in these rescue efforts meant that the Federal Government <u>couldn't
use these dollars for Other Things</u>.

But most of these Other Things <u>still</u> had to be funded, too.

Therefore, outlays for Rescue Investments had to be <u>added</u>
to **Total Federal Outlays**. <u>Increasing</u> the size of the Federal

Government's **Cash Shortfall** (commonly—but mislead-ingly—known as the "**Budget Deficit**"). So necessary fed-eral borrowing <u>increased</u> significantly. Leading to increases in **Total Federal Debt**.

In June 2009, the **Congressional Budget Office** published its projections on the potential implications of this financial pattern over the next 25 years (including the impact of the future costs of escalating Baby Boomer retirements). **Chap-ter 11** describes these projections in detail.

Basically, the Congressional Budget Office's "worst-case scenario" projects **Total Federal Outlays** growing <u>signifi-cantly faster</u> than **Total Federal Receipts**. Causing the Fed-eral Government's annual **Cash Shortfall** to grow—both in dollars, and as a <u>Percentage of Gross Domestic Product</u> (which is the most important growth measure). Requiring <u>more</u> **Federal Borrowing** each year. Leading to a disturbing growth in **Total Federal Debt** <u>as a Percentage of Gross Do-mestic Product</u>. Equivalent to an individual's outstanding Credit Card Debt growing faster than his income.

The most troubling issue this raises involves what steps the Federal Government may have to take <u>to attract sufficient lenders to buy these growing annual debt issues</u>. Will it have to offer much higher <u>interest rates</u>? Leading to higher outlays for interest payments and boosting interest rates for consumers and business firms alike? Or will it have to cover increasingly large portions of the annual Cash Short-fall with "new money" that the Federal Reserve effectively "prints" (**Chapter 7** explained how this is done)?

Obviously, the best solution is to bring the growth rates of Total Federal Outlays and Total Federal Receipts <u>much closer together</u> to slow the growth of the annual Cash Shortfall. The mechanisms discussed for accomplishing this usually involve various combinations of higher tax rates and funding cuts for popular Federal programs. But whether Congress could be induced to approve such unpopular measures is by no means certain.

Fortunately, there is another solution. It effectively involves <u>growing our way out of financial trouble</u>. By making the kind of national investments that <u>increase</u> the growth rate of Gross Domestic Product. Since Total Federal Receipts is a relatively stable <u>proportion</u> of Gross Domestic Product, <u>more</u> GDP means <u>more</u> Federal Receipts. Which would match the growth rate of Total Federal Receipts <u>more closely</u> to the growth rate of Total Federal Outlays and reduce the growth of the annual Cash Shortfall that governs Federal borrowing.

Chapter 11 explains the details of this solution. Including the potential role of investments to **Transform the Nation's Transportation Systems into Healthy Growth Generators.**

<u>POINT 3</u>: The American People owe an enormous <u>vote of thanks</u> to the **gifted Staff Professionals** in the Treasury Department, the Federal Reserve System, and other federal agencies.

These were our <u>Front-Line Combat Soldiers</u>. Who battled the **Fire Demon** round-the-clock during seven-day weeks for months on end. To engineer and implement the imaginative rescue measures that dragged the nation back from an **Abyss** of terrifying proportions.

It's become fashionable in too many circles to glibly dismiss government employees as mindless drones feeding at the public trough who could never cut it in the Real World of private business firms.

But it's difficult to see how this kind of facile sophistry applies to Staff Professionals in these federal agencies (most of whom could have earned more than 10 times their government salaries in the private sector). Why were they so dedicated?

Well, I know why. From a friend's experiences working in the governments of New York City and New York State back in the 1970s, before going on to a career in investment banking.

It turns out that there's nothing like the **thrill** you get working for a large government during a Serious Crisis when all the bureaucratic nonsense goes out the window. Economists like to call this "**Psychic Income.**" If so, my friend was made unimaginably rich with Psychic Income from these experiences. And so were the gifted government people he had the good fortune to work with.

- **POINT 4:** The <u>Political Structure</u> of the Federal Government is an antiquated relic of the Eighteenth Century. This threatens the American People with <u>dangerous levels of Governmental Dysfunction</u> in times of Crisis. All of which was demonstrated with shocking clarity in the previous section. And which we may not survive next time.

When the Founding Fathers wrote the Constitution that imposed this now-outmoded Political Structure on the nation, the only real-world model they had to guide them was the **British Government** of the time. But the British government's model was mainly concerned with attempting to use an independent <u>Legislature</u> to reign in the supposedly God-given arbitrary powers of a <u>Hereditary Monarch</u>.

So the Founding Fathers developed the principle of **Separation of Powers**. In which an independent **Legislature** would <u>make the laws</u>. An independent **Judiciary** would <u>interpret the laws</u>. And an independent **Administration** would <u>carry out the laws</u>.

<u>This</u> was the restrictive **principle** around which the Founding Fathers wrote the Constitution to dictate the structure of our national government. And which was further hamstrung by all sorts of childish visions of a "Rural American Fairyland" imposed by Colonial Schnorrers like **Thomas Jefferson**.

Ironically, all this occurred <u>even while</u> resourceful individuals in the nation's fledgling urban centers were beginning to exploit the kind of entrepreneurial commercial instincts which, over time, and often <u>despite</u> the Constitution, enabled America to become the world's most successful example of <u>Market Capitalism in action</u>.

We like to talk glibly about how we're a nation of **Laws**. But this is sentimental nonsense that ignores Reality. We're <u>actually</u> a nation of **Deals**. Between business firms and their customers. Between the hired-gun managers of these firms and the stockholders who supposedly own them. Between employers and employees. Between anyone who seeks to <u>buy</u> something (real or intangible) and anyone who's willing to <u>sell it</u> (for cash or some other "consideration," like a political vote). And so it goes.

There's nothing wrong with this. It's entirely healthy and productive, at least in spirit. Because **Deals** embody the <u>principles of free markets</u>. And as we saw in **Chapter 6,** markets arise <u>instinctively and naturally</u> whenever human beings gather together in societies.

But what about **Laws?**

Well, they're nice enough to have. Even useful. Such as when we can use them to control the anti-social behavior of hopeless lascivines. Like those who nearly brought us to **Perdition** during the **Financial Meltdown of 2008.** By all means, let's have Laws. So long as they don't get in the way of anything <u>Really Important</u>.

Meanwhile, the UK moved on from the crude government model that inspired the Founding Fathers back in the Eighteenth Century. To evolve something called the **Parliamentary Form of Government,** which is the Standard Contemporary Model for democratic government outside the United States.

The <u>most important principle</u> of Parliamentary Government is that the **Administration** (i.e., the "Head of Government" and his cabinet) is <u>contained within</u> the **Legislature.** Not <u>separate</u> from it. Or <u>independent</u> of it. As in the United States.

<u>Therefore</u>, members of the Administration are <u>also</u> members of the Legislature's majority.

This assures that the **Administration** is always <u>accountable</u> to the **Legislature.** To the point where the Legislature can even <u>fire</u> the Administration (with a "No Confidence" vote). And accept the possibility of having to <u>face the voters itself</u> in a new election on relatively short notice if a <u>new</u> Administration can't be formed within the Legislature.

Therefore, the majority members of the **Legislature** must (in their own interests) be <u>accountable</u> to the **Administration.** Accept its leadership. Support its programs. Rally to its side when the chips are down.

What a breath of fresh air it would be if the United States Congress could be counted on to behave the same way. But its Constitutionally mandated <u>separateness</u> ends up leaving it functionally accountable mainly to K Street lobbyists. Waving checkbooks overflowing with "campaign contributions" (bribes?) to lure too many members of Congress into serving the interests of fat cat lobbyist clients rather than the American People.

It would be nice if we could switch to something closer to a more sensible Parliamentary form of government. But this is probably a vain dream. At least, until Congressional dysfunction during a future national crisis (and don't kid yourself, there's <u>bound</u> to be one) shatters this country to a point where we have to hold a new Constitutional Convention to try and pick up the pieces.

And who knows? This could even make it possible for a newly elected President and Congress to take office <u>the very next day</u>.

■ ■ ■

Chapter 9
Why Markets Need Savvy Regulation

Tiger, Tiger burning bright
In the forests of the night.
What immortal hand or eye
Dare frame thy fearful symmetry?
—William Blake

To understand why, let's consider the **Siberian Tiger**. Probably the most awesome living creature on earth (as attested by the popularity of tiger exhibits in the world's major zoos and circuses).

The Siberian Tiger was brilliantly engineered by God, Ma Nature (or whatever) to be the world's ultimate **Serial Killer**. Far surpassing the shark, barracuda, and piranha fish on this score. Tigers kill other animals with their fearsome combination of size, speed, strength, and cleverness. Topped off with razor-sharp claws and nightmarish teeth.

But tigers don't kill just to meet the Darwinian imperative of satisfying their ravenous hunger. Driven by the magic of some cosmic "Invisible Hand," they also kill for the **sheer joy** of destroying life. Preferably while inflicting the maximum amount of torture and torment on their terrified victims. Because that's their **Nature**.

An example of this occurred on Christmas Day 2007 at the San Francisco Zoo. When 3 teenage boys who had consumed too much beer thought it would be great fun to tease **Tatiana**, the Zoo's four-hundred-pound female Siberian Tiger. By yelling taunts and obscenities at her while standing safely outside her enclosure.

But tigers are notoriously short-tempered. So after the boys had tired of their game and started on their way, Tatiana decided to Seek Vengeance.

She leaped to the top of the twelve-foot wall surrounding her enclosure (no great feat for any full-grown tiger, who can easily surmount such a barrier while carrying an adult deer in her teeth). Hid behind some bushes along the pathway she figured the boys would take. And leaped out at them with a mighty roar as they passed.

Tatiana killed the first boy instantly with a well-placed neck bite that severed his spinal chord. Whacked the other two into a state of semi-consciousness with blows from her powerful front paws. Then settled down to begin the delightful task of tearing their arms off with her fearsome teeth so they could slowly bleed to death while she had fun torturing them.

At which point a team of zookeepers reached the scene and killed Tatiana with a shot to the head from a high-powered rifle. Thereby saving the lives of the remaining two boys. (Whose families naturally followed the standard American practice of suing the City of San Francisco. And ultimately settled for around half a million dollars each.)

But for all their great strength, superior intelligence, and murderous natural instincts, Siberian Tigers are in danger of becoming extinct in their natural habitats. Because each adult tiger requires roughly 400 square miles of unspoiled wilderness stocked with a full range of tasty other animals to survive on its own. And in the modern world, with its burgeoning human population and development pressures, such outsized land hunger is becoming increasingly impractical to satisfy.

So the best future for Siberian Tigers is to live in **Regulated Environments** like the Bronx Zoo's *Tiger Mountain*. Where they can roam at will in large wilderness compounds that replicate their natural habitats. Are fed fresh meat daily so they no longer have to murder other animals. Have their occasional illnesses and injuries promptly treated by trained veterinarians. And are tended by skilled keepers. Who entice them into playing cleverly designed games (to the delight of human spectators) that maintain their physical fitness and fighting instincts without requiring them to indulge in the worst aspects of Serial Killer behavior.

Like Siberian Tigers, markets are "**Serial Killers**" in too many respects. And their best future from the social perspective is to exist in Regulated Environments akin to the Bronx Zoo's *Tiger Mountain*. Where their many benefits can be harnessed to serve the public good. While the anti-social downsides inherent in their nature are properly restrained.

But such Regulated Environments must be intelligently designed to avoid doing more harm than good.

■ ■ ■

The "Theory" of Regulation

In common sense terms, this "Theory" states that that the <u>Buyer</u> of something (a financial security, a car, a house, etc.) must be confident that the item he's purchasing really and truly possesses all the advantages claimed for it by the <u>Seller</u>. And that any disadvantages must be clearly identified. This assures that the Buyer can make a "prudent and rational" decision about whether the item is actually worth the price being charged him.

Many of those who labor in the ivory towers of what they imagine is "Libertarian Economic Theory" insist that the responsibility for informing the Buyer of this factual information will <u>always</u> be fully and effectively carried out by the <u>Seller</u>. Because a Seller knows that his economic success ultimately depends on his reputation among potential buyers for "honesty," "clarity," and similar desirable qualities. Therefore, he has a powerful "economic incentive" to lean over backwards to maintain such a Boy Scout Leader reputation. Even if his natural instincts may be those of a born con artist.

This philosophical concept was an important justification for the recent "**Deregulation Mania**" on Wall Street and elsewhere. Which was embraced by no less an Economic Moralist than Alan Greenspan when he was Federal Reserve Chairman. And it's obviously why General Motors is today the world's largest, most trusted, most profitable manufacturer of high-quality motor vehicles and a bulwark of America's global economic leadership.

At a more cynical (realistic?) extreme is the philosophical concept that all Sellers are inherently Times Square shell-game scammers who can't possibly be trusted to provide clear, honest, comprehensive information about the advantages and disadvantages of the products they offer in the marketplace.

So the Buyer can never afford to act like an innocent child. Instead, he must accept sole responsibility for obtaining on his own all necessary information about whatever purchase he's considering. By reading articles in *Consumer Reports*. By studying information provided by the **Better Business Bureau** and his local government's **Department of Consumer Affairs**. By performing detailed analyses of the numbers in company Annual Reports or Offering Statements for financial securities. And so on.

This is the spirit behind the old saying "**Let the Buyer Beware.**" Popularly expressed by the Latin phrase, "*Caveat Emptor.*"

But Latin is a dead language and out of touch with today's realities. Among other things, this popular Latin phrase implicitly assumes that the Buyer has unlimited time, knowledge, and resources to obtain and evaluate all necessary information to make an informed purchase decision. Which is scarcely the case in the real world.

This obvious truism has given rise to the concept of **Third-Party Regulators**. These are entities charged with the responsibility of providing buyers with the information they need to make informed purchase decisions. Of making sure this information is complete, accurate, and clear. And even (in some cases) of policing the activities of sellers to make sure their actual performance lives up to their promises.

If we accept (at least temporarily, for the sake of discussion) the

311

practical reality that many markets perform better for society generally if they have some degree of regulation by objective and independent third parties, we need to decide whether these third parties should be **Government Agencies** or **Private Sector Organizations.**

- At least in theory, a **Government Agency Regulator** inherently has the police powers that government possesses under the U.S. Constitution. This means that it can, on its own initiative, impose performance standards on those who wish to participate in markets as Sellers. Require them to provide, for the products they sell, specified quantities of information that meet specified quality standards. And sanction them for failure to comply. Including imposing both civil and criminal penalties. For under Constitutional Law, a business corporation is a "legal individual" with the same rights <u>and</u> responsibilities as a human individual.

- On the other hand, a **Private Sector Regulator** depends on the <u>willingness</u> of those it regulates to comply with the performance standards it imposes, and to accept any sanctions it may levy for failure to comply. However, this may be less weak-kneed than it sounds. Many industries go out of their way to pay great respect and deference to their private regulators (at least on paper)—if only to ward off the threat of government regulation. This can give private regulators a high degree of "<u>moral suasion</u>" in policing the behavior of industry firms. And since private regulators aren't hamstrung by civil service pay scales, they can afford to pay the kind of salaries that supposedly ensure first-class technical competence and industry knowledge among their staff members.

■ ■ ■

The FASB Model

A classic example of a private sector third-party regulator is the **Financial Accounting Standards Board,** popularly known as FASB.

Its members are drawn from the highest and most technically qualified levels of the accounting profession. And among other things, FASB has the critically important responsibility for determining how American business firms should <u>report their financial results</u>.

Normal People assume that reporting a firm's income should be a relatively simple matter.

- When the firm receives <u>Cash</u> from the sale of its products, it should report this cash inflow as a **Revenue.**

- When it pays out <u>Cash</u> to its employees or suppliers, it should report this cash outflow as a **Cost.**

- And if the firm has generated more dollars in Revenues than Costs during a month or quarter or year, it's earned a **Profit.**

What could be more obvious?

But FASB's accounting theoreticians think differently. They seem to have a <u>horror</u> of Cash. As if it's something never to mention in mixed company.

So instead of focusing on the hard reality of Cash, FASB's mavens prefer to focus on an intellectual abstraction known as the **"Economic Event."** This can be **"a customer accepting delivery of products."** Or **"employees performing work for wages."** Or **"suppliers delivering raw materials."**

And <u>when</u> such an Economic Event occurs determines the month, quarter, or year in which its <u>dollar value</u> should be reported as a Revenue or Cost. With the timing of this "When" being left to a firm's top managers to decide. So any mention of that taboo obscenity known as Cash is avoided completely.

This intellectual approach to financial reporting is called **Accrual Accounting**. It's enshrined under a formidable panoply of rules and regulations known as **"Generally Accepted Accounting Principles"**—or GAAP for short. (Which, despite the carping of cynics, does <u>not</u> refer to "the Gap between Reality and Fairyland.")

The universal use of this abstract and intellectually oriented form of accounting is why such highly respected and profitable American corporations as **Enron** and **WorldCom** continue to win awards for the completeness, clarity, and honesty of their financial reporting. And why so many firms are able to report "profits" (in the accrual sense) right up to the day when they must file for bankruptcy because they've run out of Cash. Leaving their innocent creditors and equity investors holding what's often an extremely empty bag.

The great flaw in the FASB model for private third-party regulators is obvious enough.

All the technical competence in the world among a regulator's highly paid professional staff members is no automatic protection against having their intellects confused by ivory tower "theories" that are generally clueless about real-world realities.

And if such "theories" dictate the objective standards to be applied in regulating Seller behavior, it's inevitable that Buyers will be misled. Suffering costly losses as a consequence. Thereby defeating the whole purpose of Regulation.

But it gets worse.

If we apply the principal of "what makes sense to a Normal Person" to reporting a business firm's Financial <u>Performance</u> (i.e., its profit or loss during any given period), then this should be a piece of cake. So as we've seen, the firm should report the receipt of Cash from selling its products as **Revenues**, and the payment of Cash to employees and suppliers as **Costs**. If Revenues are higher than Costs during the reporting period, it's made a **Profit**. But if Costs are higher than Revenues, it has a **Loss**.

What's so hard about that?

However, reporting a firm's Financial <u>Status</u> at any point in time in a way that makes sense to a Normal Person is more complicated. Even though Status is just as important as Performance, because it's the underlying basis for determining what the firm's <u>Value</u> is.

A firm's Financial <u>Status</u> (as opposed to its Financial <u>Performance</u>) concerns the dollar value of what the firm **Owns** versus the dollar value of what it **Owes**. Both of which are supposed to be shown on its **Balance Sheet**.

In terms of simple algebra, this means that:

The $ Value of What the Firm <u>Owns</u> = The $ Value of What the Firm <u>Owes</u>

In accounting-speak, the things a firm <u>Owns</u> are called **Assets** and the things it <u>Owes</u> are called **Liabilities**. Therefore:

Total Asset $ = Total Liability $

But there are two categories of Liabilities. <u>One</u> consists of **Dollars Owed to the firm's Creditors**. The <u>second</u> consists of **Dollars Owed to the firm's Owners** (i.e., its **Stockholders**). So:

Total Asset $ = Creditor Liability $ + Stockholder Equity $

By the process of simple algebraic manipulation, this means that:

Stockholder Equity $ = Total Asset $ - Creditor Liability $

In other words, we can increase the theoretical dollar value of **Stockholder Equity** <u>either</u> by increasing the dollar value of **Total Assets** <u>or</u> by decreasing the dollar value of **Creditor Liabilities** (or some appropriate combination of the two).

All of which underscores the importance of showing a realistic value for **Total Assets** on a firm's **Balance Sheet**.

So how do you establish the value of Assets in a way that makes sense to Normal People?

Suppose one of the firm's Assets is a **fully equipped factory** that's producing products for sale to customers. What's the <u>value</u> of this factory at any given point in time?

Here are the possibilities:

- **How much money did the firm pay to acquire the factory in the first place (its "<u>Original Cost</u>")?**

This is the standard way of reporting the factory's Asset Value because it's the simplest. The firm has records documenting the Actual Cash it paid out to buy or construct the factory building and equip it with production machinery. So it can report the factory's Asset Value this way on its Balance Sheet with the "blessings" of FASB.

However, it's standard practice to show the factory's Asset Value on a <u>Net</u> basis. This subtracts from the Actual Cash originally paid out an estimate of the factory's **Accumulated Annual Depreciation**. Depreciation is an estimate of the theoretical cost of "<u>wear and tear</u>" on the factory during each year it produces products for sale to customers. Based on an estimate of how many years of "economically useful life" it's expected to have. So estimated Accumulated Depreciation is simply the annual Depreciation estimate <u>times</u> the number of years it's been producing products. (Lots of "estimates" here.)

In theory, therefore, the factory's Net Asset Value is <u>Zero</u> at the end of its "estimated useful life" (i.e., when it's "<u>Fully Depreciated</u>"). Even if, in the real world, the factory can continue producing products for sale to customers without needing any new investment to upgrade its building and replace worn-out production equipment. So a Fully Depreciated factory may still, in fact, have meaningful Asset Value, even though FASB won't let the firm show this on its Balance Sheet. This can motivate top management to make new investments in the factory solely to avoid any decline in the theoretical value of its Total Assets ("FASB-driven investment activity"). Because such a decline would inevitably result in a decline in the theoretical value of its Stockholders' Equity.

At the same time, the "Original Cost" approach to defining a factory's Asset Value implicitly assumes that the factory didn't become "economically obsolete" more rapidly than is reflected in its estimate of Accumulated Depreciation. If this assumption is wrong, then its Net Asset Value shown on the Balance Sheet may be unrealistically high in common sense terms. This would result in an unrealistically high theoretical value for its Stockholders' Equity. Thereby misleading Normal People who might be considering buying the firm's common stock.

• **How much money would the firm have to pay today to replace the factory with a brand new one (its "Replacement Cost")?**

This is generally regarded as a more conservative approach to defining Asset Value. And it may be a sensible approach for firms in industries where rapid advances in production technology may cause the factory's production layout or equipment to become "economically obsolete" relatively quickly.

The "Replacement Cost" approach is likely to result in a higher Asset Value for the factory <u>even if</u> a new factory would be exactly the same as an old one. Because today's cost of constructing an identical new building and equipping it with identical production machinery is bound to be greater than it was 10 or 20 years ago.

Therefore, defining an existing factory's Asset Value on the basis of its Replacement Cost may appeal to top managers who wish to offset higher Liability values on their Balance Sheet (from taking on new debt, for example). Or to "artificially" boost the theoretical value of Stockholders' Equity by means of accounting trickery. All of which can mislead Normal People about the firm's true financial strength.

• **How much money could the firm sell the factory for today in the open market (its "<u>Market Value</u>")?**

If an active and liquid Secondary Market happens to exist for such factories, it should be possible (at least in theory) for the firm to use the current price at which similar factories are selling in this market as a good estimate of what its factory is actually worth as an Asset. Using this "**Mark to Market**" approach has the advantage of appearing "<u>Objective</u>" to many people and therefore seems "<u>Realistic</u>" because it reflects the ancient concept that "**a thing is worth what somebody's willing to pay for it right now.**" But it's not without its problems.

Most obviously, as far as a factory is concerned, there's unlikely to be a meaningful Secondary Market for it in the Real World. So the firm is reduced to basing the factory's

"**Market Value**" on theoretical analyses of its anticipated "Replacement Cost" at today's prices. Or the time-adjusted value of the "**Income Stream**" it can be expected to generate during the remaining years of its estimated "economically useful life" by producing products for sale to customers. If all this sounds like so much "elegant guesswork" to Normal People, they're probably right. But at least it makes work for freshly minted MBAs.

Another problem is that markets in general have a long history of going crazy at unpredictable times. As we've seen, market participants are periodically subject to irrational sheep-like manias that cause them to bid up prices to ridiculous levels. Or dump whatever they may own in a wild panic to sell out. Thereby sending prices into free fall. Many economists like to insist that markets are "<u>Rational and Objective</u>." But Normal People know "this ain't so." So how can they know whether a "Market Value" estimate of Asset Value is totally out of whack with the Real World?

• **How much money can the factory produce for the firm over its remaining useful life by producing products for sale to customers (its "<u>Income Value</u>")?**

If a factory's purpose is to produce Income for the firm, it seems reasonable that its Asset Value today should reflect today's value of this future "Income Stream." Just like for a corporate bond that makes regular payments of interest. At least, in theory.

There are various accepted procedures for estimating the current value of a future income stream. "**Discounted Cash**

Flow Analysis" is the most highly respected and is taught in all the nation's business schools. But something called **"Real Options Value"** is gaining fast. Especially among financial types who wish to appear "truly sophisticated." And all involve some heavy-duty number crunching.

More importantly, all these procedures rely on numerous assumptions about what's going to happen in the future. And everyone knows how safe and easy it is to make predictions about the future.

So in the end, a Normal Person's judgment about whether a factory's **Income Value** makes sense as a reliable measure of its Asset Value often requires a Leap of Faith that can be more than a little Heroic.

The value of a **"Hard Asset,"** like a concrete block factory building full of operating production machinery, should be relatively easy to determine. And maybe it would be, if FASB were to leave its accounting theory ivory tower long enough to provide the rest of us with some common sense advice.

Meanwhile, what about **Financial Assets?** Like plain vanilla corporate bonds? Or commercial bank loans to business firms, or home buyers, or college students? Or complex Derivatives whose income streams are based on the income streams of other financial securities (or even other Derivatives)? And so on.

These securities constitute the main asset base for many financial institutions. So being able to reliably establish sensible **Asset Values** for them is critically important to the ability of these institutions to function normally.

Fortunately, we have some guidelines to help us make these judgments. For example:

- Some of these financial assets (even including certain Derivatives) trade actively on well-managed exchanges that provide constant data about their current market price. So their Asset Value can be established by "**Marking Them to Market**" at the end of each day. Unless, of course, their secondary markets should choose this week or month to Go Crazy (up or down). In which case, all bets are off. Because their trading prices have "gone ballistic" and have no sensible meaning.

- Other financial securities trade more or less actively in established "Over-the-Counter" markets manned by reliable broker-dealers who are committed to making orderly markets in these securities. So their Asset Value can be estimated by regularly Marking Them to Market. Except when these markets Go Crazy.

- Still other securities (like commercial bank loans) are assumed to be held by their originating institutions until they mature. In which case, their Asset Value can (for practical purposes) be based on their Original Cost to the institution in question.

But these days, far too many securities don't trade at all. Or only trade "By Arrangement" (which can mean a potential buyer and seller haggling over the price for a particular security at opposite ends of a private telephone line). And far too many others have Original Costs that are meaningless in terms of current Asset Value. Or lack reliable income streams to back them up. Which makes any attempt to estimate their Income Values an exercise in futility.

All of which came to a head in the Fall of 2008, when the world's financial markets melted down more or less in unison. Causing the financial community to experience a case of **Extreme Constipation** when it came to trading securities. Because nobody knew what anything was Really Worth. In his own portfolio or anyone else's.

And where was FASB in all this?

Hiding in its ivory tower. Unwilling to take the lead in providing the financial world with any reasoned guidance about temporary ways to value assets until the markets were able to function sanely again. Bestirring itself only after considerable noodging by the feds. As in April 2009, when FASB finally agreed that "it might be okay for banks to use some judicious flexibility in their procedures for valuing certain of their financial assets."

One of the most important services we should be able to expect from private sector Third-Party Regulators is providing expert advice to society on difficult technical issues during economic emergencies. But FASB's dismal performance suggests that this may be an unrealistic dream.

■ ■ ■

The Rise of Wall Street's Rating Firms

Years ago, Wall Street's investment banking firms woke up to the fact that their credibility as sellers of financial securities to private investors could be significantly enhanced if these securities were "rated for safety" by **Independent and Objective Third Parties.**

This was especially true for debt securities like bonds. Whose likely buyers were perceived as being "very conservative." Particularly about the ability of corporations and governments issuing such securities to fulfill their promises of making scheduled payments of interest and principal on time.

Since the market for bonds and other debt securities is far larger in dollar volume than the market for common stocks, development of a third-party rating system for debt securities became a priority for Wall Street.

So in 1909, John Moody (whose firm eventually blossomed into **Moody's Investors Services**) began assigning "letter-rating grades" to railroad company bonds, which were among the most popular trading securities in those days. And in 1916, **Standard & Poor's** began selling its securities ratings directly to investors.

During the 1930s, the Federal Government began using ratings in their evaluation of banks. And in 1975, the federal **Securities and Exchange Commission** made their importance "official" by requiring ratings from a "nationally recognized statistical ratings organization" for all new issues of corporate bonds and stock to be sold to the public.

By this time, the basic business model for the ratings organizations had changed significantly. Previously, they had sold ratings directly to the buyers of securities. But now they charged fees to the sellers of securities for rating their new issues.

Three private firms emerged as the primary and most trusted "rating agencies" for debt securities. They are:

- **Moody's Investors Services, Inc.:** An independent business corporation whose common stock is traded on the New York Stock Exchange as a member of the S&P 500.

- **Standard & Poor's:** A subsidiary of the McGraw-Hill Companies that's traded on the NYSE as an S&P 500 stock.

- **Fitch, Inc.:** Which is owned by the French corporation Fimalac, SA.

These firms assign "investment ratings" to debt securities based on their analysis of relevant financial data about the issuers. The ratings themselves consist of letter combinations that define a hierarchy of "safety" ranging from *"virtually as safe as U.S. Treasury securities"* down to *"minimum investment grade"* and then down through several categories of *"questionable safety"* to the bottom category of *"issuer in default."* Rating firms may revise a security's rating (up or down) from time to time to reflect significant changes in the issuer's financial strength. Or the secondary market's perception of that strength.

Here's a list of Moody's bond-rating categories:

- **Aaa**: "Highest quality, with minimal credit risk."
- **Aa**: "High quality and subject to very low credit risk."
- **A**: "Upper-medium grade and subject to low credit risk."
- **Baa**: "Moderate credit risk, medium-grade and may possess certain speculative characteristics." (This is the lowest "Investment-Grade" rating.)
- **Ba**: "Have speculative elements and are subject to substantial credit risk."
- **B**: "Speculative and subject to high credit risk."
- **Caa**: "Poor standing and subject to very high credit risk."
- **Ca**: "Highly speculative and are likely in, or very near, default, with some prospect of recovery of principal and interest."
- **C**: "Lowest-rated class of bonds and are typically in default, with little prospect for recovery of principal or interest."

The financial community accepted this approach for providing buyers of debt securities "objective" information about their relative safety with something like a vast sigh of relief. So these rating systems became a popular shorthand way to categorize debt securities. Even to the point where investment banks would use favorable ratings as marketing tools in their sales activities.

Also, some institutional buyers of debt securities (like insurance companies with constant streams of premium income to invest) announced that they would only buy securities rated "**A**" or better. While some third-party government and private sector regulators set fairly high minimum rating levels for the securities that the firms they regulated (such as commercial banks) were permitted to buy.

■ ■ ■

The Milken Revolution

One result of these rating systems was that bonds whose ratings had declined below "Investment Grade" became increasingly difficult to sell. These "**Junk Bonds**" (as they came to be called) could only be marketed to the relatively small group of professional speculators who sought high yields and had strong stomachs for "risky" investments.

But during the 1980s, something very interesting happened.

An ambitious investment banker named **Michael Milken**, who worked for the old-line firm of **Drexel Burnham Lambert**, produced statistical data suggesting that Junk Bonds might actually be safer investments than most people realized.

Milken's data indicated that the <u>Percentage</u> of such bonds that ever actually defaulted (i.e., stopped making payments of interest and principal) was "astonishingly small." So small, in fact, that a properly diversified portfolio of Junk Bonds could provide very attractive yields to investors with <u>little practical risk</u>.

Armed with this encouraging statistical data, Milken proceeded to develop a profitable new business for Drexel selling existing Junk Bonds to a much wider market of supposedly knowledgeable investors. Then aggressively sought out corporations willing to issue <u>brand new</u> Junk Bonds through Drexel, to give himself more products to sell.

As the 1980s wore on, Junk Bonds became an increasingly important financing backbone for the well-known "**Leveraged Buyout Boom.**"

In its most highly publicized form, a Leveraged Buyout involved a **Corporate Raider** taking control of a publicly traded corporation by purchasing its common stock for an attractive price from its shareholders. And financing these stock purchases by having the corporation issue long-term Junk Bonds backed by its "assets" (which, in this context, usually included the corporation's ability to "generate cash from its operations"). A large number of well-known American corporations were "**Taken Private**" in this manner.

The Raider would profit from his Leveraged Buyout by aggressively exploiting a number of mechanisms. Such as selling off some of the corporation's real estate and other "undervalued assets" (including entire product divisions) for something closer to their current market value. Slashing its costs to the bone to pump up its cash-generating power (by cutting employee benefits or moving production to low-wage countries like Mexico). And eventually selling divisions of the corporation (or the entire corporation itself) back to the investing public by issuing new common stock.

But the Raider's whole basis for making profits was his ability to buy the target corporation with cash raised by borrowing against ("leveraging") its own assets. For which he used Michael Milken's imaginative new approach to Junk Bonds.

For the record, Milken pleaded guilty in 1990 to six counts of felony "Money Crimes" involving manipulation of the trading markets for Junk Bonds (partly in collaboration with Ivan Boesky—one of the most famous "Financial Lascivines" in American history—who sang like the proverbial canary when federal prosecutors offered him leniency for testifying against Milken). After some subsequent wheeling and dealing by his lawyers, Milken ended up serving 22 months in Federal Prison and paying several hundred million dollars in fines and penalties.

But he was able to keep most of the Billion-dollar-plus fortune he'd made as the ultimate Junk Bond maven. And after his release from prison, became a "Professional Philanthropist."

All of which is neither here nor there for our purposes. Because Milken's most important legacy may well be his influence on how "**Risk**" in debt securities is evaluated. Which had considerable impact in stoking the boom in Derivatives.

By long tradition, the rating firms had evaluated the relative safety of debt securities by using the classic Wall Street focus on "**Fundamentals.**" Each debt issue was regarded as unique. With its safety depending on the financial strength of its issuer. Most especially, on the size and reliability of the issuer's income stream. Which was the source of payments for the security's interest and principal. And therefore had to be analyzed in some detail.

But Milken's concept was radically different. It implicitly argued that, when push came to shove, <u>most debt securities were pretty much alike</u>. What really mattered in terms of safety was their "**Probability**" of defaulting. With a "<u>low Probability of default</u>" implying a "<u>high degree of Safety</u>." And Probability was something you could reliably estimate by the proper application of Gaussian statistical analysis.

In short (the argument continued), suppose you have 25 years of annual data on 1,000 different issues of Junk Bonds. You run the numbers and find that, <u>on average</u>, only 47 of these issues ever defaulted during any year in this twenty-five-year period.

Doesn't that represent an <u>annual default rate of only 4.7 Percent</u>? Of course it does.

And doesn't that suggest that the **Probability** of <u>any</u> of these bond issues ever defaulting in a given year is a <u>safely low 4.7 Percent</u>? What could be more obvious?

Needless to say, iconoclastic risk mavens like Nassim Taleb scream with outrage at this simplistic logic.

Doesn't it matter where you are in the business cycle, they remind us? Surely bonds are more likely to default during recession years than during boom years.

And doesn't the inherent <u>Riskiness</u> of the bond issuer's industry matter? Surely an issuer in a high-risk industry like <u>making movies for</u>

<u>theaters</u> is more likely to default on its bonds than an issuer in a low-risk industry like <u>distributing pharmaceutical products to drug stores</u>.

After all, just because you've never <u>seen</u> a Black Swan doesn't automatically mean that **All** **Swans are White**.

Well, maybe.

But the important thing for our purposes is how Milken's bond risk concept captured the imaginations of Wall Street's new gang of numbers-obsessed Rocket Scientists.

They quickly saw how bond risk could be expressed in all sorts of complicated Differential Equations. To form awesomely computerized mathematical **Value-at-Risk** models that could wow their bosses. (Which we looked at in **Chapter 4**.)

And the rest, as they say, is History.

■ ■ ■

"Paying Foxes to Protect Chickens"

As the 1990s wore on and turned into the current decade, the private rating firms further refined their simple business models in ways that had some interesting implications.

Here's how this new business model works.

- A **Wall Street Investment Bank** has a <u>new issue</u> of debt-based derivative securities it wants to sell to private investors (which can include both institutions and individuals). And knows this sale can happen more quickly and for a higher profit mark-up if the issue has a "<u>high investment-grade rating</u>."

- So the Investment Bank goes to one of the **Rating Firms** (which insist on calling themselves "**agencies**" because this makes them sound more "professional" and possibly even "governmental"). Puts on an elaborate presentation to lay out the details of its new derivatives. Complete with flip charts and other Show & Tell glitziness. Plus the key numbers generated by its mathematical risk model that show how "safe" the derivatives are.

- The Rating Firm takes this information in hand. And in due time, provides the Investment Bank with the high rating it's seeking. Along with a six-figure bill for its "services." Which the Bank promptly pays.

Notice the key element in this business model.

The investment bank seeking a high rating for its new derivatives <u>pays the rating firm</u> to provide this rating.

Therefore, the rating firms have an **Economic Incentive** to give investment banks the high ratings they're after. And the more such ratings they provide to their clients, the higher their profits are going to be.

How high? Well, consider these numbers provided by Moody's about its rating services:

- During 2005 to 2007, Moody's had a Return on Capital of an astonishing **140 Percent**. This was the <u>highest</u> among all publicly traded corporations listed in the S&P 500 Index.

- Its Operating Profit Margin during these years was **53.6 Percent**. This was the **Seventeenth Highest** margin among companies in the S&P Index.

- From 2005 to 2007, Moody's revenues from rating corporate

bonds grew by a total of **187 Percent**. That represents an average growth rate of nearly **37 Percent per year**.

In short, by allowing themselves to be become <u>paid handmaidens</u> for their Wall Street clients seeking high investment ratings, the rating firms made out like proverbial bandits. (Five Families take note.)

So it doesn't take much imagination to picture how all this might play out on a typical Wall Street day in 2007 as the derivatives boom was approaching its climax.

Charlene is a savvy blond Managing Director at a well-known Wall Street investment bank who's responsible for bringing a new issue of debt-based derivatives to market. And on this particular day, immaculately attired in a dark gray business suit, she hand-delivers a follow-up report detailing the risk profile for these derivatives to schlubby-looking **Aaron**—her contact guy at the rating firm from which she's seeking a high rating for her derivatives.

"I think you'll find the answers to all your questions in this report," Charlene says with a practiced smile as she hands the report to Aaron in his office.

"It describes your mathematical risk models?" Aaron says.

"Absolutely. And our models are the best in the business. Really cutting edge. The head of our Risk Research unit has a Ph.D. in Physics from MIT. And his chief analyst has a Math Ph.D. from the Courant Institute at NYU. He's the one who developed these particular models."

"So the report covers everything about them?"

"Everything you need to understand how they work."

"Including all the formulas and equations?"

"Well naturally, those are Proprietary. They won't even let me see them. Not that I could understand . . . "

"In other words, your models are simply Black Boxes as far as the Report is concerned."

"Come on, Aaron. Our risk models are . . . "

"Don't worry about it. I was just trying to push the envelop a little."

"And you have every right . . . "

"Look, Charlene. You know how busy we are these days. With the number of deals coming in for ratings."

"Everybody's overworked," she says with an understanding smile.

"Anyway, there's nothing to worry about," he says. "You'll get the rating you're looking for."

"That's very encouraging."

"Top management's going all-out to up our volume. I mean, somebody could bring us a deal structured by a . . . a cow and we'd rate it. There's no time to fuss over details these days. And by the way, your Report looks very impressive."

"I thought you'd like it."

"The way you've used three contrasting colors on the cover is quite striking."

"We have a top-notch graphic artist who designs these things."

"Incidentally, you got the word that our fees are going up Five Percent as of the first of this month?"

"Yes. No problem."

"That'll apply to your new derivative issue."

"I know. And worth every penny."

"Okay, Charlene. We've done a lot of business together the last few years, and I hope it continues."

"So do I. We need to become even closer," she says, leaning towards him.

He takes a sharp breath and clears his throat.

"Right. Absolutely," he says. "So keep bringing us your deals and we'll . . . take good care of you. You got the check we sent you on the fifteenth?"

"Yes. Thanks again."

"Fine. Let's just hope we're all nicely rich and retired when the shit finally hits the fan. As it's bound to."

"I'm keeping my fingers crossed."

We may be forgiven for seeing certain parallels here with the relationship between a Hooker and her John. Not the street corner kind of Hooker, of course. More like an elegant Call Girl from a prestige escort service. With everything very couth and kosher-looking.

Which begs the question of who's really the Hooker and who's the John.

■ ■ ■

Are Government Regulators the Answer?

This is a popular alternative to private sector third-party regulators.

Especially among those law school graduates holding top jobs on the staffs of important Senators and Members of Congress. Not to mention on key Congressional Committees. Whose natural instincts favor Leninist- and Moses-style **"Thou Shalt"** commandments to regulate human behavior. (As opposed to secular economist types who argue in favor of *"properly structured and targeted economic Incentives."* In other words, **"Bribes."**)

So why shouldn't we turn over all responsibility for regulating capitalist markets and private business firms to properly magisterial government agencies? Staffed by highly qualified managers and analysts who regard "service to the American public" as the noblest of callings and their surest path to WASP or Jewish Heaven? Like such respected American heroes of the past as W. Averill Harriman and Franklin Delano Roosevelt?

Well, there are <u>three problems</u> with this in the real world.

The **First Problem** is that it depends on an large supply of **Trust Fund Babies** to staff these government agencies. People whose Robber Baron grandfathers made such unimaginable fortunes (by hook or crook) that their descendants were forever liberated from all concerns about the grubby business of "earning a living." So they're free to devote their professional lives to "public service." As a more interesting and respectable alternative to polo or sailboat racing or chasing debutants.

But the supply of these Trust Fund Babies is nowhere near large enough to staff government regulatory agencies. Most of the intelligent and well-educated people such agencies require emerge from graduate school burdened by such crushing student loan debts that they're forced to "go where the most money is" in choosing their professional careers.

In theory, we could deal with this by addressing the economic concerns of such gifted but highly indebted people. Like subsidizing their student loan burdens in return for their committing to careers in public service. Paying them high enough salaries for government jobs so they can match the living standards of their graduate school colleagues who have chosen careers in the private sector. Offering them generous medical benefits and pensions and college scholarships for their children. And generally enabling them to match the lifestyles of their private sector colleagues. Just as the UK has always done for its senior civil servants.

But too many American elected politicians fear that voters would see this as an un-American form of "Elitist Socialism." So there's no possibility that it could ever be implemented.

The **Second Problem** flows naturally from the first.

Many gifted, well-educated, savvy young people these days see government jobs as stepping stones to lucrative careers in the private sector. Especially jobs in government regulatory agencies. Where they can develop useful contacts with key employees in the private sector firms whose behavior they're supposed to regulate. And quietly impress these contacts that their "hearts are in the right place" as far as the regulated firm in concerned.

So it's scarcely a surprise that there's a formidable parade of such people regularly marching back and forth between lavish private sector executive suites and the basic-steel-desk offices of government regulatory agencies like the Securities and Exchange Commission. Committed to serving no one's interests but their own.

The **Third Problem** arises from the Topsy-like growth of regulatory structures in federal, state, and local governments. Where irrational lines of responsibility have inevitably led to turf battles among government agencies over "who should regulate whom and what," as each agency seeks to enhance its bureaucratic clout (and the size of its budget) by increasing the extent of its turf. This is especially true when more or less routine regulatory activities expand to include the distinctly macho business of "policing."

An especially colorful example of this involves some interesting stories that circulate informally about New York City's large and aggressive Police Department. Which naturally considers itself "the Best Law Enforcement Agency in the World."

Once upon a time, the NYPD's main concern was the usual array of crimes committed within New York City's extensive borders. Which encompass five counties housing about 8.5 Million people reflecting more than 150 different ethnic backgrounds (and their multitude of different languages). So its jurisdiction was limited to the city.

But this is said to have changed after the 9/11 terrorist attack on Manhattan's World Trade Center. With its usual "we know best" provincialism, the Powers That Be in New York City's government supposedly determined that the NYPD should be given primary responsibility for protecting the city against any and all future terrorist attacks. Without regard to whatever the federal government—or any other government in the world—might (or might not) be doing in this regard.

To carry out this new responsibility, the NYPD has allegedly developed a host of sophisticated "regulatory procedures" to identify, investigate, infiltrate, frustrate, and defuse any activities that could potentially become terrorist threats to New York City. Wherever such activities might be taking place. Which therefore expanded the NYPD's <u>functional jurisdiction</u> to include the Entire World.

So it was (according to current folklore) that NYPD detectives, fully literate since childhood in appropriate local languages and cultural traditions (because of their ethnic backgrounds), quietly set up underground shop in locations throughout the world where terrorist types were known, suspected, or assumed to gather. Armed with the latest in sophisticated surveillance technology. Not to mention attaché cases stuffed full of hundred-dollar bills. To buy information, fund infiltration into possible terrorist cells by members of the local population, and assure the informal cooperation of local police officials. In short, a <u>full-court press</u>.

Inevitably, these extensive **Counterterrorist Activities** brought the NYPD into conflict with such federal agencies as the Department of Homeland Security, the FBI, the CIA, the Secret Service, and other policing organizations that might have anti-terrorism responsibilities on their plates.

In each one of which the NYPD is said to have artfully recruited or inserted secret "moles" to ensure that it promptly receives every scrap of information about potential terrorist activity that could affect New York City. While playing officials of these agencies with the street-smart con artistry that's assumed to be instinctive among native New Yorkers. Up to and including letting other agencies take credit in the media for newsworthy "terrorist busts" as they occurred. In order to keep its profile as low as possible.

But isn't there some "Third Way" to achieve the kind of effective regulation we need? A way that avoids the poisonous corruption of private sector greed and side-steps the trustworthy incompetence and turf battles of government?

Well, maybe there is.

Let's take a look.

■ ■ ■

Internal Regulation

This approach to regulation is based on the concept of **Competition**. Which is one of the most sacred principles of **Free Market Capitalism** and is highly respected as a key source of its ability to produce "the greatest good for the greatest number in a free society."

(Unless, of course, you're one of those alpha-type CEOs of a major business corporation. Who regards Competition as a "fucking waste of time" and will do anything short of committing murder to eliminate it from his business environment.)

Let's assume we have three guys (we'll call them **Tom, Dick,** and **Harry** for want of imagination) who serve as policy kingpins on the Board of Directors of an investor-owned <u>Electric Power Company</u> in a major metropolitan region.

Tom has spent most of his career in the top management ranks of one of the region's largest stock brokerage firms, which his father helped found. Belongs to an elite country club in the fashionable suburb where he lives. Is active in local alumni affairs for Yale University (which he attended after prepping at St. Paul's). And believes instinctively that *"the business of America is Business."* So his natural concern as a board member is the <u>welfare of investors</u> who provide the power company with its equity capital. Which translates into pushing policies designed to **"Maximize Stockholder Dividends."**

In Tom's ideal world, therefore, the power company would charge the <u>highest rates</u> for electricity the traffic will bear. While keeping <u>its costs as low as possible</u> by providing the least service imaginable without causing riots in the streets.

Dick is a partner in a general practice law firm. And also an elected member of the City Council in one of the region's local governments (of which there are far too many—but that's the "<u>American Way</u>"). Not to mention an important player in the region's dominant political party. And like Tom, he's an instinctive "<u>Maximizer</u>" when it comes to policy decisions by the power company's Board of Directors.

But Dick's goal is to **"Maximize Votes for his party's Elected Public Officials."** So in his ideal world, the power company would charge the <u>lowest rates</u> this side of Chapter 11. While leaning over backwards to provide its customers (the region's voters) with <u>lavish, gold-plated services</u>.

Needless to say, the radically different instincts of Dick and Tom result in some spirited debates between them during meetings of the power company's Board of Directors, when their irreconcilable views clash. In other words, real <u>Intellectual Competition</u> at the policy level.

Like most companies that generate and distribute electric power, this one tends to operate more effectively the larger it is (known in the trade as **"Economies of Scale"**). And as is so often the case, its "optimal size" turns out to mean a **"Natural Monopoly"** in the region's electric power business.

Tom naturally welcomes this because (at least in theory) it's consistent with his ideal world. Like most trust fund babies and their groupies, he's a firm believer in **"Competition"**—as the best route to achieving a <u>Monopoly for His Guys</u> (after which it should politely fade away).

Dick accepts the power company's Natural Monopoly as an unavoidable fact of life. But he would much prefer that such a monopoly be **"Owned by the People"** (which, in a functional sense, means <u>owned by his political party</u>) and operated as a Public Agency (providing lots of jobs for his party's loyal soldiers). This is naturally opposed by Tom, who regards it as (horrors) "Socialism."

So both have grudgingly accepted what seems like the only practical alternative. Regulation of the power company by a third-party government agency known as the **State Utility Commission.**

The Commission sets the electricity rates the power company can charge at levels that are theoretically designed to provide a "fair return" on its equity capital if it operates "efficiently." While exerting oversight of its operations (a polite term for "micromanagement" by civil service Commission staff personnel) to ensure that it maintains an "optimal" balance between equity capital and debt capital. Keeps its physical plant up-to-date and in good condition. And provides adequate capacity to meet the region's electric power needs.

Such government regulatory commissions are the **Standard American Model** for trying to ensure that privately owned corporations function "in the public interest" when their businesses work best as Natural Monopolies unhindered by "wasteful competition."

The natural tendency for this model is to generate top managers for these monopolies who are highly knowledgeable about the ins and outs of regulatory law. Skilled in artful ways of manipulating their accounting records to roll every conceivable expenditure into their rate bases. As persuasive as used car salesmen in convincing the chronically underpaid staff of the State Utility Commission and the legislature to "see things their way" when it comes to rate increases.

But when it comes to the critical business function of "**Creating Value for Customers**," these managers are totally clueless. Most of them have never even heard of management guru Peter Drucker. Much less knowing about his insightful views on the true goals for any enterprise that wishes to succeed in a modern economy.

Meanwhile, what about **Harry**?

In many respects, he's the most interesting of our 3 policy kingpins on the power company's Board of Directors. Bubbling over with iconoclastic ideas that are worth taking seriously.

Harry runs the region's largest and most profitable retail chain. He got his start right out of high school with a sales job in a downtown consumer electronics store. Rose through the ranks on the strength of his talent for coming up with new profit ideas at the right time. Learned how to bamboozle the region's financial establishment into supplying the capital he needed to start his own retail chain and build it into a business powerhouse. Insists on wearing off-the-rack sports jackets rather than dark gray business suits (when he's not running around in his shirt sleeves).

He has a low opinion of slow-witted commercial bank types who have trouble seeing good investment opportunities even when they smack them in the face. Has nothing but scorn for bright young MBAs from fashionable business schools, whose answer to every challenge is a new Excel spreadsheet full of neat columns and rows of numbers. Is convinced that the best training for a manager is a few years of dealing face-to-face with customers across a sales counter. (And is very careful to hide the MBA in Marketing he earned after years of attending a local public university at night).

Most of all, Harry has learned **One Big Thing** in his business career. Which is that the **growth of the region's economy is the <u>most important factor</u> in the continued growth of his retail chain.** Because after all is said and done, this is the <u>main thing</u> that determines how fast his chain's sales revenues can grow (which sharp management can leverage into even faster profit growth).

So Harry's primary goal for the electric power company is to **Maximize its Contribution to the Region's Economic Growth.** And this has positioned him as a Natural Referee on the Board of Directors between the disparate and more narrowly focused competitive goals of Tom and Dick.

He's very sympathetic to Dick's emphasis on superior service at attractive rates. Because he knows this combination creates the kind of <u>Value for Customers</u> that can stimulate healthy economic growth in the region.

But his brushes with insolvency during the early days of building his retail chain have made him very sensitive to the importance of the power company's financial stability. So he's also sympathetic to Tom's concerns for rate growth and tight cost controls.

Harry's pivotal role as a member of the power company's Board of Directors leads to an interesting climate of competitive **Internal Regulation** that's far closer to Peter Drucker's ideal for large enterprises than the standard form of External Regulation represented by the State Utility Commission.

So the power company's **Financial Management** is rationally prudent. And its **Operating Management** is appropriately tough-minded and hands-on.

But most of all, it has **Marketing Management** that's highly customer-focused and proactive.

It's all too rare for an externally regulated monopoly enterprise to have any marketing management at all. Much less one that recognizes **Creating Value for Customers** as the enterprise's top priority.

But this is the only practical way to assure that such enterprises truly serve the interests of the public. And isn't it more likely to happen under a climate of competitive **Internal Regulation** that includes influential voices like Harry's at the enterprise's policy-setting level?

In which case (the argument continues), there's no need to clutter up the landscape with State Utility Commissions and other counterproductive mechanisms involving third-party External Regulation.

Would it were so.

But can we make it so with enough huffing and puffing?

(Let's not forget the old Army motto: "*If it doesn't fit, Force It.*")

■ ■ ■

Striking the Proverbial "Right Balance"?

But let's not kid ourselves. When it comes to something as complicated as regulating economic activity, a "One-Size-Fits-All" approach is never going to work. Instead, we must examine a variety of different approaches and try to determine the most suitable mix for our increasingly diverse economy.

China's semi-autonomous metropolitan region of **Hong Kong** provides us with many interesting things to think about on this score (apart from Jackie Chan's martial arts movies, exotic food, and beautiful women with thrilling cheek bones). If we're willing to bestir ourselves and look.

For starters, Hong Kong happens to be one of the world's <u>most successful metropolitan societies</u>. With a **per capita Gross Domestic Product** that's the highest in Asia and outranks most Western European nations (except for those off-the-wall "welfare state paradises" in Scandinavia). Which is popularly attributed to its enthusiastic embrace of **Free Market Capitalism**. Uncontaminated by "cloying government regulation."

A lesson for us all?

Well, maybe. But the lesson's more complicated than it first appears.

For one thing, Hong Kong seems to have recognized implicitly the <u>critical distinction</u> between **Discretionary Activities** and **Non-discretionary Activities** as it affects the ability of Free Markets to function effectively. And one of the most obvious examples of this recognition is how Hong Kong has handled the complex issue of **housing a metropolitan population**.

Most of Hong Kong's 7 Million residents live in housing built (directly or indirectly) by its metropolitan government during the past five decades. Further, the monthly housing cost for these residents is pegged by the government at a very low **proportion** of their family incomes rather than at some fixed dollar amount. And this cost averages about **9 Percent of these family incomes**. (Which is very low by Western standards.)

In other words, government housing in Hong Kong isn't simply "welfare for the deserving poor," as in most Western societies. Rather, it reflects the **Principle** that basic affordable housing is a **Non-discretionary Need** for a metropolitan society. And one that's just as important for middle-income residents as it is for those with low incomes. All things considered, it seems easier to meet this need by having Government build or sponsor various housing programs.

Hong Kong's approach to carrying out this Principle has some interesting consequences:

- Virtually all of Hong Kong's residents are "decently housed." Though housing space per resident tends to be on the tight side compared to middle-class standards in the USA. And much of this space is in high-rise towers. Especially those located in elaborate, land-efficient, government-planned "New Towns" like Sha Tin (whose population is larger than the American city of Boston). As opposed to the standard American metropolitan pattern of single-family houses, each standing alone on its own plot of land.

- As noted, Hong Kong residents who live in government housing pay a <u>very low</u> proportion of their family incomes for housing costs. This makes available a <u>larger</u> proportion of their incomes to support **Discretionary Spending** in private free market industries like retail stores, restaurants, and various consumer services.

- Hong Kong's private <u>real estate industry</u> has been **totally liberated** from all the complicated social-welfare baggage inherent in leaving the primary responsibility for housing a metropolitan population to the private sector. This means that private real estate firms are <u>completely free</u> to maximize their profits by concentrating on providing <u>Discretionary</u> upscale housing to upper-income residents through a largely unregulated free market. And luxury housing in Hong Kong is every bit as lavish (and expensive) as its counterpart in Manhattan.

Admittedly, Hong Kong enjoys certain characteristics that make all this much easier to achieve than in American metropolitan societies.

For example:

- **Hong Kong is, for practical purposes, a <u>totally homogeneous</u> society in terms of its ethnic composition (98 Percent Cantonese at last count). Just like those "welfare state" Scandinavian societies.**

This implies a **"widespread consensus on social values"** among its residents. Which greatly facilitates implementing certain social principles. Such as access to decent and affordable housing being a citizen's "<u>Right</u>" without regard to his income. Like access to police and fire protection.

(It's interesting to contrast this with societies like the UK and France. Where some groups believe that "social consensus" is being threatened by non-European immigrants whose social values are "different" because of their ethnicity.)

- **Hong Kong has never had what Americans would regard as a "democratic" government.**

The head of the government's all-powerful Executive Branch isn't directly elected by Hong Kong's voters. Instead, he's "elected" by a panel of 800 Distinguished Citizens (whose loyalty to Beijing is beyond question) from among several candidates approved by Beijing—though there's never been more than a single candidate so far. Prior to reunification with China (when Hong Kong was a British Crown Colony), the head of the government was always a native British male appointed by the Monarch on the advice of Parliament and sent out from London. Similarly, only half the members of Hong Kong's legislature are directly elected by Hong Kong's voters.

The rest are appointed by the leadership cadres of the region's "functional constituencies"—each of which represents a particular industry, profession, or labor union. Before reunification with China, all members of the legislature were appointed by the Executive Branch.

- **Hong Kong's government "functionally owns" all the land in the metropolitan region.**

Therefore, the government controls <u>all land development</u> in Hong Kong. Which it implements by leasing land parcels on a long-term basis to private developers. With each lease specifying how the land parcel in question is to be developed. Reflecting overall development strategies determined by the government's ongoing **Regional Planning Process**. Such comprehensive government control of metropolitan development through "Central Planning" has no precedent in the United States.

Also, the government's considerable <u>income from land leases</u> (coupled with its lucrative 100 Percent monopoly over <u>all taxes collected</u> from Hong Kong residents and business firms) has made it probably the world's <u>richest</u> metropolitan government. This enables it to undertake large-scale development programs (in transportation, for example) on an as-needed basis simply by <u>writing checks</u> against its enormous accumulated <u>financial wealth</u>. Never having to issue any debt.

Clearly, these unique characteristics enable Hong Kong to accomplish things that support its thriving free market economy with an ease and flair unknown in most Western metropolitan societies.

But for our purposes, what really matters is how Hong Kong has recognized the critical distinction between **Discretionary** and **Non-discretionary Activities** in sorting out responsibilities for who does what in a capitalist society.

The record shows that free markets can do an outstanding job in meeting a society's vast array of <u>Discretionary</u> wants.

But meeting the <u>Non-discretionary</u> needs without which a free market society has trouble functioning involves too many "non-economic" considerations. These hamper the fundamental ability of private firms to maximize their profits (which, after all, is their whole reason for existing).

So if we can put aside ideological hang-ups for the moment, it often makes sense to delegate the responsibility for meeting these Non-discretionary Needs to Government. Which Hong Kong has done. With notable success.

Can we Americans apply <u>the same logic</u> to the complex task of determining:

- Whether <u>any</u> of our industries or business firms should be regulated.
- If Yes, <u>which types</u> of industries or firms should be regulated?
- <u>Who</u> should do the regulating? And <u>how</u>?

Coming to grips with the critical distinction between **Regulated** and **Non-regulated Activities** is the great challenge we face.

One of the big problems that the Economic Crisis has brought us is what to do about private business enterprises that are regarded as "**Too Big to Fail.**"

The easy answer so far is for the federal government to "Bail Them Out" in one way or another. That's what we've done with General Motors, Chrysler, AIG, Citicorp, and a host of other less-publicized sickos.

But some people will argue that "**Too Big to Fail**" really means "**Too**

Big to be Privately Owned." Therefore, they insist, such giant firms should be broken up into a number of smaller and more manageable private enterprises. Or, if the principle of Economies of Scale dictates that such giantism has too many benefits to discard in certain cases, convert them into "publicly owned" (i.e., "nationalized") enterprises.

After all, hasn't General Motors mainly been an informal "**National Jobs Program**" for years? Going through the motions of trying (with declining success) to support itself by making and selling motor vehicles? In which case, why not face reality and run it as a formal "federal jobs program"? Subsidized by taxpayers until such time as intelligent restructuring can make it sufficiently self-supporting to attract private investors to buy out taxpayers (hopefully at a profit)?

"**Public Enterprises**" is an umbrella term covering so many combinations of ownership, control, and operation that lawyers can have a field day sorting them all out:

- *Government ownership, control, and operation*
- *Government ownership and control, private operation*
- *Private ownership, government control, private operation*
- *Joint ownership and control by government and private investors, private operation . . .*
  The list of combinations goes on. And on.

In **Theory**, a large corporation is **owned** by numerous private stockholders. Who **delegate** to a Board of Directors the responsibility of looking after their ownership interests by controlling the corporation wisely. With this Board **hiring** top managers to implement the business policies and strategies it develops to serve the interests of the corporation's private owners.

In **Practice**, of course, this is largely a Fairyland ideal. The common stock of most large corporations is owned by institutions and individuals whose primary goal is to see the market price of their company shares rise (never mind how) so they can sell out at a profit and move on.

This opens a <u>very wide door</u> for hired-gun top managers to gain control of such a corporation and stuff its Board of Directors with their acquiescent cronies. Giving themselves "<u>functional ownership</u>" of the corporation. Which they can turn into a mechanism for short-term personal enrichment (with no concern for stockholders). Before moving on to their next conquest.

All of which may be something we can live with <u>if</u> (a Big If) the corporation is a "**Type A**" firm—one whose primary business is limited to providing society with purely **Discretionary Goods or Services,** preferably in a reasonably competitive environment. So that all members of society are <u>entirely free</u> to do business with this corporation whenever it can meet their needs of the moment on acceptable terms. Or look elsewhere for a better deal. Or even wait until tomorrow. Because a more or less free market usually manages to come up with something acceptable if left to its own devices (especially for those who have relaxed views about "spreading a little Green around" to grease the wheels). Without regard for the private agendas of the corporation's top managers. Or any need for noodging by Regulators.

But all bets are off if the corporation is a **Type B** firm—whose primary business involves providing society with **Non-discretionary Goods or Services,** usually in an industry composed of other Type B firms. With "Non-discretionary" being defined to include products (like bank loans to fund a retail store's inventory) for which no short-term substitutes realistically exist. And where "delivery time is often of the essence."

Members of society who <u>must</u> do business with Type B firms are effectively locked in and have no "elsewhere" to look. So they're <u>heavily dependent</u> on the corporation to behave reliably and openly. But this can expose them to various kinds of "victimization" by the corporation's top managers, whose agendas are of an entirely different order.

Unless, of course, the corporation and its industry are regulated in effective ways to produce something akin to an environment of Type A firms.

So now we begin to see the critical distinction in a capitalist society between economic activities that are **Discretionary** and those that are **Non-Discretionary**.

Regulation of the first may be nice enough to have. So long as (like Religion and the Law) it doesn't get in the way of anything <u>Really Important</u>.

But it's difficult to see how regulation of the second can be anything less than <u>Mandatory</u> if free markets are to have social credibility.

This may be easy enough in theory. But how can we put it to work in the real world?

- How can we accomplish effective top-down design of regulatory programs that target the right Non-discretionary Activities in the right ways? And have them survive emasculation by the Congressional Authorization Process (a polite name for "<u>Government By Lobbyists</u>")?

- Do we need another of those "Independent Bipartisan Commissions" to study the issues for a year or so and report back with its recommendations? While Congress jury-rigs some temporary arrangement to serve in the meantime?

- Should regulatory programs be organized on an "<u>industry-wide basis</u>" (one for Commercial Banking, another for Auto Manufacturing, and so on)? Or on an "<u>activity-wide basis</u>," in cases where certain Non-discretionary Activities are common to several different industries (Health Care, for example)?

- Is there really a place in the mix for private third-party regulators like FASB and Wall Street's rating firms? Or does the evidence indicate that this concept has become what intellectuals like to call an "Oxymoron"? Are there ways to make private third-party regulators truly viable in terms of meeting society's needs? Is there anything meaningful to be gained by doing this?

- How can we end wasteful bureaucratic turf battles between existing government regulatory agencies (like the SEC vs. the Federal Reserve Board vs. the Treasury Department)? Including growing conflicts between federal agencies (like the Department of Homeland Security) and increasingly aggressive state and local government agencies (New York City's Police Department, for example)?

- How can we ensure that government regulatory agencies have the qualified managers and staff professionals they need to function effectively? And end the all-too-common practice of having such people regard terms of service in regulatory agencies as private mechanisms for positioning themselves to move on to more lucrative careers in the industries they're supposed to regulate?

- Should we make greater use of the **"European Board Model"**? So that the Board of Directors of a corporation engaged primarily in Non-discretionary Activities includes a competitive mix of private equity stockholders, hired managers, unionized employees, major creditors, locked-in customers, government, community groups, and so on—all having different agendas? Is this the most practical way to implement the kind of meaningful Tom/Dick/ Harry Internal Regulation described above? Can this substitute for External Regulation by so-called "Independent and Objective" third parties? Do we need some combination of both?

- Should the overarching guideline for effective regulation be "Flexibility"? Reflecting the fact that each industry is "different"? With changing circumstances causing these differences to evolve over time? Even to the extent of Discretionary Activity industries becoming Non-discretionary? And vice versa (like the domestic auto industry)? Suggesting that the nation's regulatory structure needs a fast-on-its-feet ability to change with the times?

All of which suggests that we have a great deal on our plates if we're to implement the right kind of regulation of the right kind of activities in the right way.

Hard? Sure.

But who ever said Life was easy? Except, perhaps, for the guy lucky enough to have been <u>born on Third Base</u>. Who (as a wise old sports columnist is rumored to have pointed out) is able to glide through life imagining that he <u>hit a Triple</u>.

■ ■ ■

Yes But...

Oh, I know.

Self-appointed "Libertarian Mavens" in the ivory tower world are going to insist that most of what we've just been considering about Regulation is meaningless and wrongheaded. Because they argue that Markets work best when they're free of any "interference" by Government.

Well, they usually unbend enough to admit that it's a good idea to have Government standing by to "enforce contracts." That is, to "interfere" with the freedom of any buyer or seller to welch on his agreement to abide by terms of a market transaction to which he's a party.

But otherwise, it's strictly hands-off. Any other meddling by Government will inevitably make markets "less than fully efficient." And the more meddling Government does, the less efficient the market becomes. Until (in the worst case), the wide-open, Saturday-night-shoot-out, Dodge City freedom of the ideal market winds up being imprisoned in a dull-as-dishwater Sunday School where everybody goes through the motions of reading the same Bible verses at the same time (to no visible purpose).

What do they mean by "efficient markets" anyway? Well, here's one definition:

> *An "Efficient Market" successfully allocates a limited supply of goods in a manner that satisfies the wants of all individuals at the price each one is willing to pay.*

Not bad. Except for the "willing" part.

What defines "willing"? The amount of <u>Cash</u> in your pocket? Or the amount of <u>Hunger</u> in your stomach?

Makes a difference in the real world, doesn't it?

To better understand why, let's return to the subject of Tigers for a moment.

During the past century, the world's tiger population has plummeted for a variety of reasons, and tigers are now considered an "endangered species."

Currently, about half the world's tigers live in more or less **Regulated Environments** like the **Bronx Zoo's** highly popular **Tiger Mountain.** Where their **survival** as a species is pretty much assured and they don't have to engage in daily **Serial Killer** behavior as a matter of course. The rest of the world's tigers live freely in the wilderness areas of Eastern Siberia and Northern India, where survival is more like a crap shoot.

In an effort to improve these survival odds, some of the governments with jurisdiction over these wilderness areas have passed laws designed to protect tigers and assure their continued freedom. The most important of these laws make it a crime for any person to kill or otherwise mistreat a tiger. And these laws have some interesting implications.

Suppose, for example, one of these wilderness areas is experiencing a period where live prey for tigers is in short supply. Perhaps due to adverse weather conditions. Or an epidemic of fatal illness among certain species of prey. Or any one of a number of other natural scourges that regularly beset wilderness areas.

So one day, a hungry tiger in search of food happens to wander into a village within the edge of the wilderness area. Where he sees a small human child playing alone on the dirt road in front of a house. With a lightning move, the tiger pounces on the child. Knocks him flat with a heavy blow of his massive front paw. Picks up the moaning child in his mouth and starts to carry him away. Seeking a private place where he can tear off the child's arms and eat them. Drink his gushing blood. And generally feast on the child's body.

Fortunately, the child's father happens to be looking out the front window of the house and sees all this. So he immediately grabs his loaded rifle and rushes outside. Intent on shooting the tiger to save his son's life.

At that moment, half a dozen local police officers march onto the scene, and four of them manage to surround the tiger. And by making the maximum amount of noise, induce him to drop the child and flee the village. Then start giving the child First Aid.

But the other two police officers rush over to the child's father. Quickly disarm him. And place him under arrest.

"What the Hell are you arresting me for?" the father protests.

"You were going to shoot the tiger," one of the police officers explains. "That's against the law."

"But I was trying to save my son's life."

"It's still against the law."

Then the second police officer patiently explains to the father how tigers are a Protected Species. How it's against the law to harm them in any way. And how all this is necessary to assure the tigers' survival.

"Fuck the tigers," the outraged father screams. "If the price of their survival is my son's life, they're not worth it. Let them all die."

Do the father's sentiments remind you of the screams of outrage heard from auto drivers faced by four-dollar-per-gallon gasoline prices in the Spring of 2008? As they vented torrents of obscenities against the "Big Oil Companies" for <u>deliberately</u> holding gasoline supplies off the market to push up prices still further? Demanded that their elected politicians tax away the "scandalously high profits" the Exxons of the world were extorting from captive drivers?

And when ivory tower Libertarians attempted to explain to these drivers, in cool and reasoned voices, why such occasional price spikes were necessary if Free Market Capitalism is to achieve "<u>market efficiency</u>"?

"Fuck Capitalism," drivers screamed back. "If four-dollar gasoline is the price of market efficiency, it's not worth it. We need something better."

Americans are perfectly happy with Capitalism, Free Markets, and all that jazz when the result is rising incomes, full employment, homes of their own, college for their children, and prosperous retirements. But when these Libertarian icons confront us with their periodic hiccups, all bets are off. Fairly or not, Americans simply won't stand for it. They demand "<u>something better.</u>"

As the Financial Meltdown of 2008 reminded us, under-regulated markets have a long history of going on periodic murderous rampages. Just like hungry tigers roaming free in the wilderness. With their Serial Killer behavior overflowing as they rip away jobs and homes from Millions of people who depend on them. Gulp down Trillions of dollars in hard-earned life savings. Ravage the flesh of thousands of small businesses whose bones are flung on the ash heaps of Bankruptcy. Lay waste to the civilized landscape, Big Time.

And Americans simply <u>won't stand for it</u>. Not for all the fairyland Libertarian nostrums in the world.

There are two possible solutions.

One is to learn how to <u>regulate markets</u> (and their participants) in sensible ways. To rein in their Serial Killer behavior before it gets out of hand. Build the kind of Capitalist system whose ups and downs are <u>sufficiently tempered</u> to avoid destructive booms and busts.

And you don't want to know what the second solution is.

(But if you happen to be an immigrant from the former Soviet Union, you already know.)

■ ■ ■

Chapter 10
WHAT DOES IT ALL MEAN?

He that will not apply new remedies must expect new evils.
For Time is the greatest innovator.
—Francis Bacon

<u>Everybody</u> knows who caused the 2008 financial market crash. Right?
Greedy bankers. That's who.

Running wild in unregulated markets like there was no Tomorrow.

Peddling to hapless victims the world over the most <u>outrageous</u> collections of overpriced **Collateralized Mortgage Obligations, Credit Default Swaps,** and other **Toxic Derivatives.** Whose <u>real value</u> reflected the convenient "your-guess-is-as-good-as-mine" principle that lay behind Wall Street's elaborately mathematical price and risk models.

Irresponsible Lascivines all.

Driven by Scarlet Woman promises of seven-figure bonuses keyed to the <u>retail dollar volume</u> of the junk securities they sold. While the **Securities and Exchange Commission,** the **Federal Reserve,** and other government agencies with regulatory responsibilities stood by, all smiles. Bleating forth, like so many sheep, their comforting mantras about the "<u>Self-Regulating Nature</u>" of "<u>Efficient Markets</u>" in this "<u>Best of All Possible Worlds.</u>"

Until it was the **Summer of 1914** all over again. And the rest of us poor schnooks woke up to find that the Lascivines had driven the **Whole Crazy World** off an unimaginable cliff.

Leaving us up to our eyebrows in **Deep Doo-Doo.**

Wouldn't it be great if things <u>really were</u> this simple?

■ ■ ■

You Mean, There Were Other Villains?

Banks are no different from any other profit-seeking business enterprise.

Just like Siberian Tigers, they're driven by their inherent **Nature** to do whatever they can get away with to satisfy their ravenous hunger. And if this should result in **Serial Killer Behavior,** can we blame the banks alone?

Or must we also include whoever (or whatever) determined what banks should be allowed to get away with? Even encouraged to get away with?

Here's an example we already looked at in **Chapter 5**, about Housing and Mortgages. And it's worth a quick review.

- **An unquestioned All-American National Virtue is that people should own the homes they live in.** This is assumed to promote Neighborhood Stability. Family Stability. And all kinds of other Good Things.

- **But many Americans are too poor to buy homes the regular way.** Their incomes are too low and unstable for them to qualify for the mortgages that normally fund most of the purchase price of a house. Or to save up enough dollars to make a suitable down payment on a home of their own.

So how do we expand home ownership among these low-income Americans?

- **Do we launch ambitious national programs to lift them out of poverty?** Raise the Minimum Wage to higher and higher levels each year? Create large <u>Government Jobs Programs</u> to provide productive work at decent wages? <u>Subsidize Private Employers</u> dependent on cheap labor costs so they can afford to pay living wages? Provide <u>Government Grants</u> to low-income families so they can make suitable down payments on homes? Go all out to raise the functional incomes of these Americans so they can meet the financially prudent requirements for owning their own homes? Just as in one of those crazy Welfare States like Norway (whose citizens happen to enjoy higher living standards than the average American).

- **Or do we "Bend the Rules" a little?** Waive various financial requirements for home ownership so these Americans can qualify with their <u>existing</u> incomes. And push banks and other mortgage lenders to "Cooperate."

Naturally, we couldn't seriously consider the first option. Too expensive. Too much like a "reward for remaining poor." Too "Socialistic."

So we chose the second option. Bent the rules. And kept our fingers crossed that it would somehow "all work out."

Our religious institutions like to tell us that *"God must Love the Poor because he made so Many of Them."* And this seems to imply that Poverty confers some kind of **Moral Virtuousness** on those afflicted.

But the reality is, poor Americans are no more inherently virtuous than the rest of us. And a lot more "entrepreneurial" than we generally give them credit for.

So when "Bending the Rules" created opportunities for them to buy homes by lying, cheating, forging income documentation, and other human chicanery, large numbers of them took advantage of "whatever they could get away with."

Abetted, of course, by the legions of hungry lascivines in the unregulated

Mortgage Broker trade. Who could boost their fee incomes like crazy by delivering as many Warm Bodies as possible to banks and other mortgage lenders. Even if this meant surreptitiously lending these mortgage applicants the proverbial "White Tie and Tails" for the wedding. Because "they could get away with it."

All of which brought waves of existing homeowners out of the woodwork. To refinance their mortgages so they could pocket cash for Hawaiian vacations from the burgeoning equity value in their homes caused by the boom in housing prices. Or buy new (even second) homes they couldn't afford with pennies-per-day teaser-rate mortgages. Assuming that inevitably rising house prices would bail them out. Swelling the glut of new mortgage applicants even further.

Banks were all too eager to bear-hug these mortgage applicants. Because part of "Bending the Rules" meant that Congress had directed government to give the banks Brownie Points for increasing the number of mortgages they granted to low-income Americans. (And penalize them with demerits if they didn't.)

And anyway, banks wanted to originate as many new mortgages as possible so they could sell them for fast cash to the mortgage pools put together by Wall Street firms. Plus gain nice fees for collecting monthly payments from homeowners and passing them on to their Wall Street buyers.

Where they became the new "Income Streams" that investment bankers collateralized into dividend-paying **Derivative Debt Securities**. By mixing together all varieties of mortgages into bubbling stews of tainted meat and rotting vegetables. Whose funny taste they hid with copious amounts of chili powder. In the form of "Good-as-Gold" safety ratings bought and paid for from Wall Street's private rating firms. Because "they could get away with it."

Thereby giving their securities salesmen new products to sell to investors who hadn't made the cut for acceptance into Bernie Madoff's secret fraternity for the "rich and well connected." All craving attractive yields and being careful not to ask too many questions.

Of course, just because we can get away with something doesn't necessarily make it "rational." Or even in our best interests.

This is graphically illustrated in the fascinating **National Geographic** nature documentary *Tigers of the Snow*. Where a short-tempered Siberian Tiger living in a Russian wilderness preserve scrambles aggressively to the top of a tree so he can try to attack the low-flying helicopter carrying several forest rangers who want to replace the battery in his tracking radio.

If the tiger's attack had succeeded, he would have crashed the helicopter and killed the forest rangers. But he probably would have been killed too. So what would have been the point?

There was no point. At least, not "rationally." The tiger was simply doing what came naturally to him as a serial killer.

Just like all the lascivines in the Fall of 2008. Who came to grief even while they were crashing the rest of the world. Because it was their **Nature** to behave like serial killers. And they were in the habit of "getting away with it."

■ ■ ■

Derivatives

In previous chapters, we looked at the details of things that determine what lascivines can get away with and how they work.

But before we go on to Chapter 11 and see how we can solve these and other problems, let's consider the implications of these details.

(Now bear with me if some of what follows seems repetitious. Because I'll let you in on a **Secret of Effective Teaching** passed on to me by the most brilliant teacher I had in graduate school. Which is to explain each difficult concept **Three Different Times**, in **Three Different Ways**, from **Three Different Perspectives**. So that the pennies will finally drop among your students and they'll really understand it.)

So we'll begin by considering the implications of **Derivatives**.

Suppose you bought **100 shares** of Microsoft back in 2007.

That gave you possession of something <u>Tangible</u>. An owner's claim on a portion of Microsoft's profits. You could find out the Free Market Value of this Tangible Asset any time you wanted because Microsoft trades daily on an organized exchange called NASDAQ. And this Tangible Asset was yours to keep until you decided to sell it.

<u>Or instead</u>, supposed you bought a **Call Option** on 100 shares of Microsoft. That gave you the <u>Right</u> to buy those shares at a specified "**Strike Price**" any time until your Option's specified <u>Expiration Date</u>.

Somewhat less tangible. Because your Option's value was <u>derived</u> from the market price of Microsoft on NASDAQ. <u>That's</u> why it's called a **Derivative**. And its relationship to Microsoft's market price was shown by the <u>actual market price</u> of the Option itself. Because Microsoft Options are traded on an organized exchange called the **Chicago Board Options Exchange**, which posts the latest trading prices for the options it lists.

You bought the Option for a small fraction of the price of 100 shares of Microsoft. But you <u>still</u> had the same right as a full-fledged share owner to profit from a rise in Microsoft's share price on NASDAQ. <u>If</u>, that is, the share price rose <u>higher</u> than your Option's Strike Price (meaning that your Option was "In the Money"). And did so <u>on or before</u> the Option's Expiration Date.

Because <u>then</u> you could "Exercise your in-the-money Option." That is, <u>buy</u> 100 shares of Microsoft at the Option's bargain Strike Price. And turn right around and <u>sell</u> these shares on NASDAQ for their <u>higher market price</u>. Realizing an immediate profit.

Or, even easier, you could simply <u>sell</u> the Option itself for its now-higher market price on the Chicago Board Options Exchange. Realizing a profit on your original purchase of the Option.

Either way, your profit dollars gave you a <u>Higher Percentage Gain</u> on the relatively few dollars you spent to buy the <u>Option</u> than if you had spent many more dollars to buy the 100 shares in the first place. In other words, you Leveraged your few dollars by purchasing the Option to bet on a rise in the market value of Microsoft on NASDAQ.

Just like that two-dollar horse bettor we saw in **Chapter One**. Conned by the Loanshark into placing ever-larger bets on races whose outcomes had been "Arranged." With the Loanshark lending him enough cash (at the usual 6-for-5 rate) to cover these large bets.

Of course, most Call Options "**expire worthless.**" That is, they never quite end up In the Money on or before their Expiration Dates. So most of the time, the bettor loses the few dollars he spent to buy the Option. (That's why the Smarter Strategy is to Sell options rather than Buy them. So you can keep pocketing sale dollars.) But hope springs eternal among these bettors craving the occasional Big Payoff.

Now suppose you did something Really Crazy. You bought a much more complicated Derivative known as a "**Credit Default Swap.**"

The original **Issuer** of the Credit Default Swap insures its owner (you) against the possibility of any interruption in the income stream paid by another Derivative. And you paid the Issuer regular "insurance premiums" for this protection.

What other Derivative are we talking about? Well, in this case we'll assume it was a dividend-paying **Collateralized Mortgage Obligation.**

In other words, your Credit Default Swap was sort of like a Fire Insurance Policy on your house. For which you pay regular premiums to the insurance company.

But with three important differences:

- **FIRST:** The Issuer of your Credit Default Swap probably wasn't a regular insurance company. More likely a Wall Street investment bank always eager for new products to sell. Therefore, it wasn't subject to normal insurance industry government requirements that it set aside enough **Capital Reserves** to cover any likely default claims against the Derivative it was supposedly insuring. So all you really had was a don't-worry-about-it "Promise to Pay" not backed by any Tangible Dollars.

- **SECOND:** The Issuer of those Credit Default Swaps had <u>no limit</u> on the <u>number</u> of these securities it could sell against the <u>same group</u> of Collateralized Mortgage Obligations. It could sell <u>many times</u> this number in its pursuit of profits. Incurring obligations to pay off on <u>all of them</u>. Even though it hadn't been required to set aside Capital Reserves to pay off on <u>any of them</u>.

- **THIRD:** You probably didn't even own the "house being insured" (that is, the Collateralized Mortgage Obligation in question).

So <u>why on earth</u> would you want to buy "fire insurance" on a house you didn't own?

Because your Credit Default Swap had **"Tradable Market Value,"** that's why. And you, as an Aggressive Investor, hoped to sell it for a profit when (if?) this Market Value rose beyond what you paid for it. Just as when the Market Value of Microsoft's common stock rose on NASDAQ.

<u>What</u> gave your Credit Default Swap its Market Value?

We can best answer this by tracing your Credit Default Swap through its (somewhat complicated) Derivative Chain.

- The <u>Market Value</u> of your particular Credit Default Swap was <u>derived from the perceived Value</u> of the underlying **Collateralized Mortgage Obligation** it insured.

- And the <u>Value</u> of this Collateralized Mortgage Obligation was <u>derived from the perceived Value</u> of its underlying **pool of home mortgages.**

- And the <u>Value</u> of those home mortgages was <u>derived from the perceived Value</u> of the **underlying monthly payments** made by the home owners who were granted these mortgages.

- And the <u>Value</u> of those monthly payments was <u>derived from the perceived Value</u> of the ongoing **family incomes** of these home owners.

In short, your Credit Default Swap was a "**Derivative** of a **Derivative** of a **Derivative** of **Tangible Family Incomes.**" (Unlike the much simpler Microsoft Call Option, which was merely a "Derivative of Tangible Ownership Shares of Microsoft stock.")

Now let's suppose the "trading market" for Credit Default Swaps like yours perceived (for whatever reason) that the overall **Credit Quality** of these **Tangible Family Incomes** was <u>Declining</u>. Raising the <u>possibility</u> that some of these families might become unable to keep paying their monthly mortgage payments.

And that this perception rose up through the Derivative Chain. Until it raised questions about the <u>safety</u> of the dividend stream paid by those Collateralized Mortgage Obligations. Whose safety was supposedly <u>insured</u> by Credit Default Swaps like yours. Thereby making the <u>default protection</u> your Credit Default Swap provided <u>more valuable</u>. So its Market Price <u>rose</u>. And you could sell it at a <u>profit</u>. Which was your hope when you originally bought it.

But exactly <u>what market</u> are we talking about? Ah, there's the rub.

Because <u>unlike</u> Microsoft's stock or Options on Microsoft's stock, Credit Default Swaps <u>aren't</u> traded in well-organized regulated markets like NASDAQ or the Chicago Board Options Exchange.

They're <u>only</u> traded in so-called **Over-The-Counter Markets.** Which can consists of little more than Big Swing Dick Traders hondeling each other about prices via telephone or computer networks.

And these traders can, at a moment's notice and for whatever reasons they choose, stop trading Credit Default Swaps like yours. To concentrate instead on trading other securities they believe can make them more money.

Leaving you High and Dry for buyers if you should want to sell your now-unsaleable Credit Default Swap.

This is what happened in 2008 to firms like **Bear Stearns**. Which suddenly found their balance sheets crammed full of Credit Default Swaps with Zero Market Value, for all practical purposes. Because their trading markets had simply disappeared.

So these firms had no choice but to write down the balance-sheet value of these orphaned assets. Taking Big Losses in the process, which they were too undercapitalized to absorb. Thus destroying their Credit Standings and staggering into financial collapse.

As you can see, we've taken a couple of giant steps from the simple direct ownership of Tangible Shares of Microsoft stock to a complicated "Fourth-Power Derivative" known as a Credit Default Swap. Which, by the end of 2008, had been thrown on an ever-more-towering junk pile of **Toxic Securities** that were impossible to value in any objective manner because their trading markets had vanished. Helping to bring down the world's financial markets with a thunderous crash.

Why?

Simple enough.

All those buyers and sellers had ridden much too high for much too long on little more than Willy Loman's proverbial "**Smile and a Shoeshine.**" Because lack of sensible regulation, lack of competent Risk Management, and lack of elementary Common Sense left them all believing "they could get away with it."

■ ■ ■

The Housing Prices Boom

Lots of things affect the prices of houses. But at the national level, the most important is probably **Interest Rates**.

Look at it this way.

The purchase price of most houses people buy in the United States is funded primarily by a self-liquidating Mortgage. This imposes on the home buyer a fixed monthly Mortgage Payment that he compares to his monthly take-home income. So he decides how much he can pay for a house by looking at the <u>relationship</u> between monthly Mortgage Payments and his monthly income.

Monthly Mortgage Payments have two components. One is the <u>Principal Payment</u> portion (i.e., the portion of the original mortgage loan being paid back). The second is the <u>Interest Payment</u> portion (which is the income paid to the mortgage lender).

The dollar size of the Interest Payment portion depends on the Interest Rate charged by the mortgage lender. Therefore, the lower the Interest Rate is, the <u>cheaper</u> the monthly mortgage payment will be. This means that a lower interest rate will enable a home buyer to <u>pay more</u> for a house. So <u>lower</u> Mortgage Interest Rates tend to mean <u>higher</u> prices for all houses.

Like all American interest rates, Mortgage Interest Rates are ultimately based on the <u>Federal Funds Rate</u>. As we saw in **Chapter 7**, the **Federal Reserve's Open Market Committee** sets the target for the Federal Funds Rate. And this target is implemented by the **Federal Reserve Bank of New York** by means of the pace at which it buys short-term Treasury debt securities in the open market.

Therefore, the Federal Reserve's target for the Federal Funds Rate has a major influence on Mortgage Interest Rates. And inevitably (though usually as a by-product of other policy factors), on the <u>Price of Houses</u>.

Simple enough.

But now let's consider the <u>implications</u> of this relationship between interest rates and the price of houses.

On Monday, October 19, 1987, stock markets around the world suffered the most extreme one-day crash in history. In the United States, the S&P 500 Index fell a horrendous <u>20.4 Percent</u>. Ivory tower theorists (wedded to such concepts as "Efficient Markets," "Rational Investor Behavior," and "the Inherent Randomness and Normal Gaussian Distribution of Securities Prices") had insisted that a one-day decline of this magnitude was such a low-probability event that "it couldn't happen in the lifetime of the Universe."

But it <u>did</u> happen. And it had some interesting consequences.

One of which was that it caused Federal Reserve Chairman **Alan Greenspan** (in office only since August) to direct the New York Fed to buy huge amounts of Treasury Securities. Thereby flooding the credit markets with a massive volume of "liquidity" (i.e., New Money) and pushing down the Federal Funds Rate. Making it easier for banks to rush to the side of Wall Street firms badly hit by the crash and offer to lend them baskets of money to see them through. As much as they needed. For only pennies a day. The result was that <u>this</u> time, Wall Street's gigantic sneeze <u>didn't</u> cause Main Street to catch pneumonia. Or even a slight case of the sniffles. And in less than two years, a resurgent Stock Market had completely wiped out its losses.

As we've seen, Greenspan came to the Fed with "top Libertarian Republican" credentials. A man who firmly believed "Markets are Always Right." Ideally suited to keeping "Prices Under Control." And his lifelong ability to attract interesting girlfriends gave him a macho image that nicely softened the edges of his cerebral intellectual demeanor.

But Greenspan's experiences in the wake of Black Monday seemed to have had a profound effect on him. He might still have believed "***Markets are Always Right.***" But he also came to appreciate the reality of "***Except when they're Wrong.***" When Wise Men in Positions of Power (like him) had to "take corrective actions."

The one thing he <u>didn't</u> appreciate was the possibility that Black Monday might have been a **Warning Siren** of tsunamis to come.

366

But Greenspan was no different from the rest of us on that score. Virtually all of us ignored that possibility.

So he proceeded as if he'd discovered a new version of the **Philosopher's Stone**. Letting the sacred all-knowing Markets do their own thing, free from nuisances like Regulation. And if (when) they got into trouble, he'd come rushing in with New Money to refill the punch bowl and keep the party going full blast.

He did this in 1998 when the Asian financial crisis and Russian debt default blew the over-leveraged hedge fund **Long-Term Capital Management** out of the water and threatened the stability of its big name Wall Street lender banks.

And again in 2000. When the **Dot.Com Bubble** exploded. Crashing the stock market and precipitating a national recession.

And he couldn't stop doing it in the years that followed. Keeping interest rates at bargain-basement levels with fresh doses of New Money. Which, needless to say, caused housing prices to boom.

He did this because he thought he could get away with it.

We all did.

Until the gigantic bill came due in 2008.

■ ■ ■

Mortgages

Back in **Chapter 5**, we looked at the details of the Old-Fashioned Home Mortgage Model that were dramatized in Frank Capra's legendary movie *It's a Wonderful Life*.

Lead character **George Bailey** ran a modest bank in a modest All-American town. And had developed a nice business using the account balances of his depositors to fund the home mortgages he granted to aspiring home buyers. Keeping these mortgages in his bank's asset portfolio until they were paid off. And in the meantime, living off the payments these home buyers made each month on their mortgages.

These mortgages were <u>Low-Risk</u> investments for George's bank. Because they'd been granted almost exclusively to the <u>bank's own depositors</u>. And George knew them all. Knew what kind of jobs they held and how much money they made. Knew how conscientious they were about paying their bills on time. Knew which of them might drink more than was good for them in the town's various saloons and which of them stayed home playing Chinese Checkers with their families. So he had a wealth of personal information to help him decide which depositors were sufficiently "Creditworthy" to be awarded mortgages so they could buy their own homes.

Needless to say, George couldn't originate very many new mortgages each year. Because his available lending cash was limited by the number of <u>existing</u> mortgages that were paid off and the growth of his depositors' account balances. So his mortgage business was a <u>low-growth</u> enterprise. But a very <u>safe</u> one.

This low ceiling on the number of new mortgages banks like George's could award each year limited the number of families who could actually buy homes. Leading to a "low-demand climate for homes" that limited the number of new houses local construction firms were willing to build each year.

Back in the 1930s, these low limits clashed with the ambitions of President Roosevelt's New Deal to bring the nation out of the Great Depression by increasing its Gross Domestic Product. Because New Housing Construction was the kind of activity that had a considerable multiplier impact on the growth of GDP. But George Bailey's **Old-Fashioned Home Mortgage Model** kept the number of new mortgages available each year at too low a level to boost Housing Construction.

There were two possible ways to change this:

- **Create a New Federal Program to <u>directly lend</u> taxpayer funds to aspiring homeowners so they could afford to buy houses. Thereby increasing the Demand for new houses.**

Which would boost Housing Construction and therefore the Growth of GDP.

- Let the Free Market do it. And if the Free Market couldn't accomplish this on its own, goose it with "carefully targeted economic incentives" until it could.

Naturally, there was no shortage of "left-wing social-welfare types" in the New Deal who pushed for the first approach.

But the Roosevelt Administration was encountering increased resistance in the country-bumpkin Congress to "runaway Federal anti-Depression spending." So the second approach became the only practical choice. And the Administration went about it in a very interesting way.

- **FIRST:** It established a government-owned commercial corporation (called **Fannie Mae**) to buy existing home mortgages from lender banks like George's. Which gave these banks fresh cash to fund new mortgages. That they could sell to Fannie Mae for more fresh cash to fund more new mortgages.

- **SECOND:** The Administration made Fannie Mae "self-funding" (not taxpayer funded). By authorizing it to issue its own interest-paying debt securities to private investors. These were backed by Fannie Mae's income stream of monthly payments from the home mortgages it had bought. And with the cash Fannie Mae received from the sale of its debt securities, it could buy still more existing mortgages from banks like George's.

(After all, where is it written that government bureaucrats are forbidden from being as innovative as private entrepreneurs when the chips are down? How else could we have won World War II?)

And the rest, as they say, is History.

Fannie Mae's **New Deal Mortgage Model** spurred a major increase in the availability of home mortgages. This made it possible for increasing numbers of American families to buy their own homes. And the construction industry responded to this rising demand for houses to purchase by stepping up its pace of high-multiplier New Home Building.

But **Fate,** ever malicious in its Nazi-like craving to undermine human progress, determined that this was certainly one Good Deed that should absolutely Not Go Unpunished. So it encouraged the lascivines among us to corrupt the Fannie Mae concept beyond all recognition. Converting it from a Good Deed into a virulent **Curse.**

We've already seen how Wall Street types jumped on the mortgage collateralizing bandwagon to give themselves profitable new products to sell. Buying up mortgages of every description to use their monthly income streams to back imaginative new unregulated Derivatives. And in the process, casting aside Fannie Mae's high standards for mortgage credit strength. Because what mattered was **Quantity,** not Quality.

With mortgage lenders also catching the Quantity obsession. As they eagerly welcomed every Warm Body who walked in the door. And paid big fees to Mortgage Brokers to send them more. Since all that mattered was goosing the number of new mortgages they could originate, and never mind how. To sell to Wall Street for fresh cash and higher income from servicing fees.

As Alan Greenspan kept the punch bowl full with his low-interest - rate policies. Fueling an ever-rising tide of home prices to paper over any concerns about old-fashioned questions like Credit Quality and Risk.

Well, we've seen how it ended. With Fate herding the suckers into its gas chambers and opening the valves.

Because all concerned thought they could get away with it.

■ ■ ■

Leverage

Back in 2006, my friend Tyler needed to increase his family's income by a reliable $50,000 per year so he could send his eldest son to the kind of high-fashion private university where he could meet upscale people who could help his future business career.

But he only had $100,000 to invest. And there weren't any safe bonds around that paid 50 Percent interest.

So was Tyler going to have to settle for sending his son to a down-market public university where he'd only meet working-class types who wiped their noses on their sleeves?

Not necessarily.

He checked around and found he could buy nice A-rated tax-exempt hospital bonds paying Five Percent and maturing in a comfortably distant 30 years. And it occurred to him that maybe he could take out a loan to help himself buy enough of these bonds to give him the income boost he needed.

So he spent a few hours fiddling with a crude Excel model he cobbled together on his laptop. Then paid a visit to a loan officer he knew at his bank. And came up with the following investment strategy:

- He'd buy $9.1 Million worth of those 5 Percent hospital bonds. Paying for them with his $100,000. Plus the proceeds of a $9 Million four-year term loan from his bank. Thereby leveraging each dollar of his $100,000 to the tune of 90 to 1.

- He wouldn't have to pay back the term loan until his son was out of college. And he figured he'll sell the bonds at that time to raise the loan repayment cash. But in the meantime, he'd still have to pay interest on the loan. And the loan's interest rate couldn't exceed 4.5 Percent if his strategy was going to work.

- For Tyler to get a rate that low, the bank insisted that he pledge the bonds as security. Plus throw in his house to provide a margin of safety. Which was okay because his home mortgage only had another five years to run. So he'd built up a ton of equity value in a house whose market value had skyrocketed to the Moon because of the housing price boom.

So Tyler signed the necessary papers at his bank. Bought the $9.1 Million worth of 5 Percent hospital bonds by leveraging his $100,000 at the rate of 90 to 1 with his bank loan. And sent his son off to that fashionable private university.

Here's what his first year's numbers looked like:

- His $9.1 Million worth of 5 Percent hospital bonds produced an income of $455,000.

- But he had to pay $405,000 of that to the bank in interest on his $9 Million term loan.

- Leaving him with a <u>net income increase</u> of $50,000. Just what he needed to cover his son's college bills.

Pretty neat. Right?

Sure. Tyler's aggressive use of 90-to-1 <u>Leverage</u> had enabled him to parlay his $100,000 into extra income of $50,000. Which amounted to an <u>investment return</u> of a whopping <u>50 Percent</u>. At least, it was pretty neat until November 2008. When the snowballing recession cost Tyler his well-paying job.

So now that $50,000 in bond income left over after Tyler paid the interest on his bank loan was no longer available to keep his son in that upscale private university. He needed it to put food on the table. Pay his wife's medical bills (because his health insurance had disappeared with his job) and his daughter's dental bills. Cover the monthly interest payments on the credit card balances he'd run up in 2007 to pay for a family skiing vacation in Switzerland. Keep his car's clunker engine running so he could drive to job interviews.

In fact, it didn't even stretch far enough to keep Tyler current with his home mortgage payments. So he was being threatened with foreclosure. And since his house was pledged as security on his bank loan, losing it would cause the bank to call his loan for immediate repayment. Which he couldn't cover by selling his muni bonds because he needed their income to live on.

Is it any wonder that Tyler began to think seriously about declaring personal bankruptcy?

Leverage can seem like a great thing when you're running in the Winner's Lane. But it can be a disaster when you're losing.

Just as so many firms in the financial industry found out in 2008, when their off-the-wall leverage ratios turned around and bit them in the tush. Very painfully.

■ ■ ■

Risk

Since Life's really just One Big Poker Game, it naturally follows that everything in Life is "**Risky.**"

That means we have to learn all we can about what Risk is.

How it <u>really</u> works. How it <u>never</u> disappears no matter how cleverly we repackage it and try to sell it to the next guy. How it's <u>always</u> hidden away in everything we buy. How to <u>measure</u> it correctly and <u>assess</u> it sensibly. So that when the Player next to us Bets Big, we can make a smart response. To <u>See</u> his bet. Or <u>Raise</u> it. Or cut our losses and <u>Fold</u>.

Or even go <u>All-In</u> . . .

There are lots of books about Risk. One of the best is by a true guru named **Ralph Vince**.

It was published in 2007, and its title is ***The Handbook of Portfolio Mathematics***, with the intriguing subtitle of ***Formulas for Optimal Allocation & Leverage***. (But don't be scared away by the mention of "Mathematics" and "Formulas." All the math is simple Algebra and clearly explained in the highly readable text.)

Vince's lifelong schtick has been determining how <u>large a portion of your stake</u> you should bet on the next financial security. Or race horse. Or Poker card. Or new house in the suburbs. Or any other Risky investment. With the goal of maximizing the growth rate of your stake while <u>still</u> keeping your potential losses at tolerable levels.

The first few chapters explain all you really need to know about measuring and assessing Risk (which is what the forbidding subject of **Probability** is all about). Full of clear and fun-to-read examples drawn from (what else?) common gambling games.

It seems unlikely that very many Wall Street Rocket Scientists read Vince's earlier books (on the same subject) before they started engineering their hokey **Value- At-Risk** models. And it's almost certain that none of the top managers of financial firms were even aware of them (assuming they could read anything more advanced than in-house memos). Otherwise, they might not have gotten us into the mess we're currently struggling with.

Risk is the <u>Most Dangerous</u> scourge in the world around us. And the <u>only</u> way we can protect ourselves from the disasters it can clobber us with is to learn as much as we can about it.

Because such knowledge is the only way to find out what we can <u>really</u> get away with.

■ ■ ■

Well, so much for our review of the book's main points so far.

Now let's go on to the Chapter 11 and see what we can do to resolve the most serious problems bedeviling us.

And how **Transforming American Transportation** can be one of the most effective tools we have available for doing this.

■ ■ ■

Chapter 11
THE BOTTOM LINE

The trumpet shall sound, and the dead shall be
raised incorruptible. And we shall be changed.
For this corruptible must put on incorruption.
And this mortal must put on immortality.
—First Corinthians

So far, we've had great fun making snide comments from our gilded perch of Superior Hindsight. About the Appalling Sins of **Mismanagement, Greed, Ignorance, Bad Judgment,** and **Gross Immorality** (have I left anything out?) committed by the Lascivines who did so much to precipitate the current Economic Crisis.

Easy enough to do, of course. But bound to get a little tiresome after a while.

So now it's time to shift gears and become More Constructive.

Specifically, by looking at some of the things that can get us out of this mess. Especially the kind of intelligently conceived and managed **Major New Investment Programs** that can create new jobs and give the American economy a long overdue shot in the arm.

Programs that (not so incidentally) include **Transforming the Nation's Transportation Systems** in ways that can boost our rate of **Economic Growth** in the future.

So Fasten Your Seat Belts. (Thought it's not going to be <u>that</u> bumpy a night.)

■ ■ ■

Summary of the Major Issues

There are two issues that tower above all the others.

Spiraling Unemployment. This is the Economic Indicator that <u>matters most</u> to the Average American. During 2009, it reached levels not seen in more than a <u>Quarter of a Century</u>. And there were fears that its gross numbers could rise even further to challenge those of the **Great Depression.**

Long-Term Federal Budget Deficits and Outstanding Debt. In June 2009, the Congressional Budget Office published various sets of projections for these variables covering the 2009 through 2035 period and beyond. Its "<u>Alternative Fiscal Scenario</u>" projections are the most disturbing.

■ ■ ■

Major Issue: Spiraling Unemployment

Economists like to regard the **Unemployment Rate** as a "Lagging Indicator." Because its significant trend changes tend to occur well after trend changes in the growth of Gross Domestic Product.

But to Normal People, the Unemployment Rate is the **<u>Most Important</u>** indicator of what's going on in the economy <u>Right Now</u>. (<u>Are economists the "Real Lagging Indicators"?</u>) So **Unemployment** is the indicator they pay the <u>most attention</u> to.

As well they might, when you consider the following:

- **Job Losses** since the "Official Beginning" of the Recession in December 2007 reached a cumulative total of **8.2 Million** in October 2009. This is the <u>largest number</u> of total recession job losses in American history.

- The **"Official" Unemployment Rate** shot up past the terrifying **10 Percent Level** during October 2009. And closed out the month at **10.2 Percent**. This is the <u>Highest Level</u> in more than a **Quarter of a Century**. And <u>Over One-Third</u> of these unemployed workers have been jobless for <u>More Than One Year</u>.

- When "Part-Time" and "Drop-Out" workers are counted, the **"True" Unemployment Rate** reached a staggering **17.5 Percent** in October 2009. This may be the most significant measure of joblessness, since many part-timers experience the <u>same</u> negative psychological and social impacts as those who are totally unemployed.

- The **Economic Impact** of so many unemployed workers exerts a <u>Severe Drag</u> on the nation. Workers and their families who must struggle to make ends meet on traditionally low unemployment benefits are <u>no longer able</u> to participate fully in the nation's consumer economy. And since **Consumer Spending** accounts for some <u>70 Percent of GDP,</u> their enforced spending curtailments <u>further reduce</u> GDP and hold back attempts at recovery. This represents an **Economic Multiplier Effect** in reverse.

- The **Psychological** and **Social Impacts** of such widespread unemployment can be <u>even worse</u> than the economic impact. Especially among the many middle-class professionals and managers who have <u>never experienced</u> anything like this before. Greatly curtailed family incomes lead to **higher home mortgage foreclosure rates,** which can <u>Destabilize</u> entire neighborhoods. Wives who prefer to focus on raising their children may have to <u>return to the workforce,</u> and the <u>shortage of affordable Day Care</u> can impose **new burdens on children** that they're unable to handle. The rate of **family dissolution** rises at an alarming rate. And the record shows that **Roughly Half** of these middle-class unemployed workers are unlikely to **ever again** be able to resume their former careers. Settling instead for whatever Dead-End Jobs are available at a fraction of their former incomes. Thereby **Permanently Removing** themselves and their families from America's functional middle class, which is its **Economic Backbone.** Not to mention losing a whole generation of <u>fresh college graduates.</u> Who can't begin the new careers they'd hoped for because of the moribund job market. And may have to settle for something much less valuable to the future of America.

• The current **anemic economic recovery** has done little more than stem the horrendous job losses the nation suffered during the late months of 2008 and most of 2009. At this rate, it will take literally **Years** to build the employment base back to where it was in 2007. Much less increase total jobs by enough to absorb new workers pouring into the labor force as the population rises. So we face what will seem like **Permanently High Unemployment Rates.** With a **dangerously high** and **socially disruptive** proportion of the labor force reduced to shaping up on street corners at the crack of dawn each morning. Hoping for a day's work.

And things could get <u>even worse.</u>

- The **Official Unemployment Rate** could <u>remain above 10 Percent</u> for the next **Eight Years**. According to some economists, this could happen if the nation <u>slipped back into recession</u> in 2011. With the Unemployment Rate maxing out at **13 Percent** in 2011 and 2012. Perhaps because Congress <u>refuses</u> to pass New Stimulus Programs after existing programs have run out of funds. Leading to <u>New Rounds of Job Losses</u> as private firms hunker down to conserve cash by laying off employees in response to falling demand for their products and services.

- The nation would have to <u>add 250,000 jobs per month,</u> **every month,** for **Five Years** to get back to the 5 Percent Unemployment Rate we had in 2007. That's a grand total of **15 Million New Jobs**. Well, in 1999, we had that kind of healthy job growth. But <u>only</u> for that one year. How are we going to achieve that for <u>Five Years</u>?

Clearly, **Unemployment** is America's **Most Serious** current problem.

So forget "Nation-Building in Afghanistan." Or "Providing Affordable Health Care to All Americans." Or "Balancing the Federal Budget." Or "New Space Initiatives for NASA." Or "Taming the Wolves of Wall Street." These are obviously important initiatives.

<u>But they all take **Second Place**</u> to the overriding challenge of PUTTING AMERICANS BACK TO WORK.

<u>This</u> must be the Federal Government's **Number One Priority** for the foreseeable future. And carrying it out successfully will require something more than "Traditional Measures." <u>Fresh Approaches</u> are needed.

The problem with Fresh Approaches is that some of the most obvious are simply <u>Crazy</u>.

Like that Old Perennial among the Know-Nothings to erect High Tariff Walls that keep out "foreign-made products." So all products Americans buy would have to be made by "American Workers" in "American-Owned Factories" on "American Soil."

Yeah sure.

Just like we tried with the infamous **Smoot-Hawley Tariff** in 1930. That meshuga piece of destructive legislation <u>Shattered International Trade</u> for more than a generation. And became one of the <u>Midwives</u> of the **Great Depression**. Spawning innumerable gangs of homeless "*Wild Boys of the Road*." Which director William Wellman immortalized in his 1933 movie of that title.

■ ■ ■

Do We Need a New "G.I. Bill"?

As the Roosevelt Administration began planning for postwar America in 1943, it recognized the problem posed by some <u>16 Million military veterans</u> returning to civilian life all at once after the end of World War II. Their numbers were so huge relative to the size of the total work force at the time that they would totally swamp private sector job markets. Producing an <u>Unemployment Crisis</u> of Great Depression proportions that was likely to be socially destabilizing.

So the Administration decided to "<u>temporarily remove</u>" a Significant Percentage of these returning veterans from the job markets. By paying them decent salaries to attend colleges or trade schools at government expense for up to four years. With the basic salary level being adjusted upward if the veteran was married. And adjusted still further upward if he and his wife had children.

All of which produced a **New Generation** of well-educated professionals and technicians to meet the private sector's burgeoning demand for skilled workers in the late 1940s and early 1950s as the postwar economic boom took off.

These were the famous **Educational Benefits** that became a central feature of the legendary "**G.I. Bill**," which became law in 1944. Not just another so-called "New Deal Welfare Program," but a **Major Capital Investment** to raise the future productivity of the nation's "Citizen Soldiers." Which was just as important as capital investments in new plant and equipment. And paid off Big Time for the nation as a whole in new growth and prosperity.

Could we profit just as lavishly by implementing a <u>similar</u> educational program today as a first step in **Putting Americans Back to Work?** After all, it's not as if unemployment was some kind of "Just Punishment" for real or imagined sins committed by these idle workers (even though Washington too often acts as if it is).

So why not <u>temporarily remove</u> large numbers of the nation's unemployed workers from private sector job markets and send them to college or trade school to enrich their skills for the future? And pay them decent salaries in the meantime so they and their families can fully participate in the consumer economy instead of being a drag on it?

While we're at it, why not resurrect <u>another valuable feature</u> of the G.I. Bill? Have the government provide low (maybe zero) down-payment mortgages at below-market interest rates to reduce "out-of-pocket" home ownership costs to those otherwise unable to afford homes of their own.

And just as it did in the late 1940s, such a program could <u>also</u> boost the level of new housing construction. Which is a significant factor in growing the national economy. Not to mention supporting the All-American goal of expanding home ownership much more effectively than all those sub-prime mortgage scams earlier in the decade.

Finally, why not make these educational and housing benefits "Tradable"? Giving those who elect not to use them the option of selling them for <u>Cash</u> in organized markets that Wall Street would be more than happy to provide.

This "**Son of the G.I. Bill**" could focus initially on providing its benefits to veterans of the wars in Iraq and Afghanistan, many of whom have made significant <u>economic sacrifices</u> that deserve to be recognized.

But it shouldn't stop there. Ways must be found to extend these benefits to Millions of other Americans whose lives have been derailed by economic calamities they did nothing to cause.

Such a program for investing in America's future certainly makes a lot more sense than continuing to waste money on unwinnable foreign military adventures that can never produce anything but casualty lists.

(**<u>Interesting note</u>:** The text of the <u>original</u> G.I. Bill was actually written by that "flaming red bastion of social-welfare liberalism" known as the **American Legion.** No doubt in the same spirit that had previously led the Legion to name one of its posts in Brooklyn after noted American poet **Sergeant Joyce Kilmer**—best known as the author of the poem *Trees.* Who died a hero's death at age 31 on July 30, 1918 during World War I's *Second Battle of the Marne* while leading a platoon for New York's legendary "**Fighting Sixty-Ninth**" Infantry Division. And was later awarded the *Croix de Guerre* by France.)

■ ■ ■

Major Issue: Escalating Federal Budget Deficits and Debt

One lesson history has taught us is that national government measures to reverse economic adversities must be <u>large enough</u> to have the necessary impact. And must be carried on <u>long enough</u> to ensure Full Recovery.

Any attempt to cut corners or get by with halfway measures poses the danger of the government being tempted into false economies that can plunge the nation into something like Japan's **Lost Decade** of the 1990s.

Or like the **Return of the Depression** in 1937, when a weary and ignorant Congress insisted on cutting outlays for New Deal programs in an attempt to "Balance the Federal budget." Which delayed the nation's recovery for another four years. Until unavoidably huge increases in Federal Defense Spending finally put everyone back to work and brought Americans a long overdue taste of Prosperity.

So government has to do <u>enough stimulus</u> and keep doing it <u>long enough</u> for the private sector to get the traction it needs to start <u>running the ball</u> on its own. Otherwise, it ends up back where it started. With the usual naysayers (who want to win intellectual debates rather than wars) crowing about how government stimulus is a waste of time and money that <u>never</u> works.

The Obama Administration faces the same problem today as the Roosevelt Administration faced in the 1930s. Because pre-2009 policies in the White House and Congress <u>destabilized</u> the federal government's financial picture. Leading to projections of escalating **Budget Deficits** "for as far as the eye can see." Plus a growing Mount Everest of **Outstanding Federal Debt**. And spiraling **New Annual Borrowing Needs** to be met by . . . who?

Not to mention the need for the Federal Government to provide additional funds to extend <u>unemployment benefits</u> to idle workers who seem unlikely to return to work anytime soon. Plus significantly more <u>financial assistance</u> to hard-pressed state and local governments struggling to meet their legally mandated "Balanced Budget" requirements by raising taxes and cutting spending. Which can only drag down the economy still further.

All of which suggests that the Obama Administration faces a difficult **Balancing Act** replete with harsh **Trade-Offs**.

We'll look at some details of the Federal Government's dismal financial outlook in a minute. But before we do, there's something important we must keep in mind.

The Federal Government's approach to financial accounting is as <u>simple-minded and misleading</u> as that used by a group of third-grade children operating a **Sidewalk Lemonade Stand**. As a result, the Federal Government's so-called "Surplus or Deficit" is **in no way** equivalent to a private business firm's "Profit or Loss."

- The Federal Government's budget reflects the difference between its **Total Revenues** and its **Total Outlays**. And its Total Outlays include <u>both</u> Operating Costs <u>and</u> Capital Spending.

- But the budget for a private firm more logically reflects the difference between its **Total Revenues** and its **<u>Operating Costs</u>**. Because its Capital Spending is an <u>Investment</u> Activity, <u>not</u> an Operating Activity. Therefore, it's <u>never</u> included in determining whether the firm has made a Profit or Loss.

If private firms used the same <u>third-grader accounting approach</u> as the Federal Government, very few of them would ever be able to show a "Profit."

Even so, the Federal Government insists on going its own childish way. In effect, pointing to a rose bush in the White House garden and calling it the **Washington Monument**. Thereby misleading (and too often needlessly alarming) Normal People.

A more sensible (and less misleading) name for the Federal Government's so-called "Budget Deficit" would be its **Cash Shortfall**. Because this term correctly implies that this is the amount of hard cash it must raise from "outside sources" (i.e., the world's credit markets).

But we can't expect to reform the entire world with a single book. So we'll compromise and henceforth talk about the Federal Government's "**Cash Deficit.**" Always surrounding this term with quotation marks to remind ourselves that we're referring to its childishly misnamed "Budget Deficit."

Now for a look at what the numbers suggest about the fiscal future.

■ ■ ■

The Road to Perdition?

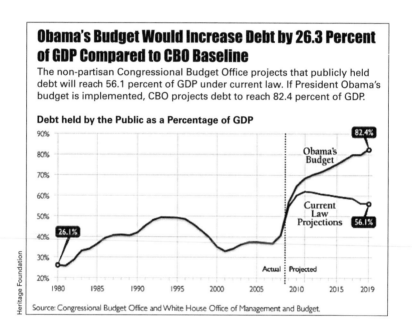

FIGURE 11.1. Two CBO "scenarios"

This chart was released in June 2009 by the **Congressional Budget Office**. It shows <u>near-term</u> (through 2019) patterns for the Federal Government's Financial Outlook. Based on annual numbers from CBO's economic models that have generated various "Scenarios" running through the middle of this century.

CBO's projections are being constantly revised to reflect changing circumstances. But its June 2009 projections constitute a useful <u>baseline</u> for our purposes.

- CBO's **"Extended Baseline Scenario"** generally reflects the assumptions in the Obama Administration's original **Fiscal Plan** for how the Federal Government's financial condition will evolve through 2035. On the chart, it's represented by the lower dotted line in the "Projected" section on the right.

- CBO's **"Alternative Fiscal Scenario"** is represented by the upper dotted line in the chart's "Projected" section. This is its "<u>Doctor Doom</u>" scenario. But many people regard it as the "most realistic" scenario because it more fully reflects what they regard as the likely escalation of necessary outlays for such high-cost budget categories as Social Security and Medicaid.

So we decided to focus on the **Doctor Doom** scenario. No Big Deal really. Something any of you could do on a rainy Sunday afternoon and still have time to watch your favorite spots teams on TV.

- <u>First</u>: We went to CBO's web site and printed out each year's projected numbers for its Key Variables through 2035. These variables included annual numbers for **Total Federal Revenues, Total Federal Outlays, Total "Cash Deficits," New Borrowing,** and **Total Debt Held By The Public.** (The "Debt-Holding Public" includes the Federal Reserve but does <u>not</u> include the Social Security Trust Fund and other "Internal Government Accounts.")

- <u>Second</u>: We laid out the projected numbers for these variables side-by-side and matched up their years. And added CBO's annual projections for **Gross Domestic Product.**

- <u>Third</u>: As we examined these numbers, certain interesting patterns began to jump off the pages. These patterns appeared to reflect what CBO was assuming about the <u>Significant Relationships</u> between these variables, as well as with **GDP**.

As its chart implies, CBO seemed to regard the <u>Relationship</u> between **Federal Debt Held By The Public** and **Gross Domestic Product** as especially important for defining the Federal Government's financial condition.

This is entirely sensible. It's like looking at your amount of outstanding credit card debt <u>relative</u> to your income. And as your income rises, you can afford to support <u>more dollars</u> of credit card debt. Just so long as the amount you owe isn't <u>growing faster</u> than your income.

Unfortunately, CBO's Doctor Doom numbers project that **Federal Debt Held by the Public** will rise <u>faster</u> than the nation's income. Growing from about:

- **37 Percent of GDP** in 2007.

- To **87 Percent of GDP** by 2019.
  After which it keeps on rising. To reach an awesome <u>180 Percent of GDP</u> in 2035.

- The comparable dollar amounts are **$5 Trillion** in Debt in 2007, **$19 Trillion** in 2019, and **$67 Trillion** in 2035.

- This rapid escalation in Outstanding Debt would represent an average increase of **9.7 Percent per year** during the twenty-eight-year period.

Some concerned observers believe that there's <u>no way</u> the U.S. Treasury can persuade the Investing Public (which includes big foreign debt buyers like China and Japan) to hold such large amounts of Federal Debt except by offering them <u>outrageously high interest rates</u>. The cost of which would boost necessary outlays for **Net Interest Payments** in the Federal Budget. So they regard CBO's Doctor Doom scenario as a <u>Warning Siren</u> of a **Tsunami Crisis** in the financial affairs of the Federal Government.

■ ■ ■

Traditional Solutions

Economic experts from respected think tanks have correctly pointed out that the **reason** for the Federal Government's dismal financial outlook is that its **<u>Outlays</u>** are<u> growing much faster </u>than its **<u>Revenues</u>**.

- For example, CBO's numbers for its Doctor Doom scenario show that the Federal Government's **Total Revenues** are projected to grow at an average rate of **<u>3.8 Percent per year</u>** during the twenty-five-year 2010–35 period.

- But its **Total Outlays** are projected to grow <u>1.4 times faster</u> during this period. At an average rate of **<u>5.3 Percent per year</u>**.

- This would cause the Federal Government's **"Cash Deficit"** to escalate during this period by an average rate of **<u>7.2 Percent per year</u>**.

Traditional solutions for this problem involve some combination of <u>Slowing</u> the growth of **Outlays** and <u>Increasing</u> the growth of **Revenues**.

This is a sound basic **Strategy**. But its **Tactical** implementation seems likely to encounter some major practical problems.

Under present circumstances, for example, "<u>Increasing the Growth of Revenues</u>" usually means **Raising Taxes** (either by boosting tax rates or by eliminating certain costly tax deductions, such as the popular middle-class deduction for home mortgage interest payments). This seems politically difficult to achieve, given the perception among many members of Congress that "Voting for Tax Increases" is tantamount to announcing your forthcoming retirement from elective politics.

Similarly, "Slowing the Growth of Outlays" in any meaningful way probably means finding ways to **Cut Back Funding** for high-dollar-payment categories like Social Security and Medicaid. Which are bound to be opposed by retirees—a large and rapidly growing component of the nation's voting-age population.

This could be further complicated by the Real Possibility that some sharp and savvy political operators may eventually grab control of major retiree associations like **AARP** as a means of making themselves lavishly paid and politically powerful "Kingmakers." They would presumably achieve this by mobilizing the enormous, growing (but still latent) Voting Power of their retired constituents to "**Demand**" that members of Congress move (on pain of losing the next election) to increase the "Living Standards of Retirees" with new and more costly federal pension and aid programs.

Are there other possible solutions to the Federal Government's fiscal problems?

Maybe so.

■ ■ ■

The "Higher Economic Growth" Solution

As we continued examining the projected numbers in CBO's Doctor Doom scenario, two other interesting patterns emerged.

One suggested that CBO was assuming a Significant Relationship between the <u>Size</u> of Current Dollar (i.e., "Actual") **Gross Domestic Product** and the <u>Size</u> of **Total Federal Revenues.**

In other words, CBO seemed to be assuming that (if tax rates remained unchanged) <u>**Total Dollars of Federal Revenues**</u> would remain pretty much a <u>**Fixed Proportion**</u> of the <u>**Total Dollar Value of the Nation's Economy.**</u> As measured by Current Dollar GDP.

So as GDP <u>**grows**</u> **in Total Dollar Value,** the dollar size of Federal Revenues <u>**will grow**</u> **at more or less the same rate.** Even while tax rates remain unchanged. With Federal revenues maintaining their <u>same</u> fixed proportion of GDP.

The other interesting pattern that emerged from CBO's projections suggested that it was assuming a <u>Linked Set of Relationships</u> between **GDP, Total Federal Revenues,** the **Federal "Cash Deficit,"** new **Federal Borrowing,** and **Total Federal Debt Held By The Public.**

More specifically, CBO's <u>Relationship Links</u> imply that:

- <u>Higher</u> **GDP** results in <u>higher</u> **Federal Revenues.**

- <u>Higher</u> **Federal Revenues** directly affect the <u>size</u> of the **"Cash Deficit."**

- The <u>size</u> of the **"Cash Deficit"** determines the <u>amount</u> of new **Federal Borrowing** needed.

- And the <u>amount</u> of new **Federal Borrowing** in any given year directly affects the <u>amount</u> of **Federal Debt Held By The Public.**

As we thought about the implications of these CBO assumptions, we couldn't help asking ourselves an interesting question:
WHAT WOULD HAPPEN IF GROSS DOMESTIC PRODUCT <u>GREW FASTER</u> THAN CBO WAS PROJECTING?

So we played around with some possibilities for alternative GDP Growth Rates. Temporarily holding **Total Federal Outlays** at CBO's projected Doctor Doom levels so the results would be clearer. And these results were very interesting.

Here's one example. It assumes that Current Dollar ("Actual") GDP grows **One Percentage Point** <u>Faster</u> than CBO is projecting. What happens?

Let's start with the Federal Government's annual "**Cash Deficit**":

- <u>By 2020</u>, faster GDP growth would boost Federal Revenues sufficiently to cause the "Cash Deficit" to **grow more slowly** than in CBO's Doctor Doom scenario. So that it would reach just under $2 Trillion in 2020. (Or only 88 Percent as high as CBO's $2.2 Trillion projection). **Reducing** its Percentage of GDP to 8.3 Percent (vs. CBO's 10.2 Percent).

- <u>By 2035</u>, the "Cash Deficit" would grow to $5.3 Trillion. (Only 78 Percent as high as CBO's projected $6.7 Trillion). **Falling** to 11.4 Percent of GDP (rather than CBO's projected 18.1 Percent).

Since CBO assumes that <u>smaller</u> annual cash deficits mean <u>less borrowing</u> by the U.S. Treasury, the results for projected levels of **Total Outstanding Federal Debt Held By The Public** are equally interesting:

- <u>By 2020</u>, Total Debt would reach $18.4 Trillion (only **96 Percent as high** as CBO's $19.1 Trillion projection). Falling to **78 Percent of GDP** (vs. CBO's Doctor Doom projection of 88 Percent).

- <u>By 2035</u>, Total Debt would have grown to $57 Trillion (only **85 Percent as high** as CBO's projected $67 Trillion).

Falling to **123 Percent of GDP** (rather than CBO's record-setting 180 Percent).

These numbers seemed to be going in an encouraging direction.

So we expanded our sights a little. By looking at what would happen if GDP grew **Two Percentage Points Faster** than CBO is projecting.

Again starting with the Federal Government's projected annual "**Cash Deficit**":

- By 2020, faster GDP growth would cause this to grow only to $1.7 Trillion (75 Percent as high as CBO's $2.2 Trillion Doctor Doom projection). **Reducing** its Percentage of GDP to 6.5 Percent (vs. 10.2 Percent in CBO's projections).

- By 2035, the "Cash Deficit" would only reach $3.5 Trillion (52 Percent as high as CBO's projected $6.7 Trillion). **Falling further** to only 6.1 Percent of GDP (rather than CBO's projected 18.1 Percent).

With less borrowing by the U.S. Treasury to cover the "Cash Deficit," the results for projected levels of **Total Outstanding Federal Debt Held By The Public** were equally encouraging.

- By 2020, Total Debt would reach $18 Trillion (or **92 Percent as high** as CBO's $19 Trillion projection). Falling to **69 Percent of GDP** (vs. CBO's Doctor Doom projection of 88 Percent).

- By 2035, Total Debt would only have grown to $46 Trillion (**68 Percent as high** as CBO's projected $67 Trillion). Falling still further to **79 Percent of GDP** (rather than rising to CBO's whopping 180 Percent).

Obviously, there was a favorable trend here.

So we decided to let it all hang out and try growing GDP **Three Percentage Points Faster** than CBO was projecting.

Starting with the "**Cash Deficit**":

- <u>By 2020</u>, this would have <u>ceased to grow</u> during the previous decade. Remaining at a virtually flat $1.2 Trillion (and only 53 Percent as high as CBO's $2.2 Billion Doctor Doom projection). **Reducing** its Percentage of GDP to 4.1 Percent (vs. 10.2 Percent in CBO's projections).

- <u>By 2035</u>, the "Cash Deficit" would actually **decline** to $853 Billion (only 13 Percent as high as CBO's projected $6.7 Trillion). **Falling** to only 1.1 Percent of GDP (rather than CBO's projected 18.1 Percent).
And what about **Total Outstanding Federal Debt Held By The Public?**

- <u>By 2020</u>, Total Debt would reach $16 Trillion (only **83 Percent as high** as CBO's $19.1 Trillion projection). Falling to **56 Percent of GDP** (vs. CBO's Doctor Doom projection of 88 Percent).

- <u>By 2035</u>, Total Debt would only have grown to $28 Trillion (only **42 Percent as high** as CBO's projected $67 Trillion). Falling still further to **38 Percent of GDP** (rather than rising to CBO's enormous 180 Percent). Back to pre-2008 levels.

Wow.

Numbers like these suggested that a **Large Enough Boost** in the GDP **Growth Rate** could actually make it possible for the Federal Government to **Grow Its Way Out Of Financial Trouble**. Without increasing taxes. Or cutting popular spending programs.

But then we had to ask ourselves the next obvious question:

WHAT COULD BE DONE TO <u>BOOST</u> THE ANNUAL GROWTH RATE OF GDP TO HIGHER LEVELS LIKE THESE?

To answer this question, we turned to **Mainstream Economic Reasoning** for a list of widely accepted candidates.

Of course, one candidate for growing Current Dollar GDP is to have the **Federal Reserve** work overtime <u>pumping up the nation's Money Supply</u> (**Chapter 7** explained how the Fed can do this). If this leads to a rise in Price Levels, then (for example) the same number of Widgets sold tomorrow at higher prices will produce <u>more dollars</u> of sales revenue for the Widget firm.

But at the national level, this simple-minded approach is inherently <u>self-defeating</u>.

Yes, inflating the Current Dollar value of GDP in this way will generate <u>more total dollars</u> of revenue for the Federal Government with no change in tax rates (which is why it's been so popular throughout history among many national governments).

<u>However,</u> the rise in Price Levels will reduce the <u>Buying Power</u> of dollars already targeted for Federal Outlays. So total dollars of outlays will have to be <u>increased</u> to compensate. Leaving us right back where we started.

So we need a candidate that can increase the <u>Constant Dollar Value</u> of GDP (known as "Real GDP" or "Inflation-Adjusted GDP"). Because growth in Real GDP is mirrored by a similar growth in Current Dollar GDP <u>even when there's Zero increase in Price Levels</u>.

Therefore, measures to increase Real GDP <u>also</u> increase Current Dollar GDP and therefore <u>total dollars</u> of Federal revenues. And if there's <u>no</u>

increase in Price Levels, then total dollars of Federal Outlays will still have the same Buying Power as before and therefore don't have to be increased. This can progressively narrow the gap between the growth of total Outlay dollars and the growth of total Revenue dollars. Reflecting the sound, basic **Strategy** recommended by the experts at various think tanks.

This would be the macroeconomic equivalent of being **Home Free**.

So we turned back to Mainstream Economic Reasoning to find GDP Growth-Boosting candidates that also boosted Productivity sufficiently to hold Price Levels more or less steady.

And a leading candidate was **Major Capital Investments**. The kind that can create New Jobs. Boost Productivity. And generally Grow the Economy Faster without causing Inflation.

A too-often forgotten legacy of President Roosevelt's New Deal to "**Save Capitalism in America**" was the massive capital investments by the Federal Government in huge economic growth projects. Like:

- **Rural Electrification.**

- **The Tennessee Valley Authority.**

- **Boulder Dam** in Arizona, the **Grand Coulee Dam** in the State of Washington, and other monumental hydroelectric generating facilities.

- Not to mention hundreds of commercial airports like **La-Guardia** and **JFK** in New York City, thousands of modern post offices, schools, local courthouses, and the like.

- Culminating in the construction of the forty-one-thousand mile **Interstate Highway System,** begun in the 1950s by President Eisenhower (the "Republican New Dealer") because of what he'd learned from his military experiences leading the armies of the Western Allies in smashing Germany during World War II.

- With the **G.I. Bill's** capital investments to educate returning war veterans providing the "<u>Human Resources</u>" equivalent of the "<u>Brick and Mortar</u>" products of other Federal capital programs.

America has been living off these Federal capital investments ever since. In fact, their contribution to decades of job growth and increasing national prosperity has been <u>so enormous</u> that we've come to take them for granted as "cost-free gifts from a beneficent God." Like the unimaginably bountiful resources of crude oil discovered under that legendary East Texas hill called **Spindletop**. Which came exploding out of the Lucas Number 1 oil-drilling well in 1901 with a <u>roar that shook the world</u>.

So why hasn't the Obama Administration made any serious "New Deal"-style capital investments to assure the nation's future prosperity?

Admittedly, the Administration's initial funding for economic stimulus had to focus on "shovel-ready" <u>Emergency Room projects</u> that could put people to work right away. Projects like repaving potholed highways and making overdue repairs to bridges.

But let's not kid ourselves. Spending for these projects scarcely represents "<u>Investments in the Future</u>."

They're simply the kind of ongoing maintenance activities that <u>should have been funded</u> out of current revenues (like replacing burned-out light bulbs in a factory) if we were operating our roadway systems in a sensible manner.

In other words, we've just been playing <u>Catch-Up Ball</u>.

So now's the time for the Administration to develop a series of **Major Capital Programs** (equivalent to Rural Electrification or the Tennessee Valley Authority) to create new jobs and build a better, stronger, more prosperous nation.

Because, interestingly enough, capital investment programs like these can <u>also</u> generate the kind of <u>near-term, non-inflationary economic growth</u> needed to solve the Federal Government's looming financial problems. <u>Without</u> having to do such politically difficult things as raising tax rates or cutting outlays for popular middle-class benefit programs.

Such capital investment programs can, in fact, enable us to **Grow Our Way Out of Financial Trouble**.

The obvious problem, of course, is <u>where the actual dollars can come from</u> to get such ambitious capital programs started.

As we've seen, projections for escalating Federal budget deficits and skyrocketing levels of Federal debt are bound to raise questions in Congress and among the public about the Federal Government's <u>ability</u> to come up with the necessary start-up dollars.

Yes, the ultimate payoff from these growth-oriented programs could go a long way towards solving Federal financial problems. But that wouldn't happen for a few years. So what do we do for <u>hard cash</u> in the meantime?

<u>One solution</u> is to recruit **private firms** as <u>active partners</u> to help start, fund, and run as many of these programs as possible.

If properly structured, such **Public-Private Partnerships** could tap into the **Billions of dollars in private capital** sloshing restlessly throughout the world and hungering for low-risk investment opportunities able to offer decent rates of return. Which these New Deal-style programs could provide. Thereby <u>greatly minimizing</u> the need for scarce government dollars to get these programs under way.

This means designing such Partnerships as overtly "**Commercial Enterprises**." Able to demonstrate reasonable prospects for earning <u>reliable income streams</u> of sufficient size to pay consistent dividends to their private partners.

Not a simple challenge, to be sure. But scarcely one that's beyond the capabilities of Wall Street's more innovative investment bankers.

But making this work on a sufficiently large scale would require some significant <u>Rethinking</u> of how government deals with private firms in the Real World (which may be overdue anyway). Because some of these Partnerships may need to involve the **User Charge Principle** (as employed by movie theaters, for example) to generate their necessary income streams. Which, if approached creatively, could actually <u>enhance</u> the likelihood that the activities of these Partnerships would fully meet environmental goals and other regulatory mandates that serve the Public Interest.

Remember the Electric Power Company example we looked at in **Chapter 9**? And its three Kingpin board members who had such very different policy agendas?

- **Tom** was a stock broker. So his agenda was driven by a wish to <u>maximize the Dividends</u> the Power Company paid to its <u>Private Investors</u>. Which meant charging the highest possible rates while providing as little service as it could get away with. Period.

- **Dick** was a leading light of the region's dominant political party. So naturally he wanted to <u>maximize votes</u> for his party's elected officials. By having the Power Company deliver lots of service at bargain rates. While standing with the Angels when it came to "acting Green" on environmental matters and proudly waving the flag in its highly visible commitment to serve other popular aspects of the "Public Interest."

- **Harry** ran the region's largest and most successful consumer retail chain. And he knew that his chain's sales growth ultimately depended on the growth of the region's economy. Which the Power Company could best serve by enhancing its financial stability and "sound management" stance, on the one hand. While at the same time, delivering good service at what were perceived as "affordable rates" and supporting so-called "non-economic goals" that would help the region become a better place to do business. In other words, striking a sensible balance between the polar opposite agendas of Tom and Dick.

This may be an effective **Governance Model** for any Public-Private Partnership that truly wants to succeed.

Alternative models based on elaborate legislative mandates can often accomplish the same thing. Assuming, of course, that the necessary legislation can be passed without being riddled with compromises, trade-offs, escape clauses, and weasel language.

But in many cases, the Tom/Dick/Harry model may be the most reliable way to be sure that, for example:

- The Original Cost of every facility is evaluated on a proper Lifecycle basis. So customers and operators alike don't wind up being confronted by expensive ongoing maintenance nightmares.

- There's certainty of Long-Term Financial Commitment. So the public never has to deal with the problem of "Orphaned Facilities."

- The responsibility for Sound Asset Management is clear and unambiguous. There are minimum chances for abuse by limited-life warranties, guarantees written by "paper companies" that melt into the woodwork when push comes to shove, and the kind of multi-party finger-pointing that only ends up enriching the legal profession.

- Commitments to <u>Fairness</u> and <u>Affordability</u> in the operation of integrated facility networks are transparent and meaningful. Customers are less likely to be subject to discrimination because of their individual physical, social, or economic challenges.

These are realities not likely to be lost on the relevant parties, once they get their acts together. In fact, some creative states like Texas have found that properly structured Public-Private Partnerships can successfully attract private capital to transportation projects <u>without</u> compromising meaningful local decision making and other built-in mechanisms to protect the public interest.

Actually, such "Everybody Wins" thinking may be less radical than it may at first appear. Many of the principles these Partnerships need to incorporate can be found in the New Deal programs. Not to mention other examples of how government led the way in investing in America's future. Like:

<u>Building</u> the **Panama Canal.**

<u>Developing</u> the nationwide system of **Land Grant Colleges,** which became the <u>backbone</u> of higher education in America.

<u>Partnering</u> with private firms to build the **First Transcontinental Railroad.**

<u>Building</u> the legendary **Erie Canal** early in the Nineteenth Century. So a fledgling nation previously confined to the Atlantic Coast could expand into the untapped, resource-rich hinterlands west of the Appalachian Mountains.

And, of course, <u>building</u> the Interstate Highway System.

Let's look at an example of how such an ambitious, high-payoff capital program might work.

■ ■ ■

The Potential Impact of Transforming Transportation

Estimates already exist from various sources about the <u>Dollar Size</u> of the **Capital Investment Programs** needed to transform America's transportation systems to meet the mobility needs of the Twenty-First Century.

But for our purposes here, the questions we need to answer are:

- *HOW MANY <u>NEW JOBS</u> CAN THESE PROGRAMS CREATE AND HOW SOON?*

- *HOW MANY <u>PERCENTAGE POINTS</u> CAN THESE PROGRAMS <u>ADD</u> TO THE <u>GROWTH RATE</u> OF GROSS DOMESTIC PRODUCT?*

- *WHAT WOULD THEIR IMPACT BE ON <u>NATIONAL PRODUCTIVITY</u>?*

So far, **No Serious Number Crunching** appears to have been done to give us a clear and well-defined picture of the "Pot of Gold" growth potential of these Capital Investment Programs for transportation. Including <u>full-scale application</u> of breakthrough **Intelligent Transportation Technology** to greatly improve Customer Service, make possible expanded Operating Efficiencies, and generate New Revenues.

This apparent lack of Solid Numbers is a **Grave Omission** and one that should be <u>rectified immediately</u> by the Federal Government and the various trade associations representing the Transportation industry.

We need **Definitive Number Crunching** to give us reliable answers as soon as possible (like the proverbial "Yesterday") to such questions as:

- *HOW MANY NEW JOBS CAN BE CREATED BY EACH $1 BILLION OF NEW INVESTMENT IN TRANSPORTATION? WHAT KIND OF NEW JOBS? HOW QUICKLY?*

- *HOW MANY <u>PERCENTAGE POINTS</u> CAN BE <u>ADDED</u> TO THE <u>GROWTH RATE</u> OF GDP BY <u>EACH</u> $1 BILLION OF NEW INVESTMENT IN TRANSPORTATION? HOW QUICKLY? FOR HOW LONG?*

Without reliable answers to these questions, we're left struggling with one hand tied behind our back to develop meaningful transportation programs that generate Serious Economic Growth <u>even as</u> they address our Mobility needs. And Congress will have all the excuses it needs to diddle around with <u>inadequate Same Old/Same Old proposals</u> in any legislation to "renew" broken and obsolete existing Federal Transportation Programs.

So until Solid Numbers become available, all we can do is look to **Mainstream Economic Reasoning** for a general picture of what major Transportation Capital Investment Programs could <u>potentially</u> accomplish on the Economic Front. But lack of precise numbers at this stage <u>doesn't compromise</u> the inherent logic of the link between Enhancing Infrastructure and Boosting Economic Prosperity.

For example:

The **American Association of State Highway and Transportation Officials** (AASHTO) estimates that we'd need to invest about **$6 Trillion** over 25 years just for the nation's roadway and mass-transit systems. This roughly translates into investments levels of nearly **$250 Billion** per year.

But in addition to giving us the kind of improved mobility we need, this kind of ambitious **Transportation Transformation** could <u>also</u> give the growth rate of the nation's economy a vital shot in the arm by creating new jobs and helping to solve the Federal Government's worrisome financial problems.

According to generally accepted Mainstream Economic Reasoning, it could do this in <u>three ways</u>:

- **<u>FIRST</u>:** The <u>process</u> of transforming our transportation systems can create large numbers of **New Jobs** within the transportation community. The people holding these new jobs would spend most of their new income buying consumer goods and services. And such Consumer Spending accounts for some 70 Percent of GDP. Which gives this boost in Consumer Spending a healthy **Economic Multiplier Effect.**

- **<u>SECOND</u>:** This initial Multiplier Effect would <u>expand</u> business activity in consumer industries. Creating **New Jobs** <u>outside</u> the transportation community. And again, the people holding these jobs would spend most of their income on consumer products and services. Further boosting Consumer Spending. Which produces a **Secondary Economic Multiplier Effect.**

- **<u>THIRD</u>:** The **Improved Mobility** provided by transportation transformation can have a <u>positive impact</u> on the revenue and cost structures of millions of business firms in hundreds of industries throughout the nation's economy. Causing many of them to <u>expand their operations</u>. Thereby creating **still more New Jobs.** Whose holders would spend most of their incomes on consumer products and services. Providing <u>another</u> boost to Consumer Spending, and therefore generating **Additional Economic Multiplier Effects.**

Could this **Three-Fold Effect** of AASHTO's recommended **$250 Billion** annual investment in roads and mass transit add a cumulative total of **Three Percentage points to the Growth Rate of GDP**? Or **half that much**? Or **even more than Three Percentage points?**

We won't know until the Right Experts do the Right Kind of **Serious Number Crunching.**

But let's remember an important fact.

AASHTO's estimates cover investments only for the nation's roadway and mass-transit systems. Imagine the larger job creation and economic growth impact of adding investments to improve other transportation systems.

- Like our badly shrunken Freight Rail systems. Whose private owners have torn out some 41 Percent of their rail networks since they became deregulated in 1980.

- And our Domestic Airlines. Still flying obsolete, inefficient, and fuel-guzzling airplanes. While their clueless managers wonder why they continue adding to their amazing record of having lost more money than they've ever made.

- Plus Inland Waterways . . . (Well, you get the idea.)

Clearly, we might be looking at the kind of potential economic growth impact that could rival what was produced by the New Deal's capital investment programs. Which gave us two generations of Record Prosperity.

So it's imperative that we turn these sample illustrations into **Seriously Crunched Numbers** as quickly as possible. "Toot Sweet," as the French say. (And anyone who's recently visited France knows how superlative French technology and massive capital investments have made it a world leader in transportation services.)

But there's another interesting benefit that transforming the nation's transportation systems could have.

The capital funds needed to support an investment program of this magnitude <u>need not</u> be largely dependent on the flow of scarce government dollars. Building such a program around properly structured **Public-Private Partnerships** could make it possible to tap **Billions of dollars** in <u>private</u> capital throughout the world. Which the global economic crisis has left hungering for low-risk investments producing decent returns.

Some European banks and construction companies have <u>already</u> done Public-Private Partnership transportation deals in the U.S. But this represents only the tip of an exceedingly massive iceberg.

To those who feel frustrated by the seeming impossibility of funding meaningful Transportation Transformation Programs from traditional government sources because of the Federal Government's breadline financial outlook, <u>this potential</u> can seem like the next thing to a **Free Lunch.**

■ ■ ■

Is Our Future an Open Book?

Many of us believe that a better future for Transportation in America must involve greater reliance on:

- **Up-to-date financing mechanisms** based on <u>sensible user charges</u> that ensure adequate funds for asset maintenance. For timely replacement of worn-out plant and equipment. And for investments in new technology and other capacity enhancements to support national economic growth.

- **Skilled managers** who are committed to <u>Creating Value for Customers</u>. To riding herd intelligently on operating costs. And

406

to exploiting the best of new technology to achieve both goals.

- **A host of other beneficial features of Market Capitalism** practiced by the most enlightened American commercial enterprises. Which brought us so much prosperity in the past.

The most practical way to accomplish all this is to end our dependence on the overstuffed basket of <u>existing public and private institutions</u> as sole owners and operators of vital transportation facilities like metropolitan roadway networks and transit systems, freight railroads, and airlines. Institutions like:

- **Tax-supported government agencies,** such as classic "state transportation departments."

- So-called **"public authorities"** that try to blend politically constrained user charges with taxpayer subsidies.

- **Privately owned corporations** run by top managers whose main concern is Wall Street's response to their latest quarterly earnings. Which determine the value of their stock options (except in the domestic airline industry, which has lost more money than it ever made).

This traditional model may have served its purpose in the past. But its horse-and-buggy characteristics now seem to have run out of steam and can't cope with the realities of today's world.

Rather than waste money and time tinkering with this antiquated model in a vain effort to make it more responsive, we should move to replace it with a **New Model.** One that properly reflects Twenty-First Century challenges.

At the heart of this New Model should be government-chartered, commercially oriented, market-focused transportation enterprises that are jointly owned by:

- **State and Local Governments,** whose elected leaders depend on the support of the voting public.

- **Private Investors** (institutional and individual), seeking fair and low-risk investment returns.

- **Major Business Corporations** whose sales revenues depend primarily on the <u>level of economic activity</u> in the regions where their customers live and work (and that are aware of Transportation's critical role in helping economic activity grow).

Inevitably, the most efficient size for many of these new transportation enterprises would cause them to enjoy **Functional Monopolies** in the regions where they operate. This reality should be formally recognized by government, through the established practice of granting such enterprises "monopoly franchises."

But whether or not these enterprises have service monopolies, all of them should be <u>intelligently regulated</u> to assure that they serve the interests of the public. Which could mean **Internal Regulation,** as in the power company example described in **Chapter 9.** Rather than relying solely on the outdated tradition of External Regulation by bureaucratic government commissions.

Such Internal Regulation might best be accomplished by a <u>properly competitive balance</u> in their Boards of Directors among representatives from all **Three Owner Groups** with their understandably different agendas (i.e., "the right mix of Toms, Dicks, and Harrys"). In other words, through **Healthy Competition** at the policy level. Where it matters most.

Possible?

Maybe.

But let's not forget that we have <u>only four options</u> for dealing with the nation's transportation crisis:

- **<u>Do nothing</u>. Muddle along rearranging deck chairs. And watch America descend into a swamp of lower living standards and political irrelevancy in the world.**

- **<u>Accept the inevitable</u>. Adopt a national policy of Planned Shrinkage to spread the pain of economic decline more equitably among the American people.**

- **<u>Convert our major metropolitan regions into true twenty-four-hour societies</u>. Make productive use of existing transportation capacity now lying idle during the nighttime hours when most people are asleep. Require half the population in these regions to live by night. Rather than continuing the Nineteenth-Century rural farm practice of everyone living by daylight.**

- **<u>Transform our transportation systems into strong economic growth generators</u>. Invest in a vibrant future of rising living standards and world leadership. Demonstrate that the American Experiment is still alive and thriving.**

Obviously, Options 2 and 3 are **Straw Men**. Fun topics for debates in ivory tower seminars and speculative journals. But no one is going to take them seriously as real-world policy options.

That leaves us with a choice between <u>Options 1 and 4</u>. Letting American society decline. Or making sure it grows in sensible ways.

A tall order?

Maybe.

Especially in view of the dim prospect for overhauling in meaningful ways the generally dysfunctional Federal Government (which is, after all, <u>our</u> "dysfunctional Federal Government").

But <u>how else</u> are we going to transform Transportation into a healthy generator of Economic Growth? Able to help us bring our rising national debt under control. The growing cost of supporting Baby Boom retirees. And all our other socioeconomic challenges.

Without being forced onto an exceedingly painful austerity diet.

Those of us blessed with working-class grandparents may remember the carefully framed photographs of **Franklin Delano Roosevelt** hanging in Places of Honor on the walls of their living rooms. Like veritable <u>Religious Icons</u>.

Religious Icons indeed. Because our grandparents <u>knew in their bones</u>, with a wisdom born of their hardscrabble battle for a decent life against all manner of adversities, that this astonishing National Leader saved the America of their dreams from **Armageddon**. With his remarkable combination of creative intelligence, sound judgment, personal charm, indomitable courage, brilliant con artistry, and warmhearted love for his countrymen.

Rising <u>far taller</u> than all the mountain ranges of critics and naysayers. Even while trapped in his wheelchair.

And <u>all of us</u>, regardless of our political preferences, are the Offspring of this **Great American Hero**.

So can we do any less than accept the <u>**Torch of Wisdom**</u> passed on to us from our grandparents? And set to work doing the **Right Things**?

For a change.

> *Remember ye not the Former Things. Neither consider the Things of Old. Behold, I will do a New Thing. Now it shall spring forth. Shall ye not know it? I will even make a Way in the Wilderness, and Rivers in the Desert.*
> *—Isaiah*

■ ■ ■

Chapter 12
WANT TO KNOW MORE?

You'll notice I've done something very radical for a book of this type.

I haven't included either the traditional **End Notes** or the traditional **Bibliography.**

But if I had, would you bother giving either one so much as a glance? Of course not. Normal People rarely do.

The only people who look at End Notes are classic academic types who want to count the number of times and ways the author has recycled Old Ideas. They call this "**Scholarship.**" But Normal People may wonder if a more accurate term might be "**Plagiarism.**"

As for Bibliographies (terrible word), they're worse than useless for anyone who actually wants to find anything worthwhile. Their standard pattern is to list books in alphabetical order by the Author's Last Name. Not by Subject Matter, which is what everyone but the author's mother is most interested in. So why should Normal People bother struggling through the usual Bibliography?

Anyway, there are lots of Books and Movies you may find helpful to find out more about any of the subjects (and their implications) discussed in these pages. So I've listed some of the best. And grouped them By Chapter so you can more easily find those dealing with subjects that have perked your interest. Along with brief comments to help you decide whether their content and perspective may be worth your time.

Yes, Movies too. Because this Great American Art Form can often tell us a good deal about ourselves. Why we get into such messes. And how we can recover.

CHAPTER 1: TRANSFORMING WHAT?

Full discussions of America's transportation problems and ways to re-solve them are contained in my two earlier books: *Mobility* (2005) and *Driving Questions* (2007). Both were published by the Hudson Institute. And are easily available Online from Hudson and Amazon.

For a more "novel" presentation of this material, see my 2008 book *Judges of the Secret Court.* Also published by the Hudson Institute and available Online. This is "entertaining fiction" in which two admitted rogues and con artists (with some compelling personal hang-ups) from different parts of that exotic land called Brooklyn discuss transportation problems and their solutions. Against the larger background of such is-sues as Free Market Capitalism (and how to seduce it into serving the public), Morality vs. Legality, and some fascinating Judeo-Christian "Heresies."

Gordon Gekko's spirited defense of **Greed** is a highlight of Oliver Stone's 1987 movie *Wall Street.* It's widely available on DVD from On-line sources like **Movies Unlimited.**

Emphasizing the same theme is **Ayn Rand's** "Libertarian" novel *Atlas Shrugged* (1996, Penguin). Originally published in 1957.

In the same vein is Rand's 1943 novel *The Fountainhead.* This was made into an interesting movie in 1949, directed by King Vidor. Avail-able on DVD.

The whole issue of **Incentives** has a solid basis in mainstream eco-nomic theory. For an irreverent and illuminating look at this, read *Su-perFreakonomics: Global Cooling, Patriotic Prostitutes, and Why Suicide Bombers Should Buy Life Insurance* by **Steven D. Levitt and Stephen J. Dubner** (2009, HarperCollins). Full of amusing stories about the seemingly crazy things people do simply because the Incentive Struc-tures they confront cause them to perceive, as "rational beings," that such behavior is in their own best interests.

On the other hand, the comparatively new field of **Behavioral Economics** argues that people often behave in short-sighted, emotional, irrational ways that turn out to be <u>against</u> their best interests (does that remind you of the Stock Market?). *Predictably Irrational: The Hidden Forces That Shape Our Decisions* by **Dan Ariely** (2008, HarperCollins) discusses the surprising finds of recent research in this area.

Contrary to popular opinion, **Bernard Madoff** is <u>Not</u> one of the people who helped cause the current Economic Crisis. But his Ponzi Scheme activities (for which he's currently serving 150 years in Federal Prison) have come to symbolize many of the abuses that led to it. Therefore his personal story is both fascinating and relevant.

Two recent books by experienced contemporary journalists dig into this. They are *Too Good to be True: The Rise and Fall of Bernie Madoff* by **Erin Arvedlund** (2009, The Penguin Group), and *Betrayal: The Life and Lies of Bernie Madoff* by **Andrew Kirtzman** (2009, HarperCollins).

Both books explore the "sociology" of Madoff's life and career in entertaining fashion. And they explain the details of his Ponzi Scheme's "marketing plan" for suckering investors into his web. Which concentrated first on rich members of the American Jewish small-business community. Then WASP trust fund babies. Then rich European aristocrats.

But neither book explains how Madoff's Ponzi Scheme <u>actually worked</u> (apart from the usual throw-away allusions to "using cash from new investors to pay dividends to existing investors"). Or why he got involved in it in the first place and went on for so long, seemingly without a clear Exit Strategy. (<u>Any</u> Ponzi Scheme is destined to blow up eventually. So a Really Smart Operator has to have an effective Exit Strategy ready ahead of time.) On the other hand, the details of these things are still in the process of being unraveled. So maybe it's simply <u>too soon</u> for any book to explain them.

Nor does either book explain the <u>Exotic Options Strategy</u> that Madoff vaguely claimed (when pressed hard enough) was the basis for his being able to pay investors "attractively high and steady" returns. But the authors may have felt that its details were "too technical" for the mass market readers they were trying to reach.

(For the record, Madoff's alleged strategy involved <u>buying</u> a common stock. Then turning around and <u>selling</u> call options on this stock to earn premium income. Then turning around again and <u>buying</u> put options on this stock to hedge against a possible decline in its price. The profit secret lies in achieving the "Right Balance" between the strike prices of the two sets of options. But financial professionals familiar with this strategy claimed all along that "it couldn't consistently produce the kind of returns" Madoff claimed. Though nobody listened.)

If Bernie Madoff symbolizes an "All-American Villain," then his obvious counterpart as "All-American Hero" is **Rick Blaine**—the lead character in the classic movie *Casablanca* (1942, Warner Brothers), widely available in a restored print on DVD from Online sources like **Movies Unlimited.**

Rocket Scientists became a fact of life on Wall Street as investment banks hungered for complicated, high-profit new products to sell. For a perceptive take on what these guys (no gals needed apply) were "really like" see **Emanuel Derman's** autobiographical *My Life as a Quant: Reflections on Physics and Finance* (2004, John Wiley & Sons).

Derman got himself a Ph.D. in Theoretical Physics from Columbia University (one of the classic degrees for "Bright Jewish Boys" with a taste for math and science). After struggling for a few years to make a decent living in a series of grant-funded academic physics projects, he drifted for financial reasons in the general direction of Wall Street. By 1985, he had become a Rocket Scientist at Goldman Sachs, where his career in "financial engineering" flourished.

Reading this book is like having a leisurely dinner with a decent, agreeable, intellectual powerhouse whose superior talents could have produced some of the technological tools needed for a better America if he hadn't been waylaid by Wall Street.

You can see how (regrettably) typical Derman's story is by reading

How I Became A Quant: Insights from 25 of Wall Street's Elite by **Richard R. Lindsey** and **Barry Schachter** (2007, John Wiley & Sons). This series of interviews with Wall Street Rocket Scientists underscores how America's self-defeating insistence on nickel-and-diming serious scientific research has forced too many gifted people to (mis)apply their scientific talents to earning Big Dollars on Wall Street by developing chrome-plated Derivative products—because after all, they have <u>families</u> to support.

CHAPTER 2: THE "GUNS OF AUGUST" ALL OVER AGAIN

There's certainly no shortage of books about **World War I**. Not as many as about **World War II**, perhaps. But this may be at least party because World War II is a "<u>Success Story</u>" (certainly from the perspective of the United States and its Allies, and maybe of humanity in general), while World War I is a story of <u>Failure</u>. And Success is always more fun to read about than Failure.

The paperback edition of Barbara Tuchman's classic *The Guns of August* (1994, Random House) will tell you all you want to know about how Europe melted down during the Summer of 1914. Originally published in 1962, the book covers the basic causes leading up to the Meltdown, details the key incidents, and climaxes with France and the UK finally halting the German onslaught at the First Battle of the Marne.

A top-notch chronological history of the entire War is military historian **John Keegan**'s magnificent *The First World War*. The original hardcover edition was published in 1999 by Alfred A. Knopf and covers everything with great eloquence. But you may prefer the large-format paperback revision published in 2000 by Random House because some of the material has been rearranged in the interest of greater clarity.

Once you have a sense of "what happened and when," you may find two "revisionist" books about World War I especially interesting.

The Pity of War by **Niall Ferguson** (1999, Basic Books) argues that

415

World War I was entirely <u>Britain's fault</u>. Because general British stupidity and mismanagement turned what could have been a fairly standard European conflict between Germany, France, and Russia into a worldwide disaster (does this sound like 2008?).

The Myth of the Great War by **John Mosier** (2001, HarperCollins) documents why the <u>German Army</u>'s much better training, tactics, and leadership enabled it to win most of its battles. While the British and French generally did everything "all wrong," hid their constant failures behind elaborate PR spin, and had to be bailed out in the end by the United States.

Here are several entertaining and informative journalistic accounts of <u>what actually happened</u> during the Great Meltdown of 2008. These books tend to use some of the techniques of Fiction (like reconstructed dialogue, revealing the inner thoughts of the people involved, etc.) to give readers "fly on the wall" pictures of some very dramatic events in these all-too-human tragedies.

- *House of Cards: A Tale of Hubris and Wretched Excess on Wall Street* by **William D. Cohan** (2009, Doubleday)
  The story of the Bear Stearns collapse in 2008.

- *Street Fighters: The Last 72 Hours of Bear Stearns, the Toughest Firm on Wall Street* by **Kate Kelly** (2009, Portfolio)
  Focusing on the sad End Game of this legendary investment bank.

- *A Colossal Failure of Common Sense: The Inside Story of the Collapse of Lehman Brothers* by **Lawrence G. McDonald** (2009, Crown Business)
  The title says it all.

- *In Fed We Trust: Ben Bernanke's War on the Great Panic* by **David Wessel** (2009, Crown Business) Spine-tingling adventures of Fed Chairman Bernanke, Bush's Treasury Secretary Hank Paulson, New York Fed President (and now Obama's Treasury Secretary) Tim Geithner, and their colleagues during the nation's 2008 financial showdown version of The Battle of Britain.

For helpful information about the broader picture, basic causes, and key implications of what happened during 2008, the following books are worth looking into:

- *The Return of Depression Economics and the Crisis of 2008* by **Paul Krugman** (2009, W. W. Norton) This updated and expanded edition of a 1999 book by the winner of the 2008 Nobel Memorial Prize in Economics covers all the issues. And does so in the highly accessible "twinkling eyes and droll smile" literary style that's made his regular *New York Times* column a <u>must read </u>in New York, Washington, and the rest of the world. So arm yourself to sound "really with-it" at the next wine-and-cheese party in Manhattan's Upper West Side or Washington's Georgetown.

- *The Origin of Financial Crises: Central Banks, Credit Bubbles, and the Efficient Market Fallacy* by **George Cooper** (2008, Vintage) Challenges the so-called "Economic Orthodoxy" that helped precipitate the current worldwide crisis. Also contains an excellent summary of Monetary Theory that will be very useful when you get to **Chapter 7** about the "Secrets of Money."

417

- *The Two Trillion Dollar Meltdown: Easy Money, High Rollers, and the Great Credit Crash* by **Charles R. Morris** (2008, Public Affairs)
Armed with a Common Sense awareness of economic reality and a hard-hitting writing style, the author tackles some of the key issues that brought on the Meltdown of 2008.

- *Money, Greed, and Risk: Why Financial Crises and Crashes Happen* by **Charles R. Morris** (1999, Times Business)
In this book, Morris provides an essential (and all too rarely discussed) run-down on America's economic evolution since Colonial days. And shows how it left the nation sitting on top of the economic equivalent of a dangerous "Subduction Zone" (the kind of geological fault that caused the devastating 2004 Indonesian earthquake and tsunamis).

- *Bailout Nation: How Greed and Easy Money Corrupted Wall Street and Shook the World Economy* by **Barry Ritholtz** with **Aaron Task** (2009, John Wiley & Sons)
Begins with an excellent historical review of past Federal Government bailouts. Then discusses the causes and events of the 2008 "bailout boom."

- *A Demon of our Own Design: Markets, Hedge Funds, and the Perils of Financial Innovation* by **Richard Bookstaber** (2007, John Wiley & Sons)
The author is a top Wall Street Rocket Scientist who admits to being one of the people "fiddling with the controls" during the shattering Black Monday stock market crash in 1987 and the collapse of the Long-Term Capital Management hedge fund in 1998. The traumatic impact of these

disasters caused him to rethink his personal view of the boom in financial engineering that produced ever-more-arcane Derivative products during the years leading up to 2008. And to come up with some devastating conclusions that he discusses in this book. Also useful while you read the last section of <u>Chapter 7</u>.

CHAPTER 3: WHAT HAPPENED: OIL PRICES

The definitive story of oil's complicated impact on the world we live in remains **Daniel Yergin**'s Pulitzer Prize book *The Prize: The Epic Quest for Oil, Money, and Power* (1991, Touchstone). Long, thorough, and fascinating.

Like most extractive resources, oil often winds up being seen as a **Curse of God** by many of its producers and consumers. As noted in the text, John D. Rockefeller's solution was to turn his **Standard Oil Company** into a monopoly that could "regulate the supply of oil" for the benefit of all concerned. But government had no patience with self-appointed monopoly regulators. So Standard Oil was broken up.

As the chapter describes, this left oil producers subject to periodic panic attacks when surges in the unregulated supply of oil undercut their pricing power and left them terrified that their revenues wouldn't be able to keep pace with their costs. While consumers were subject to panic attacks at other times when oil shortages threatened their oil-dependent lifestyles.

Curse of God indeed.

CHAPTER 4: WHAT HAPPENED: DERIVATIVES

Two fascinating books by **Espen Gaarder Haug** will tell you all you want to know about the astonishing varieties of Options and their countless derivative offsprings.

First out of the gate is the Second Edition of *The Complete Guide to Option Pricing Formulas* (2007, McGraw-Hill), which comes with a free CD containing a complete set of Excel spreadsheets. The author's opening words best describe this book's content and its fresh-air style.

> *"Some people collect stamps. Others collect coins, matchboxes, butterflies, or cars. I collect option pricing formulas. The book you have before you is a copy of this collection."*

Building on the mine of information collected in the first book is Haug's *Derivatives: Models on Models* (2007, John Wiley & Sons), which also comes with a free CD containing usable Excel spreadsheets with the relevant mathematical models already built in. The author uses a variety of narrative techniques (including comic strips) to explain concepts. And the book is peppered with illuminating interviews with such luminaries as **Nassim Taleb** (on Black Swans), **Edward Thorp** (on Gambling and Trading), **Emanuel Derman** (on life as a Wall Street Rocket Scientist), and **Aaron Brown** (on Gambling, Poker, and Trading).

In the same vein and equally valuable is *Paul Wilmott Introduces Quantitative Finance* (2007, John Wiley & Sons), covering "just about everything" in the field of Derivatives with great clarity. But an easier way into Wilmott's mind is his pocket-sized *Frequently Asked Questions in Quantitative Finance* (2007, John Wiley & Sons). Fun to read and skip around in while waiting in the doctor's office for your inevitably delayed appointment.

Bargain-priced copies of the Chinese paperback edition (with English text) are available on eBay for *Investment Science* by **David G. Luenberger** (1997). This is a standard, thorough, clearly written "textbook" on the subject as taught (uncritically) in the nation's leading graduate business schools. Good presentation of the "mainstream view" of things.

For the specific subject of **Credit Default Swaps**, see journalist **Gillian**

Tett's fascinating *Fool's Gold: How the Bold Dream of a Small Tribe at J.P. Morgan Was Corrupted by Wall Street Greed and Unleashed a Catastrophe* (2009, Free Press). Provides lots of detail to flesh out the Story Summary presented in this book's <u>Chapter 4</u>.

I'll bet you savvy types have been wondering how long it would take me to get around to Real McCoy **Gambling**. Specifically, **Poker**. America's <u>Ultimate Gambling Game</u> and a vital part of our national folklore.

Well, wonder no longer.

Even if you consider yourself a "pretty good Poker player," I <u>still</u> recommend that you at least skim through either of two terrific "books for raw beginners" (or even both). One is *Poker For Dummies* by **Richard D. Harroch** and **Lou Krieger** (2000, Wiley). The other is *The Complete Idiot's Guide to Poker* by **Andrew N. S. Glazer** (2004, Alpha Books). Both are great fun to read and crammed full of information. Especially about the rules and basic strategies for **Texas Hold'Em Poker**, currently the Most Popular version of the game.

Then (take a deep breath) you'll be ready to take on the monumental (and very advanced) *Doyle Brunson's Super System 2: A Course in Power Poker* (2005, Cardoza Publishing). Doyle Brunson is the unchallenged "Greatest Poker Player of All Time." With a homey Texas Cowhand personal style that masks a highly intellectual strategic mind. He assembled ten of the world's best Poker Professionals to contribute chapters to this book. Including **Jennifer Harman**, whose must-read chapter on the presumably arcane subject of *Limit Hold'Em* betting strategies shows a truly great Poker mind in action.

Needless to say, Poker is highly popular among Wall Street types. So it's only natural that there'd be more than a few books that apply the principles of Poker to securities trading. And two of the most interesting are *The Poker Face of Wall Street* by **Aaron Brown** (2006, John Wiley & Sons), and *Poker, Sex & Dying: The Heart of a Gambler* by **Juel E. Anderson** (1998, Marketplace Books). Both will open your eyes to some compelling ideas.

Maybe Doyle Brunson said it best in one of his favorite lines: *"We don't stop playing Poker because we get old. We get old because we stop playing Poker."*

An especially fascinating (but challenging) book dealing with **Value-at-Risk** issues is *Iceberg Risk: An Adventure in Portfolio Theory* by Wall Street Rocket Scientist **Kent Osband** (2002, Texere). The "iceberg" in question is the one that sank the ocean liner *Titanic*. This was an extremely low-probability event that had a catastrophic impact (and therefore qualifies as one of Nassim Taleb's **Black Swans**).

The author alternates technical chapters (full of calculus-level math) with very readable "novel-style" chapters. In which a Rocket Scientist and his boss debate various issues involved in making their firm's Risk Models more effective. And since their respective personal agendas are radically different, these conversational debates are fun to read and very illuminating. In fact, they're so informative you can skip the technical chapters and simply read the conversation chapters as an interesting novel (in the same vein as my 2008 novel *Judges of the Secret Court*).

CHAPTER 5: WHAT HAPPENED: HOUSING AND MORTGAGES

For the two or three of you who've <u>never seen</u> Frank Capra's classic movie *It's A Wonderful Life* (1946, RKO), it's available on DVD from any number of standard Online sources. And shown on TV (several times usually) each year during the Holiday season.

For more details about the causes and impacts of the so-called "Subprime Mortgage Crisis," read **Robert J. Shiller**'s short, snappy *The Subprime Solution: How Today's Global Financial Crisis Happened, and What to Do About It* (2008, Princeton). The author is probably the nation's leading maven on housing markets and what causes them to behave the way they do. He also resists being conned by any of the "Efficient Markets" and "Rational Investors" tooth-fairy illusions.

CHAPTER 6: IS MARKET CAPITALISM STILL ALIVE?

Probably the best (and shortest) book explaining what **Free Market Capitalism** is <u>really</u> all about is *How Markets Work: Disequilibrium, Entrepreneurship, and Discovery* by **Israel M. Kirzner** (1997, The Institute of Economic Affairs).

Kirzner is Emeritus Professor of Economics at New York University, protégé of the legendary Libertarian philosopher Ludwig von Mises, and a leading theoretician of the "Austrian" school of Free Market Economics. Also an ordained Orthodox Rabbi in Brooklyn and distinguished Talmudic scholar. Plus a brilliant teacher who's helped to make the English language a major tool of <u>Intellectual Discovery</u> (far surpassing on this score the fashionable mathematical nonsense practiced by so many ivory tower economists).

<u>All</u> Kirzner's books are worth reading by anyone who wants to get behind the childish illusions that stuff the pages of standard economics textbooks and learn how Free Markets actually work in the <u>Real World</u>. And this is the book to begin with.

Taking off from Kirzner and Austrian economic theory in general is *Patterns in the Dark: Understanding Risk and Financial Crisis with Complexity Theory* by **Edgar E. Peters** (1999, John Wiley & Sons).

Among other things, the author contends that Free Markets are inherently <u>Self-Organizing</u> despite being beset by Uncertainty (i.e., Risk that can't be quantified mathematically) and never achieve the classroom nirvana of Perfect Equilibrium. And that's one of their great strengths. Not that any of this would come as a surprise to the Prisoners of War described in this chapter. Who were too busy <u>practicing</u> Free Market Economics with the contents of their Red Cross packages to ponder such theoretical issues.

Just in case **Paul Krugman**'s "playing to the liberal galleries" *New York Times* column has left you wondering just how <u>serious and incisive</u> an economist he really is, any doubts will vanish as you read his short and highly perceptive *The Self-Organizing Economy* (1996, Blackwell).

As a committed **Keynesian,** Krugman obviously sits at an entirely different table from Kirzner and Peters. Yet he's fascinated by the principles of Self-Organization in markets. And goes further to describe how these principles aren't just confined to economics but are natural phenomena on a much larger stage. He explains their common links to economic recessions, hurricanes, earthquakes, urban growth, the development of embryos, segregated neighborhoods, and a host of other Self-Organizing Systems in the world. A real eye-opener.

Adam Smith is beyond question the Patron Saint of Free Market Capitalism. But his interests were considerably larger than so-called "Invisible Hands" and such things.

The following books can give you a more complete picture of what Smith was really all about and the true nature of his influence on economics and social morality.

- *The Authentic Adam Smith: His Life and Ideas* by **James Buchan** (2006, W. W. Norton)

- *Adam's Fallacy: A Guide to Economic Theology* by **Duncan K. Foley** (2006, Harvard University Press)

- *The Worldly Philosophers: The Lives, Times, and Ideas of the Great Economic Thinkers* by **Robert L. Heilbroner** (1999, Touchstone)

- *The Theory of Moral Sentiments* by **Adam Smith** (2006, Dover)

So why isn't John Maynard Keynes's monumental *General Theory of Employment, Interest and Money* on this "recommended" list? Because it's "too hard and time-consuming a read" for Normal People.

Lord Keynes wrote English with a clarity, brilliance, and wit that's rarely been matched by other economists (see his *Economic Consequences of the Peace*). But in writing the *General Theory*, he seems to have deliberately adopted a strategy of making it a "long tough read". Presumably, so that dedicated young economists would force themselves to devote the time and intellectual resources to understand it. And in so doing, become so "emotionally committed" to its ideas that they'd be driven to express them in articles and books of their own.

Which is exactly what happened. So Keynes was certainly no dummy. With the *General Theory* going on to become one of the **Most Important** (if least read) books of the Twentieth Century. With "fresh relevance" to the problems we're facing today.

So the next time you're confronting a few weeks in traction because of a skiing accident, you might want to have the *General Theory* handy. The world will never look the same to you again if you can manage to get through it.

CHAPTER 7: THE "SECRETS OF MONEY"

John Kenneth Galbraith is always a delight to read. And the popularity of his books among Normal People aroused such envious fury in traditional academic circles during his career that his reputation as a "Serious Economist" suffered accordingly. Nor did it help that his lifelong commitment to **Lord Keynes**'s view of the world permeates all his books.

So it's no surprise that Galbraith's *Money: Whence It Came, Where It Went* (1975, Houghton Mifflin) is one of the very few books on **Monetary Theory** you can bother reading. It's out of print, but sold so well that secondhand copies are readily available among various Online sources of used books.

For an example of the other kind of books on Monetary Theory, see any cheap secondhand edition of *Principles of Money, Banking, and Financial Markets* by **Lawrence S. Ritter**, **William L. Silber**, and **Gregory**

F. Udell (my copy of the tenth Edition was published in 2000 by Addison-Wesley). This is a standard, comprehensive college textbook you probably won't want to read straight through. But dipping into it here and there will give you a good laugh as you see what a Big Forbidding Deal the authors make of Monetary Theory (presumably so Normal People will be in awe of them for having mastered it).

Also (to be fair), it contains very detailed technical explanations of such monetary topics as **Bank Deposit Expansion.** Not to mention **Derivatives, Modern Portfolio Theory,** and similar financial items (as taught in graduate business schools) that relate to other chapters in this book.

What happens when Central Bankers really screw up in managing a nation's Money Supply? You can find out in *Lords of Finance: The Bankers Who Broke the World* by British investment manager **Liaquat Ahmed** (2009, Penguin Press).

During the 1920s, four Central Bank managers in the United States, Britain, France, and Germany struggled to restore the structure of international finance that World War I had shattered. Mainly by getting everyone back on the commodity money **Gold Standard,** which they regarded as the next thing to God's Holy Writ.

But commodity money currencies lack the strength and flexibility to meet such challenges. So these bankers stumbled through a series of increasingly bad events that culminated in the economic meltdown of 1929, which became the Great Depression. And ended up looking like total idiots.

The quasi-sexual passion for Gold as the Ultimate Money among people who should know better is explored in detail in *The Power of Gold: The History of an Obsession* by **Peter Bernstein** (2000, John Wiley & Sons). The author traces the history of this passion from Biblical times to the present day and shows how much trouble it's caused along the way.

There are two excellent books that provide further details about Capitalist Hero **A. P. Giannini** and San Francisco's astonishingly rapid recovery from the **1906 Earthquake and Fire.**

The first is the "company authorized" *Biography of a Bank: The Story of Bank of America* by **Marquis James** and **Bessie Rowland James** (1954, Harper). Giannini originally founded Bank of America as "The Bank of Italy" to serve the otherwise ignored small-business operators among the Italian colony in San Francisco's North Beach (where Joe DiMaggio grew up). Covers his early life, take-charge entrepreneurial activities in the wake of the Earthquake, and imaginative management in growing the bank (after its requisite name change) into one of the nation's largest financial institutions. Too bad he wasn't around in 2008 when his idiot WASP successors mismanaged Bank of America into a disaster that required a Federal bailout.

The second book is *The Economics of Localized Disasters: The 1906 San Francisco Catastrophe* by **Christopher Morris Douty** (1977, Arno Press). Based on the author's doctoral dissertation at Stanford University, this book contains a wealth of time-series data tracing the impact of the Earthquake and the city's rapid recovery on its economic performance from 1905 through 1912. Excellent factual demonstration of John Stuart Mills's contention that major disasters have surprisingly little impact on a developed society's economy. They just "speed up the pace of capital replacement." In which case, how do we explain the laggard recovery of New Orleans from Hurricane Katrina? Was it a "doomed society" to begin with? Or did it suffer from the **Curse of Bush II**'s flawed perception of government responsibilities? And what does this imply about the major earthquake disasters destined to strike the metropolitan regions of Los Angeles, San Francisco, and Seattle during our lifetimes?

Meanwhile, what about **Niall Ferguson**'s recent book *The Ascent of Money: A Financial History of the World* (2008, Penguin Press)?

Well, despite its main title, this readable and informative book isn't really about Monetary Theory at all. As its more accurate subtitle suggests, it's about **Capital**. And we can define "Capital" as "the portion of our income stream that's left over after we pay our current bills"—so we save it, in the hopes of being able to <u>invest</u> it to earn a profit. As such, the book is a fine account of how Capital has been used, abused, squandered, and swindled away by con artists throughout history. So you'll find it very illuminating for many of the topics discussed in this book.

CHAPTER 8: WHO ARE THE VILLAINS?

Speaking of con artists, the world of business and finance has produced an impressive share of gifted superstars who commit "Crimes in the Suites."

A good place to begin learning about them is *Frankensteins of Fraud: The 20th Century's Top Ten White-Collar Criminals* by **Joseph T. Wells** (2000, Obsidian). It contains fascinating stories about well-known rogues from the all-time Lascivine Hit Parade. Including such notables as "Crazy Eddie" Antar ("His Prices Are Insane"), Charles Ponzi (of "Scheme" fame), "Ultimate Flight Risk" Robert Vesco, and "Junk Bond King" Michael Milken.

For an exciting and detailed account of one of Wall Street's "Ultimate Insider Trading Scandals," you can do no better than read **James B. Stewart**'s Pulitzer Prize winner *Den of Thieves* (1991, Simon & Schuster). It's all-star cast includes such luminaries as Ivan Boesky, Michael Milken, Martin Siegel, and Dennis Levine.

We all know about **Enron** and its larger implications. Or think we do.

Anyway, the definitive story is found in *The Smartest Guys in the Room: The Amazing Rise and Scandalous Fall of Enron* by **Bethany McLean** and **Peter Elkind** (2004, Penguin). This updated and expanded paperback edition covers all the details of how a crew of "respectable corporate managers" perpetrated a series of Multibillion-dollar scams on American society.

As my book notes, most economists studiously ignore a Major American Industry that accounts for a significant share of the nation's Gross Domestic Product. Popularly known as the **Mafia** (but more accurately as "The Five Families" or simply "Organized Crime"), the influence of this huge multi-ethnic "business cartel" reaches into virtually every corner of American life in ways that will astonish you.

The most comprehensive source of information about its history, key players, operating structure, and multitude of business activities (illicit and kosher) is the updated second edition of *The Mafia Encyclopedia* by **Carl Sifakis** (2005, Facts on File).

The author has organized the book alphabetically by topic and personality. So it's easy to dip into. And dip you will as you become entranced by its wealth of material about how rival Sicilians, Neapolitans, Jews, Irishmen, Blacks, and Hispanics managed to put aside their instinctive ethnic hatreds to make fortunes building a great national industry by exploiting the average American's instinctive greed and subterranean cravings.

It covers such major figures as organizational genius **Charles** ("Lucky," but never to his face) **Luciano**, financial maven **Meyer Lansky** (who grew up with Luciano), "intellectual fountainheads" **Johnny Florio** and **Arnold Rothstein**, "Prime Minister" **Frank Costello** (who perfected the mechanisms for controlling political establishments), and charismatic "top managers" like **Al Capone, Longy Zwillman, Carlo Gambino**, and **John Gotti**.

Plus all-important business and operational topics like **Gambling, Banking** (i.e., "Loansharking"), **Prostitution, Bootlegging, Drug Distribution, High-Value Hijacking, Political Influence, Exploiting Wall Street** and other supposedly kosher industries, and **Managerial Control** (including Assassinations and other bloodbath activities).

American business is clearly no Sunday School. And this book shows how the organized crime cartel epitomizes this. Unfettered by the usual Chamber of Commerce hypocrisy.

All the movies mentioned in the text that have **Barbara Stanwyck** playing unforgettable Scarlet Women are available on DVD or VHS from various Online sources like *Movies Unlimited* or (in a pinch) eBay retailers.

Ditto the two "Scarlet Women" movies **Joan Bennett** made in the mid-1940s for director Fritz Lang. And, of course, **Joan Crawford**'s memorable performance as the Ultimate Schnook in *Mildred Pierce*.

To help you understand why you should dismiss the "Myths and Enchantment Tales" surrounding contemporary **Finance** as a so-called "Science," there's a really Great Read to get you started. It's *Fortune's Formula: The Untold Story of the Scientific Betting System that Beat the Casinos and Wall Street* by **William Poundstone** (2005, Hill and Wang).

The savvy and popular-voice author gives you the Real Skinny on how **Paul Samuelson, Harry Markowitz, William Sharpe,** and other math-oriented economists Took Over the World with their "Efficient Markets" theories.

While Bell Labs geniuses **Claude Shannon** and **John Kelly** teamed up with Blackjack maven **Edward Thorp** to adapt concepts of Information Theory (which Shannon had developed) into betting techniques that could beat the Casinos at their own games. Before moving on to Wall Street's games with the same techniques. Where they Won Big (and didn't have to worry about getting their knees broken by Casino goons) by demonstrating that the Efficient Markets Cosa Nostra in the academic world were teaching hogwash.

Other colorful characters include **Moses Annenberg**, whose mob-sponsored horse racing wire businesses became AT&T's biggest customers and inspired Shannon, Kelly, and Thorp to develop their bet-winning concepts. And **Rudy Guiliani** (in his racket-busting days), who bullied Thorp into closing down his hedge fund because its consistently high returns seemed "suspicious." And super-bookie **Manny Kimmel** who financed Thorp's earlier efforts to beat the Casinos. And **J. Edgar Hoover, Michael Milken, Ivan Boesky,** among other rogues.

An altogether delightful and informative book.

Poundstone's more sober and couth (but equally informative) counterpart is *The (Mis)Behavior of Markets: A Fractal View of Risk, Ruin, and Reward* by **Benoit Mandelbrot** and **Richard L. Hudson** (2004, Basic Books)

This book was actually "written <u>for</u> Mandelbrot" by *Wall Street Journal* reporter and editor Hudson. Which is all to the good, because Mandelbrot's native language is French, which is too "toy-like" and hamstrung by the French Academy to deal with ideas as profound as his. He applies the concepts of **Chaos Theory** and **Fractal Analysis** to explain how financial markets <u>really work</u>. And in the process, demolishes the Efficient Markets hypothesis and the math-oriented Finance models it's sired.

The first part of the book tells the down-to-earth story of how Harry Markowitz's **Modern Portfolio Theory** and William Sharpe's **Capital Asset Pricing Model** were developed and are supposed to work. Plus the impact they had on the **Black-Scholes-Merton Options Pricing Model**, which provided the whole basis for developing most of Wall Street's favorite Derivative products (which turned out to be so much toxic waste in 2008).

Then the book goes on to blow the entire Efficient Markets edifice out of the water by showing how it has no relevance to Real Markets. And replaces it with a More Realistic View of markets based on Chaos Theory and Fractal Analysis. Building on studies of a century's worth of daily price movements in the commodity Cotton. And the lifetime work of British hydrologist **Harold Edwin Hurst** evaluating data going back to Biblical times on annual flood levels in the Nile Valley.

Challenging ideas indeed. Which took a long time to reach the economics community because the Efficient Markets Cosa Nostra that ruled the academic world <u>wouldn't allow</u> Mandelbrot's "heretical" articles to be published in the standard scholarly journals.

So much for "academic freedom."

These two books will get you ready to go a few rounds with the "Muhammad Ali" champ of them all. It's the monumental second edition of *Chaos and Order in the Capital Markets: A New View of Cycles, Prices, and Market Volatility* by **Edgar E. Peters** (1996, John Wiley & Sons).

Peters rejects the conventional view of markets as "static linear systems," so childishly diagrammed in the multitudes of standard economics text-books that college students are conned into buying (at ridiculously inflated prices). Like Kirzner, Krugman, and a few others with grown-up minds, he finds real markets to be "dynamic non-linear systems" whose multi-dimensional nature can only be understood through Chaos Theory. (This doesn't mean that markets are "patternless." Rather, they reflect <u>Fractal</u> patterns instead of those of two-dimensional Plane Geometry.)

A simple analogy may help make this difference clearer.

Suppose you're serving as Navigator on a forty-eight-foot sailboat in the Newport-to-Bermuda race. As you sail out of Narragansett Bay, you discover that the Skipper's expensive new GPS electronic navigation system has stopped working. So if you're to go on with the race, you'll have to navigate the sailboat's course to Bermuda using old-fashioned, tried-and-true Plane Trigonometry. Which you learned in high school and has worked perfectly for short cruises along the East Coast within sight of land. So you go to it.

And guess what? You miss the island of Bermuda completely and the crew has to be rescued.

Why?

Because the earth <u>isn't flat</u>. It's <u>round</u> (actually an oblate spheroid, but round is close enough). Therefore, Plane Trigonometry can <u>never</u> give you an accurate course over such a distance as that from Newport to Bermuda. Instead, you must use the more sophisticated <u>Spherical Trigonometry</u>. Which can deal with curved surfaces.

Meanwhile, Peters doesn't simply rely on abstract discussions to convey his ideas. He actually <u>demonstrates</u> how they work. By applying them to <u>actual</u> long-term time-series data of returns for the S&P 500 Index, four well-known individual stocks, thirty-year Treasury Bonds, and 4 major currency pairs. Using the same **Rescaled Range Analysis** methodology Harold Hurst developed for his studies of Nile Valley flood levels.

And <u>all</u> of these examples showed marked <u>Persistence</u> in the direction of their returns. <u>None</u> of them showed Randomness (which the Efficient

Markets crowd insists should be the case). Or Mean Reversion ("Up today implies Down tomorrow"). So a higher return is normally followed by a still-higher return. All consistent with a Fractal view of how markets actually work.

The free disk accompanying the book contains various sets of time-series data. Plus the software for performing Rescaled Range Analysis on them. So you don't have to take the author's word for all this. You can see for yourself.

CHAPTER 9: WHY MARKETS NEED SAVVY REGULATION

There are two fine books that demonstrate how clueless FASB is with its fairyland "GAAP accrual accounting" dictates for financial reporting.

Creating Shareholder Value: The New Standard for Business Performance by Northwestern University accounting guru **Alfred Rappaport** (1986, The Free Press), turns FASB's ivory tower financial reporting standards upside down in this clearly written discussion of what financial information people really need to assess the performance of private business firms.

Free Cash Flow: Seeing Through the Accounting Fog Machine to Find Great Stocks by financial pro **George C. Christy** (2009, John Wiley & Sons) seems aimed at the "poor schnook amateur investor" market. But it's a great read for anyone interested in learning how to track actual dollars through the pointless maze of standard FASB income statements and balance sheets. The author demolishes the entire accrual accounting edifice and replaces it with straightforward, down-to-earth financial reporting procedures that make sense to Normal People.

For some "great stories" about the New York City Police Department's "War on Terrorism" see *Securing the City: Inside America's Best Counterterror Force—The NYPD* by **Christopher Dickey** (2009, Simon & Schuster). New York City folklore at its best.

CHAPTER 10: WHAT DOES IT ALL MEAN?

This chapter has already mentioned **Ralph Vince**'s outstanding *The Handbook of Portfolio Mathematics: Formulas for Optimal Allocation & Leverage* (2007, John Wiley & Sons) as an excellent source of information about **Risk** and its inevitable handmaiden, **Probability**.

Equally useful is Vince's latest book *The Leverage Space Trading Model: Reconciling Portfolio Management Strategies and Economic Theory* (2009, John Wiley & Sons). Among other virtues, this short book confronts the reality that Normal People define "Risk" as "the chance of losing your shirt" and explains why such ivory tower concepts as **Modern Portfolio Theory** (taught as "Holy Writ" in the nation's leading graduate business schools) are congenitally unable to deal with the Real McCoy dangers of Risk.

The standard "popular history" of Risk and Probability is *Against the Gods: The Remarkable Story of Risk* by **Peter L. Bernstein** (1998, John Wiley & Sons). The author traces how some of history's greatest mathematical minds struggled to define and understand what Risk was all about and how it could be quantified through "the Science of Probability." Because of their fascination with (surprise?) gambling games. Concludes with an illuminating discussion of the impact this had on Wall Street's boom in Derivatives.

Now hold your breath for this next book. Because it's the answer to the prayers you uttered in frustration as you struggled to master the bewildering "Gaussian" concepts taught in your college Statistics courses. Which your gut told you seemed like "so much over-mathematized nonsense." (And your gut was Right.)

The book in question is *The Black Swan: The Impact of the Highly Improbable* by **Nassim Nicholas Taleb** (2007, Random House). The author is a successful commodity trader, self-appointed "public intellectual," and arrogant iconoclast with an amusing talent for invective. And

Lebanese to boot (which is enough to make anyone suspicious of "Received Wisdom"). Who seeks to demolish the whole edifice of Gaussian Statistics as a "great intellectual fraud" that has little value in the Real World.

Instead, Taleb goads us to be sensitive to **"Black Swans."** Which he defines as low-probability events (like 9/11, or Black Monday's one-day stock market decline of more than 20 Percent on October 19, 1987). Whose impact can be <u>so catastrophic</u> that we damn well better be prepared to deal with them. And get over such flat-earth illusions as "security price changes being Random and Independent, with frequencies that nicely fit the Normal Gaussian Bell-Shaped Curve." A very challenging and enjoyable read.

CHAPTER 11: THE BOTTOM LINE

Since this payoff chapter is devoted to <u>Solutions</u> to the problems that previous chapters went on about at such length, you might like to see what the Usual Suspects think the best solutions are.

Naturally, each suspect has his own pet cure. Some are even interesting. And how better to get a sense of their thinking than to open a single book that contains a <u>collection</u> of their ideas, all in one place?

Such a book is *Restoring Financial Stability: How to Repair a Failed System* edited by **Viral V. Acharya** and **Mathew Richardson** (2009, John Wiley & Sons). Its contents is the result of a large-scale hurry-up project undertaken at the beginning of 2009 by 33 faculty members of the **Leonard N. Stern School of Business** at **New York University** under the direction of Dean **Thomas Cooley** and Vice Dean **Ingo Walter**. The result was 18 "Policy Papers" collected in this book that span the fields of economics, finance, and accounting.

As noted, the authors of these papers are Professional Academics. And a taken-for-granted requirement for membership in this elite fraternity is a demonstrated inability to write the English language ("the immortal tongue of Shakespeare, Milton, and the King James Bible") any better than the average high school dropout. So don't look for the linguistic clarity and brilliance of a Keynes or Kirzner or Krugman as you struggle your way through many of these Policy Papers. But the effort (if you really want to bother making it) will pay dividends in terms of learning what Mainstream Conventional Thinking has to say about Solutions to the mess we're in.

Few of which, needless to say, have much to do with the Solutions discussed in this chapter. But that's another matter.

In much the same vein (but reflective of a single mind and voice) is *The Road to Financial Reformation: Warnings, Consequences, Reforms* by **Henry Kaufman** (2009, John Wiley & Sons). As Chief Economist at the late and much-lamented investment banking firm of **Salomon Brothers**, the author developed a prized reputation as **Doctor Doom** for his endless jeremiads about how bad things were. His latest book doesn't disappoint on this score.

Very different, blessedly shorter, and a lot more fun to read is *Bold Endeavors: How Our Government Built America, and Why It Must Rebuild Now* by **Felix Rohatyn** (2009, Simon & Schuster). Formerly "New York's best-known investment banker" during his long career at Lazard Freres & Company, the author tells us the story of major events in the Federal Government's highly successful "Venture Capitalist" career—from the Louisiana Purchase through the Interstate Highway System. And argues that government must undertake similar initiatives in these times of trouble. A breath of fresh air after so many years of fashionable nonsense about "government is the problem" and "private enterprise is the solution."

This chapter describes the **G.I. Bill** as one of the most important and successful investment programs—by government or private enterprise—in the nation's history. If you want to fill yourself in about the too-long forgotten details of this monumental undertaking that helped build the **Greatest Generation,** here are two worthwhile books:

436

1. *Over Here: How the G.I. Bill Transformed the American Dream* by **Edward Humes** (2006, Harcourt).

2. *Soldiers to Citizens: The G.I. Bill and the Making of the Greatest Generation* by **Suzanne Mettler** (2005, Oxford).

Anyway, enjoy.

AFTERWORD: JUST IN CASE YOU WONDERED...

You've probably noticed that this book <u>wasn't written</u> like the standard dull academic textbooks you had to study in college so you could pass your courses. In fact, it was more like reading a really good sports column in one of the better tabloid newspapers that you could breeze through enjoyably while traveling to work.

This was <u>deliberate</u>.

As you must have sensed by now, my reason for writing this book was to show you <u>why</u> the Transportation ideas in my previous books have gained fresh <u>urgency</u> and <u>importance</u> because of the current **Economic Crisis** and the **2008 Financial Meltdown** that led to it.

But this meant I had to give you a really good <u>working understanding</u> of how and why the Economic Crisis and Meltdown came about. And I couldn't do that by using the kind of dull textbook prose that makes people's eyes glaze over. I had to make the book a <u>fun read</u> for you, as well as an <u>enlightening read</u>. So I had to <u>clearly explain</u> in down-to-earth, reader-friendly language such heavy stuff as:

- **Financial Derivatives.**
- **The Housing and Mortgage Mess.**
- **How Free Markets Work in the Real World.**
- **Monetary Theory.**
- **The True Meaning and Implications of "Risk."**
- **Regulating Financial Markets and Financial Firms.**
- **The Federal Government's Budget Deficit and Outstanding Debt.**

All of which you're now at least "Lay Experts" in. Right?

(And remember: You can always go back to the book's technical chapters to get back up to speed on the details. If nothing else, sounding like a Real Maven about these things will make the more interesting people you meet take you seriously. Not to mention your bosses.)

Most of you have educational backgrounds in Engineering. Or Law. Or Public Administration. Some of you work in and around the world of Practical Politics. Others are college students majoring in fields like Economics and Finance. Where you have to be ready to parrot back what your professors and textbooks tell you. Even when they're Wrong.

The so-called Experts who make their livings in the technical areas listed above <u>don't want</u> Normal People like you to understand those things. They'd much prefer that you simply "take their word for it." Admire them for seeming to understand what they make incomprehensible. And not ask a lot of annoying questions.

But that's not good enough anymore. The challenges we face in getting America back on track demand that people like you put your street-smarts to work full-time. And you can do this more effectively by understanding those technical things.

Therefore, a book written in <u>standard academic prose</u> would be of little value to you. You'd quickly become lost and bored. And end up putting the book aside before you get very far. So the book would, at best, become one of those tomes that "everybody buys but nobody reads." Which, for my purposes, would make it a failure.

So this couldn't be a book that readers like you had to <u>study</u> like a textbook so you could pass a college course (after which you're free to forget the material). Rather, it had to be one that <u>grabbed your attention</u> on the first page. Kept you eagerly <u>turning the pages</u> as with an entertaining novel to find out what comes next. And was <u>instantly understandable</u>. The book had to leave you with a sense of having a <u>functional grasp</u> of the technical material. And an <u>easily accessible</u> source of further details.

This meant that the book had to be written in a style that's <u>entirely different</u> from most non-fiction books.

And now I'm going to tell you how I did it. ("Sawed the Woman in Half," as it were.)

The Book's Basic Narrative Style

This pretty much models itself on the writing style you'd expect from a really good <u>sports columnist in a popular tabloid newspaper</u> who's under constant pressure to grab the attention of as many casual readers as possible while they're riding the subway. Supplemented by certain other narrative tricks to enhance accessibility, clarity, and general reader friendliness.

So the book depends heavily on:

- **Short, punchy sentences.**
- **Short paragraphs,** to clearly separate individual points and give the pages lots of eye-friendly "white space."
- **Simple punctuation** (limited to Periods and Commas for the most part).
- **Colorful, contemporary metaphors** (often with attention-grabbing sexual overtones, since most of you are male).
- **Lots of "bullets"** to make "logical sequences" visually clear.
- **Little "stories"** (**often with dialogue**) to illustrate complex issues and avoid abstractions.
- **Analogies to historical events** (like those involving World War I, which was as badly mismanaged as the events leading to the Economic Crisis).
- **References to popular classic movies** (like Frank Capra's *It's a Wonderful Life* and Billy Wilder's *Double Indemnity*).

Typographical Tricks

To further enhance clarity, reading speed, and general reader-friendliness for you, I used certain "Typographical Tricks" to <u>emphasize</u> key terms or phrases. Just as if we were sitting face-to-face and I was <u>telling you</u> these things. Using normal body language and vocal tricks to help get my points across.

Anyway, here are the typographical tricks (alone or mixed together) you saw me use:

- Capitalizing the Initial Letters of certain Key Terms Or Phrases (as here).
- Capitalizing ALL the letters of certain KEY TERMS OR PHRASES.
- Showing certain **key terms or phrases** in **bold-face type**.
- <u>Underlining</u> certain <u>key terms or phrases</u> (so the book <u>doesn't</u> use this old typewriting convention to indicate that the <u>underlined term or phrase</u> should be set in italics).
- Setting certain *key terms or phrases* in *italics*.
- Surrounding certain "key words or phrases" with "quotation marks."

And if all this should make you want to go back and re-read certain portions of the book . . . ?

Well, I'm no dummy. That's good for both of us.

So tell your friends.